Nuisances

FOR MY PARENTS

Nuisances

First Edition

Editor

Gordon Wignall MA

Barrister, Chambers of Lord Thomas of Gresford QC

Published by
Sweet & Maxwell Limited of
100 Avenue Road
London NW3 3PF

Printed in Great Britain by Bell & Bain

A CIP catalogue record for this book
is available from the British Library

ISBN 075200 4751

No natural forests were destroyed to make this product,
only naturally farmed timber was used and re-planted.

Editor

Gordon Wignall MA, Barrister, Chambers of Lord Thomas of Gresford QC

Contributors

Vivien King BA, Solicitor, SJ Berwin

Christopher Hancock LLB, Solicitor, DJ Freeman

Jacqui O'Keeffe LLB, Assoc MInstWM, Solicitor, Denton Hall

David Powell FRICS, Surveyor, David J Powell Surveys Ltd

Kaivin Wong BSc, ARICS, Surveyor, Malcolm Hollis

Contents

Foreword		xiii
Preface		xv
Table of Cases		xvii
Table of Statutes		xxx
Table of Statutory Instruments		xxxix
Table of European Provisions		xli
Abbreviations		xliii

1	**Private Nuisance**	1
1.1	Overview	1
1.2	The plaintiff	3
1.3	Damage – introductory	5
1.4	Damage – physical damage	6
1.5	Damage – encroachment	7
1.6	Damage – intangible damage	7
1.7	Damage incapable of amounting to a nuisance	17
1.8	Damage – foreseeability of damage	20
1.9	The defendant	21
1.10	Dangerous hazards on land	26
1.11	Defences	29

2	**Public Nuisance**	32
2.1	Overview	32
2.2	Common law actions in public nuisance	32
2.3	The highway	34

3	**Statutory Nuisances**	41
3.1	Overview	41
3.2	Environmental Protection Act 1990, Part III	41
3.3	Smoke from premises	43
3.4	Fumes or gases	44
3.5	Dust, steam, smell or other effluvia from industrial, trade or business premises	45
3.6	Any accumulation or deposit	45
3.7	'Any animal kept in such a place or manner'	45
3.8	Noise emitted from premises	46
3.9	Noise emitted from or caused by a vehicle, machinery or equipment in a street	46

3.10 Any other matter declared by any enactment to be a statutory
nuisance 47
3.11 Enforcement by a local authority – introduction 48
3.12 Issue and service of abatement notices 49
3.13 Appealing against an abatement notice 50
3.14 Offences in connection with abatement notices 52
3.15 Local authority self-help 55
3.16 Injunctive relief 56
3.17 Private remedies against the local authority 56
3.18 Instituting private proceedings for an abatement order 57

4 **The Rule in *Rylands v Fletcher* and Liability for Fire** 60
4.1 Overview 60
4.2 Liability in *Rylands v Fletcher* 60
4.3 Fire 66

5 **Trespass** 70
5.1 Overview 70
5.2 Trespass to land – introductory 71
5.3 The plaintiff 73
5.4 The defendant 73
5.5 Remedies available to the individual 76
5.6 Police and local authority powers 83
5.7 Adverse possession 88
5.8 Occupiers' duties to trespassers on land 91

6 **Boundaries** 93
6.1 Overview 93
6.2 New boundaries 94
6.3 Fences 95
6.4 Walls 100
6.5 Hedges 100
6.6 Ditches 102
6.7 Trees 107
6.8 Highways 110
6.9 Railways 111
6.10 The seashore 114
6.11 Lakes and rivers 114
6.12 Evidence 116

7 **Party Walls** 124
7.1 Overview 124
7.2 Structures covered by the 1996 Act – definitions 125
7.3 The rights and duties of owners 130
7.4 Notification 135

7.5	Dispute resolution	137
7.6	Security for expenses	138
8	**Withdrawal of Support and Interference with Light**	140
8.1	Overview	140
8.2	Establishing the existence of an easement	141
8.3	Withdrawal of support	145
8.4	Interference with light	149
9	**Animals**	156
9.1	Overview	156
9.2	Common law liability for damage caused by animals	156
9.3	Liability for animals under the Animals Act 1971	158
9.4	Trespassing livestock	164
9.5	Animals straying on to the highway	167
9.6	Dangerous dogs	168
9.7	Pit bull terriers and dogs bred for fighting	171
9.8	Liability for injury caused by dogs to livestock	172
9.9	Liability for the killing of or injury to dogs worrying livestock	173
9.10	Strays	173
10	**Stalkers and Nuisance Telephone Calls**	175
10.1	Overview	175
10.2	Criminal offences	177
10.3	Civil remedies apart from s 3 Protection from Harassment Act 1997	184
10.4	The Protection from Harassment Act 1997	188
10.5	Family law remedies	191
11	**Wheel Clamping**	199
11.1	Overview	199
11.2	Police powers	199
11.3	Wheel clamping on private land	199
12	**Noise**	202
12.1	Overview	202
12.2	Street noise as statutory nuisances	203
12.3	Construction works	206
12.4	Building control under the Building Regulations 1991	210
12.5	Noise from plant or machinery	210
12.6	Loudspeakers	211
12.7	Burglar alarms	212
12.8	Road vehicle noise	213
12.9	Aircraft noise	213
12.10	Late night revellers and night time neighbour noise	214
12.11	Entertainment licences	219

12.12   Waste management licences and integrated pollution control   219
12.13   Noise abatement zones   220
12.14   Planning control and noise   221
12.15   Major projects   222

13   Air Pollution   223
13.1   Overview   223
13.2   Part I, Environmental Protection Act 1990   223
13.3   Dark smoke   226
13.4   Smoke, grit, dust and fumes   229
13.5   Smoke control area   231
13.6   Traffic orders   231
13.7   Agricultural practices   232
13.8   Air quality monitoring   232

14   Waste on Land and Litter   234
14.1   Overview   234
14.2   Enforcement bodies   234
14.3   The prohibition against unauthorised or harmful deposits,
        treatment or disposal etc of waste   236
14.4   The duty of care as respects waste   237
14.5   Fly-tipping   238
14.6   Removal of refuse/rubbish   240
14.7   Abandoned vehicles   243
14.8   Litter   245
14.9   Abandoned shopping and luggage trolleys   253

15   Water and Sewage   255
15.1   Overview   255
15.2   Water pollution – Part II of the Water Resources Act 1991   255
15.3   Remedial works and other pollution powers   258
15.4   The supply of drinking water   259
15.5   Sewage and effluent disposal   263

16   Remedies   269
16.1   Overview   269
16.2   Actual damage to land and its appurtenant rights – the correct
        measure of damages   270
16.3   Damages for annoyance, inconvenience and distress   272
16.4   Consequential loss   272
16.5   Damages in trespass where there has been no actual damage   273
16.6   Damages for interference with light   273
16.7   Continuing damage   274
16.8   Recovering compensation for damage occurring after the issue
        of proceedings but before judgment   274
16.9   'Nominal damages'   274

16.10   Injunctions – introductory   275
16.11   Final prohibitory injunctions and damages in lieu   276
16.12   Mandatory injunctions   279
16.13   Mandatory *quia timet* injunctions   280
16.14   Mandatory *quia timet* injunctions at an interlocutory stage   281
16.15   Injunctions and trespass to land   282

Appendices

Appendix A1   Environmental Law – Regulatory Bodies and
                   Enforcement   283
Appendix A2   Environmental Law and Access to Information   289
Appendix A3   A Note on Disputes Involving Trees   298
Appendix A4   Standard Scale of Fines in the Magistrates' Courts   301
Appendix A5   Precedents and Specimen Forms   302

Index   325

Foreword

Gordon Wignall in his preface describes private nuisance as a robust tort. And so indeed it is. It has survived more or less intact since the earliest origins of the common law. It has survived attempts to make it part of the modern law of negligence, to which (on one view) it may be said to have given birth. It has survived association, by name if not by nature, with the myriad topics discussed in this admirable book. To one who was becoming footsore and weary in the search to define the boundaries of negligence, it was refreshing to take part in the hearing of *Hunter v Canary Wharf Ltd*. Our decision in that case would not have come as any surprise to Blackstone, or even Glanvil. For the action on the case for nuisance is still much as it was in the time of the Statute of Westminster II. I hope this is not regarded as a matter for criticism.

The merit of this book is that it deals clearly and concisely with private and public nuisance, but also with the myriad of other topics which I have mentioned. The format is excellent. In particular I like the 'Overview' with which each chapter is introduced. Gordon Wignall and his team of specialist contributors are to be congratulated on producing a book which will prove indispensable to the practitioner.

In his celebrated article in 1949 LQR vol 65, Professor FH Newark described nuisance as the least satisfactory branch of the law of tort. This book goes far to disprove that view.

The Right Honourable Lord Lloyd of Berwick
11 June 1998

Preface

This book is intended to serve several purposes. First, it seeks to provide the reader with a clear and succinct guide to the principles of private nuisance and its related common law torts: public nuisance, trespass and *Rylands v Fletcher*. Secondly, it attempts to show how these torts have a practical application, for instance in boundary disputes, liability for damage caused by fire and liability for injury on the highway. Thirdly, it endeavours to act as an exegesis of a number of disparate statutory rules which govern the complexities of contemporary life and which can be said to supplement the common law previously considered.

Private nuisance is a robust tort which protects the rights of a person who enjoys the exclusive possession of land. It is inextricably connected with real property. Periodically, however, litigants come before the courts attempting to make private nuisance do more than it can. In 1949 Professor Newark called for a notice to be erected at the law courts to remind lawyers of the elements and purpose of the tort. Recently in *Hunter v Canary Wharf* [1997] AC 655 the House of Lords had reason to restate its essential principles. If this book succeeds only in directing the reader towards a better understanding of the workings of private nuisance or any of the other common law causes of action, then the contributor's labours will have been justified.

Much of this work is given over to statute. Parliament has made increasing provision for matters relating to the neighbouring use of land, for instance the Access to Neighbouring Land Act 1992 and the Party Wall etc. Act 1996. So too the law relating to animals has been codified and amended by the Animals Act 1971. Specific modern problems addressed by Parliament are dealt with in various chapters. These include raves, travellers and trespassory assemblies (under the Criminal Justice and Public Order Act 1994), pit bull terriers and dogs bred for fighting (the Dangerous Dogs Act 1991) and stalkers (the Protection from Harassment Act 1997).

Above all Parliament has introduced legislation designed to safeguard us and our enjoyment of the land around us from the effects of pollution. Part III of the Environmental Protection Act 1990 lays down a code granting powers to both local authorities and individuals in respect of many forms of pollution which are 'prejudicial to health or nuisance'. Further, detailed rules govern a myriad of subjects which can be a source of real irritation. Burglar alarms, late-night revellers, stubble burning, fly tipping, litter, poor quality drinking water: these and many others are nuisances which are subject to their own legislative rules and which have a place in this book.

I hope that no-one will cavil at the title. Although the starting point has been the tort of private nuisance, some subjects have been incorporated on the basis solely of expediency. I have sought to select topics which the lay person might ordinarily recognise as 'nuisances', applying everyday, rather than legal, notions.

I must express my gratitude to all the contributors. They are some of the foremost experts in their various specialist fields. Most were involved in the planning and structure of the book. Whilst it is difficult to attribute different chapters to individuals, since many made significant contributions to a variety of sections, their formidable backgrounds give clues to the areas with which they were mainly concerned. Of the lawyers, Vivien King has a special interest in trespass and boundary disputes and is a well known lecturer at the RICS and the Law Society, as well as to local authorities on their liabilities under the Criminal Justice and Public Order Act 1994. Chris Hancock provided an all-round property litigator's experience. Jacqui O'Keeffe is a prominent environmental lawyer as well as being the head of a very busy department.

The book has benefited from the practical input of two leading surveyors. Although many surveyors manage to tackle several areas of expertise, our own contributors are closely linked with specific areas. There are few real right to light experts in the country. Kaivin Wong succeeds in combining real specialism in right to light issues with an exhaustive knowledge of party walls, being a member of the Pyramus and Thisbe Club. We also had the advantage of a major contribution from David Powell, a boundary surveyor and founder member of the RICS' Boundary and Party Walls Practice Panel. During the writing of this book he became known to many when he was filmed taking part in a popular television series, *Neighbours at War*.

For all their contributions I am extremely grateful. I must extend my profound thanks to them for their patience, since they offered their manuscripts promptly and then had to wait for me to fulfil my own part.

To the publishers too I wish to offer my thanks. In particular, Hugo de Rijke was always at hand to offer advice and handled any difficulties with skill and diplomacy.

I must also thank Lord Thomas of Gresford QC and the members of his chambers since they allowed me to use the excellent facilities at our Reading Annex without apparently examining too closely the extent of my contributions to our practice during the writing of the book. In particular Peter Digney read some of the manuscript and made useful observations.

Finally, I am grateful to the librarians at the Bodleian Library, Oxford for their assistance; to the partners at Dexter Montague, Reading, who answered many practical questions; to Darren Crispin, barrister, for this help in correcting errors; and especially to Christopher Sheffield of Peter Kingshill & Co, Grays Inn. I must take the blame for any mistakes which remain.

The text seeks to state the law as applied on 1 May 1998.

Gordon Wignall
1 Dr Johnson's Buildings,
Temple

Table of Cases

All references are to paragraph number. Those prefixed A refer to the Appendices.

Aitken v South Hams DC [1994] 3 WLR 333; [1994] 3 All ER 400; (1994) *The Times*
8 July 3.14.12
Alan Wibberley Building Ltd v Insley (1997) LSG Reports 26 November; (1997)
The Times 24 November 6.6.4
Aldham v United Dairies (London) Ltd [1940] 1 KB 507; [1939] 4 All ER 522;
109 LJKB 323 . . . . 9.2.2
Allen v Greenwood [1980] Ch 119; [1979] 2 WLR 187; [1979] 1 All ER 819,
CA 8.4.12
Allen v Gulf Oil Refining Ltd [1981] AC 1001; [1981] 2 WLR 188, HL; rvsg [1980]
QB 153, CA 1.6.24, 1.6.25, 1.11.9
Alphacell v Woodward [1972] AC 824; [1972] 2 WLR 1320; [1972] 2 All ER 475,
HL 15.2.4
Anchor Brewhouse Developments v Berkley House (Docklands) Developments Ltd
(1987) 38 Build LR 82; (1988) 4 Const LJ 29. . . . . 16.11.6, 16.11.13
Andreae v Selfridge & Co [1938] Ch 1; [1937] 3 All ER 255; 107 LJ Ch 126. . . 1.6.6,
1.6.27–1.6.29
Anglo-Cyprian Trade Agencies v Paphos Wine Industries [1951] 1 All ER 873;
95 SJ 336; [1951] WN 205 . . . . 16.9.4, 16.9.5
Ankerson v Connelly [1907] 1 Ch 678; 76 LJ Ch 402; 23 TLR 486, CA. 8.4.19
Armstrong v Sheppard & Short Ltd [1959] 2 QB 384; [1959] 3 WLR 84; [1959]
2 All ER 651, CA. 16.9.5, 16.10.1
Arthur v Anker [1997] QB 564; [1996] 2 WLR 602; [1996] 3 All ER 783,
CA 11.3.4, 11.3.5, 11.3.9
Ashby v White (1703) 2 Ld Raym 938; 6 Mod Rep 45; 92 ER 126. . . . . 5.2.1
Attorney-General's Reference (No 1 of 1994) [1995] 1 WLR 599, CA. 15.2.4
Attorney-General v Beynon [1970] Ch 1; [1969] 2 WLR 147; [1969] 2 All ER
263 . . . . 6.8.4
Attorney-General v Corke [1933] Ch 89; [1932] All ER Rep 711; 102 LJ
Ch 30 . . . . 4.2.6
Attorney-General v Gastonia Coaches [1977] RTR 219. . . . . 1.6.6, 1.6.10, 2.2.2
Attorney-General v PYA Quarries Ltd *ex rel* Glamorgan CC 1957] 2 QB 169;
[1957] 2 WLR 770; [1957] 1 All ER 894, CA. 1.7.7, 2.2.1
Attorney-General v Roe [1915] 1 Ch 235; [1914-15] All ER Rep 1090; 84 LJ
Ch 322 . . . . 6.3.9
Attorney-General for Southern Nigeria v John Holt & Co (Liverpool) Ltd [1915]
AC 599; 1914-15] All ER Rep 444; 84 LJPC 98, PC 6.11.3
Backhouse v Bonomi (1861) 9 HL Cas 503; [1861-73] All ER Rep 429; 34
LJQB 181, HL 8.3.2
Balfour v Barty-King [1957] 1 QB 496; [1957] 2 WLR 84; [1957] 1 All ER 156,
CA 4.3.4, 4.3.5
Bamford v Turnley [1861-73] All ER Rep 706; 3 B & S 66; 10 WR 803 . . . . 1.6.3

Banque Bruxelles Lambert SA v Eagle Star Insurance Co Ltd [1997] AC 191;
  [1996] 3 WLR 87; [1996] 3 All ER 365, HL........................... 1.8.2
Barker v Herbert [1911] 2 KB 633; [1911-13] All ER Rep 509; 80 LJKB 1329,
  CA 1.9.6, 1.9.8, 1.9.9, 1.10.11
Barton v Armstrong [1969] 2 NSWR 451; [1976] AC 104; [1975] 2 WLR 1050;
  [1975] 2 All ER 465, PC 10.2.11
Baten's Case (1610) 9 Co Rep 536; 77 ER 810 .... 1.5.1
Bativala v West [1970] 1 QB 716; [1970] 2 WLR 8; [1970] 1 All ER 332...... 9.2.1,
                                                                     9.5.3
Beaulieu v Finglam (1401) YB 2 Hen 4, fo 18, pt 6 .... 4.3.7
Beaumont v Greathead (1846) 2 CB 494; 15 LJCP 130; 135 ER 1039 .... 16.9.2
Behrens v Bertram Mills Circus Ltd [1957] 2 QB 1; [1957] 2 WLR 404; [1957]
  1 All ER 583 .... 9.2.3, 9.3.6, 9.3.8, 9.3.21
Benjamin v Storr (1874) LR 9 CP 400; [1874-80] All ER Rep Ext 2000;
  43 LJCP 162.. 2.2.3, 2.3.10
Betts v Penge UDC [1942] 2 KB 154; [1942] 2 All ER 61; 111 LJKB 565...... 3.2.7
Birmingham DC v McMahon (1987) 151 JP 709; (1987) 19 HLR 452; (1988)
  86 LGR 63 .... 3.18.4
Black v Carmichael (1992) *The Times* 25 June........................... 11.3.8
Black v Christchurch Finance Co [1894] AC 48; [1891-4] All ER Rep Ext 1498;
  63 LJPC 32, PC 1.9.17
Blundell v Catterall (1821) 5 B & Ald 268; 106 ER 1190 .... 5.2.6
Bolton v Stone [1951] AC 850; [1951] 1 All ER 1078; 95 SJ 333, HL 1.8.3
Bond v Norman; Bond v Nottingham Corporation [1940] Ch 429; [1940]
  2 All ER 12; 109 LJ Ch 220, CA 8.3.2, 8.3.7
Bone v Seale [1975] 1 WLR 797; [1975] 1 All ER 787; 119 SJ 137, CA....... 1.6.6,
                                                           1.6.22, 1.6.26, 16.3.1
Botross v Hammersmith and Fulham LBC (1994) 16 Cr App Rep (S) 622;
  27 HLR 179 .... 3.18.7
Bower v Peate (1876) 1 QBD 321; [1874-80] All ER Rep 905; 45 LJQB 446 .. 1.9.17
Bracewell v Appleby [1975] Ch 408; [1975] 2 WLR 282; {1975] 1 All ER 993
  .... 16.11.8, 16.11.13
Bradburn v Lindsay [1983] 2 All ER 408; (1983) 268 EG 152 .... 8.3.7
Bradford Corporation v Pickles [1895] AC 587; [1895-9] All ER Rep 984;
  64 LJ Ch 759, HL... 1.6.11
Bridlington Relay Ltd v Yorkshire Electricity Board [1965] Ch 436; [1965]
  2 WLR 341; [1965] 1 All ER 264 .... 1.7.4
Brine v Great Western Railway Co (1862) 2 B & S 402; 31 LJQB 101; 10 WR
  341 .... 5.2.2
Bristol City Council v Higgins (1994) (unreported)...................... 3.16.1
British Celanese Ltd v A H Hunt (Capacitors) Ltd [1969] 1 WLR 959; [1969]
  2 All ER 1252; 113 SJ 368 .... 1.7.7
British Road Services Ltd v Slater [1964] 1 WLR 498; [1964] 1 All ER 816;
  108 SJ 357 .... 6.7.10
Broder v Saillard (1876) 2 Ch D 692; 24 WR 1011; 45 LJ Ch 414........ 1.4.1, 1.6.5,
                                                                1.6.7, 1.6.22
Bromley v Mercer [1922] 2 KB 126; 91 LJKB 577; 127 LT 282, CA.......... 2.3.8
Bucks CC v Moran [1990] Ch 623; [1989] 3 WLR 152; [1989] 2 All ER 225,
  CA 5.7.7
Buckley v United Kingdom [1996] JPL 1018; [1995] JPL 633 .... 5.4.10
Bunclark v Herts CC (1977) 243 EG 455; [1977] 2 EGLR 114........ 16.2.6, 16.3.1
Burnett v George [1992] 1 FLR 525; [1992] Fam Law 156; 1 FCR 1012, CA .. 10.3.8
Burris v Azadani [1995] 1 WLR 1372; [1995] 4 All ER 802, CA 10.3.10

Burton v Winters [1993] 1 WLR 1077; [1993] 3 All ER 847, CA 5.5.7
Butler v Standard Telephones and Cables Ltd [1940] 1 KB 399; [1941] 1 All ER
   121; 109 LJKB 238 . . . . 1.5.3
Butuyuyu v Hammersmith and Fulham LBC [1997] Env LR D13. . . . . 3.14.7
C v C [1998] 2 WLR 599; [1998] 1 FLR 554 . . . . 10.5.6
Cambridge Water Co Ltd v Eastern Counties Leather plc [1994] 2 AC 264; [1994]
   2 WLR 53; [1994] 1 All ER 53 . . . . 1.8.1, 1.8.2, 2.3.9, 4.1.2, 4.2.5, 4.2.13
Caminer v Northern and London Investment Trust Ltd [1951] AC 88; [1950]
   2 All ER 486; 94 SJ 518, HL 1.9.9
Canterbury CC v Ferris [1997 Env LR D14; (1996) *The Independent*
   11 November 3.14.2
Canvey Island Commissioners v Preedy [1922] 1 Ch 179; 91 LJ Ch 203; 66 SJ
   182 . . . . 5.3.1
Carlgarth, The; Otarama, The [1927] P 93; 96 LJP 162; 136 LT 518. . . . . 5.2.4
Carr-Saunders v Dick McNeil Associates [1986] 1 WLR 922; [1986] 2 All ER 888;
   130 SJ 525 . . . . 16.6.4, 16.11.8
Chapman v Gosberton Farm Produce Co [1992] COD 486; Env Law 1992-93 4(3),
   63. . . . . 3.14.5
Charing Cross West End and City Electric Supply Co v Hydraulic Power Co [1914]
   3 KB 772; [1914-15] All ER Rep 85; 83 LJKB 1352 . . . . 4.2.8
Christie v Davey [1893] 1 Ch 316; 62 LJ Ch 439; 3 R 210 . . . . 1.6.12
City of London Brewery Co v Tennant (1873) 9 Ch App 212; 43 LJ Ch 457; 22
   WR 172 . . . . 8.4.2
City of London Corporation v Bovis Construction Ltd [1992] 3 All ER 697; 49
   BLR 1; 86 LGR 660, CA 1.6.27, 12.3.14
City of London Land Tax Commissioners v Central London Railway Co [1913]
   AC 364; 82 LJ Ch 274; 57 SJ 403, HL 6.8.3
Coffee v McEvoy [1912] 2 IR 95 . . . . 5.4.1
Colls v Home and Colonial Stores Ltd [1904] AC 179; [1904-7] All ER Rep 5; 73
   LJ Ch 484, HL 1.6.8, 1.6.18, 8.1.2, 8.4.2, 8.4.3
Colwell v St Pancras BC [1904] 1 Ch 707; 73 LJ Ch 275; 52 WR 523. . . . 1.6.6, 1.6.7,
                                                               1.6.26
Cooke v Adatia (1989) 153 JP 129; [1989] COD 327; (1989) 153 LG Rev 189 . . 3.8.3
Cooper v Railway Executive [1953] 1 WLR 223; [1953] 1 All ER 477. . . . . 9.5.2
Courtauld v Legh (1869) LR 4 Exch 126; 38 LJ Ex 45; 17 WR 466 . . . . 8.2.16
Coventry CC v Cartwright [1975] 1 WLR 845; [1975] 2 All ER99; 119 SJ 235 . . 3.6.1
Cowper v Laidler [1903] 2 Ch 337; 72 LJ Ch 578; 89 LT 469. . . . . 16.11.3
Cross v Kirklees MBC [1998] 1 All ER 564, CA 2.3.19
Crow v Wood [1971] 1 QB 77; [1970] 3 WLR 516; [1970] 3 All ER 425, CA . . . 9.4.6
Crump v Lambert (1867) LR 3 Eq 403; 15 WR 417; 15 LT 600 . . 1.6.5, 1.6.10, 1.6.19
Cudmore-Ray v Pajouheshnia [1993] CLY 4040 . . . . 16.5.1
Cummings v Granger [1977} QB 397; [1976] 2 WLR 842; [1977] 1 All ER 104,
   CA 9.3.16, 9.3.23, 9.3.25, 11.3.7
Cunard v Antifyre Ltd [1933] 1 KB 551; [1932] All ER Rep 558; 103 LJKB
   321 . . . . 1.2.3, 1.7.2, 1.7.7
Cunliffe v Bankes [1945] 1 All ER 459 . . . . 1.10.12, 2.3.13
Cunningham v Birmingham CC (1997) *The Times* 9 June 3.2.7
Curtis v Betts [1990] 1 WLR 459; [1990] 1 All ER 769; 134 SJ 317, CA 9.3.11,
                                                      9.3.13, 9.3.15, 9.3.16
Cushing v Peter Walker & Son (Warrington and Burton) Ltd [1941] 2 All ER
   693 . . . . 1.10.10, 1.10.11
Dalton v Angus (1881) 6 App Cas 740; [1881-5] All ER Rep 1; 30 WR 191. . . . 1.7.3,
                                                                1.9.17

Daniel v Ferguson [1891] 2 Ch 27; 39 WR 599, CA 16.14.2
Darley Main Colliery Co Ltd v Mitchell (1886) 11 App Cas 127; [1886-90] All ER
    Rep 449; 55 LJQB 529, HL...................................... 8.3.2, 16.7.1
Davey v Harrow Corporation [1958] 1 QB 60; [1957] 2 WLR 941; [1957] 2 All ER
    305, CA 6.12.13
Davies v Davies [1975] QB 172; [1974] 3 WLR 607; [1974] 3 All ER 817,
    CA 9.5.1, 9.5.4
Davis v Johnson [1979] AC 264; [1978] 2 WLR 553, HL; [1978] 1 All ER 841,
    CA 10.1.8, 10.5.6
Davis v Whitby [1974] Ch 186; [1974] 2 WLR 333; [1974] 1 All ER 806, CA .. 8.2.7
Deakins v Hookings [1994] 14 EG 133............................... 16.6.4
Didow v Alberta Power [1988] 5 WWR 606 (Alberta CA) 5.2.5
Diment v N H Foot Ltd [1974] 1 WLR 1427; [1974] 2 All ER 785; 118 SJ 810.. 8.2.7
Dodd Properties (Kent) v Canterbury CC [1980] 1 WLR 433; [1980] 1 All ER 928;
    13 BLR 45, CA 1.4.1, 16.2.6
Dollman v A & S Hillman Ltd [1941] 1 All ER 355, CA................... 2.3.12
Draper v Hodder [1972] 2 QB 556; [1972] 2 WLR 992; [1972] 2 All ER 210... 9.2.1,
                                                                9.2.2, 9.3.17
Drinking Water Inspectorate and Secretary of State v Severn Trent Water (1995)
    The Independent 24 April 15.4.8
Dymond v Pearce [1972] 1 QB 496; [1972] 2 WLR 633; [1972] 1 All ER 1142,
    CA 2.3.11, 2.3.14
East Northamptonshire DC v Fossett [1994] Env LR 388 .... 3.8.1
Easton v Richmond Highway Board (1871) LR 7 QB; 36 JP 485; 20 WR 203 ... 6.8.1
Edwards (Job) Ltd v Birmingham Navigations [1924] 1 KB 341; 93 LJKB 261;
    68 SJ 501 .... 1.10.3
Egerton v Harding [1975] QB 62; [1974] 3 WLR 437; [1974] 3 All ER 689,
    CA 6.3.9
Elliott v Islington LBC [1991] 1 EGLR; [1991] 10 EG 167; (1990) *The Times* 6 July,
    CA 16.11.10, 16.12.4
Ellis v Johnstone [1963] 2 QB 8; [1963] 2 WLR 176; [1963] 1 All ER 286,
    CA 9.5.1
Emanuel (H & N) v Greater London Council [1971] 2 All ER 835; 69 LGR 346;
    [1971] 2 Lloyd's Rep 36, CA.............................. 4.3.4, 4.3.7, 4.3.8
Emms v Polya (1973) 227 EG 1659 .... 1.6.15
F v F (Protection from Violence: Continuing Cohabitation) [1989] 2 FLR 451;
    [1990] Fam Law 224 .... 10.5.6
Fardon v Harcourt-Rivington (1932) 146 LT 391; {1932] All ER Rep 81; 76 SJ 81,
    HL 9.2.1
Farrell v Mowlem (John) & Co Ltd [1954] 1 Lloyd's Rep 437 .... 1.9.4, 2.3.9
Fay v Prentice (1845) 1 CB 828; 14 LJCP 298; 135 ER 769 .... 1.5.2
Filburn v People's Palace & Aquarium Co Ltd (1890) 25 QBD 258; 59 LJQB 471;
    38 WR 706, CA 9.3.6
Filliter v Phippard (1847) 11 QB 347; 17 LJQB 89; 116 ER 506.............. 4.3.9
Fisher v Winch [1939] 1 KB 666; [1939] 2 All ER 144; 108 LJKB 473, CA.... 6.6.4,
                                                                6.12.13
Fitzgerald v E D & A D Cooke Bourne (Farms) Ltd [1964] 1 QB 249; [1963]
    3 WLR 522; [1963] 3 All ER 36, CA 9.3.14
Fitzhardinge (Lord) v Purcell [1908] 2 Ch 139; 77 LJ Ch 529; 72 JP 276...... 6.10.3
                                                                6.11.6
Foster v British Gas [1991] 2 AC 306; [1991] 2 WLR 1075; [1991] 2 All ER 705,
    HL A1.23

Foster v Warblington UDC [1906] 1 KB 648; [1904-7] All ER Rep 366; 54 WR 575,
    CA 1.2.5
Fowley Marine (Emsworth) Ltd v Gafford [1968] 2 QB 618; [1968] 2 WLR 842;
    [1968] 1 All ER 979, CA 6.10.12
Fresh Fruit Wales Ltd v Halbert (1991) *The Times* 9 January; (1991) *The Daily*
    Telegraph 7 February, CA 10.3.7
Gafford v Graham (1998) *The Times* 1 May 16.11.8, 16.11.12
Gaunt v Fynney [1872] 8 Ch App 8; 42 LJ Ch 122; 21 WR 129 . . . . 1.6.8
Geddis v Bann Reservoir (Proprietors) (1878) 3 App Cas 430, HL 1.11.7, 1.11.9
Giles v Walker (1890) 24 QBD 656; [1886-90] All ER Rep 501; 59 LJQB
    416 . . . . 1.10.5
Gillingham BC v Medway (Chatham) Docks Co Ltd [1993] QB 343; [1992] 3
    WLR 449; [1992] 3 All ER 923 . . . . 1.6.24, 1.6.25
Goldman v Hargrave [1967] 1 AC 465; [1966] 3 WLR 513; [1966] 2 All ER 989,
    PC 1.10.6, 1.10.7, 1.10.8, 4.3.4
Gomberg v Smith [1963] 1 QB 25; [1962] 2 WLR 749; [1962] 1 All ER 725 . . . . 9.2.1
Gould v McAuliffe [1941] 2 All ER 527; 57 TLR 468, CA 9.2.1
Gravesham Borough Council v British Railways Board [1978] Ch 379; [1978] 3
    WLR 494; [1978] 3 All ER 853 . . . . 2.3.1
Great Northern Railway v M'Alister [1897] 1 IR 587 . . . . 6.9.7
Greater London Council v Tower Hamlets LBC (1984)15 HLR 54 . . . . 3.2.7
Greenock Corporation v Caledonian Railway Co [1917] AC 556; [1916-17] All
    ER Rep 426; 86 LJPC 185, HL 4.2.14
Griffin v South West Water (1994) 25 August (unreported) A1.23, A2.6
Griffiths v Kingsley-Stubbs [1987] CLY 1277; (1986) CAT No 506, 3 June . . . 16.5.3
Grigsby v Melville [1974] 1 WLR 80; [1973] 3 All ER 455; 117 SJ 467 . . . . . . 6.12.5
Gyle-Thompson v Wall Street (Properties) Ltd [1974] 1 WLR 123; [1974] 1 All
    ER 295; 117 SJ 526 . . . . 7.3.7
Hadwell v Righton [1907] 2 KB 345; 76 LJKB 891; 51 SJ 500 . . . . 2.3.3
Hale v Jennings Bros [1938] 1 All ER 578; 82 SJ 193, CA 4.2.6, 4.2.9, 4.2.11
Halsey v Esso Petroleum Co Ltd [1961] 1 WLR 683; [1961] 2 All ER 145; 105 SJ
    209 . . . . 1.6.4, 1.6.6, 1.6.18, 1.7.1, 1.9.5, 2.1.1, 4.2.12, 16.3.1
Hammersmith and City Railway Co v Brand (1869) LR 4 HL 171; 38 LJQB 265;
    21 LT 238, HL 1.11.7
Hampstead & Suburban Properties Ltd v Diomedous [1969] 1 Ch 248; [1968]
    3 WLR 990; [1968] 3 All ER 545 . . . . 1.6.7, 1.6.9
Harbutt's 'Plasticine' v Wayne Tank and Pump Co [1970] 1 QB 447; [1970]
    2 WLR 198; [1970] 1 All ER 225, CA 16.2.4
Harper v G N Haden & Sons [1933] Ch 298; [1932] All ER Rep 59; 76 SJ 849,
    CA 2.2.3, 2.3.4, 2.3.7, 2.3.8
Harris v James [1874-80] All ER Rep 1142; (1876) 45 LJQB 545; 35 LT 240 . . 1.9.3,
    1.9.14
Harrison v Rutland (Duke of) [1893] 1 QB 142; [1891-4] All ER Rep 514; 62
    LJQB 117, CA 2.3.2
Harrison v Southwark and Vauxhall Water Co [1891] 2 Ch 409; [1891-4] All ER
    Rep 372; 60 LJ Ch 630 . . . . 1.6.28
Harrold v Watney [1898] 2 QB 320; 67 LJQB 771; 42 SJ 609, CA 6.3.10
Harrow LBC v Donohue [1993] NPC 49; [1995] EGLR 257, CA 16.15.1
Hay, *ex p* (1886) 3 TLR 24 . . . . 9.6.2
Heap v Ind Coope & Allsopp Ltd [1940] 2 KB 476; [1940] 3 All ER 634; 109
    LJKB 274 . . . . 1.9.11, 2.3.18
Henderson v M'Kenzie (1876) 3 R 623; 13 SLR 393 . . . . 9.6.2
Henniker v Howard (1904) 90 LT 157 . . . . 6.6.6

Hickman v Maisey [1900] 1 QB 752; 69 LJQB 511; 44 SJ 326, CA 2.3.5
Hindson v Ashby [1896] 2 Ch 1; 65 LJ Ch 515; 40 SJ 417, CA. 6.11.3
Hoare & Co v McAlpine [1923] 1 Ch 167; [1922] All ER Rep 759; 92 LJ Ch
    81 . . . . 4.2.6
Hobbs v The Baxendale Chemical Co Ltd [1992] 1 Lloyd's Rep 54 . . . . 4.3.5
Hobson v Gledhill [1978] 1 WLR 215; [1978] 1 All ER 945; 121 SJ 757 . . . . . . 9.6.13
Hodgson v York Corporation (1873) 28 LT 836; 37 JP 725. . . . . 1.10.5
Hole & Son (Sayers Common) Ltd v Harrisons of Thurnscoe Ltd [1973] 1 Lloyd's
    Rep 345; (1972) 116 SJ 922. . . . . 16.2.5
Hollebone v Midhurst and Fernhurst Builders Ltd [1986] 1 Lloyd's Rep 38; (1968)
    118 NLJ 156. . . . . 16.2.4
Holliday v National Telephone Co [1899] 2 QB 392; 68 LJQB 1016; 47 WR 658,
    CA 2.3.12
Holling v Yorkshire Traction Co Ltd [1948] 2 All ER 662, 206 LT 240 . . . . 2.3.7
Hollis v Dudley MBC (1997) The Times 12 December 3.18.7
Hollywood Silver Fox Farm Ltd v Emmett [1936] 2 KB 468; [1936] 1 All ER 825;
    105 LJKB 829 . . . . 1.6.13
Horner v Horner [1982] Fam 90; [1982] 2 WLR 914; [1982] 2 All ER 495,
    CA 10.5.2, 10.5.6
Horton v Colwyn Bay & Colwyn UDC [1908] 1 KB 327; 77 LJKB 215; 52 SJ 158,
    CA 16.4.1
Horton's Estate v James Beattie Ltd [1927] 1 Ch 75; 996 LJ Ch 15; 70 SJ 917. . . 8.4.3
Hubbard v Pitt [1976] QB 142; [1975] 3 WLR 201; [1975] 3 All ER 1, CA 2.2.2,
    2.3.3, 2.3.12
Hunter v Canary Wharf [1997] AC 655; [1997] 2 WLR 684;[1997] 2 All ER 426,
    HL 1.1.2,1.2.1, 1.2.4, 1.7.3, 1.7.5, 1.7.6, 10.3.4
Hurst v Hants CC [1997] NPC 99; (1997) LGR 27; (1997) The Times 6 June . . 6.7.11,
    A3.6–A3.7
Ibbotson v Peat (1865) 3 H & C 644; 159 ER 684; 34 LJ Ex 118 . . . . 1.6.14
Inland Revenue Commissioners v National Federation of Self Employed and Small
    Businesses [1982] AC 617; [1981] 2 WLR 722; [1981] 2 All ER 93, HL 3.18.4
Isaac v Hotel de Paris [1960] 1 WLR 239; [1960] 1 All ER 348; 104 SJ 245,
    PC. 5.3.1
Isenberg v East India House Estate Co Ltd (1863) 3 De G J & Sm 263; 33 LJ Ch
    392; 46 ER 637 . . . . 16.12.1–16.12.3
Jacobs v London CC [1950] AC 361; [1950] 1 All ER 737; 94 SJ 318, HL 2.3.12
Jaggard v Sawyer [1995] 1 WLR 269; [1995] 2 All ER 189, CA 16.11.4, 16.11.8,
    16.11.9, 16.11.13, 16.11.14
Janvier v Sweeney [1919] 2 KB 316; [1918-19] All ER Rep 1056; 88 LJKB 1231,
    CA 10.3.2, 10.3.8
Job Edwards Ltd v Birmingham Navigations. See Edwards (Job) Ltd v Birmingham
    Navigations
Johnson v Walton [1990] 1 FLR 350; [1990] Fam Law 260; [1990] FCR 568,
    CA 10.3.9, 10.5.2, 10.5.6
Jones v Chappell (1875) LR 20 Eq 539, 44 LJ Ch 658. 1.2.2
Jones v Gooday (1841) 8 M & W 146; 10 LJ Ex 275; 151 ER 985 . . . . 16.2.3
Jones v Price [1965] 2 QB 618; [1965] 3 WLR 296; [1965] 2 All ER 625, CA. . . 6.3.9
Jordeson v Sutton, Southcoates & Drypool Gas Co [1899] 2 Ch 217; 68 LJ Ch 457;
    63 JP 692, CA 8.3.3
Keddle v Payn [1964] 1 WLR 262; [1964] 1 All ER 189; 107 SJ 911 . . . . 9.6.2
Keeble v Hickeringill (1706) 11 East 574; [1558-1774] All ER Rep 286; 11 Mod
    Rep 73 . . . . 1.6.14

Kelsen v Imperial Tobacco Co [1957] 2 QB 334; [1957] 2 WLR 1007; [1957] 2 All
ER 343 . . . . 5.2.2, 16.11.10, 16.11.12, 16.12.2
Kennaway v Thompson [1981] QB 88; [1980] 3 WLR 361; [1980] 3 All ER 329,
CA 16.3.1, 16.11.4
Khorasandjian v Bush [1993] QB 727; [1993] 3 WLR 476; [1993] 3 All ER 669,
CA 10.3.4, 10.3.8
King v Harrow LBC [1994] EGCS 76 . . . . 15.5.3
King v Liverpool CC [1986] 1 WLR 890; [1986] 3 All ER 554;130 SJ 505,
CA 1.10.11
Kirklees MBC v Field (1997) The Times 26 November 3.12.3
Lambeth LBC v Mullings (1990) RVR 259; (1990) The Times 16 January 3.12.7
Lambeth LBC v Stubbs [1980] JPL 517; (1980) 78 LGR 650; (1980) 255 EG
789 . . . . 3.14.6
Land v Sykes [1992] 1 EGLR 1; [1992] 03 EG 115; [1991] EGCS 98, CA 5.4.2
Lavender v Betts [1942] 2 All ER 72; 167 LT 70 . . . . 5.2.3
League Against Cruel Sports v Scott [1986] QB 240; [1985] 3 WLR 400; [1985]
2 All ER 489 . . . . 5.2.2
Leakey v National Trust for Places of Historic Interest or Natural Beauty [1980] QB
485; [1980] 2 WLR 65; [1980] 1 All ER 171, CA 1.10.7, 3.2.3, 6.7.5, 8.3.7
Leanse v Lord Egerton [1943] KB 323; [1943] 1 All ER 489; 112 LJKB 273 . . . 1.9.10
Leeds Industrial Co-operative Society v Slack [1924] AC 851; [1924] All ER Rep
259; 93 LJ Ch 436 . . . . 16.11.9
Leigh v Jack (1879) 5 Ex D 264; 49 LJQB 220; 28 WR 452, CA 5.7.7
Lemmon v Webb [1895] AC 1; [1891-4] All ER Rep 749, HL; affg [1894]
3 Ch 1 . . . . 1.5.2, 6.7.4, 6.7.6
Letang v Cooper [1965] 1 QB 232; [1964] 3 WLR 573; [1964] 2 All ER 929,
CA 10.3.2
Lilly (Walter) & Co Ltd v Westminster CC (1996) The Times 1 March 12.3.4
Llandudno UDC v Woods [1899] 2 Ch 705; [1895-9] All ER Rep 845; 98 LJ Ch
623 . . . . 16.11.5
Lloyd v Director of Public Prosecutions [1992] 1 All ER 982; (1992) 156 JP 342;
(1992) 156 JPN 284 . . . . 11.3.2–11.3.4
Lloyds Bank v Guardian Assurance plc 17 October 1986 (unreported) 12.3.10
Locobail International Finance Ltd v Agroexport [1986] 1 WLR 657; [1986]
1 All ER 901; 130 SJ 245, CA 16.14.1
London and Manchester Assurance Co Ltd v O & H Construction Ltd (1989)
29 EG 65; (1990) 6 Const LJ 155 . . . . 5.2.2
London and North Western Railway Co v Westminster Corporation. See Westminster
Corporation v London and North Western Railway Co
Lonrho v Fayed (No 2) [1992] 1 WLR 1; [1991] 4 All ER 961; (1991) The Guardian
16 April 10.3.3
Lonsdale (Earl) v Nelson [1814-23] All ER Rep 737; 2 B & C 302; 107 ER
396 . . . . 1.5.2
Loseby v Newman [1996] 1 FCR 647; [1995] 2 FLR 754, CA 10.5.21
Lotus v British Soda Co Ltd [1972] Ch 123; [1971] 2 WLR 7; [1971] 1 All ER
265 . . . . 8.3.3, 8.3.5
Lowe v South Somerset DC [1997] EGCS 113 . . . . 3.12.4
Lyons, Sons & Co v Gulliver [1914] 1 Ch 631; [1911-13] All ER Rep 537; 83 LJ
Ch 281, CA 2.3.10
M v Home Office [1992] QB 270, CA; [1993] 3 WLR 433; [1993] 3 All ER 537,
HL 10.3.9
Maberley v Peabody & Co of London [1946] 2 All ER 192 . . . . 1.4.1, 1.9.2,
1.9.7, 1.9.16

McColl v Strathclyde Regional Council [1984] JPL 351 . . . . 15.4.4
McCombe v Read [1955] 2 QB 429; [1955] 1 WLR 635; [1955] 2 All ER
    458 . . . . 6.7.6, 16.8.1
McGillivray v Stephenson [1950] 1 All ER 942; 48 LGR 409; [1950] WN
    209 . . . . 3.12.4
McGrath v Munster and Leinster Bank [1959] IR 313; (1959) 94 ILTR 110. . . . 16.2.3
McPhail v Persons, Names Unknown [1973] Ch 447; [1973] 3 WLR 71; [1973]
    3 All ER 393, CA 5.4.5, 5.5.7
McQuaker v Goddard [1940] 1 KB 687; [1940] 1 All ER 471; 109 LJKB 673,
    CA 9.3.6
McVittie v Bolton Corporation [1945] KB 281; [1945] 1 All ER 379, CA 14.6.9
Mace v Philcox (1864) 15 CBNS 600; 33 LJCP 124; 12 WR 670 . . . . 5.2.2
Maher v Nazir (1977) Construction Industry Law Leter 1257, May 1977 . . . . . . 16.5.2
Maitland v Raisbeck [1944] 1 KB 689; [1944] 2 All ER 272;113 LJKB 549,
    CA 2.3.12, 2.3.14
Malone v Laskey [1907] 2 KB 141; [1904-7] All ER Rep 304; 76 LJKB 1134,
    CA 1.2.3, 1.7.2
Manchester Corporation v Farnworth [1930] AC 171; [1929] All ER Rep 90; 99
    LJKB 83, HL 1.11.7
Mappin Bros v Liberty & Co Ltd [1903] 1 Ch 118; 72 LJ Ch 63; 47 SJ 71 . . . . . . 6.8.3
Marshall v Blackpool Corporation [1935] AC 16; [1934] All ER Rep 437; 103
    LJKB 566, HL 2.3.10
Mason v Levy Auto Parts of England Ltd [1967] 2 QB 530; [1967] 2 WLR 1384;
    2 All ER 62 . . . . 4.2.4, 4.2.6, 4.3.1, 4.3.3, 4.3.5, 4.3.9, 4.3 10
Matania v National Provincial Bank and Elevenist Syndicate [1936] 2 All ER 633;
    106 LJKB 113; 80 SJ 532, CA 1.6.29, 1.9.17
Mediana, The [1900] AC 113; [1900-3] All ER Rep 126; 44 SJ 259, HL 16.9.3,
                                                                                          16.9.5
Meggs v Liverpool Corporation [1968] 1 WLR 689; [1968] 1 All ER 1137; 111 SJ
    742, CA 2.3.19
Mellor v Walmesley [1905] 2 Ch 164; 74 LJ Ch 475; 49 SJ 565, CA 6.10.2
Metropolitan Asylum District Managers v Hill (1881) 6 App Cas 193; 50 LJQB 353;
    29 WR 617 . . . . 1.7.6, 1.11.7, 1.11.8
Metropolitan Properties v Jones [1939] 2 All ER 202; 83 SJ 399 . . . . 1.6.6
Midland Bank v Bardgrove Property Services Ltd (1992) 60 BLR 1; (1992) 65
    P & CR 153; [1992] NPC 83, CA 16.5.2
Midwood & Co v Manchester Corporation [1905] 2 KB 597;1904-7] All ER Rep
    Ext 1364; 74 LJKB 884, CA 1.7.7
Miliangos v George Frank Textiles [1976] AC 443; [1975} 3 WLR 758; [1975]
    3 All ER 801 . . . . 16.2.6
Miller v Jackson [1977] QB 966; [1977] 3 WLR 20; [1977] 3 All ER 338,
    CA 1.11.6
Mills v Brooker [1919] 1 KB 555; [1918-19] All ER Rep 613; 88 LJKB 950. . . . 6.7.4
Milton v Proctor (1989) NSW Conu R 55-450 . . . . 5.7.5
Ministry of Defence v Thompson (1993) 25 HLR 552; [1993] 40 EG 148; [1993]
    2 EGLR 107, CA 5.5.2
Minting v Ramage [1991] EGCS 12, CA 6.8.4
Morgan v Fry [1968] 2 QB 710; [1968] 3 WLR 506; [1968] 3 All ER 452,
    CA 10.3.3
Morrice v Evans (1989) The Times 27 February, CA 5.7.6
Morris v Blaenau Gwent District Council (1982) 80 LGR 793; (1982) The Times
    6 July 9.4.10

Mount Carmel Investments Ltd v Peter Thurlow Ltd [1988] 1 WLR 1078; [1988] 3
     All ER 129; (1989) 57 P & CR 396, CA 5.7.4, 5.7.5
Mulholland & Tedd Ltd v Baker [1939] 3 All ER 252; 161 LT 20 . . . . 4.3.4
Musgrove v Pandelis [1919] 2 KB 43; [1918-19] All ER Rep 589; 88 LJKB 915,
     CA 4.2.6, 4.3.1, 4.3.10
National Coal Board v Neath BC [1976] 2 All ER 748; sub nom National Coal
     Board v Thorne [1976] 1 WLR 543; 120 SJ 234. . . . . 3.2.6
National Rivers Authority v Alfred McAlpines Homes East Ltd [1994] 4 All ER 286;
     [1994] Env LR D5; [1994] NPC 6. . . . . 15.2.6
National Rivers Authority v Egger (UK) Ltd [1992] Water Law 169 . . . . 15.2.9
National Rivers Authority v Wright Engineering Co Ltd [1994] 4 All ER 281;
     [1994] Crim LR 453; (1993) The Independent 19 November. 15.2.5
National Telephone Co v Baker [1893] 2 Ch 186; 62 LJ Ch 699; 9 TLR 246 . . . . 4.2.6
Neath RDC v Williams [1951] 1 KB 115; [1950] 2 All ER 625; 94 SJ 568. . . . . . 4.2.7
Network Housing Association v Westminster City Council (1994) The Times
     8 November 3.12.3
Newcastle-under-Lyme Corporation v Wolstanton Ltd [1947] Ch 427; [1947] 1
     All ER 218, CA; rvsg [1947] Ch 92. . . . . 1.2.5
News of the World Ltd v Allen Fairhead & Sons Ltd [1931] 2 Ch 402; [1931] All
     ER Rep 630; 100 LJ Ch 394 . . . . 8.4.16, 8.4.18
Nichols v Marsland (1876) 2 Ex D 1; [1874-80] All ER Rep 40; 46 LJQB 174,
     CA 4.2.14
Nisbet and Potts' Contract, Re [1906] 1 Ch 386; [1904-7] All ER Rep 865; 75 LJ
     Ch 238 . . . . 5.7.12
Noble v Harrison [1926] 2 KB 332; [1926] All ER Rep 284; 70 SJ 691. . . 1.9.8, 1.9.9,
                                                                          1.10.12, 2.3.13, 3.2.3
Northern Ireland Trailers Ltd v County Borough of Preston [1972] 1 WLR 203;
     [1972] 1 All ER 260; 116 SJ 100, CA. 3.14.6
Northwestern Utilities Ltd v London Guarantee and Accident Co [1936] AC 108;
     [1935] All ER Rep 196; 105 LJPC 18, PC 4.2.8
Nor-Video Services Ltd v Ontario Hydro (1978) 84 DLR (3d) 221 . . . . 1.7.4
O'Fee v Copeland BC (1995) 94 LGR 115; (1995) The Times 22 April 13.3.5
Ough v King [1967] 1 WLR 1547; [1967] 3 All ER 859; 111 SJ 792, CA 8.4.3,
                                                                                8.4.8, 16.2.3
Pamplin v Express Newspapers [1988] 1 All ER 282; (1985) 129 SJ 190; (1985)
     82 LSG 1417, CA. 16.9.3, 16.9.4
Patel v Patel [1988] 2 FLR 179; (1988) 18 Fam Law 213; [1988] LSG
     23 March 10.3.6
Patel v Smith [1987] 1 WLR 853; [1987] 2 All ER 569; 131 SJ 888, CA 16.15.2
Perry v Kendricks Transport Ltd [1956] 1 WLR 85; [1956] 1 All ER 154; 100 SJ
     52, CA 4.2.10, 4.2.15, 4.2.16
Phipps v Pears [1965] 1 QB 76; [1964] 2 WLR 996; [1964] 2 All ER 35, CA . . . 7.3.7
Pidduck v Molloy [1992] 2 FLR 202; [1992] Fam Law 529; (1992) The Times
     9 March, CA. 10.3.8, 10.3.11
Polsue and Alfieri Ltd v Rushmer [1907] AC 121; [1904-7] All ER Rep 586, HL;
     affg sub nom Rushmer v Polsue and Alfieri Ltd [1906] 1 Ch 234. . . . . . 1.6.5, 1.6.8,
                                                                1.6.10, 1.6.17, 1.6.20, 1.6.23
Polychronakis v Richards & Jerrom Ltd (1997) The Independent 22 October. . . 3.14.5
Pontardawe RDC v Moore-Gwyn [1929] 1 Ch 656; 27 LGR 493; 98 LJ Ch
     242 . . . . 4.2.7
Practice Note (Family Division: Ex parte injunction) [1978] 1 WLR 925; [1978] 2
     All ER 919; (1978) SJ 460. . . . . 10.5.21
Price v Cromack [1975] 1 WLR 988; [1975] 2 All ER 113; 119 SJ 458 . . . . 15.2.7

Price v Hilditch [1930] 1 Ch 500; 99 LJ Ch 299; 143 LT 33 . . . . 8.4.9, 8.4.14
Proffitt v British Railways Board (1985) CLY 2302; (1985) *The Times*
   4 February 6.9.9
R v British Coal Corporation *ex p* Ibstock Building Products Ltd [1995] Env LR 277;
   [1994] NPC 133 . . . . A2.9
R v Burstow [1997] 1 Cr App R 144, CA 10.2.2, 10.2.7
R v Chan-Fook [1994] 1 WLR 689; [1994] 2 All ER 552; (1994) 99 Cr App R 147,
   CA 10.2.7, 10.2.8
R v Cramp [1880] 5 QBD 307; 39 LJMC 44; 28 WR 701 . . . . 15.2.10
R v Dorset CC *ex p* Rolls. *See* R v South Hams DC *ex p* Gibb
R v Dovermoss Ltd [1995] Env LR 258 . . . . 15.2.9
R v Dunmow Justices *ex p* Anderson [1964] 1 WLR 1039; [1964] 2 All ER 943;
   108 SJ 179 . . . . 9.6.4
R v Ealing Justices *ex p* Fanneran (1996) 8 Admin LR 351; (1995) *The Times*
   9 December 9.7.5
R v Greenwich LBC *ex p* W (a minor) [1997] Env LR D2, CA 13.6.1
R v Ireland [1997] QB 114; [1996] 3 WLR 650; [1997] 1 All ER 112, CA. . . . 10.2.12
R v Johnson [1997] 1 WLR 367; [1996] 2 Cr App R 434, CA 2.2.2, 10.2.16
R v Jones *ex p* Daunton [1963] 1 WLR 270; [1963] 1 All ER 368; 107 SJ 76. . . . 9.6.3
R v Knightsbridge Crown Court *ex p* Dunne [1994] 1 WLR 296; [1993] 4 All
   ER 491; 158 JP 213 . . . . 9.7.4
R v Leicester Justices *ex p* Workman [1964] 1 WLR 707; [1964] 2 All ER 346;
   108 SJ 358 . . . . 9.6.3
R v Lincolnshire CC *ex p* Atkinson [1997] JPL 65 . . . . 5.6.21
R v London Boroughs Transport Committee *ex p* Freight Transport Association
   Ltd [1991] 1 WLR 828; [1991] RTR 337; (1992) 156 JP 69, HL 12.8.1
R v Madden [1975] 1 WLR 1379; [1975] 3 All ER 155; 119 SJ 657 . . . . 10.2.14,
                                                             10.2.16
R v Millward (1986) 8 Cr App R(S) 209, CA 10.2.16
R v Norbury [1978] Crim LR 435 . . . . 10.2.15
R v Nottingham Justices *ex p* Brown [1960] 1 WLR 1315; [1960] 3 All ER 625;
   104 SJ 1036 . . . . 9.6.1
R v Secretary of State for Transport *ex p* Factortame [1992] QB 680; [1991] 3
   WLR 288; [1991] 3 All ER 769, ECJ A1.24
R v Smith [1997] QB 836; [1997] 2 WLR 588; [1997] 1 Cr App R 390, CA . . . 10.2.2
R v Southend Stipendiary Magistrates *ex p* Rochford DC 1994] Env LR D15;
   (1994) *The Times* 10 May 3.13.7
R v South Hams DC *ex p* Gibb [1995] QB 158; [1994] 3 WLR 1151; [1994] 4 All
   ER 1012, CA *sub nom* R v Dorset CC *ex p* Rolls [1994] EGCS 13 . . . . 5.4.7
R v Venna [1975] 3 WLR 737; [1975] 3 All ER 788; 119 SJ 679, CA 10.2.7
R v Wolverhampton MBC *ex p* Dunne (1997) *The Times* 2 January 5.6.21
Rainham Chemical Works v Belvedere Fish Guano Co Ltd [1921] 2 AC 465;
   [1921] All ER Rep 48; 90 LJKB 1252, HL 4.2.6
Rapier v London Tramways Co [1893] 2 Ch 588; [1891-4] All ER Rep 204; 63
   LJ Ch 36 . . . . 1.6.5, 1.6.9, 1.6.22
Read v J Lyons & Co Ltd [1947] AC 156; [1946] 2 All ER 471; 91 SJ 54,
   HL 4.2.5, 4.2.6, 4.2.10, 4.2.11
Redland Bricks Ltd v Morris [1970] AC 652; [1969] 2 WLR 1437; [1969] 2 All
   ER 576, HL 8.3.3, 16.13.1
Reinhardt v Mentasti (1889) 42 Ch D 685; 58 LJ Ch 787; 38 WR 10 . . . 1.6.15, 1.6.22
Rickards v Lothian [1913] AC 263; {1911-13] All ER Rep 71; 82 LJPC 42,
   PC 4.2.3, 4.2.4, 4.2.15

Rider v Rider [1973] 1 QB 505; [1973] 2 WLR 190; [1973] 1 All ER 294,
CA 2.3.19
Robinson v Kilvert (1889) 41 Ch D 88; 58 LJ Ch 392; 37 WR 545 . . . . 1.6.16
Rookes v Barnard [1964] AC 1129; [1964] 2 WLR 269; [1964] 1 All ER 367,
HL 10.3.3
Ross v Evans [1959] 2 QB 79; [1959] 2 WLR 699; [1959] 2 All ER 222 . . . . . . 9.6.12
Rouse v Gravelworks Ltd [1940] 1 KB 489; [1940] 1 All ER 26;109 LJKB 408,
CA 1.11.3, 6.6.4, 8.3.4
Rover International v Cannon Film Sales Ltd [1987] 1 WLR 1597; [1987] 3 All
ER 986; 131 SJ 1591 . . . . 16.14.1
Rushmer v Polsue and Alfieri Ltd. See Polsue and Alfieri Ltd v Rushmer
Russell v Barnet LBC (1894) 271 EG 699; 83 LGR 152; [1984] 2 EGLR 44. . . . 6.7.6,
6.7.10
Rylands v Fletcher (1868) LR 3 HL 330; [1861-73] All ER Rep 1; 14 WR 799, *sub*
nom Fletcher v Rylands (1866) 3 H & C 774 . . . . . . 1.7.1, 4.1.1–4.3.10, 9.2.3, A5.7
Sack v Jones [1925] Ch 235; [1925] All ER Rep 514; 94 LJ Ch 229. . . . . 8.3.2
Saddleworth UDC v Aggregate & Sand Ltd (1970) 114 SJ 931; 69 LGR 103. . . 3.14.6
St Edmundsbury & Ipswich Diocesan Board of Finance v Clark (No 2) [1973] 1
WLR 1572; [1973] 3 All ER 903; 117 SJ 793. . . . . 6.8.2
St Helens Smelting Co Ltd v Tipping [1862] 11 HL Cas 642; [1861-73] All ER
Rep Ext 1389; 13 WR 1083. . . . . 1.6.2, 1.6.5, 1.6.9, 1.6.10
Salford CC v McNally [1975] 3 WLR 87; [1975] 2 All ER 860; 119 SJ 475,
HL 3.2.7
Salsbury v Woodland [1970] 1 QB 324; [1969] 3 WLR 29; [1969] 3 All ER 863,
CA 2.3.18
Sampson v Hodson-Pressinger [1981] 3 All ER 710; 12 HLR 40; 125 SJ 623,
CA 1.6.6, 1.9.13, 1.9.14
Sampson Associates v British Railways Board [1983] 1 WLR 170; [1983] 1 All
ER 257; 126 SJ 836 . . . . 6.9.7
Schulman Incorporated Ltd v National Rivers Authority [1992] 1 Env
LR D2. . . . . 15.2.8, 15.2.11
SCM (UK) Ltd v W J Whittall & Son Ltd [1970] 1 WLR 1017; [1970] 2 All ER
417; 114 SJ 268 . . . . 1.9.5
Scott v Pape (1886) 31 Ch D 554; 55 LJ Ch 426; 34 WR 465, CA 8.4.17
Searle v Wallbank [1947] AC 341; [1947] 1 All ER 12; 15 SJ 40, HL 9.5.1
Sedleigh-Denfield v O'Callaghan [1940] AC 880; [1940] 3 All ER 349; 84 SJ 657,
HL 1.9.2, 1.10.4, 1.10.6, 1.10.9, 2.3.13
Sheffield Masonic Hall Co Ltd v Sheffield Corporation [1932] 2 Ch 17; [1932]
All ER Rep 545; 101 LJ Ch 328 . . . . 8.4.8, 8.4.11
Shelfer v City of London Electric Lighting Co [1895] 1 Ch 287; [1891-2] All ER
Rep 838; 43 WR 238, CA 1.2.7, 6.11.3, 6.11.4, 6.11.12, 6.15.1
Shiffman v Venerable Order of the Hospital of St John of Jerusalem [1936] 1 All
ER 557; 80 SJ 346 . . . . 4.2.9, 4.2.11, 4.2.16
Sinclair-Lockhart's Trustees v Central Land Board (1950) 1 P & C R 320; 1951
SC 258; 1951 SLT 121 . . . . 6.12.5
Siskina, The [1979] AC 210; [1977] 3 WLR 818; [1977] 3 All ER 803, HL. . . . 10.3.6
Slater v Worthington's Cash Stores (1930) Ltd [1941] 1 KB 488; [1941] 3 All ER
28; 111 LJKB 91, CA 1.9.12, 2.3.15
Smith v Baker [1961] 1 WLR 38; [1960] 3 All ER 653; 105 SJ 17 . . . . 9.6.4
Smith v Baker & Sons [1891] AC 325; [1891-4] All ER Rep 69; 60 LJQB 683,
HL 11.3.7
Smith v Baxter [1900] 2 Ch 138; 69 LJ Ch 437; 44 SJ 393 . . . . 8.2.16

Smith v Chief Superintendent Woking Police Station (1983) 76 Cr App R
234 . . . . 10.2.10
Smith v Giddy [1904] 2 KB 448; [1904-7] All ER Rep; 73 LJKB 894 . . . . 1.5.3, 6.7.5
Smith v Littlewoods Organisation Ltd [1987] AC 241; [1987] 2 WLR 480; [1987]
1 All ER 710, HL 1.10.11
Smith v Scott [1973] Ch 314; [1972] 3 WLR 783; [1972] 3 All ER 645 . . . . . . 1.9.14
Sochacki v Sas [1947] 1 All ER 344; 63 LQR 148; 11 Conv 281 . . . . 4.3.3, 4.3.8
Southport Corporation v Esso Petroleum Co Ltd [1954] 2 QB 182; [1954] 3 WLR
200; [1954] 2 All ER 561, CA ; [1953] 2 All ER 1204, QBD 1.9.5
Spicer v Smee [1946] 1 All ER 489; 175 LT 163 . . . . 1.9.11, 1.9.17
Stagecoach Ltd v McPhail [1988] SCCR 289 . . . . 3.14.7
Sterling Homes (Midlands) Ltd v Birmingham CC [1996] Env LR 121 . . . . 3.12.3,
3.14.7
Stoke-on-Trent CC v W & J Wass Ltd [1988] 1 WLR 1406; [1988] 3 All ER 394;
132 SJ 1458, CA 5.5.2
Strand Electric and Engineering Co v Brisford Entertainments [1952] 2 QB 246;
[1952] 1 All ER 796; 96 SJ 260, CA 5.5.2, 16.5.1
Sturges v Bridgman (1879) 11 Ch D 852; 48 LJ Ch 785; 28 WR 200, CA 1.6.18,
1.11.5, 1.11.6
Swordheath Properties Ltd v Tabet [1979] 1 WLR 285; [1979] 1 All ER 240;
122 SJ 862, CA 16.5.1
Tapling v Jones (1865) 11 HL Cas 290; 34 LJCP 342; 144 ER 1067, HL 8.4.1,
8.4.17
Tarry v Ashton (1876) 1 QBD 314; 45 LJQB 260; 34 LT 97 . . . . 2.3.16
Tate & Lyle Food and Distribution Ltd v GLC [1983] 2 AC 509; [1983] 2 WLR
649; [1983] 1 All ER 1159, HL 1.2.6, 1.11.9
Taylor (CR) (Wholesale) Ltd v Hepworths Ltd [1977] 1 WLR 659; [1977] 2 All
ER 784; (1976) 121 SJ 15 . . . . 16.2.2, 16.2.5
Tetley v Chitty [1986] 1 All ER 663; (1985) NLJ 1009 . . . . 1.9.15
Theyer v Purnell [1918] 2 KB 333; 88 LJKB 263; 119 LT 285 . . . . 16.4.1
Thomas v Sorrell (1673) Vaugh 330; [1558-1774] All ER Rep 107; 124 ER
1098 . . . . 5.3.1
Thompson-Schwab v Costaki [1956] 1 WLR 335; [1956] 1 All ER 652; 100 SJ
246, CA 1.6.6, 1.6.8
Tower Hamlets LBC v Manzoni and Walder (1984)148 JP 123; [1984] JPL
436 . . . . 3.2.3
Trevett v Lee [1955] 1 WLR 113; [1955] 1 All ER 406; 99 SJ 110, CA 2.3.6,
2.3.7, 2.3.11
Turberville v Stampe (1697) 12 Mod Rep 152; 92 ER 944; 1 Ld Raym 264 . . . . 4.3.6,
4.3.7
Turner v Coates [1917] 1 KB 670; [1916-17] All ER Rep; 86 LJKB 321 . . . . 9.2.1
Vanderpant v Mayfair Hotel Co Ltd [1930] 1 Ch 138; [1929] All ER Rep 296;
99 LJ Ch 84 . . . . 1.6.5, 1.6.6, 1.6.9, 1.6.22
Vaughan v Biggs [1960] 1 WLR 622; [1960] 2 All ER 473; 104 SJ 508 . . . . 14.8.2
Vaughan v McKenzie [1969] 1 QB 557; [1968] 2 WLR 1133; [1968] 1 All ER
1154 . . . . 5.2.4
Vaughan v Menlove (1837) 3 Bing NC 468; [1835-42] All ER Rep; 132 ER
490 . . . . 4.3.8
Vaughan v Vaughan [1973] 1 WLR 1159; [1973] 3 All ER 449; 117 SJ 583,
CA 10.5.6
Wagon Mound (No 2), The [1967] 1 AC 617; [1966] 3 WLR 498; 110 SJ
447 . . . . 1.8.1, 1.8.2, 1.8.3, 1.10.1, 2.2.3, 2.3.9
Wallace v Newton [1982] 1 WLR 375; [1982] 2 All ER 106; 126 SJ 101 . . . . . . 9.3.13

Walker & Sons v British Railways Board [1894] 1 WLR 805; [1984] 2 All ER 249;
    128 SJ 383 . . . . 6.9.9
Walter v Selfe (1851) 4 De G & Sm 315; 20 LJ Ch 433; 64 ER 849 . . . . 1.6.9
Walter Lilly & Co v Westminster CC. *See* Lilly (Walter) & Co Ltd v Westminster CC
Ware v Garston Haulage Co [1944] 1 KB 30; [1943] 2 All ER 558; 113 LJKB 45,
    CA 2.3.12
Wellingborough DC v Gordon [1991] JPL 874; [1991] COD 154; (1991) 155 LG
    Rev 408 . . . . 3.14.12
Welsh v Holst & Co [1958] 1 WLR 800; [1958] 3 All ER 33; 102 SJ 559,
    CA 2.3.16, 2.3.18
Wentworth v Wiltshire CC [1993] QB 654; [1993] 2 WLR 175;[1973] 2 All ER
    256, CA 2.3.20
West v Bristol Tramways Co [1908] 2 KB 14; [1908-10] All ER Rep 215; 77
    LJKB 684 . . . . 4.2.8, 4.2.12
West Mersea UDC v Fraser [1950] 2 KB 119; [1950] 1 All ER 990; 94 SJ 271 . . 3.2.3
Westminster Corporation v London and North Western Railway Co [1905] AC
    426; 74 LJ Ch 629, HL; affg *sub nom* London and North Western Railway Co
    v Westminster Corporation [1902] 1 Ch 629, CA 6.8.3
Wheat v E Lacon & Co [1966] AC 552; [1966] 2 WLR 581; [1966] 1 All ER 582,
    HL 5.8.2
Wheeldon v Burrows (1879) 12 Ch D 31; [1874-80] All ER Rep 669; 48 LJ Ch
    853, HL 8.2.5
Wheeler v J J Saunders Ltd [1996] Ch 19; [1995] 3 WLR 466; [1995] 2 All ER
    697 . . . . 1.6.6, 1.6.25
White v Taylor (No 2) [1969] 1 Ch 160; [1967] 3 WLR 1246; [1967] 3 All ER
    349 . . . . 6.3.7
Whitwham v Westminster Brymbo Coal & Coke Co [1896] 2 Ch 538; 65 LJ Ch
    741; 40 SJ 620, CA 16.5.1
Whycer v Urry [1956] JPL 365, CA 1.6.15
Wilchick v Marks & Silverstone [1934] 2 KB 56; [1934] All ER Rep 73; 103
    LJKB 372 . . . . 1.9.12
Wilkins v Leighton [1932] 2 Ch 106; [1932] All ER Rep 55; 101 LJ Ch 385 . . . 1.4.1,
                                                                                                        1.9.8, 1.9.9
Wilkinson v Downton [1897] 2 QB 57; [1895-7] All ER Rep 267; 66 LJQB
    493 . . . . 10.3.2, 10.3.8
Wiltshire Bacon v Associated Cinema Properties Ltd [1938] Ch 268; [1937] 4 All
    ER 80; 107 LJ Ch 49, CA 16.11.4
Wivenhoe Port v Colchester BC [1985] JPL 396, CA; affg 1985] JPL 175 . . . . . . 3.5.4
Wood v Conway Corporation [1914] 2 Ch 47; All ER Rep 1097; 83 LJ Ch 498,
    CA 1.2.7, 1.4.1
Woollerton and Wilson v Costain Ltd [1970] 1 WLR 411; 114 SJ 170 . . . . 16.11.6
Wringe v Cohen [1940] 1 KB 229; [1939] 4 All ER 241; 109 LJKB 227 . . . . . 1.10.10,
                                                                                                        2.3.15
Wrotham Park Estate Co Ltd v Parkside Homes [1974] 1 WLR 798; [1974] 2 All
    ER 321; 118 SJ 420 . . . . 16.11.13

Table of Statutes

All references are to paragraph numbers. Those prefixed A refer to the Appendices.

Access to Neighbouring Land Act
1992—
  s 1 . . . . A3.9
    (4)(c) A3.9
    (7) 6.4.2, A3.9
Ancient Monuments and Archæological
Areas Act 1979 . . . . 5.6.4
Animals Act 1971 . . . . 9.1.1, 9.2.1,
                    9.2.3, 9.3, 9.4.1
  s 1(1)(a) 9.3.1
    (c) 9.4.1
  s 2 . . . . 9.3.6
    (1) 9.3.5, 9.3.9, A5.11
    (2) 9.3.9, A5.11
      (a) 9.3.9, 9.3.11
      (b) 9.3.9, 9.3.12, 9.3.13,
                        9.3.15
      (c) 9.3.9, 9.3.18, 9.3.19
  s 3 . . . . 9.8.1
  s 4 . . . . 9.4.7, 9.4.8, 9.4.11
    (1) 9.4.2, 9.4.5
      (a) 9.4.4
      (b) 9.4.7, 9.4.9
  s 5(1) 9.3.22, 9.8.1, A5.12
    (2) 9.3.23, A5.12
    (3) 9.3.25, 9.9.2
    (4) 9.8.1
  s 6 . . . . A5.11
    (2) 9.3.6
      (a)–(b) 9.3.6
    (3) 9.3.2, 9.3.3
      (a) 9.3.2
      (b) 9.3.2
    (4) 9.3.4
    (5) 9.3.24
  s 7 . . . . 9.4.7, 9.4.8
    (1) 11.3.5
      (a) 9.4.7
    (3)(b)–(c) 9.4.7
    (4)–(5) 9.4.8
    (6) 9.4.11

Animals Act 1971—*contd.*
  s 8 . . . . 9.5.3
    (1) 9.5.1
    (2)(a)–(b) 9.5.4
  s 9(1)(a) 9.9.1
    (b) 9.9.2
    (2)(a)–(b) 9.9.2
    (3)(a)–(b) 9.9.1
    (4) 9.9.1
  s 11 . . . . 9.3.22, 9.4.3
Building Act 1984—
  s 59 . . . . 15.5.18
    (1) 15.5.17
  s 62 . . . . 15.5.14
    (2) 15.5.14
  s 63(1) 15.5.17
  s 79(2) 14.6.9
  s 101 . . . . 15.5.13
Caravan Sites Act 1968—
  Part II 5.4.9
  s 16 . . . . 5.4.7
Caravan Sites and Control of
  Development Act 1960 . . . . 5.4.9,
                         5.4.10
Channel Tunnel Act 1987—
  s 6(3) 12.15.1
  Sched 2, Part III 12.15.1
Civil Aviation Act 1982 . . . . 12.9.3
  s 76 . . . . 12.9.1
    (1) 5.2.5
  s 77 . . . . 12.9.1
  s 78 . . . . 12.9.2
Civil Evidence Act 1995 . . . . 6.12.2
  s 4(2) 6.12.2
Clean Air Acts 1956–1968 . . . . . . 13.3.1
Clean Air Act 1993 . . . . 3.3.3, 13.3.1
  Parts I–III 13.3.3
  Part I 13.3.1
  s 1 . . . . 13.3.2, 13.3.10, 13.3.11
    (1)–(2) 13.3.4
    (4)(a)–(c) 13.3.11

Clean Air Act 1993—*contd.*
s 1(5) 13.3.10
s 2 .... 13.3.2, 13.3.8,
                    13.3.10, 13.3.12
  (1) 13.3.9
  (3) 13.3.8
  (4) 13.3.12
  (6) 13.3.7
s 3. .... 13.3.5
  (1) 13.3.5
  (2) 13.4.5
Part II. 13.4.1, 13.4.2
s 4(1) 13.4.3
  (2) 13.4.2, 13.4.4
  (4) 13.4.3
s 5. .... 13.4.6
  (1) 13.4.5
s 6. .... 13.4.7
  (4) 13.4.1
ss 14–15. .... 13.4.8
Part III 13.5.1
ss 18–29. .... 13.5.1
s 19. .... 13.5.1
s 20(1)–(2). 13.5.2
  (5) 13.5.2
Part V. A2.16
Part VI. 13.3.3
ss 41–46. .... 13.3.3
s 52. .... A1.14
s 55. .... 13.3.2
s 64. .... 13.4.1
  (1) 13.3.6, 13.3.7, 13.3.11
  (6) 13.4.1
Scheds 1–2. .... 13.5.1
Control of Pollution Act 1974. .... 3.2.6
s 23. .... 14.7.12
s 60 .... 3.13.3, 3.14.9, 12.2.16,
                12.3.1, 12.3.7, 12.3.10,
                12.3.11, 12.3.13, 12.3.14
  (1) 12.3.2
  (2) 12.3.4
  (4) 12.3.5, 12.3.7
  (7) 12.3.6
s 61 .... 3.13.3, 3.14.9, 12.2.16,
                12.3.1, 12.3.14, 12.3.15
  (6) 12.3.16
s 62. .... 12.2.5
  (1) 12.6.1
ss 63–67. .... 12.13.1
s 63. .... 12.13.3, A2.16
s 65. .... 3.14.9, 12.13.6
  (1) 12.13.5
s 66. .... 3.13.3, 3.14.9

Control of Pollution Act 1974—*contd.*
s 68. .... 12.5.1
  (3) 12.5.1
s 69. .... 12.13.9
s 74. .... 12.3.15, 12.5.1
  (1) 12.3 11
Part IV 13.3.1
s 79(2) A2.16
s 80–81. .... A2.16
s 81(2) A2.16
s 87. .... 12.3.12
Control of Pollution (Amendment) Act
1989—
  s 6. .... 14.5.2
    (9) 14.5.4
  s 7. .... A1.14
Countryside Act 1968—
  s 10(2) 14.8.9
County Courts Act 1984—
  s 38. .... 10.3.5
Criminal Damage Act 1971—
  s 1(1) 11.3.3
Criminal Justice Act 1982—
  s 70. .... 10.2.19
Criminal Justice Act 1988—
  s 39. .... 10.2.5, 10.2.6
Criminal Justice and Public Order Act
1994 .... 5.1.3
Part V. 5.1.6, 5.5.15, 5.6.1
s 61. .... 5.6.2, 5.6.5
  (4) 5.6.3
s 61(9) 5.6.4, 5.6.8
s 62. .... 5.6.2, 5.6.8
ss 63–66. .... 5.6.6
s 63. .... 5.6.6
  (2) 5.6.8
  (6) 5.6.8
  (10) 5.6.7
s 64–66. .... 5.6.8
s 65(4) 5.6.8
s 68–69. .... 5.6.10
s 68(2) 5.6.10
  (3) 5.6.12
  (5) 5.6.10
s 69(1) 5.6.11
  (3) 5.6.12
ss 70–71. .... 5.6.13
s 72. .... 5.5.9
s 73. .... 5.5.14
s 74. .... 5.5.11
s 75. .... 5.5.12, 5.5.29, 5.5.35, 5.5.40
s 76. .... 5.5.29, 5.5.35
ss 77–79. .... 5.4.11, 5.6.18

Criminal Justice and Public Order Act
1994—*contd.*
s 77(1) 5.6.18
   (2)–(3). 5.6.19
s 78(1). 5.6.20
   (2)(b). 5.6.20
   (4) 5.6.20
s 79(2)–(3). 5.6.19
s 80. . . . . 5.4.9
s 154. . . . . 10.2.24
Criminal Law Act 1977. . . . . 5.4.3
s 6. . . . . 5.5.8
   (1A). 5.5.9
s 7. . . . . 5.5.14
s 12(3)–(4). 5.5.10
s 12A 5.5.11
s 51. . . . . 10.2.5, 10.2.20
Dangerous Dogs Act 1989—
s 1(1)(a) 9.6.5
    (b). 9.6.1, 9.6.5
   (2) 9.6.6
   (3) 9.6.5
   (4)–(5). 9.6.6
s 2. . . . . 9.6.5
Dangerous Dogs Act 1991—
s 1. . . . . 9.7.6
   (2) 9.7.2
   (d). 9.7.2
   (3) 9.7.7
s 3(1) 9.6.8
   (2) 9.6.9
   (3) 9.6.10
   (5) 9.6.7
    (b). 9.6.7
   (6) 9.6.7
s 4. . . . . 9.7.5
s 4A 9.7.6
s 4B 9.7.7
s 10(3) 9.6.8
Dangerous Dogs (Amendment) Act 1997
. . . . 9.7.1
Distress for Rent Act 1737—
s 18. . . . . 5.5.4
Dogs Act 1871—
s 2. . . . . 9.6.1, 9.6.2, 9.6.5, 9.8.2
Dogs Act 1906—
s 1(4) 9.6.2
s 3. . . . . 9.10.1
   (1) 9.10.2
   (1A). 9.10.2
   (2) 9.10.2
   (4) 9.10.2
   (6) 9.10.3

Dogs Act 1906—*contd.*
s 4 (2)–(3) 9.10.4
Dogs (Fouling of Land)
Act 1996. . . . . 14.8.9
Dogs (Protection of Livestock)
Act 1953—
s 1(2) 9.8.3
   (2A)(b) 9.8.4
s 2. . . . . 9.8.2
Domestic Proceedings and Magistrates'
Courts Act 1978. . . . . 10.5.4
Domestic Violence and Matrimonial
Proceedings Act 1976 . . 10.5.4, 10.5.6
Environment Act 1995—
s 4(1) A1.7
s 9. . . . . A1.8
Part II. 3.2.2, 15.3.3
Part IV 13.8.2
s 80. . . . . 13.8.2
ss 82–84. . . . . 13.8.2
s 87(1) 13.6.2
Sched 22 . . . . 14.3.2, 15.3.3
    para 89(3) 3.2.2
    para 103. . . . . 15.5.7
Sched 24 . . . . 14.3.2
Environmental Protection Act 1990—
Part I 3.3.4, 13.1.2, 13.2.1,
        13.2.2, 13.2.3, A2.16
s 5. . . . . 14.2.2
s 12. . . . . 13.2.4
s 14. . . . . 13.2.4, 13.2.5
s 20. . . . . A2.16
s 23(1) 13.2.4
   (2) 13.2.7
s 24. . . . . 13.2.8
s 26. . . . . 13.2.7
Part II. 14.6.3, A2.16
s 32. . . . . 14.2.2
s 33. . . . . 14.1.1, 14.5.2
   (1). 14.3.1, 14.3.5,
              14.3.7, 14.5.1
   (2)–(3). 14.3.3
   (6) 14.3.5
   (7) 14.3.4
   (9) 14.3.6
s 34. . . . . 14.1.1, 14.5.1
   (1) 14.4.1, 14.4.2
   (5) 14.4.2
   (6) 14.4.2, 14.4.3
   (7)–(8). 14.4.3
s 35. . . . . 14.3.2
ss 45–47. . . . . 14.2.3
s 45. . . . . 14.2.3

Environmental Protection Act
1990—*contd.*
s 45(1)(a)–(b). 14.2.4
   (2). 14.2.4
s 48(1) 14.2.3
s 49. 14.2.3
s 51. 14.2.2
s 55. 14.2.2
s 63(2) 14.3.7
ss 64–67. . . . . A2.16
s 64. 14.2.1
   (4) 14.2.3
   (6) 14.2.3
s 73. A1.15
   (6) 14.3.7
   (8) 14.3.7
s 75. 14.3.2
Part IIA 3.2.2
Part III. 1.6.30, 3.1.2, 3.2.1, 3.2.3,
          3.3.4, 3.14.4, 3.18.2,
         13.1.1, 13.2.2, 14.6.15
ss 79–82. . . . . 3.11.1, 12.7.1
s 79. . . . . . . 3.2.2, 3.2.4, 12.2.2, 12.7.3
   (1). 3.10.2, 3.11.2,
             3.14.8, 12.2.2
   (a). 3.2.1, 3.13.3
   (b). 3.2.1, 3.13.3
   (c). 3.2.1, 3.4
   (d) 3.2.1, 3.5, 3.13.3
   (e). 3.2.1, 3.6, 3.13.3
   (f). 3.2.1, 3.7, 3.13.3
   (g) 3.2.1, 3.7.1, 3.8.1,
             3.8.4, 3.13.3
   (ga) 3.2.1, 3.7.1, 3.9, 3.9.2,
     3.13.3, 3.14.8, 12.2.2, 12.2.3
   (h) 3.2.1, 3.10
   (2) 3.3.2, 3.8.2
   (3) 3.3.3
   (i)–(iv) 3.3.3
   (6A). 12.2.4
   (7). 3.2.5, 3.3.1, 3.4.1,
        3.12.6, 3.14.3, 12.3.1
   (8) 3.2.3
   (9) 3.14.4
   (12) 3.2.3
s 80. . . . . 12.2.6, 12.3.10
   (1) 3.11.2, 3.12.1
   (2)(a)–(c). 3.12.5, 3.18.6
   (3) 12.2.11
   (4) 3.14.1, 3.14.2, 12.2.13
   (5) 3.14.2, 3.14.3
   (7) 3.14.4, 3.14.5, 3.14.8
   (8) 3.14.8, 12.2.14

Environmental Protection Act
1990—*contd.*
s 80(9) 3.14.9, 12.2.16
s 80A 12.2.6
   (2)(a) 12.2.7
   (b). 12.2.8
   (3)–(4) 12.2.8
   (7)–(8) 12.2.12, 12.2.14
s 81. 12.3.10
   (3) 3.8.4, 3.14.1, 12.7.3
   (5) 3.16.1, 12.3.13
s 81A 3.15.2
   (6) 3.15.2
   (8) 3.15.2
   (9) 3.12.5
s 81B 3.15.3
s 82 . . . . 3.18.3, 12.1.2, 12.3.10,
                  12.3.14
   (2) 3.18.2, 3.18.5, 3.18.10
   (3) 3.18.5
   (8) 3.18.8
   (9)–(10) 3.18.9
   (11) 3.18.10
   (12) 3.18.7
   (13) 3.18.11
Part IV. 14.8.1, 14.8.3, 14.8.9,
       14.8.16, 14.8.17, 14.8.20
s 86(4) 14.8.11
s 87. . . . . 14.8.5, 14.8.7
   (1) 14.8.6
   (3)–(4) 14.8.6
s 89. 14.8.16
   (1) 14.8.10, 14.8.24
   (2) 14.8.12
   (10) 14.8.18
s 90(3) A2 16
s 90(4) 14.8.26
s 91(1) 14.8.13
   (5) 14.8.14
s 93. A2.16
s 95. A2.16
s 99. 14.9.1
Part VI A2.16
s 118. A2.16
s 149. 9.10.1
   (1) 9.10.2
   (3)–(7) 9.10.2
   (8) 9.10.3
s 150. 9.10.4
   (1) 9.10.4
   (5) 9.10.4
s 152. 13.7.2
s 157. A1.14

Environmental Protection Act
1990—*contd.*
Sched 1, para 1(3) A2.16
Sched 3 .... 3.13.2, 12.7.3
para 2(3) 3.11.3
para 2A 12.2.10
(3)......... 12.2.10
para 5........... 3.14.11
para 6........... 12.2.11
Sched 4 .... 14.9.1, 14.9.2
Family Law Act 1996.......... 10.1.8,
10.5.1, 10.5.5
Part IV 10.5.4
ss 33–41.................. 10.5.13
s 33.................... 10.5.13
(2) 10.5.18
(3)(g)................ 10.5.19
s 35.............. 10.5.13, 10.5.15
(5)(d) 10.5.19
(6)(e)–(f) 10.5.17
s 36................... 10.5.13
(4)(d)............... 10.5.19
(6)(e)–(h)........... 10.5.16
s 37.................... 10.5.13
(3)(d)............... 10.5.19
s 40................... 10.5.20
s 41................... 10.5.17
s 42............. 10.5.6, 10.5.7
(1)(a) 10.5.8
(b)............... 10.5.9
(2)(a)–(b)............. 10.5.10
(4) 10.5.8
(5) 10.5.11
(7)–(8)............... 10.5.12
s 43(1)–(2)............... 10.5.10
s 46................... 10.5.22
(1) 10.5.22
(3)–(4)............... 10.5.22
s 47................... 10.5.23
(2) 10.5.23
(3)(b)............... 10.5.24
(6) 10.5.25
(7)(a)–(b)............. 10.5.25
(8) 10.5.26
(9)(a)–(b)............. 10.5.26
s48 .... 10.5.27
s 50................... 10.5.28
s 62(3) 10.5.8
(a)–(e).............. 10.5.8
Fire Precautions Act 1971 .... A2.16
Fires Prevention (Metropolis)
Act 1774—
s 86...................... 4.3.8

Forestry Act 1967—
s 9(1)–(2).................. A3.4
(4) A3.8
Guard Dogs Act 1971
s 1(1) 9.6.13
Health and Safety at Work Act 1974
.... A2.16
s 37...................... A1.14
Highways Act 1980—
s 1....................... 2.3.19
s 41...................... 2.3.19
s 58...................... 2.3.20
(1) 2.3.20
s 96.................. A3.6, A3.7
(1) 6.7.11, A3.4, A5.13
(6) 6.7.11, A3.7, A5.13
(7) A3.7
s 112..................... 14.8.9
Part VIII................. 2.3.10
s 141..................... 6.7.9
s 142(9) 6.7.9
s 149............ 14.6.11, 14.6.13
(2) 14.6.12
s 151.................... 14.6.14
(3) 14.6.14
s 154(1)–(2)............... 6.7.8
(4) 6.7.8
s 185.................... 14.8.3
s 305(5) 14.6.13
s 329(1) 2.3.20
Housing Act 1988—
ss 27–28................. 5.5.13
Land Charges Act 1972......... A2.16
Land Compensation Act 1973... 12.15.1
s 20...................... 12.15.1
Land Registration Act 1925—
s 70(1)(f) 5.7.12
s 75(1)–(2)............... 5.7.11
Landlord and Tenant Act 1730—
s 1....................... 5.5.4
Landlord and Tenant Act 1954 .... 5.4.1
Law of Property Act 1925 .... 7.1.1,
7.1.3, 7.1.2, 7.1.4, 7.2.3
s 62................ 8.2.5, 9.4.6
s 205..................... 6.12.5
(1)(ix) 5.2.5
Law Reform (Contributory Negligence)
Act 1945.................. 1.12.10
s 1(1) 5.5.5
s 4....................... 9.3.22
s 10...................... 9.8.1
Limitation Act 1980 .... 5.7.11
s 15(1) 5.7.3, 5.7.4, 5.7.8

Limitation Act 1980—*contd.*
Sched 1, para 4 . . . . 5.7.9
Litter Act 1983 . . . . 14.8.1, 14.8.3, 14.8.4
s 10 . . . . 14.8.3
Local Government Act 1972—
s 222 . . . . 3.16.1, 12.3.13
s 235 . . . . 3.7.1, 13.7.2
Local Government (Access to
Information) Act 1985 . . . . A2.16
Local Government Finance
Act 1988 . . . . 5.6.4
Local Government (Miscellaneous
Provisions) Act 1982 . . . 5.6.6, 12.11.1
Local Government Planning and Land
Act 1980 . . . . 15.5.5
London Building Acts (Amendment)
Act 1939 . . . . 7.1.1, 7.1.5, 7.1.6,
7.2.15, 7.3.7
s 46(1) 7.2.15
London Government Act 1963 . . . . 5.6.6,
12.11.1
London Local Authorities Act 1991—
s 23 . . . . 12.7.2, 12.7.3
London Local Authorities Act 1996—
s 25 . . . . 12.7.2
Magistrates' Courts Act 1980—
s 43(3) 10.2.19
s 63(3) 10.5.28
s 121(5) 10.2.19
Malicious Communications
Act 1988 . . . . 10.2.21
Matrimonial Homes Act 1983 . . . . 10.5.4
s 1(3) 10.5.14
Metropolitan Police Act 1839—
s 54 . . . . 9.6.11
Mines and Quarries Act 1954—
s 151 . . . . 6.3.9
s 181 . . . . 6.3.9
Mines and Quarries (Tips)
Act 1969 . . . . 6.3.9
Noise Act 1996 . . . . 3.8.4, 12.10.1,
12.10.2, 12.10.10
s 2(4) 12.10.5
s 3 . . . . 12.10.5, 12.10.8
s 4 . . . . 12.10.11, 12.10.15
s 5 . . . . 12.10.6
s 7 . . . . 12.10.13
(2)–(3) 12.10.13, 12.10.14
s 8 . . . . 12.10.15
(3)(b) 12.10.19
s 10 . . . . 12.10.20
s 11 . . . . 12.10.4
Schedule 12.10.20, 12.10 27

Noise Act 1996—*contd.*
Schedule, para 2 . . . . 12.10.23
para 3 . . . . 12.10.25
Noise and Statutory Nuisance
Act 1993 . . . . 3.8.1, 3.9.1, 3.9.4,
3.12.5, 12.2.6, 12.3.1
ss 2–5 . . . . 12.2.2
s 2 . . . . 3.9.1
s 7 . . . . 12.6.1
s 8 . . . . 12.6.3
s 9 . . . . 12.7.3
s 10 . . . . 3.15.2, 3.15.3
Sched 2 . . . . 12.6.3, 12.6.4, 12.6.6
Para 1 . . . . 3.13.3
Sched 3 . . . . 12.7.3
Nuclear Installations Act 1965—
s 12 . . . . A1.15
Occupiers Liability Act 1957 . . . . . 5.5.6,
5.8.1
Occupiers Liability Act 1984 . . . . . 5.1.6,
5.8.1, 5.8.2
s 1(3) 5.8.3
(5)–(7) 5.8.4
Offences Against the Person Act 1861
. . . . 10.2.3
s 16 . . . . 10.2.5, 10.2.18
s 18 . . . . 10.2.6
s 20 . . . . 10.2.6, 10.2.7
s 47 . . . . 10.2.6, 10.2.12
Party Wall, etc. Act 1996 . . . 7.1.1, 7.1.5,
8.1.1, 8.3.9, 8.3.10, 8.3.16
s 1 . . . . 7.1.8, 7.3.1, A5 .20
(2) 7.3.2, 7.4.5, A5.20
(3) 7.3.2, 7.3.3, 7.3.4
(4) 7.3.5
(5)–(6) 7.3.5, A5.20
(7) 7.3.6
s 2 . . . . 7.1.8, 7.2.12, 7.2.14,
7.3.3, 7.3.7, 8.3.9
(1) 7.2.14
(2) 7.2.14, 7.3.7, 7.3.8, A5.21
(a) 7.3.7, 7.3.9, 7.3.10
(b) 7.3.7, 7.5.13
(c)–(d) 7.3.7
(e) 7.3.7, 7.3.9, 7.3.10
(f)–(h) 7.3.7, 7.3.10
(i) 7.3.7
(j) 7.3.7, 7.3.10
(l)–(m) 7.3.7
(n) 7.3.7, 7.6.2
(3)–(4) 7.3.9
s 3 . . . . 7.4.7, 7.4.9, A5.21
(1) 7.4.2

Party Wall, etc. Act 1996—*contd.*
s 3(2)(a) 7.4.5
　(3)–(8) 7.3.8
s 4 . . . . 7.4.9
　(1)–(2) 7.4.8
s 5 . . . . 7.4.9, A5.21
s 6 . . . . 8.3.11, 8.3.12, 8.3.13,
　　　　　　　　　　8.3.17, A5.22
　(1)–(2) A5.22
　(5) 8.3.15
　(7) A5.22
s 7 . . . . 7.3.6
　(4) A5.20
s 10 . . . . . . 7.5.2, 7.5.10, A5.21, A5.22
　(1) 7.5.2
　(3) 7.5.3
　(4) 7.5.4
　(5) 7.5.5
　(6)–(7) 7.5.6
　(8) 7.5.7
　(9) 7.5.8
s 11 . . . . 7.3.3, 7.5.11
　(6) 7.3.7
　(11) 7.3.4
s 12(1)–(2) 7.6.1
s 15 . . . . 7.4.6
　(2) 7.4.6
s 20 . . . . 7.2.1, 7.2.2, 7.2.10,
　　　　　　　　7.2.13, 7.4.4, 7.4.6
Police and Criminal Evidence
　Act 1984—
　s 24(2) 10.4.5
Power of Criminal Courts Act 1972—
　s 35 . . . . 3.13.4
Prescription Act 1832 . . . . 8.2.10
s 2 . . . . . . 8.2.11, 8.2.13, 8.2.14, A5.10
s 3 . . . . 8.2.1, 8.2.15, 8.2.17,
　　　　　　　　　8.4.17, A5.9
s 4 . . . . 8.2.12
ss 7–8 . . . . 8.2.14, 8.2.17
Private Places of Entertainment
　(Licensing) Act 1967 . . . . 5.6.6
Protection from Eviction
　Act 1977 . . . . 5.4.3
Protection from Harassment Act 1997
　. . . . . 10.1.6, 10.1.8, 10.4, 10.5.5
s 1 . . . . . . 10.4.1, 10.4.3, 10.4.5, 10.4.8
s 1(1) 10.4.2, 10.4.3
　(2) 10.4.2
　(3) 10.4.3
　　(a)–(c) 10.4.3
s 2 . . . . 10.2.4, 10.4.5
　(3) 10.4.5

Protection from Harassment Act
　1997—*contd.*
　s 3 . . . . 10.1.6, 10.3.1, 10.4.8
　　(1)–(2) 10.4.8
　　(3)–(9) 10.1.6
　　(3) 10.4.9, 10.5.1
　　(4)(a)–(b) 10.4.9
　　(5)(a) 10.4.9
　　(6) 10.2.4, 10.4.11, 10.4.12
　　(7) 10.4.12
　　(8) 10.4.10, 10.4.12
　s 4 . . . . 10.2.4
　s 5(1)–(4) 10.4.6
　　(5) 10.4.7
　　(6)(a) 10.4.7
　s 7(2)–(4) 10.4.2
Public Health Act 1936 . . . . 3.2.6, 3.10.1
　s 48 . . . . 15.5.12, 15.5.16
　s 278 . . . . 15.5.13
Public Health Act 1961—
　s 17 . . . . 15.5.18
　　(1) 15.5.18
　　(3) 15.5.18
　s 34 . . . . 14.6.3, 14.6.4
　　(2)(a)–(b) 14.6.4
　　(3) 14.6.4
Public Health (Control of Disease)
　Act 1984 . . . . 3.2.3
Public Health (Recurring Nuisances)
　Act 1969 . . . . 3.2.6
Public Order Act 1986 . . . . 10.2.5,
　　　　　　　　　10.2.17, 10.2.22
　s 4(1) 10.2.23
　s 4A(1) 10.2.24
　s 5(1) 10.2.25
　Part II 5.6.13
　s 14(1) 5.6.17
　s 14(A)(4) 5.6.15
　s 14(B) 5.6.16
　s14(C)(5) 5.6.17
Radioactive Substances Act 1993
　. . . . . A2.16
　s 12(4) A2.16
　s 36 . . . . A1.14
Railways Clauses Consolidation Act
　1845—
　s 68 . . . . 6.9.5, 6.9.6, 6.9.9
Refuse Disposal (Amenity) Act 1978
　. . . . . 14.7.1
　s 2 . . . . 14.7.2
　　(2) 14.7.2
　s 3(1) 14.7.3
　　(3) 14.7.3

Refuse Disposal (Amenity)
Act 1978—*contd.*
s 3(5) 14.7.3
s 4. . . . . 14.7.7
s 4(1)(a) 14.7.8
s 6(1)–(2). 14.6.2
s 8. . . . . 14.6.2
Rights of Light Act 1959. . . . . 8.4.26
Road Traffic Reduction Act 1977—
s 2. . . . . 13.6.2
Road Traffic Regulation Act 1984 12.8.1
s 1(1)(f) 12.8.1
s 2(4) 12.8.1
s 14. . . . . 13.6.1
s 91. . . . . 14.7.4
ss 99–103. . . . . 14.7.1
s 99(4) 14.7.3
s 100. . . . . 14.7.6
s 101. . . . . 14.7.4, 14.7.7
(3)(a), (h). 14.7.8
s 104. . . . . 11.2.1
s 105. . . . . 11.2.2
s 106. . . . . 11.2.1
s 121A 13.6.2
Supreme Court Act 1981—
s 37(1) 10.3.5, 10.3.6
Telecommunications Act 1984—
s 43. . . . . 10.2.5, 10.2.13
Torts (Interference with Goods)
Act 1977. . . . . 5.5.6, 11.3.10
s 1(b) 10.3.2
Town and Country Planning Act 1990—
ss 197–214 . . . . A.3.8
s 198. . . . . 6.7.7
s 215. . . . . 14.6.5
(4) 14.6.5
s 216(2)–(3). 14.6.7
(4) 14.6.7, 14.6.8
(5) 14.6.8
s 217. . . . . 14.6.6
(1) 14.6.6
s 219. . . . . 14.6.8
s 331. . . . . A1.4
Town Police Clauses Act 1847—
s 28. . . . . 9.6.12
Vagrancy Act 1824—
s 4. . . . . 10.2.5, 10.2.10, 10.2.19
Visiting Forces Act 1952. . . . . 3.8.2
Water Industry Act 1991—
s 6. . . . . 15.4.1, 15.5.1
s 18. . . . . 15.5.3
ss 23–24. . . . . 15.5.3
Part III 15.4.14

Water Industry Act 1991—*contd.*
s 37. . . . . 15.4.2
Part III, Ch II 15.4.15
s 40–41. . . . . 15.4.15
s 41(4) 15.4.16
ss 42–44. . . . . 15.4.17
ss 45–46. . . . . 15.4.18
s 52. . . . . 15.4.19
s 55. . . . . 15.4.19
s 60. . . . . 15.4.20
ss 61–63. . . . . 15.4.21
ss 64–66. . . . . 15.4.22
s 67. . . . . 15.4.3
s 68. . . . . 15.4.7
s 70. . . . . 15.4.8
(2) 15.4.8
(3) 15.4.9
ss 71–76. . . . . 15.4.10
s 72. . . . . 15.4.10, 15.4.11
s 73–75. . . . . 15.4.12
s 76. . . . . 15.4.13
ss 80–81. . . . . 15.4.6
Part IV 15.5.1
s 94. . . . . 15.5.2
(2) 15.5.2
s 97. . . . . 15.5.3
s 98. . . . . 15.5.6
(1) 15.5.4
(2) 15.5.5
(4) 15.5.6
s 101. . . . . 15.5.6
s 101A 15.5.7
(2) 15.5.7
s 106(1) 15.5.8
(2)(a) 15.5.8
(3)–(4). 15.5.9
(5)–(6). 15.5.10
s 108. 15.5.14
s 109. 15.5.11
s 114(1)–(2). 15.5.12, 15.5.13
s 116. 15.5.19
(3) 15.5.19
Part IV, Ch III A2.16
s 118(1) 15.5.20
s 132. A2.16
s 196. A2.16
s 209. A1.15
s 210. A1.14
Water Resources Act 1991—
Part II. 15.2.1
s 85. . . . . 15.1.2, 15.2.3, 15.2.4
(1) 15.2.3, 15.2.9
(2)–(6). 15.2.3

Water Resources Act 1991—*contd.*
s 86 . . . . 15.2.3
ss 88–89 . . . . 15.2.12
s 90B A2.16
s 91 . . . . A2.16
ss 92–97 . . . . 15.3.4
s 104(1) 15.2.2
s 159(6)(b) 15.3.4
s 161 . . . . 15.3.1, 15.3.2
s 161A 15.3.3

Water Resources Act 1991—*contd.*
s 162 . . . . 15.3.1
 (1) 15.3.4
s 189 . . . . A2.16
s 197 . . . . A2.16
s 208 . . . . A1.15
s 217 . . . . A1.14
Sched 10, para 1 . . . . A2.16
 para 7 . . . . A2.16

Table of Statutory Instruments

All references are to paragraph numbers. Those prefixed A refer to the Appendices.

Air Navigation Noise Certification Order
  1990 (SI No 1514) 12.9.3
Air Quality Regulations 1997 (SI
  No 3043) 13.8.3
Building Regulations 1991
  (SI No 2768). 12.4.1
  Sched 1, Part E2. . . . . 12.4.1
Burning of Crop Residues (Repeal of
  Byelaws) Order 1992
  (SI No 893). 13.7.2
Clean Air (Emissions of Dark Smoke)
  (Exemption) Regulations 1969 (SI
  No 263) 13.3.9
Collection and Disposal of Waste
  Regulations 1988 (SI No 819)—
  reg 3 . . . . 14.2.4
  Sched 1 . . . . 14.2.4
Control of Noise (Appeals) Regulations
  1975 (SI No 2116) 12.3.7, 12.3.16
  reg 10(2) 12.3.9
Control of Noise (Code of Practice for
  Construction and Open Sites) Order
  1987 (SI No 1730) 12.3.5
Control of Noise (Measurement and
  Registers) Regulations 1976
  (SI No 37)—
  reg 64 . . . . A2.16
Control of Pollution (Applications,
  Appeals and Registers) Regulations
  1996 (SI No 2971) A2.14
Controlled Waste (Registration of
  Carriers and Seizure of Vehicles)
  Regulations 1991 (SI No 16) . . . A2.16
  regs 19-24 . . . . 14.5.2
  reg 22(1) 14.5.5
  reg 23 . . . . 14.5.5
County Court Rules 1981 (SI No
  1687)—
  Ord 3, r 4(4)(b) A5.19
  Ord 24 . . . . 5.1.6, 5.5.29, 5.6.5,
                    A5.18, A5.19

County Court Rules 1981 (SI No
  1687)—*contd.*
  Part I 5.5.16, 5.5.29, 5.5.30,
        5.5.31, 5.5.32, 5.5.33, 5.5.38
  r 1 . . . . A5.18
  r 4 . . . . A5.19
  Part II . . . 5.5.16, 5.5.29, 5.5.34–5.5.46
Crop Residues (Burning) Regulations
  1993 (SI No 1366) 13.7.2
Dark Smoke (Permitted Periods)
  Regulations 1958 (SI No 498) . . 13.3.9
Environmental Information Regulations
  1997 (SI No 3420). A1.6, A2
  reg 2(1). A2.8
    (c) A2.2
    (2)(a)-(b) A2.7
    (4). A2.8
  reg 3(1). A2.3, A2.13
    (2). A2.10
    (3). A2.12
  reg 4 . . . . A2.14
Environmental Protection (Applications,
  Appeals and Registers) Regulations
  1991 (SI No 507) 13.2.6
  reg 15 . . . . A2.16
Environmental Protection (Duty of
  Care) Regulations 1991
  (SI No 2839). 14.4.2
Environmental Protection (Stray
  Dogs) Regulations 1992
  (SI No 288). 9.10.3, 9.10.4
Genetically Modified Organisms
  (Deliberate Release) Regulations
  1992 (SI No 3280) A2.16
Land Registration Rules 1925 (SR & O
  1925 No 1093)—
  r 276. . . . . 6.12.16
  r 278. . . . . 6.12.15
  rr 298-299 . . . . 6.12.16
Litter (Animal Droppings) Order 1991
  (SI No 961). 14.8.9

Litter Control Areas Order 1991 (SI
  No 1235). 14.8.28, A2.16
Litter (Fixed Penalty Notices) Order
  1991 (SI No 111) 14.8.7
Local Land Charges Rules 1977 (SI
  No 985). A2.16
Noise Insulation (Railways and
  Other Guided Transport Systems)
  Regulations 1996
  (SI No 428). 12.15.1
Noise Insulation Regulations 1975
  (SI No 1763). 12.15.1
Planning (Hazardous Substances)
  Regulations 1992
  (SI No 656). A2.16
Private Water Supplies Regulations
  1991 (SI No 2790) 15.4.5
Radioactive Substances (Records of
  Convictions) Regulations 1992 (SI
  No 1685). A2.16
Removal and Disposal of Vehicles
  Regulations 1986 (SI No 183)—
  Part II. 14.7.3
  reg 9(2) 14.7.5
  Part III 14.7.7
  reg 12(2) 14.7.10
  regs 13-14 . . . . 14.7.10
  Sched 2 . . . . 14.7.2
Removal, Storage and Disposal of
  Vehicles (Prescribed Sums and
  Charges etc) Regulations 1989 (SI
  No 744) 14.7.11
Road Traffic (Vehicle Emissions)
  (Fixed Penalty) Regulations 1997
  (SI No 3058). 13.6.3

Road Vehicles (Construction and Use)
  Regulations 1986 (SI No 1078)—
  reg 61. 13.6.3
  reg 98. 13.6.3
Rules of the Air Regulations 1991 (SI
  No 2437) 12.9.4
  reg 5. . . . . 12.9.4
Rules of the Supreme Court (Revision)
  1965 (SI No 1776)—
  Ord 113. . . . . 5.1.6, 5.5.16,
                          5.5.18–5.5.34, 5.5.38,
                          5.6.5, A5.14–A5.17
  r 2. . . . . A5.14
  r 6. . . . . A5.16
  r 7. . . . . A5.17
Special Waste Regulations 1996 (SI
  No 972) 14.3.6
Statutory Nuisance (Appeals)
  Regulations 1995
  (SI No 2644). 12.2.11, 3.13.2
  reg 3. 12.2.11
Street Litter Control Notices Order
  1991 (SI No 1324) . . . 14.8.25, 14.8.29
Town and Country Planning (Control
  of Advertisements) Regulations 1992
  (SI No 666). A2.16
Town and Country Planning (General
  Development Procedure) Order 1995
  (SI No 419). A2.16
Waste Management Licensing
  Regulations 1994 (SI No 1056)—
  reg 10. A2.16
Water Supply (Water Quality)
  Regulations 1989 (SI No 1147)
  . . . . 15.4.4, 15.4.5, A2.16

Table of European Provisions

All references are to paragraph numbers. Those prefixed A refer to the Appendices.

Convention for the Protection of Human Rights and Fundamental Freedoms (Rome, 4 November 1950)—
    art 8 . . . . 5.4.10, A1.26
First Protocol (Paris, 20 March 1952)—
    arts 1-3 . . . . A1.26
Directive 80/778 EC (Drinking Water Quality) 18.4.4
Directive 90/313 EC (Information on Environmental Matters) A2.1

Abbreviations

CCR	County Court Rules
CJA	Criminal Justice Act 1988
DoE	Department of the Environment
EA	Environment Agency
EHO	Environmental Health Officer
EPA	Environmental Protection Act 1990
EDM	Electronic Distance Measurement
IPC	Integrated Pollution Control
HMLR	Her Majesty's Land Registry
HWM	High Water Mark
LRR	Land Registration Rules
LWM	Low Water Mark
NRA	National Rivers Authority
OAPA	Offences Against the Person Act 1861
Ord	Order
OS	Ordnance Survey
para	paragraph
r(r)	rules
reg(s)	regulation(s)
RSC	Rules of the Supreme Court
s(s)	section(s)
Sched	Schedule
SI	Statutory Instrument
TPO	Tree Preservation Order
VME	Vehicle, Machinery or Equipment
WCA	Waste Collection Authority
WDA	Waste Disposal Authority
WIA	Water Industry Act 1991
WRA	Water Resources Act 1991

Chapter 1

Private Nuisance

1.1 Overview

1.1.1 Private nuisance is a cause of action relied on by a plaintiff who has suffered some injury in the use and enjoyment of his land. It is a tort which protects interests in real property, the underlying principle being that a person who has exclusive possession of land should be entitled to make use of that land and all its appurtenant rights without interference or hindrance.

1.1.2 In order to succeed in an action, a plaintiff must be able to demonstrate exclusive possession of the land affected, whether *de jure* or *de facto*. Ordinarily this will be proved by reference to title, so that the plaintiff will be either the freeholder or tenant. In rare cases an occupier who can show that his occupation amounts to exclusive possession will also be able to sue. Mere permissive occupation of premises cannot give a plaintiff any rights in private nuisance. Although recent cases have seen an attempt to extend the ambit of private nuisance so that it would be available to protect plaintiffs who do not enjoy exclusive possession of land, the traditional role of the tort has been reasserted by the House of Lords in *Hunter v Canary Wharf* [1997] AC 655.

1.1.3 The fact that private nuisance is concerned with interests in real property is manifest at every stage. 'Damage' to the land must always be proved. This may take the form of some real physical injury to property, in which case private nuisance has been described as a tort of strict liability. It may take the more remote form of some intangible interference with the use and enjoyment of the land in question, in which case the courts have adopted a series of control mechanisms for determining the justice of the plaintiff's cause. At the other extreme, an allegation that the plaintiff has suffered some bodily injury or damage to goods, without damage to real property, is so far from being a complaint connected with the use and enjoyment of land that it does not give rise to a valid claim.

1.1.4 Private nuisance has not been unaffected by other developments in the law. The rise of negligence in particular has seen a recognition that, in some aspects of private nuisance, a duty of care is owed by one owner of land to another, notably where a defendant has a duty to ensure that some special hazard which has accumulated on his land does not escape on to his neighbours'

1

premises. A plaintiff, however, must be able to prove that the damage which has been caused to his property was reasonably foreseeable.

1.1.5 This chapter will consider the following topics:

The plaintiff

Who can sue? A plaintiff must be able to demonstrate exclusive possession of land in order to succeed.

Damage

(1) A private nuisance is only actionable if the plaintiff has suffered some damage. This must fall into one of three recognised categories:
   (a) physical damage
   (b) encroachment
   (c) 'intangible damage' (that is, some 'inconvenience materially interfering with the ordinary comfort physically of human existence'). Special rules apply to such an action.
(2) Damage incapable in itself of constituting the cause of action (such as personal injury or damage to chattels).
(3) Damage and foreseeability.

The defendant

Who can be sued?

(1) the original tortfeasor
(2) the current occupier
(3) the absent owner
(4) landlords and tenants
(5) servants, agents and independent contractors.

Private nuisances caused by dangerous hazards on land

(1) The existence of a duty to abate a hazard
(2) Responsibility for the acts of trespassers
(3) Natural hazards
(4) The scope of the duty of care and related issues.

Defences and supposed defences

(1) Trespassers
(2) Act of God
(3) Independent contractors
(4) 'Coming to a nuisance'
(5) Statutory authority
(6) Contribution.

Private nuisance is also the appropriate cause of action where a plaintiff complains of an interference with an easement. This book considers two such interferences, those involving rights of support and those concerned with rights to light. The relevant principles will be found at chapter 8. Guidance on the appropriate remedies in private nuisance will be found elsewhere, at chapter 16.

1.2 The plaintiff

The plaintiff's possessory interest in land

1.2.1 The right which is protected by the tort of private nuisance is the freedom of a person with exclusive possession of land to enjoy his premises undisturbed. It has been described as 'a tort directed against the plaintiff's enjoyment of his rights over land' (see Lord Goff in *Hunter v Canary Wharf* [1997] AC 655 at 687H, citing *The Boundaries of Nuisance*, Professor Newark, (1949) 65 LQR 480).

1.2.2 It can be said that save for exceptional circumstances, in which the courts will recognise the interest of an occupier as the equivalent of ownership (see 1.2.5), only a person with a proprietary interest, whether by virtue of his freehold or leasehold interest, can bring proceedings. Any period of proprietorship will be sufficient, so that in *Jones v Chappell* (1875) LR 20 Eq 539 a weekly tenant was able to claim in private nuisance. Mere occupation of premises without a proprietary interest or equivalent will not give rise to a cause of action. Husbands, wives, partners, children, lodgers, and any other individuals who are present solely by reason of the permission of the owner, will have no cause of action.

1.2.3 Amongst the older authorities, the principle that a plaintiff needs to be able to demonstrate a possessory interest in the land affected is demonstrated by *Malone v Laskey* [1907] 2 KB 141, in which the wife of the manager of a company entitled to live in the premises as his employer's licensee was held to be unable to sue in private nuisance. At 151 Sir Gorell Barnes P stated:

> no . . . principle of law [can] be formulated, to the effect that a person who has no interest in property, no right of occupation in the proper sense of the term, can maintain an action for nuisance.

See also *Cunard v Antifyre Limited* [1933] 1 KB 551.

1.2.4 The traditional role and function of the tort has now been decisively reasserted by the Judicial Committee in *Hunter v Canary Wharf* [1997] AC 655. See Lord Goff at 692C–D:

> An action in private nuisance will only lie at the suit of a person who has a right to the land affected. Ordinarily, such a person can only sue if he has the right to exclusive possession of the land, such as a freeholder or a tenant in possession, or even a licensee with exclusive possession. Exceptionally however . . . this category may include a person in actual possession who has no right to be there; and in any event a reversioner can sue in so far as his reversionary interest is affected. But a mere licensee on the land has no right to sue.

In order to succeed, therefore, a plaintiff must be able to show either title to the land said to be affected or some form of exclusive possession of the land in question.

De facto possession

1.2.5 Although an action for private nuisance is usually brought by the person with a proprietary right in the land in question such as a freeholder or tenant, *de facto* possession by way of exclusive occupation may be sufficient (*Newcastle-under-Lyme Corp v Wolstanton Limited* [1947] Ch 92, 106–108). In *Foster v Warblington UDC* [1906] 1 KB 648 an oyster merchant who had set up a business on the lord of the manor's shore was able to sue the defendant for damage caused by the discharge of sewage. He had carried on his trade removing and selling oysters for such a length of time that the court was willing to grant him relief. Fletcher Moulton LJ held (at 679) that:

> it is an unquestionable principle of our law that, where there has been long-continued enjoyment of an exclusive character of a right or a property, the law presumes that such enjoyment is rightful, if the property or right is of such a nature that it can have a legal origin.

(Vaughan Williams LJ noted (at 659) that given the period of time over which the plaintiff and his predecessors had occupied the oyster beds, the plaintiff could, if necessary, probably prove title.)

Rights and privileges in land not sufficient

1.2.6 A party seeking to exercise a general right or privilege which is open to all has no such exclusive possession and cannot maintain an action in private nuisance. In *Tate & Lyle Food and Distribution Ltd v GLC* [1983] 2 AC 509 the GLC constructed two ferry terminals on the banks of the Thames. These terminals caused siltation in a channel dug by the plaintiff for the purposes of making use of their own jetties. The plaintiff sought to recover the cost of redredging the channel. The plaintiff's claim in private nuisance was rejected since the plaintiff could not prove any private right over the bed of the River Thames (see Lord Templeman at 536C–537A).

The landowner who has parted with possession

1.2.7 An owner of land who has let his premises is entitled to complain of a nuisance so long as it can be demonstrated that the value of his interest has been substantially affected (*Wood v Conway Corporation* [1914] 2 Ch 47 at 58). There must have been a 'serious and permanent injury to the reversion', for instance by way of physical damage, such as cracks in the walls (*Shelfer v City of London Electric Lighting Co* [1895] 1 Ch 287 at 312).

Checklist – is the plaintiff entitled to sue?

- The plaintiff must have exclusive possession of the land affected, for instance as:
  — the freeholder
  — the leaseholder

— an occupier with *de facto* possession of the land.
- Rights or privileges in land are not sufficient.
- A landowner who has parted with possession must demonstrate 'serious and permanent' damage to the reversion.

1.3 Damage – introductory

Introductory – the need to prove damage

1.3.1 A cause of action in the tort of private nuisance is not available to a plaintiff until some damage has been sustained. It may take one of the following forms:

(1) Tangible physical damage to land
(2) Encroachment onto the plaintiff's land
(3) Intangible damage (being 'any inconvenience materially interfering with the ordinary comfort physically of human existence').

Culpability and private nuisance – the rules relating to damage

1.3.2 A plaintiff who alleges that he can maintain an action in private nuisance because there has been either some form of physical damage or encroachment must also be able to demonstrate that the damage in question was foreseeable (see 1.8). Foreseeability is a test established by the courts in order to establish culpability.

1.3.3 In the case of actions where it is said that there has been some intangible damage, that is, some material inconvenience with the use or enjoyment of land (for instance by noise, smell or dust), a judge is required to balance the competing rights of the plaintiff and the defendant according to certain control mechanisms recognised by the courts. These include rules relating to the standard of tolerance to be expected of a plaintiff, the nature and character of the area in which the complaints are made and the use of the land by the defendant. Since these rules are relevant only in cases of intangible damage they are set out in full in that section (1.6).

Some miscellaneous points

1.3.4 Several rules and their consequences must be remembered throughout. These include the following:

(1) Since private nuisance is a tort protecting the exclusive possession and enjoyment of land, damage not connected with land (such as personal injury or damage to chattels) is not capable on its own of giving rise to an action (although compensation for such damage may be recoverable as consequential loss);
(2) At common law an owner of property can build what he likes on his land, so that (in the absence of an easement) the mere presence of a

building is not actionable, however annoying or irritating the consequences of its existence;

(3) In the case of intangible damage, the source of the nuisance will ordinarily 'emanate from' the defendant's land.

1.3.5 The sections of this chapter dealing with matters concerning damage are arranged as follows:

1.4   Physical damage
1.5   Encroachment
1.6   Intangible damage
1.7   Damage incapable of being actionable
1.8   Damage and foreseeability.

Checklist – the importance of damage in private nuisance

- There is no cause of action in private nuisance if damage cannot be proved.
- 'Damage' for the purposes of establishing a cause of action may constitute
  — actual physical damage
  — encroachment (a type of actual physical damage)
  — intangible damage ('any inconvenience materially interfering with the ordinary comfort physically of human existence').
- The rules relating to damage are the means of establishing culpability:
  — actual physical damage and damage by encroachment are subject to the rules on foreseeability
  — special rules apply where it is said that there has been some intangible damage (see 1.6).
- The underlying principles must not be forgotten, eg:
  — damage not connected with land is not recoverable (save as consequential loss) – such as personal injury or damage to chattels
  — the mere presence of a building is not actionable
  — in the case of intangible damage, it will ordinarily 'emanate from' the defendant's land.

1.4   Damage – physical damage

1.4.1 The following have been held to constitute direct material harm:

(1) Wallpaper affected by damp from a neighbouring soil heap (*Broder v Saillard* (1876) 2 Ch D 692);

(2) Disintegration of bricks and lime mortar (*Maberley v Peabody & Co* [1946] 2 All ER 192);

(3) The collapse of a retaining wall as a result of 'thrust' caused by the weight of a neighbouring dwelling (*Wilkins v Leighton* [1932] 2 Ch 106);

(4) Decreased fertility of agricultural land (*Maberley v Peabody & Co* [1946] 2 All ER 192);

(5) Structural damage as a result of pile-driving (*Dodd Properties v Canterbury CC* [1980] 1 WLR 433);

(6) Damage to a plantation of trees as a result of fumes from a gasworks (proved by bringing the blackened tops to court) (*Wood v Conway Corp* [1914] 2 Ch 47).

Whether there has been actual physical damage to premises is a matter of fact for the tribunal. Whereas direct evidence from the plaintiff and his witnesses may be sufficient to prove the physical nature of the damage, expert evidence will often be required to demonstrate that the defendant's action has caused the damage which is the subject of the complaint.

1.5 Damage – encroachment

1.5.1 Encroachment over or under the plaintiff's land is enough to found a cause of action in private nuisance. This is because a landowner is presumed to own the space vertically above and below the surface of his land. An encroachment over the plaintiff's land is considered objectionable because it prevents an owner from raising the height of his premises (*Baten's case* (1610) 9 Co Rep 53b, 77 ER 810). The rule is identical to that which applies in trespass (see chapter 5).

1.5.2 The following have been considered to constitute nuisance without proof of any other damage:

(1) A cornice projecting over the garden of the plaintiff (*Fay v Prentice* (1845) 1 CB 828, 135 ER 769);

(2) Branches overhanging a private garden (*Earl of Lonsdale v Nelson* (1823) 2 B & C 302, 107 ER 396, 399–400; *Lemmon v Webb* [1894] 3 Ch 1 (affirmed at [1895] AC 1));

(3) Tree roots penetrating private land (*Lemmon v Webb* [1894] 3 Ch 1 at 14–15 (affirmed at [1895] AC 1)).

1.5.3 If some physical damage to land can be identified, then it is better modern practice to rely on the damage caused rather than on an allegation of encroachment (see for instance *Smith v Giddy* [1904] 2 KB 448 – overhanging branches causing damage to crops, and *Butler v Standard Telephones and Cables Ltd* [1940] 1 KB 399 – damage caused by abstraction of water by roots of trees burrowing into the plaintiff's land).

1.6 Damage – intangible damage

Introduction – the contents of this section

1.6.1 Actions in private nuisance where it is said there has been some intangible damage by way of an interference with the use and occupation of land (such as inconvenience caused by smoke, noise, dust) are subject to specific rules not relevant to actions involving physical damage or damage by encroachment. This is because, in general, the parties are involved in activities which, taken in isolation, are totally lawful (see 1.6.21). The rules governing cases of intangible damage operate to assist the judge in determining the reasonableness of the defendant's use of land as against the plaintiff's. Because these rules are unique to actions involving allegations of intangible damage they are set out within this section.

The nature of an action alleging intangible damage

1.6.2 There is a great difference between a private nuisance which is said to have been occasioned because of some material damage to the plaintiff's premises and that which arises by reason of some intangible interference with the use and enjoyment of property. The distinction between the two was clearly drawn in the leading case of *St Helen's Smelting Co Ltd v Tipping* (1862) 11 HL Cas 642, 11 ER 1483:

> It is a very desirable thing to mark the difference between an action brought for a nuisance upon the ground that the alleged nuisance produces material injury to the property, and an action brought for a nuisance on the ground that the thing alleged to be a nuisance is productive of sensible personal discomfort. With regard to the latter, namely, the personal inconvenience and interference with one's enjoyment, one's quiet, one's personal freedom, anything that discomposes or injuriously affects the senses or the nerves, whether that may or may not be denominated nuisance, must undoubtedly depend greatly on the circumstances of the place where the thing complained of actually occurs.

1.6.3 Physical damage, such as a cracked wall or mouldy wallpaper can be measured and assessed. Some of the underlying causes of what are said to amount to an interference with the use and enjoyment of premises (such as noise and smoke) may also be susceptible to scientific assessment. The underlying principle of the tort of private nuisance where it is alleged that some intangible damage has been sustained by the plaintiff is that an individual is entitled to the peaceful enjoyment of his premises for the purposes for which he intends them. At the same time, he is expected to tolerate these inconveniences and discomforts caused by the reasonable activities of his neighbours. Accordingly, the courts' approach is a 'rule of give and take, live and let live' (*Bamford v Turnley* 3 B & S 66, 84, 122 ER 27, 33 (Bramwell B)).

1.6.4 In a contested case involving an allegation of intangible damage, both the plaintiff and defendant will generally be engaged in activities which are in themselves entirely lawful and unobjectionable. In determining the competing rights of plaintiff and defendant the central focus of the court's inquiry is therefore the reasonableness of the plaintiff's complaint compared with the defendant's interest in making use of his land as he wishes:

> the law must strike a fair and reasonable balance between the right of the plaintiff on the one hand to the undisturbed enjoyment of his property, and the right of the defendant on the other hand to use his property for his own lawful enjoyment.

(Veale J in *Halsey v Esso Petroleum Co Ltd* [1961] 1 WLR 683, 692).
Once satisfied that an act or omission may give rise to an incidence of intangible damage, a variety of mechanisms are adopted by the courts in order to

assist it in its determination whether the plaintiff has a reasonable complaint. These include:

  (1) A robust approach to the measure of tolerance to be applied to the complaint, which is to be assessed according to the standards of the ordinary reasonable man;

  (2) An assessment of the expectations of the occupants of the locality in question, remembering in every case that the cumulative effect of a trade or occupation otherwise characteristic of the area may render the defendant's activities intolerable.

Determining what may constitute intangible damage

1.6.5 The nature of the interference with the plaintiff's use and enjoyment of his premises has been variously described. As an alternative to the test set out above in the extract from *St Helen's Smelting Co Ltd v Tipping* (ie whether 'the thing alleged to be a nuisance is productive of sensible personal discomfort') (see 1.6.2), a common formula is to determine 'whether the annoyance is such as materially to interfere with the ordinary comfort of human existence' or similar (see *Crump v Lambert* LR 3 Eq 409, 413, *Rushmer v Polsue and Alfieri Ltd* [1906] 1 Ch 234 and *Vanderpant v Mayfair Hotel Co Ltd* [1930] 1 Ch 138). Such a nuisance is actionable because 'every person is entitled as against his neighbour to the comfortable and healthful enjoyment of the premises occupied by him' (*Vanderpant's* case at 165; see also *Rapier v London Tramways Co* [1893] 2 Ch 588 at 600). Thus in a residential context it has been said in *Broder v Saillard* ((1876) 2 Ch D 692) that:

> I take it the law is this, that a man is entitled to the comfortable enjoyment of his dwelling-house. If his neighbour makes such a noise as to interfere with the ordinary use and enjoyment of his dwelling-house, so as to cause serious annoyance and disturbance, the occupier of the dwelling-house is entitled to be protected from it.

Some examples

1.6.6 The following have been said to amount to intangible damage:

  (1) Vibration and noise from an electrical generating station (*Colwell v St Pancras BC* [1904] 1 Ch 707);

  (2) The noise of an electric heating apparatus in an adjoining flat (*Metropolitan Properties v Jones* [1939] 2 All ER 202);

  (3) Noise from a busy hotel kitchen (*Vanderpant v Mayfair Hotel Co* [1930] 1 Ch 138);

  (4) The noise of revving engines and diesel fumes from a local coach business run in a residential area (*A-G v Gastonia Coaches* [1977] RTR 219);

  (5) The pungent smell of an oil depot (*Halsey v Esso Petroleum Co Ltd* [1961] 1 WLR 683);

  (6) The smell of pigs (*Bone v Seale* [1975] 1 WLR 797 and *Wheeler v JJ Saunders Ltd* [1996] Ch 19);

(7) Noise and dust from building operations (*Andreae v Selfridge & Co* [1938] Ch 1);

(8) The sound of footsteps and conversation penetrating through badly laid roof tiles on a roof terrace into the sitting room below (*Sampson v Hodson-Pressinger* [1981] 3 All ER 710);

(9) The sight of prostitutes and their clients going to and from a brothel (*Thompson-Schwab v Costaki* [1956] 1 WLR 335).

Evidence of financial loss in a claim by a landlord

1.6.7 In a case where intangible damage has been caused affecting the use and enjoyment of premises, a landlord may sue as well as the tenant who is in actual occupation and affected by the interference. However, evidence must be available to support a landlord's contention that the value of the property has been affected. This may be difficult to achieve since there must be a serious and permanent injury to the reversion (see 1.2.7). In *Broder v Saillard* (1876) 2 Ch D 692 the difficulty was overcome by adding the tenants in occupation as co-plaintiffs. Megarry J rejected a submission that there was insufficient evidence of loss in *Hampstead & Suburban Properties Ltd v Diomedous* [1969] 1 Ch 248. (See also *Colwell v St Pancras BC* [1904] 1 Ch 707, 712–713.)

A flexible test

1.6.8 It is recognised that the approach of the courts to such cases is an elastic one (*Colls v Home and Colonial Stores* [1904] AC 179 at 185 and *Polsue and Alfieri v Rushmer* [1907] AC 121 at 123). Whether or not a person's activities constitute a nuisance will always vary according to the 'usages of civilised society as they may be at the relevant date' (*Thompson-Schwab v Costaki* [1956] 1 WLR 335 at 338). The determination whether a court should intervene because there has been some intangible interference with the enjoyment of property is a matter entirely of fact and degree in each case (*Gaunt v Fynney* (1872) 8 Ch App 8 at 11–12, *Colls v Home and Colonial Stores* [1904] AC 179 at 185).

The appropriate standard of tolerance

1.6.9 The courts take a robust approach to the issue whether there has been an interference with a landowner's use and enjoyment of his property. The correct approach of the courts today derives from the question originally posed (and answered positively) by the judge in *Walter v Selfe* (1851) De G & Sm 315 at 322 (64 ER 849 at 852):

> Ought this inconvenience to be considered in fact as more than merely fanciful, more than one of mere delicacy or fastidiousness, as an inconvenience materially interfering with the ordinary comfort physically of human existence, not merely according to elegant or dainty modes and habits of living, but according to plain and sober and simple notions among the English people?

The test is that of the ordinary reasonable man (see Lord Wensleydale in *St Helen's Smelting Co v Tipping* (1862) 11 HL Cas 642 at 653–654, 11 ER 1483, 1487–1488, Kekewich J in *Rapier v London Tramways Co* [1893] 2 Ch 588 at 600, Luxmoore J in *Vanderpant v Mayfair Hotel Co Ltd* [1930] 1 Ch 138 at 165 and Megarry J in *Hampstead & Suburban Properties Ltd v Diomedous* [1969] 1 Ch 248 at 258B–C.

1.6.10 This test has also been adapted and expressed in a variety of other more succinct forms. A 'trivial' interference therefore is not enough (*A-G v Gastonia Coaches* [1977] RTR 219 at 243K). It has been said that: 'The law does not regard trifling and small inconveniences, but only regards sensible inconveniences, injuries which sensibly diminish the comfort, enjoyment or value of the property affected' (*St Helen's Smelting Co Ltd v Tipping* (1862) 11 HL Cas 642 at 653–654, 11 ER 1483 at 1488). The nuisance therefore has to be 'substantial' (*Crump v Lambert* (1867) LR 3 Eq 409) or a 'serious and not merely a slight interference' (cf *Rushmer v Polsue and Alfieri Ltd* [1906] Ch 234 at 248).

The relevance of malice

1.6.11 Evidence of malice on the part of a defendant is only useful because it may provide evidence of unreasonableness, especially in a case of nuisance by noise. This is because the lawful use of property is not rendered unlawful because of some improper or malicious motive behind the actions which form the subject of a complaint (*Bradford Corporation v Pickles* [1895] AC 587). This can be demonstrated by two well-known cases, the facts of which are worth citing in some detail.

1.6.12 In *Christie v Davey* [1893] 1 Ch 316, No 68 Angell Road Brixton was occupied by Mr JF Holder-Christie ('who, perhaps fortunately for himself, is very deaf') and his wife, a teacher of music and singing who gave private lessons at home. Her daughter came to live with her and gave piano and violin lessons at the home. Another musician came to live with them, and their son played the cello up to eleven o'clock ('but he was only an amateur'). Next door lived a wood engraver. They had lived harmoniously together for three years and the defendant had never complained. Relations deteriorated very quickly and the defendant and his family started banging on trays, whistling, shrieking and imitating the music from next door. Both sides asked for injunctions. North J held that the defendant's family's noises were made 'deliberately and maliciously for the purpose of annoying the plaintiffs'. It was 'not a legitimate use of the defendant's house'. The noises were to be regarded as excessive and unreasonable. There was no evidence to suppose that what the plaintiff's family was doing was malicious. They had not gone beyond a legitimate use of their house. There was nothing unreasonable in what they were doing.

1.6.13 In *Hollywood Silver Fox Farm Ltd v Emmett* [1936] 2 KB 468 the plaintiff established a silver fox farm. He erected a notice visible from a field owned by the defendant, who was intending to develop the field as a building estate. The plaintiff refused to take down the notice. The defendant maliciously sent his son on to his land near to that of the plaintiff to fire bird-scaring cartridges. At trial the defendant claimed that he was attempting to keep down the rabbit population. The vixens in the pens were very scared and would not breed. The court accepted the plaintiff's submissions that malice was an indication that the amount of noise generated was not reasonable since there was no need for it.

1.6.14   So too in *Ibbotson v Peat* (1865) 3 H & C 644, 159 ER 684 it was a nuisance to make bangs (fireworks, missiles, projectiles and combustibles) to frighten away game on the plaintiff's land. In *Keeble v Hickeringill* (1706) 11 East 573, 103 ER 1127 it was held to be a nuisance to discharge a gun to drive ducks away from a decoy pond.

Hypersensitive plaintiffs and delicate trades

1.6.15   Since the relevant test for judging whether a plaintiff should tolerate the activities of the defendants is that of the ordinary reasonable man (1.6.9), it follows that a hypersensitive plaintiff will not succeed (see *Emms v Polya* (1973) 227 EG 1659 and *Whycer v Urry* [1956] JPL 365).

1.6.16   In *Robinson v Kilvert* (1889) 41 Ch D 88 the plaintiff was unable to recover compensation for heat damage caused to brown paper which was kept on his premises since his trade was 'exceptionally delicate'; any ordinary business would not have been affected.

Nature and character of the area

1.6.17   Locality is a significant consideration in the assessment as to the reasonableness of the plaintiff's complaint. Thus in *Rushmer v Polsue* and *Alfieri Ltd* [1906] 1 Ch 234 Vaughan Williams LJ stated at 245:

> If a man lives in a town, it is necessary that he should subject himself to the consequences of those operations of trade which may be carried on in his immediate locality, which are actually necessary for trade and commerce, and also for the benefit of property, and for the benefit of the inhabitants of the town and of the public at large. If a man lives in a street where there are numerous shops and a shop is opened next door to him, which is carried on in a fair and reasonable way, he has no ground for complaint, because to himself individually there may arise much discomfort from the trade carried on in that shop.

Putting it more succinctly, Cozens-Hardy LJ said (at 250):

> the standard of comfort differs according to the situation of the property and the class of people who inhabit it.

1.6.18   This means that a town-dweller is expected to be more tolerant of those disturbances and annoyances characteristic of a town; he cannot expect the conditions of the countryside (*Colls v Home and Colonial Stores* [1904] AC 179, 185 and *Halsey v Esso Petroleum Co Ltd* [1961] 1 WLR 683, 692). Of course the precise nature of the area itself is relevant. See *Sturges v Bridgman* (1879) 11 Ch D 852, 865:

Whether anything is a nuisance or not is a question to be determined, not merely by an abstract consideration of the thing itself, but in reference to its circumstances; what would be a nuisance in Belgrave Square would not necessarily be so in Bermondsey; and where a locality is devoted to a particular trade or manufacture carried on by the traders or manufacturers in a particular and established manner not constituting a public nuisance, judges and juries would be justified in finding, and may be trusted to find, that the trade or manufacture so carried on in that locality is not a private or actionable wrong.

In preparing their evidence the parties must prepare for the closest possible scrutiny of the characteristics of the immediate locality.

Cumulative effect

1.6.19 It does not follow that activities cannot be a nuisance because they are already carried out by others in the area. Although a resident of a certain area must put up with an amount of discomfort or inconvenience characteristic of the area in question, a substantial additional nuisance will be actionable. Thus the plaintiff owner of a house in Walsall which had occasionally been affected by a great deal of smoke and some noise from factories in the Walsall area was entitled to succeed against a defendant who had erected a works in the adjacent grounds (*Crump v Lambert* (1867) LR 3 Eq 409). The smoke from the defendant's factory had 'produced a completely new state of things as regards the plaintiff's house and grounds'.

1.6.20 So too in *Rushmer v Polsue and Alfieri Ltd* [1906] 1 Ch 234 the plaintiff milkman lived on the middle of a part of London occupied by the printing trade. He himself was engaged in the business of supplying members of the printing trade with his milk and there were very few other residents in the area. However, 'whatever the standard of comfort in a particular district may be, the addition of a fresh noise caused by the defendant's works may be so substantial as to create a legal nuisance'. Cozens-Hardy LJ continued at 250:

> It does not follow that because I live in Sheffield I cannot complain if a steam-hammer is introduced next door, and so worked as to render sleep at night almost impossible, although previously to its introduction my house was a reasonably comfortable abode, having regard to the local standard.

In approving the above passage, the House of Lords held that the plaintiff succeeded because, taking into consideration the locality and the noises there prevailing, 'a serious addition had been caused by the defendants' (*Polsue and Alfieri Ltd v Rushmer* [1907] AC 121 at 123).

Reasonable user by the defendant

1.6.21 Characteristically in an action where the nuisance is said to have arisen because of some interference with the plaintiff's use and enjoyment of his property, neither the plaintiff nor the defendant will be doing anything unlawful with his land. As has been pointed out, much depends on the nature and character of the area. A properly run hotel, for instance, will inevitably have a noisy kitchen. A noisy kitchen is not a nuisance in itself, but whilst it may give rise to a complaint to its residential neighbours, set on its own in the countryside it is unlikely to pose a problem.

1.6.22 In assessing whether the use to which he puts his land is a nuisance, the court is not concerned with the reasonableness of the use to which the defendant puts his property taken in isolation. See *Reinhardt v Mentasti* (1889) 42 Ch D 685 at 690:

> The application of the principle governing the jurisdiction of the Court in cases of nuisance does not depend on the question whether the defendant is using his own reasonably or otherwise. The real question is does he injure his neighbour?

In *Broder v Saillard* (1876) 2 Ch D 692 Jessel MR stated (at 701):

> The law is this, that a man is entitled to the comfortable enjoyment of his dwelling-house. If his neighbour makes such a noise as to interfere with the ordinary use and enjoyment of his dwelling-house, so as to cause serious annoyance and disturbance, the occupier of the dwelling-house is entitled to be protected from it. It is no answer to say that the Defendant is only making a reasonable use of his property, because there are many trades and occupations which are not only reasonable, but necessary to be followed, and which still cannot be allowed to be followed in the proximity of dwelling-houses, so as to interfere with the comfort of their inhabitants.

Thus in *Bone v Seale* [1975] 1 WLR 797, although the defendant pig farmer had taken steps to reduce the smell of boiling pig swill, he had created and continued a nuisance (mainly by more than doubling the size of his herd) and could not avoid liability for the offensive smell caused by his pigs. The reasonableness of the defendant's conduct will be weighed against all the factors, including the degree of suffering and inconvenience undergone by the plaintiff.

1.6.23 In addition to suggesting that they have not committed a nuisance because the use to which they put their land is itself reasonable, defendants are also often inclined to argue that they should not be held liable because they have done their best to minimise or prevent the inconvenience to the plaintiff. This is not a good defence. Thus in *Vanderpant v Mayfair Hotel Co Ltd* [1930] 1 Ch 138 at 139 it was said that:

> It is no answer to say that the best known means have been taken to reduce or prevent the noise complained of, or that the cause of the nuisance is the exercise of a business or trade in a reasonable and proper manner.

So too in *Rapier v London Tramways Co* [1893] 2 Ch 588 at 600 the court held that:

> If I am sued for nuisance and the nuisance is proved, it is no defence on my part to say, and to prove, that I have taken all reasonable care to prevent it.

(See also *Rushmer v Polsue and Alfieri Ltd* [1906] 1 Ch 234 at 250.)

The effect of planning permission

1.6.24 The nature and character of an area is not immutable. It may change radically and dramatically, especially by the grant of planning permission. Such a grant, however, is not a licence to commit nuisance (*Gillingham BC v Medway (Chatham) Dock Co Ltd* [1993] QB 343 at 359G (Buckley J). A planning authority 'has no jurisdiction to authorise nuisance' (*Allen v Gulf Oil Refining Ltd* [1980] QB 156 at 174H). At the same time, where planning consent has been given for a development or change of use, the question of nuisance 'will thereafter fall to be decided by reference to a neighbourhood with that development or use and not as it was previously' (*Gillingham BC v Medway (Chatham) Dock Co Ltd* [1993] QB 343 at 361E (Buckley J)). Only to this extent can it be said that a planning authority has any statutory power to permit the change of a character of a neighbourhood (*Allen v Gulf Oil Refining Ltd* [1980] QB 156 at 174G–H).

1.6.25 In *Wheeler v Saunders* [1996] Ch 19 the defendants obtained planning permission for two pig houses, each to house 20 pigs. One of the houses was to be sited 11 metres from the plaintiffs' holiday homes. The plaintiffs had objected to the defendants' application and then sued for damages and an injunction to restrain the defendants from keeping their pigs in the units. They claimed that the smell constituted a nuisance. Applying the principles of *Allen's* and of *Gillingham's* cases, the Court of Appeal upheld the trial judge's decision to grant the plaintiffs the relief they sought. Notwithstanding that the nuisance was the inevitable consequence of the use of the planning permission, that permission had not licensed the defendants' nuisance.

Temporary interferences

1.6.26 A defendant to an action in private nuisance often seeks to assert that the inconvenience about which the plaintiff complains is only temporary and so not objectionable. This is an unattractive argument and the courts will go some way in order to defeat it. In *Colwell v St Pancras BC* [1904] 1 Ch 707 it was suggested that an admitted nuisance by way of vibration and noise was not offensive because it would only last a few months. This did not find much favour with the trial judge who considered the proposition 'novel and strange' since it would render the neighbourhood uninhabitable for the period. Moreover an intermittent nuisance cannot be divided into a series of temporary and therefore irrelevant wrongs (*Bone v Seale* [1975] 1 WLR 797).

Building and demolition operations

1.6.27 Although building and demolition works are temporary operations they can take a considerable time to complete and they can involve a great deal of disturbance to neighbouring residents. The courts recognise that the use of land will develop and that new technology may mean increased disturbance to those who have to put up with such activities (see *Andreae v Selfridge & Co*

Ltd [1938] Ch 1, 6). At common law the problem is resolved by attempting to strike a balance between the interests of local inhabitants and the desirability of developing sites (see Bingham LJ in *City of London Corp v Bovis Construction Ltd* [1992] 3 All ER 697, 712j).

1.6.28   In an action for private nuisance the courts will expect some consider-able tolerance on the part of the aggrieved plaintiffs. The approach adopted by the courts in reconciling the conflicting interests of the parties is not to hold a defendant responsible 'if he uses all reasonable skill and care to avoid annoy-ance to his neighbour by the works of demolition' (Vaughan Williams J in *Harrison v Southwark and Vauxhall Water Co* [1891] 2 Ch 409, 414).

1.6.29   The result of this test is generally that the burden falls on the defendant to demonstrate that he has taken all reasonable steps to avoid unnecessary noise, dirt and dust (see *Andreae's* case at 9). In order to discharge this burden the defendant will have to show for instance that the hours during which work was done was restricted, that limits were placed on the amount of a particular type of work which is done simultaneously (*Andreae v Selfridge & Co Ltd* at 10) or that some special arrangement could not have been made to accommo-date any particular needs of the plaintiff (see *Matania v National Provincial Bank* [1936] 2 All ER 633, 643–4). Consultation with the people affected is always helpful. At the same time the courts will not expect the defendant to take steps which are prohibitively expensive or time-consuming. (Reference should also be made to 3.2, 12.3 and 12.4 (environmental controls on building and demolition operations).)

Statutory nuisances

1.6.30   In any action in which there has been some material discomfort which is prejudicial to health or a nuisance, it is important to ascertain whether there has been a nuisance contrary to the provisions of Part III of the Environmental Protection Act 1990. These are considered in detail in chapter 3.

Checklist – intangible damage

- The underlying test is one of fact and degree. Has there been:
    - any 'personal inconvenience and interference with one's enjoy-ment, one's quiet, one's personal freedom, anything that discom-poses or injuriously affects the senses or the nerves'?
    - an activity 'productive of sensible personal discomfort'?
    - an annoyance such as 'materially to interfere with the ordinary comfort of human existence'?
- The nature of the action is governed by uncertainties. It is a flexible test:
    - intended to balance the otherwise lawful acts of the litigants
    - subject to a 'rule of give and take'
    - which varies according to the 'usages of civilised society as they may be at the relevant date'.

- The standard of tolerance to be expected of the parties:
  — is that of 'plain and sober and simple notions'
  — does not concern itself with 'trivial interferences'
  — concerns itself with 'substantial' and 'serious' interferences, not the merely 'trivial' or 'slight'
  — recognises malice on the part of a defendant as an indication of unreasonableness
  — does not protect the hypersensitive plaintiff or exceptionally delicate trades.
- The locality is an important consideration:
  — standards will vary from area to area
  — what is appropriate in the town may not be appropriate in the country
  — what is appropriate in one region may not be appropriate in another
  — the nature of the locality can change
  — the grant of planning permission may affect the nature of an area.
- 'Bad' defences
  — 'although I am driving the plaintiff mad by my activities, I am only doing exactly what everyone else in the neighbourhood is doing'
  — 'I was using my land for an entirely lawful activity'
  — 'I was using my land entirely reasonably'
  — 'I have done my best to minimise or prevent the inconvenience'.
- Special rules apply to building and demolition operations
  — the builder must use reasonable skill to avoid unnecessary noise, dirt and dust
  — the burden of proof that all reasonable steps were taken to avoid unnecessary inconvenience generally falls on the defendant
  — consider whether any environmental controls apply (3.2, 12.3, 12.4).
- Other causes of action
  — there are now many statutory nuisances intended to capture the circumstances otherwise governed by private nuisance at common law (see chapter 3).

1.7 Damage incapable of amounting to a nuisance

Chattels

1.7.1 Damage to chattels on their own cannot constitute the tort of nuisance. In *Halsey v Esso Petroleum Co Ltd* [1961] 1 WLR 683 the plaintiff owned a car which he kept on the highway. Acid smuts and oily drops fell from the defendant's oil depot on to its paintwork. Veale J allowed a claim in public nuisance (see chapter 3) and under the principle of *Rylands v Fletcher* (see chapter 4), but did not give a remedy at private nuisance in respect of this head of damage.

Personal injury

1.7.2 As with injury to chattels, personal injuries cannot constitute the tort of private nuisance. Thus in *Cunard v Antifyre Ltd* [1933] 1 KB 551 the defendant's guttering fell through a glass ceiling causing personal injury. Talbot J held at 556–7:

> We think that 'nuisance' (we are speaking of private nuisance only) is correctly confined to injuries to property, whether to easements such as the obstruction of light or of rights of way, or the diversion of water courses, or the withdrawal of support from a house; or to other kinds of property, as by noise, noxious vapours, smoke or the like. In all such cases the plaintiff in order to maintain an action must show some title to the thing to which the nuisance is alleged to be and this follows from the nature of such actions.

See also *Malone v Laskey* [1907] 2 KB 141 (1.2.3).

Rights to a view; interference with surrounding light and air

1.7.3 When considering the question of damage it is important to keep in mind the dominance of the principle that an individual should be entitled to use and enjoy his land without restriction. In the absence of direct physical damage or encroachment and without any intangible inconvenience arising from activities carried out on the defendant's land, a plaintiff has no redress in private nuisance if his neighbour erects some structure which obscures his view or interferes with his enjoyment of the surrounding light or air. The right to a view (a 'right of prospect'), for instance, is not actionable (*Dalton v Angus* (1881) 6 App Cas 740). The house-owner who finds that his fine view of the South Downs has been ruined by the building of his neighbour has no right to sue at common law in private nuisance (see Lord Lloyd in *Hunter v Canary Wharf* [1997] AC 655 at 699C). Such inconveniences are not actionable because they are not sufficiently connected with the plaintiff's land. Protection against the obstruction of a view is available only under planning legislation or by express grant or covenant. A right to air or light can only be obtained by the acquisition of an easement (whether by grant or prescription). Chapter 8 considers the principles relevant to interferences with rights of support and rights to light.

Television signals

1.7.4 The common law tort of private nuisance has not been particularly accommodating towards contemporary forms of life. Interference with television signals does give rise to an action in nuisance under Canadian law (*Nor-Video Services v Ontario Hydro* (1978) 84 DLR (3d) 221 at 231). In the United Kingdom, however, an attempt by an organisation to claim a right to sue in private nuisance over interference with the signals emitted by a commercial television aerial failed in *Bridlington Relay Ltd v Yorkshire Electricity Board* [1965] Ch 436. The court held that an interference with a purely recreational facility did not 'detract from the beneficial use and enjoyment by neighbouring owners of their properties to such an extent as to warrant their protection by the law'.

1.7.5 In *Hunter v Canary Wharf* [1997] AC 655 an attempt by private individuals to sue for interference with the reception of television signals also failed.

Consequential damages

1.7.6 Although damages for injury to chattels or the person cannot give rise to an action in private nuisance, compensation for such loss may be available in the usual way as consequential damages where some other damage founding the tort has been established. This was made clear by Lord Hoffman in *Hunter v Canary Wharf* [1997] AC 655 at 706F–G:

> There may of course be cases in which, in addition to damages for injury to his land, the owner or occupier is able to recover damages for consequential loss. He will, for example, be entitled to loss of profits which are the result of inability to use the land for the purposes of his business. Or if the land is flooded, he may also be able to recover damages for chattels or livestock lost as a result.

Such damage must be truly consequential to the damage founding an action in tort, so that a fall in letting values (because of the construction of a lunatic asylum) without any damage affecting the land does not give rise to the tort (*Metropolitan Asylum District Managers v Hill* (1881) 6 App Cas 193 at 206).

Isolated incidents

1.7.7 It is sometimes said that an isolated incident cannot found the tort of private nuisance. This is generally a question of degree since a private nuisance is an interference for 'a substantial length of time' with the use and enjoyment of property (*Cunard v Antifyre Ltd* [1933] 1 KB 551 at 557) (see also 1.6.26 – Temporary interferences). The single blast of a trumpet will not constitute a nuisance, whereas repeated blasts may well do so. (Thus in *A-G v PYA Quarries ex rel Glamorgan CC* [1957] 2 QB 169, Denning LJ stated 'a private nuisance always involves some degree of repetition or continuance'.)

1.7.8 Where, however, there has been an escape of a dangerous item from a defendant's land the position is otherwise. Such an event can constitute a nuisance. In *Midwood & Co Ltd v Manchester Corpn* [1905] 2 KB 597 an electric main installed by the defendants fused. This caused bitumen in the main to volatilise into a cloud of gas. The gas exploded and a fire damaged the plaintiff's goods. The Court of Appeal held that the defendants were liable. So too in *British Celanese Ltd v Hunt (Capacitors) Ltd* [1969] 1 WLR 959 the defendants allowed strips of metal foil to escape from their yard, causing a black-out at the local substation. This isolated incident was sufficient to found an action in nuisance.

Checklist – damages irrecoverable in private nuisance

- Damages incapable of constituting the completed tort:
  — damage to chattels
  — personal injury
  — rights to a view
  — television signals.
- Consequential damages can include:
  — damage to chattels
  — personal injury
  — economic loss.

1.8   Damage – foreseeability of damage

1.8.1   Under the law of private nuisance as understood today, it is necessary to prove foreseeability of damage on the part of a defendant in order to establish liability. This is the case whether a defendant is said to have created, continued or adopted a nuisance. It is not necessary to ascertain whether there is a concurrent duty to a plaintiff in negligence since it is now settled that a plaintiff should not be in a stronger position to sue in nuisance than if he were to sue in negligence. These principles can be derived from *The Wagon Mound (No 2)* [1967] 1 AC 617 and *Cambridge Water Co Ltd v Eastern Counties Leather plc* [1994] 2 AC 264 (see especially 300–301).

1.8.2   *The Wagon Mound (No 2)* [1967] 1 AC 617 was concerned with an oil spill in Sydney Harbour. Engineers on board the *Wagon Mound* allowed fuel oil on board the vessel to flow into the harbour. The fuel oil ignited and destroyed the plaintiff's vessels. In an appeal before the Privy Council the respondents argued that although foreseeability is an essential element in assessing compensation it was not relevant to the issue of liability. The argument was rejected by Lord Reid, stating (at 640) that:

> It could not be right to discriminate between different cases of nuisance so as to make foreseeability a necessary element in determining damages in those cases where it is a necessary element in determining liability but not in others. So the choice is between it being a necessary element in all cases of nuisance or none. In their lordships' judgment the similarities between nuisance and other forms of tort to which *The Wagon Mound (No 1)* applies far outweigh any differences, and they must therefore hold that the judgment appealed from is wrong on this branch of the case. It is not sufficient that the injury suffered by the respondents' vessels was the direct result of the nuisance, if that injury was in the relevant sense unforeseeable.

Lord Goff cited this passage with approval in *Cambridge Water Co v Eastern Counties Leather plc* [1994] 2 AC 264 at 301C–D:

> It is widely accepted that this conclusion, although not essential to the decision of the particular case, has nevertheless settled the law to the effect that foreseeability of harm is indeed a prerequisite of the recovery of damages in private nuisance.

A defendant in a private nuisance action should be no more in the position of an insurer than if he were the defendant in any other case. 'Normally the law limits liability to those consequences which are attributable to that which made the act wrongful' (*Banque Bruxelles Lambert SA v Eagle Star Insurance Co* [1997] AC 191 at 213C).

The standard of foreseeability

1.8.3 The general principle is that a foreseeable risk is a risk which can be described as 'real' rather than as a mere possibility which would never influence the mind of a reasonable man. The qualification is that it is justifiable not to take steps to eliminate a real risk if the risk is small and the circumstances are such that a reasonable man, mindful of the safety of his neighbour, would think it right to neglect it (see *The Wagon Mound (No 2)* at 642G). This qualification is justified since 'in the crowded conditions of modern life even the most careful person cannot avoid creating some risks and accepting others' (Lord Reid in *Bolton v Stone* [1951] AC 850 at 867).

1.9 The defendant

Overview

1.9.1 Liability for nuisance can lie with several parties at the same time. The immediate target for an action in nuisance is the person who created the nuisance, and he will remain liable even when he has left the scene. Beyond the original perpetrator, however, the court will hold anyone liable whom it identifies as a person who had sufficient control over the land from which the nuisance arose to be able to abate it. An absent owner as well as an occupier may therefore be liable, whether or not he created the nuisance. The fact that the nuisance was actually caused by a party's servants or agents, or even by an independent contractor, will generally not protect a defendant. Accordingly, a landlord will often be liable for a nuisance which existed at the commencement of a tenancy, since the court will be willing to impute knowledge of the nuisance to the owner.

The original tortfeaser

1.9.2 The original wrongdoer will always remain liable for a nuisance (see *Maberley v Peabody & Co* [1946] 2 All ER 192 for an example).

1.9.3 A person who authorises and requires another to commit a nuisance is also liable for the nuisance as an original tortfeasor (*Harris v James* (1976) 45 LJQB 545).

1.9.4 Whilst the law of nuisance is that a party is generally responsible for the acts of his independent contractors, it is quite possible to proceed against the contractors alone (*Farrell v John Mowlem & Co Ltd* [1954] 1 Lloyd's Rep 437).

Is a nuisance required to emanate from the tortfeasor's land?

1.9.5 The question arises (especially in relation to an original wrongdoer) whether activities said to amount to a nuisance must emanate from a defendant's land. Support for this proposition can be found in the speech of Lord Wright in *Sedleigh-Denfield v O'Callaghan* [1940] AC 880 (at 903):

> the ground of responsibility is the possession and control of land from which the nuisance proceeds.

So too in *SCM v Whittall* [1970] 1 WLR 1017 Thesiger J dismissed the plaintiff's action because *inter alia* the plaintiff had failed to prove (see 1031D–E):

> that the nuisance arose from the condition of the defendant's land or premises or property or activities thereon that constituted a nuisance.

On the other hand, the authorities provide support for the contrary position. In *Halsey v Esso Petroleum* [1961] 1 WLR 683 Veale J was content to find the defendant liable in private nuisance for noise created outside its premises (see 699–700). He preferred the *dicta* of Devlin J reported at *Esso Petroleum Co Ltd v Southport Corp* [1956] AC 218, 224:

> It is clear that to give a cause of action for private nuisance the matter complained of must affect the property of the plaintiffs. But I know of no principle that it must emanate from land belonging to the defendant.

(Cf. Denning LJ at *Southport Corp v Esso Petroleum Co Ltd* [1954] 2 QB 182, 196.)

The current occupier of land

1.9.6 A current occupier of land who did not create a nuisance will be liable if he (a) had actual or constructive knowledge of the nuisance and (b) had time to abate it but failed to do so (*Barker v Herbert* [1911] 2 KB 633).

1.9.7 A case of actual knowledge will arise ordinarily where the occupier is told by the complainant or some third party of the existence of the nuisance. Thus in *Maberley v Peabody & Co* [1946] 2 All ER 192 S created a nuisance by piling up a mound of earth against M's wall, which began to crack and shift. S left the premises and P took on the tenancy. M made his complaints known to P as the new tenant. The court found all three liable – P, S and the absent landlord (see 195A):

> I am satisfied that P did not create [the nuisance] or add to it in any shape or form, but the fact of its existence had been brought very pointedly to their notice. They are in occupation of the property; they have had ample time, if they were minded to put the matter right, so to do, and they have done nothing; and I think in law they are equally responsible with the owner of the freehold and with the actual tortfeasor.

1.9.8 Whether a court is willing to find that an occupier had constructive knowledge of a nuisance is a matter of fact. What may amount to constructive knowledge has not been analysed in great detail and the courts prefer to use expressions such as 'imputed' (*Noble v Harrison* [1926] 2 KB 332) and 'attributed' (*Barker's* case). In *Wilkins v Leighton* [1932] 2 Ch 106 the court asked itself whether the defendant 'ought with reasonable care to have known of the nuisance.' An occupier who has not created a nuisance is only culpable because he has allowed the nuisance to continue. In the case of an occupier without actual knowledge of the nuisance, therefore, the primary issue is the question whether knowledge should be attributed to the occupier, since only then can he be said to have allowed the nuisance to continue (*Barker's* case).

1.9.9 Applying these principles the courts have held variously that knowledge could not be imputed to defendants in respect of the following:

(1) A crack in a tree which was not observable by any reasonably careful inspection (*Noble's* case);
(2) Elm butt rot in the roots of a tree which would not have been discoverable by any reasonable examination (*Caminer v Northern and London Investment Trust Ltd* [1951] AC 88);
(3) Sideways thrust on to the foundations of a brick wall caused by the weight of a neighbouring dwelling (*Wilkins's* case);
(4) Railings broken by boys playing football in the street three days before the plaintiff's accident (*Barker's* case).

(These cases can also be relied on in support of the propositions that an occupier will not be liable for a latent defect (*Noble's* and *Caminer's* cases) or for the acts of trespassers (*Barker*).)

The absent owner

1.9.10 An absent owner of premises will be liable for a nuisance if the court determines that he should have known of its existence. The standard of action required is high. In *Leanse v Lord Egerton* [1943] 1 KB 323 the defendant's house in Curzon Street was hit by an enemy bomb on Friday. The defendant lived out of London. Nobody lived in the house. On Monday the defendant's agents made efforts to secure a builder to repair the damage. Before they could do that, a passer-by was hit by a piece of glass. Knowledge was imputed to the defendant on the Saturday morning (see 325):

> In my view . . . the house should not have been left as it was just because it was inconvenient or difficult or troublesome to make arrangements with regard to it.

Someone could at least have told the police so that they stopped people from passing underneath. The difficulty of getting work done on a Saturday did not assist the defendant.

Landlords and tenants: responsibilities to third parties

1.9.11 In the case of a landowner who has let premises to a tenant, if he has created a nuisance then he will be liable to any third party plaintiffs as the original tortfeasor in the ordinary way. The terms of the lease may be important, so that where the landlord has retained an obligation to repair the premises this may be evidence establishing liability (*Spicer v Smee* [1946] 1 All ER 489). In *Heap v Ind Coope and Allsopp Ltd* [1940] 2 KB 476 it was sufficient that the landlord had reserved the right to enter on and view the premises and to do all necessary repairs.

1.9.12   Conversely, the fact that the lease may contain a covenant on the part of the landlord to repair the premises does not absolve the occupiers (*Slater v Worthington's Cash Stores (1930) Ltd* [1941] 1 KB 488, 490). Both landlord and tenant may be proper defendants (see *Wilchick v Marks and Silverstone* [1934] 2 KB 56).

1.9.13   A landlord who acquires a reversion knowing that the previous landlord has created or authorised a nuisance will be liable to a third party (*Sampson v Hodson-Pressinger* [1981] 3 All ER 710).

Liability of a landlord for the acts of a tenant

1.9.14   A landlord will not be liable in nuisance to a third party for the acts of its tenants (*Smith v Scott* [1973] Ch 314). The exception is where the landlord has expressly or impliedly authorised the acts of its tenants (*Harris v James* (1876) 45 LJQB 545). Where the injury complained of by the plaintiff was the natural and necessary consequence of the purpose for which the premises were let, the landlord will be taken to have authorised the nuisance and will be liable to the plaintiff (see *Harris v James* (1876) 45 LJQB 545 and *Sampson v Hodson-Pressinger* [1981] 3 All ER 710). Where the authorisation is said to have been implied, the plaintiff must prove that there was a very high degree of probability that a nuisance would result from the purposes for which the property is let. In *Smith v Scott* the plaintiffs sued the local authority which had accommodated a 'large and unruly' family in temporary accommodation in the adjacent premises. Pennycuick VC found that the authority knew that the family were likely to cause a nuisance. He held, however, that notwithstanding this, since the terms of the tenancy expressly prohibited the tenants from committing a nuisance, it was 'not legitimate to say that the corporation impliedly authorised the nuisance' (at 321F).

1.9.15   An example of implied authority arises in *Tetley v Chitty* [1986] 1 All ER 663. In that case the local authority granted the defendant seven years to use premises for the purposes of go-kart racing. Three local residents sued the authority to restrain them from granting a lease or licence in respect of the land which permitted the use of the land for go-kart racing and for damages. McNeill J held that the noise was an ordinary and necessary consequence of the activity of go-kart racing so that the authority was liable. He granted a permanent injunction and damages.

1.9.16   If the servants or agents of the landlord knew of the nuisance then the servant's knowledge will be imputed to the landlord. Where there has been some latent nuisance which the landlord or his agents could not have discovered, however, then there will be no liability on the part of the landlord. Thus in *Maberley v Peabody & Co* [1946] 2 All ER 192, S was liable because his letting agent was permanently on the site and knew of the mound damaging

M's wall. Neither S nor his agent could have realised the effect of chemicals seeping through the mound so that only the party causing the damage was liable.

Servants, agents and independent contractors

1.9.17 Although there is no recent decision clearly on the point, authority suggests that an employer will generally be liable in private nuisance for the acts and omissions of an independent contractor in addition to those of a servant or agent (see *Spicer v Smee* [1946] 1 All ER 489 at 495E). Where dangerous consequences are likely to result from an activity unless preventive measures are adopted the duty to ensure that such steps are taken cannot be delegated (see *Bower v Peate* (1876) 1 QBD 321, 326–327 and *Dalton v Angus* (1881) 6 App Cas 740, 829). Thus in cases of a dangerous hazard arising on land (see 1.10) it can be said with some certainty that an employer will generally be liable for a nuisance created by a private contractor. In *Black v Christchurch Finance Co* [1894] AC 48 the defendants sought to avoid liability by claiming that their contractors had acted outside the terms of their agreement, which prohibited the contractors from burning timber at certain times. Lord Shand stated (at 48):

> Having authorised and entrusted the operation of burning to another they must answer for his proceedings, however much he may have violated their instructions or the detailed conditions of his contract with them.

There are other grounds too on which an employer might be held liable for the acts of an independent contractor. In *Matania v National Provincial Bank* [1936] 2 All ER 633 the landowners were liable for nuisance created as a result of dust and noise through building operations since the very operations required by the owners were hazardous and involved the risk of damage being done to the plaintiff.

Checklist – identifying the defendant

- The original tortfeasor:
    - is always liable even if no longer at the premises
    - includes one who has authorised or required another to commit the wrongful acts.
- The current occupier is liable if:
    - he has actual or constructive knowledge of the nuisance
    - he had time to abate the nuisance but did not do so.
- The absent owner is liable if it can be demonstrated that he should have known of the existence of the nuisance.
- A landlord who has let premises on a lease is liable to third parties if:
    - he created the nuisance
    - the terms of the lease render him liable

— he has acquired a reversion knowing that the previous landlord has
created or authorised a nuisance.
- A party is liable for the acts of tenants if:
— he has expressly or impliedly authorised the acts of his tenants.
- A landlord is generally liable for the acts of his servants or agents and
independent contractors.

1.10 Dangerous hazards on land

1.10.1 Special rules exist where a private nuisance consists of some dangerous hazard which has accumulated on a land without the owner's active
participation. Although negligence is not ordinarily an essential element in
nuisance (*The Wagon Mound (No 2)* [1967] 1 AC 617 at 639C), in the case of a
hazardous accumulation, a duty of care does exist concurrently in negligence
and in nuisance. In such a case a plaintiff will have to prove a breach of duty as
well as foreseeability of damage.

1.10.2 This duty of care is recognised by the courts because it is considered
iniquitous that, once such a hazard has arisen on a person's land (an event in
itself to which no culpability can attach), a property owner should be allowed
to let it continue if he becomes aware that it threatens to damage the property of
another. Such a state of things constitutes a nuisance and gives rise to a duty on
the landowner to take steps to remove it. It makes no difference whether the
hazard has accumulated by the act of a third party such as a trespasser or by
reason of some natural action, such as the effect of fire or rain.

A duty not to continue a nuisance

1.10.3 The *fons et origo* of these principles is generally accepted to be the
dissenting judgment of Scrutton LJ in *Job Edwards Ltd v Birmingham Navigations* [1924] 1 KB 341. In that case refuse was carried on to the plaintiff's land
from the defendant's by a trespasser. It caught fire and was extinguished by the
defendant, who was paid half the cost by the plaintiff (without prejudice to the
parties' various rights). The plaintiffs subsequently sought a declaration that
they were not liable to the defendants and that they should be repaid their
contribution. Scrutton LJ approved (at 360) the following proposition from
Salmond on Torts (fifth edition), 258–265:

> When a nuisance has been created by the act of a trespasser, or otherwise without the
> act, authority, or permission of the occupier, the occupier is not responsible for that
> nuisance unless, with knowledge of its existence he suffers it to continue without
> taking reasonably prompt and efficient means for its abatement.

The essence of the duty is that when an occupier of land becomes aware (or
ought to become aware) of a hazard which has arisen on his land, he is under an
obligation not to allow that state of things to continue.

Liability for the acts of trespassers

1.10.4 Scrutton's dissenting judgment was first approved in *Sedleigh-Denfield v O'Callaghan* [1940] AC 880, which involved a drain constructed by trespassers on the defendants' land. The defendants maintained the drain themselves for a period of three years, when the opening became blocked and flooded. The defendants had not caused the nuisance, but they knew of its existence, had the means to correct it and failed to do so. In finding against the defendants, the House of Lords' decision established an occupier's liability for a hazard created on his land by a trespasser where the occupier knew of the hazard and then allowed it to continue by failing to take reasonable steps to remove it:

> An occupier 'continues' a nuisance if, with knowledge or presumed knowledge of its existence, he failed to take any reasonable means to bring it to an end

(Viscount Maugham at 894). Foreseeability of the type of damage that would be sustained by the plaintiff if the drain became blocked and flooded gave rise to the defendants' culpability because they were accordingly under a duty to take reasonable steps to abate the nuisance.

Liability for the acts of natural hazards

1.10.5 In the older authorities it was taken for granted that there could be no liability on the part of a landowner for any damage arising out of a naturally growing hazard. Thus in *Giles v Walker* (1890) 24 QBD 656 there was no liability for thistles which grew on the defendant's land after tree clearance and which spread to the plaintiff's property. So too in *Hodgson v York Corporation* (1873) 28 LT 836 the defendant had no duty to clear either siltation or weeds from a channel which was thereby unable to carry off excess rainwater as before from the plaintiff's premises.

1.10.6 In *Goldman v Hargrave* [1967] 1 AC 645 a redgum tree on the defendant's land was struck by lightning and caught fire. The defendant cleared the land round the tree, felled it and cut it up. The trial judge held that if he had taken reasonable care he would have put the fire out by using water. Several days after the tree was axed, strong gusts revived the fire and it spread to the plaintiff's property. The Privy Council held that the plaintiff had succeeded in establishing a duty of care on the part of the defendant to act with reasonable prudence to remove the hazard which had accidentally arisen on his land, and had failed to do so. An attempt by the defendant to draw a distinction between liability for acts of trespassers (*Sedleigh's* case) and liability for hazards which arose naturally, did not succeed (see 661G–662A):

> their Lordships find in the opinions of the House of Lords in *Sedleigh-Denfield v O'Callaghan* and in the statements of the law by Scrutton LJ and Salmond, of which they approve, support for the existence of a general duty upon occupiers in relation to hazards occurring on their land, whether natural or man-made.

The existence of a duty to remove such a hazard is based on knowledge of the hazard, the ability to foresee the consequences of not checking or removing it and the ability to abate it (see 663D).

1.10.7 The decision in *Goldman's* case became part of English law in *Leakey v National Trust for Places of Historic Interest or Natural Beauty* [1980] QB 485. In that case a conical hill, Barrow Mump, was owned by the defendant. Two houses belonging to the plaintiffs lay to the west. After the dry summer and wet autumn of 1976 there was a slip of part of the Mump on to the plaintiffs' properties. The defendant claimed that this was natural movement so that it was not required to do anything about it. The Court of Appeal disagreed, approving the principle set out in *Goldman's* case: the defendant had a duty to avert the hazard.

The scope of the defendant's duty

1.10.8 The standard of care to be expected of a defendant where a hazard arises unexpectedly on his land is to be assessed according to what can be reasonably expected of him in his individual circumstances. Where some physical effort of which the defendant is not capable or excessive expenditure of money would be required to abate the hazard, the courts will be sympathetic to the defendant. Less will be expected of the infirm than of the able-bodied, and the owner of a small property with scant resources will not be expected to do as much as the owner of a large, wealthy estate. It may well be enough for a defendant who has done his insufficient best to go to his neighbour and call on him to provide additional resources. These principles are carefully set out in *Goldman's* case at 663–664C.

Adopting a hazard

1.10.9 As well as being held liable for continuing a nuisance an occupier will also be found culpable if he adopts a nuisance. Whereas a person 'continues' a nuisance if he merely fails to abate it after discovering its existence as a hazard, he 'adopts' a nuisance if it is a physical object which the defendant uses for his own purposes in the knowledge that it causes or is likely to cause a hazard to another owner of land (see Viscount Maugham in *Sedleigh's* case at 894). A person who adopts a nuisance is inevitably continuing it.

Knowledge of the existence of the hazard

1.10.10 Knowledge by a defendant of a hazard which has arisen on his land is all important. It may be actual or imputed. Whereas it is irrelevant whether an occupier of land who caused a nuisance knew or ought to have known of the existence of circumstances constituting a nuisance (*Wringe v Cohen* [1940] 1 KB 229), a person can only be said to have continued a nuisance if he was aware or ought to have been aware of the existence of the hazard (*Cushing v Peter Walker & Son* [1941] 2 All ER 692).

Ignorance of the acts of trespassers

1.10.11 It follows that where a slate on a roof has become loose by the act of a trespasser but the occupier would not have realised this on a reasonable inspection of his premises, the occupier is not liable for damage caused when the slate works loose (*Cushing's* case). So too an occupier will not be liable for the acts of vandals who, unknown to the occupier, have created dangerous premises (*Barker v Herbert* [1911] 2 KB 633, *King v Liverpool CC* [1986] 1 WLR 890, *Smith v Littlewoods Organisation Ltd* [1987] AC 241).

Latent defects

1.10.12 In cases of naturally occurring hazards the same principles apply. Where damage has been caused by a falling tree or branch, the occupier of the land where the tree is sited is not liable where the collapse is due to some latent defect (*Noble v Harrison* [1926] 2 KB 332) or to a disease which would not have been detected by any reasonable examination (*Cunliffe v Bankes* [1945] 1 All ER 459).

Checklist – nuisance and dangerous hazards

- Private nuisance affords a remedy for damage caused by a dangerous hazard arising accidentally on land. NB:
  - a landowner has a duty to take steps not to adopt or continue a hazard
  - the landowner must have actual or constructive knowledge of the hazard
  - there is no liability for a latent defect
  - the damage must be foreseeable
  - the standard of care will be measured according to the means and resources of the parties at the time of the incident.
- Are other causes of action available? Consider:
  - public nuisance
  - trespass
  - *Rylands v Fletcher*.

1.11 Defences

1.11.1 Most defences are established by demonstrating that a plaintiff does not satisfy the necessary criteria which he has to prove in order to succeed, for instance that the plaintiff has no possessory interest in the land affected or that the damage sought to be recovered is not connected with the land (for instance if it is for personal injury). Most of these issues should be checked by consulting the relevant sections set out above.

Trespassers

1.11.2 It is difficult to imagine circumstances in which a trespasser might cause a nuisance which was anything other than a physical hazard. Where a defendant was not in a position to do anything to avert a hazard, that is to say in this context that he did not know, or could not reasonably have known, of the hazard, then the defendant is not liable. The real question is whether the defendant continued or adopted the nuisance, and the rules which are relevant to that question are set out at 1.10.

Act of God

1.11.3 Caution should be taken by a defendant seeking to raise this defence. As with trespassers, the defence is usually attempted where some natural hazard has arisen on a defendant's land (see 1.10). Relevant principles concerning this reference are set out at 4.2.14.

Independent contractors

1.11.4 In cases of private nuisance the courts are not sympathetic to attempts to shift the blame on to an independent contractor. It can be said that in private nuisance the general rule is that an owner of land cannot escape liability where works have been carried out by an independent contractor (see 1.9.17).

'Coming to a nuisance'

1.11.5 It is no defence for the defendant to say that the plaintiff has come to the nuisance. Thus in *Sturges v Bridgman* (1879) 11 Ch D 852 the defendant was a confectioner in business in Wigmore Street, London. He had a kitchen at the back of his house which was equipped with two mortars used for breaking up hard substances and for pounding meat. These worked between 10 am and 1 pm. The plaintiff doctor built a consulting room up against the wall of the defendant's kitchen and brought an action in private nuisance. He claimed that he was unable to embark on any occupation which required thought and attention. The courts both at first instance and on appeal found for the plaintiff. See Jessel MR at 863:

> The fact that the man has made a noise which has not injured me or interfered with my comfort or enjoyment in anyway, cannot deprive me of my right to the land, or interfere with my right to come to the Court when it does seriously interfere with my comfortable enjoyment.

1.11.6 The underlying principle appears to be a desire to support a person's freedom at common law to do what he will with his land. In *Sturges'* case Jessel MR chose (at 859) an example of a blacksmith who has a forge on a moor. If a town is built:

is it to be said that the owner has lost the right to this barren moor, which has by now become worth perhaps hundreds of thousands of pounds by being unable to build upon it by reason of this noisy business?

So too in the Court of Appeal it was held (at 865) from a public point of view to be 'unjust' and 'inexpedient':

> that the use and value of the adjoining land should, for all time and under all circumstances, be restricted and diminished by reason of the continuance of acts incapable of physical interruption, and which the law gives no power to prevent.

(See also Geoffrey Lane LJ in *Miller v Jackson* [1977] QB 966 at 986 in support of this proposition.)

Statutory authority

1.11.7 Where a defendant can show that a statute required or authorised works to be carried out which were inevitably going to cause a nuisance, the nuisance is not actionable. This principle was largely developed in railway cases in the 19th century (see *Hammersmith and City Railway Co v Brand* (1869) LR 4 HL 171 at 196) but has been applied in other contexts (see *Geddis v Proprietors of Bann Reservoir* (1878) 3 App Cas 430, *Metropolitan Asylum District Managers v Hill* (1881) 6 App Cas 193, *Manchester Corporation v Farnworth* [1930] AC 171).

1.11.8 Whether a defendant can rely on the defence is always a matter of construction of the relevant statute. Where an Act expressly provides that certain works will be carried out, for instance by the annexation of plans and specifications, or by a declaration as to the use or purpose of those works, the defence will succeed. Where there is no such express grant, then the defence of statutory authority applies if the court concludes that 'it can be shown as a matter of plain and necessary implication from the language of the statute' that Parliament intended the works or the use causing the nuisance as though express words were set out in the Act (*Metropolitan Asylum District Managers v Hill* (1881) 6 App Cas 193 at 212).

1.11.9 Where the defence is raised it can be successfully defeated if the plaintiff can show that:

(1) Any nuisance caused by the activities apparently granted by the statute exceeded those for which the immunity was conferred (*Allen v Gulf Oil Refining Ltd* [1981] AC 1001).

(2) The acts otherwise authorised by the statute had been carried out negligently, that is without reasonable regard and care for others (*Geddis v Proprietors of Bann Reservoir* (1878) 3 App Cas 430 at 455–456, *Tate & Lyle Food and Distribution Ltd v GLC* [1983] 2 AC 509 at 538), *Allen v Gulf Oil Refining Ltd* [1981] AC 1001).

Contribution

1.11.10 A defendant can rely on the provisions of the Law Reform (Contributory Negligence) Act 1945.

Chapter 2

Public Nuisance

2.1 Overview

2.1.1 A public nuisance is an activity which 'materially affects the reasonable comfort and convenience of life of a class of Her Majesty's subjects'. It is a criminal offence actionable in civil proceedings by a plaintiff who can show some special damage beyond any inconvenience suffered by the others who have been affected. Public nuisance has no real similarity with the tort of private nuisance. It is often combined with a claim in private nuisance where a plaintiff seeks to recover compensation for some injury which is not strictly connected with damage to the use and enjoyment of land (see *Halsey v Esso Petroleum Co* [1961] 1 WLR 683). It has a particular relevance in the special rules involving the highway.

2.1.2 This chapter will consider the nature and character of a public nuisance in general. It will then set out the main rules relating to a public nuisance on the highway, especially in relation to

    (1) rights of access to and egress from property adjoining the highway

    (2) obstructions on the highway and

    (3) dangerous premises abutting the highway.

2.2 Common law actions in public nuisance

Public nuisance as an actionable civil wrong

2.2.1 A public nuisance only exists where a plaintiff can prove the existence of a class of people affected by the defendant's activities. What constitutes a 'class' of people is matter of fact and degree. In addressing the difficulty posed by the question what is a public nuisance, Lord Denning stated (in *A-G v PYA Quarries* [1957] 2 QB 169 at 191):

> a public nuisance is a nuisance which is so widespread in its range or so indiscriminate in its effect that it would not be reasonable to expect one person to take proceedings on his own responsibility to put a stop to it, but that it should be taken on the responsibility of the community at large.

Romer LJ (in the same case at 184) described a public nuisance as an activity which materially affects the reasonable comfort and convenience of life of a class of Her Majesty's subjects.

This and similar expressions have come to describe what is meant by a public nuisance.

Examples of public nuisance

2.2.2 A public nuisance has included:
  (1) Local residents inconvenienced by the partial obstruction of a rural road alongside common land (*A-G v Gastonia Coaches* [1977] RTR 219);
  (2) The staff and clients of an estate agents whose access to the premises was restricted by protestors (*Hubbard v Pitt* [1976] QB 142);
  (3) 13 ladies in the South Cumbria area subjected to obscene telephone calls (*R v Johnson* [1997] 1 WLR 367).

Public nuisance as an actionable civil wrong – special damage

2.2.3 A plaintiff cannot succeed in public nuisance unless he can prove some special damage. This has been expressed to be:

some particular, direct and substantial loss or damage beyond what is suffered by him in common with all other members of the public affected by the nuisance

(Lawrence LJ in *Harper v Haden & Sons* [1933] Ch 298 at 308). The fact that such damage is required to be 'beyond' that suffered by others entails proof of some damage which is different in quality from that suffered by the class of subjects affected. Thus in *Benjamin v Storr* (1874) LR 9 CP 400 a series of vans in the street obstructed the highway, but the plaintiff could succeed because he had to burn gas all day and lost customers. Brett J said (at 406):

it is not enough for him to show that he suffers the same inconvenience in the use of the highway as other people do.

As to the need to prove that special damage is a 'direct' loss, this means only that the loss must not be merely consequential (*The Wagon Mound (No 2)* [1967] AC 617, especially 635–6).

Damage not restricted to the use and enjoyment of land

2.2.4 Unlike an action in private nuisance, a plaintiff does not have to show any interest in land. It follows that he is not restricted to recovering damages intended to compensate him for an injury to real property, so that there is no objection to recovering damages for some personal injury or injury to a chattel.

Checklist – public nuisance

- Important features
  - — a 'class of Her Majesty's subjects' must have been affected
  - — the class of generally affected people must have been 'materially affected' in the 'reasonable comfort and convenience of life'
  - — public nuisance is a tort which only becomes actionable as a civil wrong when a plaintiff can demonstrate some special injury distinct from any suffered by the general class.
- Differences from private nuisance
  - — any damage is compensatable (for instance personal injury or damage to a chattel)
  - — the plaintiff does not have to show an interest in land

2.3 The highway

Introductory – the nature of a nuisance on the highway

2.3.1 Although a highway can take a variety of different forms (for instance the public ferry service in *Gravesham BC v British Railways Board* [1978] Ch 379), its most common form in an action for nuisance is the public road and footpath. This section is concerned primarily with actions based on the use and enjoyment of highways on land. These are primarily of two types:

(1) rights of access to and egress from property adjoining the highway

(2) obstructions on the highway and

(3) dangerous premises abutting the highway.

This chapter will also consider the most relevant statutory provisions, especially those governing the duties and liabilities of local highway authorities to maintain the highway.

Highway nuisance is a nuisance which concerns an easement

2.3.2 It is important to understand the nature of a common law action in respect of the highway. Although it is primarily an action in public nuisance, at the same time it is based on a right acquired by the public for a particular use of the way in question. That is to say that it is a cause of action based on an interference with a certain type of easement. It is therefore subject to certain rules characteristic of private as well as public nuisance.

The nature of the easement – the purpose of the use of the highway is relevant

2.3.3 The easement over a highway which is enjoyed by members of the public is a right of passage and repassage for the purpose of travel (see *Harrison v Duke of Rutland* [1893] 1 QB 142 at 154). As it was said in *Hubbard v Pitt* [1976] QB 142 at 149D:

The vital characteristic of a highway is that it is land dedicated for a purpose; that purpose is for use by the public for passage to and fro

The right includes the right to use the highway for any strictly incidental purposes (*'eundo, redundo* and . . . *morando'*) (*Hadwell v Righton* [1907] 2 KB 345 at 348). Any other activity on, or use of, the land is a trespass (*Harrison's* case).

Reasonable user

2.3.4 It follows that the reasonableness of the plaintiff's purpose in using the highway is therefore relevant. Like an action in private nuisance where there has been some intangible damage (see 1.6), the law of nuisance relating to highways is a law of give and take. Where the owner or occupier of premises adjacent to the highway creates an obstruction for instance, the question whether he is liable in public nuisance will depend on the reason for the obstruction. This is because:

No member of the public has an exclusive right to use the highway. He has merely a right to use it subject to the reasonable user of others, and if that reasonable user causes him to be obstructed he has no legal cause of complaint

(Romer LJ in *Harper v GN Haden & Sons Ltd* [1933] Ch 298 at 317).

2.3.5 Moreover the circumstances which render such a nuisance actionable will change with the times:

the right of the public to pass and repass on a highway is subject to all those reasonable extensions which may from time to time be recognised as necessary to its existence in accordance with the enlarged notions of people in a country becoming more populous and highly civilised, but they must be such as are not inconsistent with the maintenance of the paramount idea that the right of the public is that of passage

(*Hickman v Massey* [1900] QB 752).

2.3.6 Reasonableness of user is not an issue which is prevalent in obstruction cases on the road, since it is rarely alleged that a plaintiff's use of the highway is unreasonable. In cases involving rights of access or of obstruction of the footpath, however, the court seeks to balance two competing rights:

(1) the right of the ordinary member of the public to use the highway for the purposes of passage; and

(2) the right of the householder to use the highway for the purposes of access to his house and for other purposes connected with his property (see *Trevett v Lee* [1955] 1 WLR 113 at 119).

2.3.7 Accordingly actions in respect of the following have failed because the court thought the defendant's activities eminently reasonable:

(1) Scaffolding erected for the construction of an additional storey to premises (*Harper's* case);

(2) A hosepipe bringing water from a water supply to a house in times of drought (*Trevett's* case).

Actions which have failed because the defendant's activities could not be justified include *Holling v Yorkshire Traction Co Ltd* [1948] 2 All ER 662 in which clouds of smoke and steam were blowing on to the highway from nearby coke ovens.

Damage – rules deriving from the law relating to public nuisance

2.3.8   In order to succeed in a claim for nuisance in respect of the highway, many of the rules of public nuisance apply. A plaintiff must prove some material inconvenience suffered by a class of members of the public and some special damage distinct to the plaintiff (*Harper v G N Haden & Sons Ltd* [1933] Ch 298 at 302–304). In cases of rights of access, special damage may take the form of loss of trade profits. In cases of obstruction and of hazards it is normally demonstrated by some personal injury or damage to property. Such injury must take place whilst the plaintiff is on the highway and not, for instance, in some private yard (*Bromley v Mercer* [1922] 2 KB 126). Characteristically such injury is caused by some vehicle or other obstruction placed on the roadway (such as a skip or parked lorry) or by some item which has fallen from the defendant's property on to the highway (for instance a tree or roof tile).

Foreseeability

2.3.9   In order to recover, damage of the kind suffered must have been foreseeable. Older cases stating that foreseeability is not a requirement of public nuisance must be treated with great caution after *The Wagon Mound (No 2)* [1967] 1 AC 617 and *Cambridge Water Co Ltd v Eastern Counties Leather plc* [1994] 2 AC 264 (see for instance *Farrell v John Mowlem & Co Ltd* [1954] Lloyd's Rep 437).

Rights of access and egress

2.3.10   At common law the owner of adjoining land has a right of access to the highway from any part of his premises (*Marshall v Blackpool Corporation* [1935] AC 16 at 22). This means that a queue or crowd, whether or not marshalled by the police, may amount to an actionable nuisance if it prevents the public from gaining access to a shop and its shop front (*Lyons, Sons & Co v Gulliver* [1914] 1 Ch 631). A plaintiff may be able to claim damages in such circumstances as compensation for damage to his business (*Benjamin v Storr* (1874) LR 9 CP 400). It should be added that statutory powers are available under Part VIII, Highways Act, 1980 which permit the stopping up of means of access to highways.

Obstructions on the highway

2.3.11   An obstruction to the highway has been described as:

something which permanently or temporarily removes the whole or part of the highway from the public use together

(Lord Evershed MR in *Trevett v Lee* [1955] 1 QB, 113 at 117). Liability under this heading conventionally includes anything which renders the highway dangerous (see *Dymond v Pearce* [1972] 1 QB 496 at 501).

2.3.12 In describing the nature of such a cause of action, the definition set out in *Pratt and Mackenzie's Law of Highways* is generally accepted by the courts as an accurate summary:

> Nuisance may be defined, with reference to highways as any wrongful act or omission upon or near a highway, whereby the public are prevented from freely, safely, and conveniently passing along the highway

(see *Hubbard v Pitt* [1976] QB 142 and Lord Simonds in *Jacobs v London CC* [1950] AC 361 at 375). Obstructions which fall within this definition include:

(1) Fat from a butcher's shop flying on to the pavement (*Dollman v Hillman Ltd* [1941] 1 All ER 355);

(2) An unlit lorry left stationary on the road (*Ware v Garston Haulage Co Ltd* [1944] 1 KB 30 (cf *Maitland v Raisbeck* [1944] 1 KB 689)).

It should be noted that an employer will be liable for a nuisance created by an independent contractor on the highway where the act was one which was likely to involve danger to others using the highway (*Holliday v National Telephone Co* [1899] 2 QB 392).

Natural hazards causing an obstruction

2.3.13 Where an object obstructing the highway is a hazard which naturally arises on or near land, the rules relating to hazards in private nuisance apply (see 1.10). Accordingly, where the low bough of a tree overhanging the highway caused an obstruction to highway users, it was not held to be actionable as a nuisance since the owners of the tree could not be said to have continued the nuisance in the sense required by *Sedleigh-Denfield v O'Callaghan* (see 1.10.4) (*BRS v Slater* [1964] 1 WLR 498). So too the widow of a motorcyclist failed to recover because the owner of a diseased tree which fell on to the highway could not have made any reasonable examination which would have discovered the disease (*Cunliffe v Bankes* [1945] 1 All ER 459). The relevant law was originally set out in *Noble v Harrison* [1926] 2 KB 332 and has not been changed by *Sedleigh's* case. Thus the headnote in *Cunliffe's* case reads:

> a person is not liable for a nuisance constituted by the state of his property unless (a) he causes it; or (b) by the neglect of some duty he allows it to arise; or (c) when it has arisen without his own act or default, he omits to remedy it within a reasonable time after he became or ought to have become aware of it.

Discontinuing or abating an obstruction

2.3.14 The user of a highway is not an insurer for wrongs suffered by a plaintiff. Once a nuisance is created without the fault of the defendant, the defendant will be allowed a reasonable time in which to discontinue or abate the nuisance (*Maitland v Raisbeck and Hewitt Ltd* [1944] 1 KB 689). In *Maitland's* case itself the driver of a lorry was not liable to the defendant when the defendant ran into him. There was no evidence that the lorry driver knew or should have known that his lights had failed. (See also *Dymond v Pearce* [1972] 1 QB 496 in which the plaintiff pillion rider was injured by a collision with a lorry parked on the highway for the night. It was held that the cause of the accident was the failure of the motorcyclist to notice the lorry.)

Dangerous premises abutting the highway

2.3.15 Liability for dangerous premises abutting the highway is set out in *Wringe v Cohen* [1940] 1 KB 229 at 233:

> In our judgment, if, owing to want of repair, premises on a highway become dangerous and, therefore, a nuisance, and a passer-by or an adjoining owner suffers damage by their collapse, the occupier or the owner if he has undertaken the duty of repair, is answerable whether he knew or ought to have known of the danger or not. The undertaking to repair gives the owner control of the premises, and a right of access thereto for the purpose of maintaining them in a safe condition. On the other hand, if the nuisance is created, not by want of repair, but, for example, by the act of a trespasser, or by a secret and unobservable operation of nature, such as a subsidence under or near the foundations of the premises, neither an occupier nor an owner responsible for repair is answerable, unless with knowledge or means of knowledge he allows the danger to continue. In such a case he has in no sense caused the nuisance by any act or breach of duty.

Thus in *Slater v Worthington's Cash Stores (1930) Ltd* [1941] 1 KB 488 the defendants were liable because they failed to abate a nuisance consisting of an accumulation of snow which fell from their shop roof on to the plaintiff. They had taken no steps to remove the snow over a period of four days and did nothing to warn passers-by.

2.3.16 It follows that in such cases the relevant questions are whether the occupier or owner owes a duty to the user of the highway and whether he is in breach of the duty. Such issues were prevalent in the following:

(1) A person who maintains a lamp projecting over the highway has a duty to maintain it so as not to be a danger to passers-by (*Tarry v Ashton* (1876) 1 QBD 314);

(2) An owner converting premises into offices owes a duty to users of the highway to ensure that they had taken all reasonable steps to prevent injury (by falling bricks) (*Walsh v Holst Co Ltd* [1958] 1 WLR 800).

2.3.17 Where such a duty is owed it is non-delegable, so that it is no defence for an employer to say that he employed an independent contractor (*Tarry's* case and *Walsh v Holst & Co Ltd* [1958] 1 WLR 800) (cf. *Salsbury v Woodland* [1970] 1 QB 324).

2.3.18 It may be possible to sue an absent landowner rather than his tenant (see *Heap v Ind Coope and Allsopp Ltd* [1940] 2 KB 476). Another alternative may be to sue in negligence (see *Walsh v Holst & Co Ltd* [1958] 1 WLR 800).

Failure to maintain the highway

2.3.19 The Highways Act 1980 now governs many actions brought in respect of a public road. By s 41 the highway authorities (created by s 1) have a duty to maintain all highways maintainable at public expense. The duty is reasonably to maintain and repair the highway so that it is free of foreseeable danger to all users who use the highway in the way normally to be expected of them (*Rider v Rider* [1973] QB 505). A plaintiff must be able to demonstrate that the relevant part of the highway was dangerous in any action for non-repair (*Meggs v Liverpool Corporation* [1968] 1 WLR 689). Whether a defendant authority is in breach of duty depends on all the circumstances (*Cross v Kirklees MBC* [1998] 1 All ER 564).

2.3.20 A statutory defence is available under s 58 of the 1980 Act, allowing the authority to assert that it took such care as in all the circumstances was reasonably required to secure that the part of the highway to which any action relates was not dangerous to traffic (which includes animals and pedestrians by s 329(1)). It has been held that in enacting the 1980 Act it was intended that the plaintiff must be able to prove either personal injury or some damage to property. Accordingly, where the Milk Marketing Board refused to collect any more milk from the plaintiff because of the condition of the highway, the plaintiff was not able to recover his loss of profits (*Wentworth v Wiltshire CC* [1993] QB 654). A plea in contributory negligence will also be available to the authority (see s 58(1)).

Checklist – public nuisance on the highway

- Essential characteristics for establishing a highway nuisance
  - the highway may take many forms, for instance a public road, the footpath or a public ferry service
  - a highway is a form of easement
  - it is necessary to consider whether an activity on a highway is an accepted or reasonable activity for the highway in question. The normal purposes of a highway are for passage to and fro and for strictly incidental purposes
  - if a defendant can show reasonable user of the highway he is likely to succeed
  - special damage must always be shown
  - damage must be foreseeable
- Rights of access and egress
  - the owner of land adjoining the highway has a right of access and egress

- damages may be awarded where a business cannot use its right of access or egress
- there are statutory limitations on the right
- Obstructions on the highway
  - an obstruction may be temporary or permanent
  - the relevant question is whether the public has free, safe and convenient passage along the highway
  - if the obstruction is caused by a natural hazard there is a duty on the landowner to take steps to discontinue or avoid the nuisance
  - an obstructor has a reasonable time to remove the obstruction if it occurred without his fault
- Dangerous premises abutting the highway
  - an occupier or owner of premises adjoining the highway has a duty to keep them in a good state of repair
  - an occupier or owner with the responsibility of such a duty must have knowledge or means of knowledge of any defect in order to be liable
  - in such a case a principal will be liable for the acts of an independent contractor
  - it may also be possible to use an absent landlord or to frame a cause of action in nuisance
- Highways Act 1980
  - highway authorities have a duty under s 41 to maintain public highways
  - there is a statutory defence under s 58
  - compensation is recoverable where there has been some personal injury or damage to property.

Chapter 3

Statutory Nuisances

3.1 Overview

3.1.1 Liability under the common law tort of private nuisance arises where some unlawful interference with the use or enjoyment of another person's property has occurred (see chapter 1). However, certain types of nuisance are also the subject of statutory controls owing to their potential to cause interference with health or some other nuisance. These are collectively referred to as statutory nuisances.

3.1.2 A range of statutes formerly governed what constituted a statutory nuisance. The Environmental Protection Act 1990 Part III has consolidated earlier legislation and introduced a more streamlined procedure and a new regime of summary offences.

Contents of this chapter

3.1.3 Statutory nuisances under the 1990 Act are enforceable either by local authorities, or, in more limited circumstances, by aggrieved individuals. This section reviews the types of statutory nuisance and the rights and duties of both local authorities and private individuals as enforcers. At the centre of the relevant legislative provisions is the abatement notice (in the case of enforcement by local authorities) and the abatement order (in the case of individuals). The correct procedure governing such notices and orders will be identified, as will any related criminal offences, defences, rights of appeal and the consequences of non-compliance.

3.2 Environmental Protection Act 1990, Part III

The ambit of the Environmental Protection Act 1990, Part III

3.2.1 The ambit of statutory nuisance under the 1990 Act is wide. Any of the following matters will constitute a 'statutory nuisance', so long as they are such as to be 'prejudicial to health or a nuisance':
  (1) the state of any premises (s 79(1)(a));
  (2) smoke emitted from premises (s 79(1)(b));

(3) fumes or gases emitted from premises which are private dwellings (s 79(1)(c));

(4) any dust, steam, smell or other effluvia arising on industrial, trade or business premises (s 79(1)(d));

(5) any accumulation or deposit (s 79(1)(e));

(6) an animal kept in any place or manner (s 79(1)(f));

(7) noise emitted from premises (s 79(1)(g));

(8) noise emitted from or caused by a vehicle, machinery or equipment in a street (s 79(1)(ga));

(9) any other matter declared by any enactment to be a statutory nuisance (s 79(1)(h)).

Contaminated land as a statutory nuisance

3.2.2 When the provisions contained in Part II of the Environment Act 1995 and Sched 22, para 89(3) come into force they will amend the provisions in s 79 to exclude contaminated land. The new provisions specifically dealing with contaminated land and contained in a new Part IIA of the 1990 Act will then apply.

'Premises'

3.2.3 'Premises' includes the following:

Land
Land, including land in its 'natural state' (*Noble v Harrison* [1926] 2 KB 332, *Leakey v National Trust* [1980] QB 485) as well as buildings. It does not include streets and public places (*Tower Hamlets v Manzoni* (1984) 148 JP 123).

Boats and sailing vessels
Any vessel unless 'powered by steam reciprocating machinery' (s 79(12)). Consequently, the powers of local authorities to deal with statutory nuisances extend to boats and other sailing vessels in certain areas. Where a Port Health Authority has been established under the Public Health (Control of Disease) Act 1984 then the functions of the local authority as regards Part III, EPA 1990 will pass to that authority (s 79(8) EPA).

Mobile plant and homes
Mobile plant and homes so long as 'used as domestic premises with some degree of permanency' (*West Mersea Urban District Council v Fraser* [1950] 2 KB 119).

'Prejudicial to health or nuisance'

3.2.4 All of the situations detailed in s 79 must be 'prejudicial to health or a nuisance'. The essence of this is the concept of personal discomfort. It is not necessary to show that personal health is being damaged for a statutory nuisance claim to succeed.

3.2.5 'Prejudicial to health' is defined in s 79(7) as being 'injurious, or likely to cause injury, to health' although actual evidence of injury or ill health is not absolutely necessary. The risk of physical injury is enough.

3.2.6 Nuisance is not defined in the Act and most cases rely on this limb. For assistance on what is meant by 'nuisance' in this context, regard must be paid to the common law (*National Coal Board v Neath BC* [1976] 2 All ER 478). In addition, cases based on earlier legislation that has been consolidated may also be relevant (for instance the Public Health Act 1936, Public Health (Recurring Nuisances) Act 1969 and Control of Pollution Act 1974).

3.2.7 For a long time following the decision of *Betts v Penge UDC* [1942] 2 KB 154 a statutory nuisance had to be something that interfered with someone's personal comfort. But doubts about this decision were expressed *obiter* by the House of Lords in *Salford City Council v McNally* [1976] AC 379 and the matter was reviewed in *National Coal Board v Thorne* [1976] 1 WLR 543. There must be some evidence of circumstances prejudicial to health or a nuisance at common law for this subsection to apply. In particular the alleged nuisance must interfere with a neighbouring property. Cases involving local authority landlords in London have held that the consequences of condensation and the lack of noise insulation in a property adjacent to a railway have been held to be prejudicial to health (see *GLC v Tower Hamlets LBC* (1984) 15 HLR 54). See also the recent case of *Cunningham v Birmingham City Council* (Ends Report 269 p 47, and *The Times*, 9 June 1997) where both 'prejudicial to health' and 'nuisance' were considered.

Distinguishing a statutory nuisance from an unfit property

3.2.8 It is important to consider the difference between a statutory nuisance and an unfit property (which is governed by the Housing Acts) since the works necessary to abate a statutory nuisance may not be as extensive and more of a 'patch and repair' job, rather than works necessary to make a house fit. Examples of some of the conditions that may result in premises being a statutory nuisance include dampness, defective sanitary fittings, defective windows, doors, leaking rainwater pipes, leaking roof, defective premises, defective plasterwork and general disrepair.

3.3 Smoke from premises (EPA 1990, s 79(1)(b))

'Smoke'

3.3.1 By s 79(7), 'smoke' includes soot, ash, grit and gritty particles emitted in smoke (including dust).

Crown property

3.3.2 By s 79(2) the provisions relating to smoke as a statutory nuisance do not apply to Crown properties occupied by or used for the navy, military, air force, the Ministry of Defence or any visiting force (as defined in the Visiting Forces Act 1952).

Other exclusions

3.3.3 Section 79(3) sets out various other exceptions to the smoke provisions of s 79(1)(b). This is to avoid overlap with other legislation such as the Clean Air Act 1993. The exceptions are:

(1) 'smoke emitted from a chimney of a private dwelling within a smoke control area' (s 79(3)(i));

(2) 'dark smoke emitted from a chimney of a building or a chimney serving the furnace of a boiler or industrial plant attached to the building or for the time being fixed to or installed on any land' (s 79(3)(ii));

(3) 'smoke emitted from a railway locomotive steam engine' (s 79(3)(iii));

(4) 'dark smoke emitted... from industrial or trade premises' (s 79(3) (iv)).

The effect of the exclusions is to limit the application of the provisions to fires in the open air.

Part I and Part III of the 1990 Act – integrated pollution control

3.3.4 There is potential for an overlap between the provisions of Part I of the 1990 Act and Part III in relation to emissions into the air. Part I is regulated by two enforcement bodies: the Environment Agency (EA) in relation to integrated pollution control and local authorities in relation to emissions into the air. Part I regulates prescribed processes and substances. Where the industrial processes are governed by Part I of the Act a local authority is precluded from taking summary proceedings for a statutory nuisance without the consent of the Secretary of State (s 79(10)). This is because in most situations the relevant enforcement bodies under Part I will have power to deal with any circumstances amounting to a statutory nuisance under that regime. Copies of the authorisation will be kept on a public register (see also Appendix A2.16).

3.4 Fumes or gases (EPA 1990, s 79(1)(c))

3.4.1 Unlike the nuisance of emitting smoke, this category of statutory nuisance only applies to private dwellings. 'Fumes' are defined to mean 'any airborne solid matter smaller than dust' (s 79(7)). 'Gas' includes vapour and moisture precipitated from vapour (s 79(7)).

3.5 Dust, steam, smell or other effluvia from industrial, trade or business premises (EPA 1990, s 79(1)(d))

3.5.1 Presumably, instances of fumes or gases arising from non-domestic premises which would give rise to a nuisance will be caught by this head of statutory nuisance. The definition of 'dust, steam, smell or other effluvia' in this context is subject to several limitations. It does not include any emissions which can be dealt with under any other head of statutory nuisance, nor does it apply to steam from a railway locomotive engine.

3.5.2 This head of statutory nuisance is also limited since the local authority may not institute summary proceedings without the consent of the Secretary of State where action under the local authority air pollution control regime is possible (see 13.2). It is also curious that this head is the only one dealing exclusively with 'industrial, trade or business premises', which is quite widely framed.

3.5.3 As in other cases of statutory nuisance, an instance of any dust, steam or other effluvia on a property will not of itself give rise to a statutory nuisance. There must be some element of interference with the personal comfort of the person or persons bringing the complaint (*Wivenhoe Port v Colchester BC* [1985] JPL 175 & 396).

3.6 Any accumulation or deposit (EPA 1990, s 79(1)(e))

3.6.1 A mere deposit or accumulation on land is not sufficient. In *Coventry City Council v Cartwright* [1975] 1 WLR 845 it was held that in order to claim a statutory nuisance under this head there must be 'an accumulation of something which produces a threat to health in the sense of a threat of disease, vermin or the like'. Consequently, the accumulation of certain types of matter such as building materials or broken glass have not been held to be a nuisance while there are a host of examples where accumulations of foul or offensive smelling matter have been held to be a statutory nuisance.

3.7 'Any animal kept in such a place or manner . . .' (EPA 1990, s 79(1)(f))

3.7.1 The circumstances in which an animal might give rise to a statutory nuisance would seem relatively limited. They might include being kept in unsanitary conditions or being kept so that they give rise to disturbing odours. Until the 1990 Act it was thought that noisy animals could not give rise to a statutory nuisance. However, if the noise travels due to the way or conditions in which the animal is kept, there is scope for such a claim under s 79(1)(g). There may also well be an overlap with local government byelaws if still in existence (see also s 235 Local Government Act 1972).

3.8 Noise emitted from premises (EPA 1990, s 79(1)(g))

3.8.1 'Noise' is defined to include vibration and model aircraft (but not the real thing). For any action under this sub-section to succeed, the noise must be emitted from premises. This means that it will not extend to noise made in streets or public places, which is now largely caught by the Noise and Statutory Nuisance Act 1997 (see chapter 12). In common with other categories of statutory nuisance, the noise must either be prejudicial to health or unduly interfere with the comfort and convenience of the neighbouring occupiers. A single event may constitute a noise nuisance (*East Northamptonshire DC v Fossett* [1994] Env LR 388 – an all night rave).

3.8.2 By s 79(2) the provisions relating to noise as a statutory nuisance do not apply to Crown properties occupied by or used for the navy, military, air force, the Ministry of Defence or any visiting force (as defined in the Visiting Forces Act 1952).

Evidence

3.8.3 In proving a noise nuisance it may be sufficient for an environmental health officer to provide noise measurements in decibels without calling neighbours to give evidence proving how it interfered with their reasonable comfort or enjoyment (*Cooke v Adatia* (1989) 153 JP 129).

Seizing equipment from domestic premises

3.8.4 Under the Noise Act 1996 (the 1996 Act), local authority officers and agents are empowered to enter domestic premises to seize and remove equipment used in the emission of the noise. The 1996 Act amends s 81(3) of the 1990 Act to permit such seizure and removal where a statutory nuisance is being or has been committed under s 79(1)(g).

3.9 Noise emitted from or caused by a vehicle, machinery or equipment in a street (EPA 1990, s 79(1)(ga))

3.9.1 This category of statutory nuisance was introduced into the 1990 Act by the Noise and Statutory Nuisance Act 1993 (the 1993 Act). 'Street' is defined to include a highway and any other road, footway, square or court that is for the time being open to the public (Noise and Statutory Nuisance Act 1993, s 2 and Environment Circular 9/97 (WO Circular 42/97)).

3.9.2 Noisy activities not previously regulated because they occurred in a street rather than from premises will now be covered. These may include noisy DIY car repairs to a car in the street, roadworks, loudspeakers, tannoys, radios and ghetto blasters. Offending items are subject to the statutory nuisance provisions and can be seized by local authority officers. Section 79(1)(ga) does not extend to noise made by traffic, the military or air force of the Crown or by a visiting force, by a political demonstration, or by a demonstration supporting or opposing a cause or campaign.

3.9.3 The 'person responsible' for a statutory noise nuisance is stated to include the person in whose name the vehicle is for the time being registered and any other person who is for the time being the driver or the operator.

3.9.4 Local authority officers have been given extensive powers to enter or open vehicles, machinery or equipment to stop the nuisance and if necessary for security reasons he may take all necessary steps to immobilise it and remove it to a secure place under para 2A of Schedule 3. The 1993 Act provides a special abatement procedure to deal with noise in streets described at 12.2 below.

3.10 Any other matter declared by any enactment to be a statutory nuisance (EPA 1990, s 79(1)(h))

3.10.1 The final heading of a statutory nuisance in s 79(l) of the 1990 Act is a miscellany, all of which have been taken from the Public Health Act 1936 and have been declared by case law to be statutory nuisances. They include:

(1) storage containers for water which may render the water liable to contamination and prejudicial to health;

(2) any foul watercourse prejudicial to health or a nuisance;

(3) any watercourse which is not normally navigated by goods-carrying vehicles which is so choked up or silted that it obstructs or impedes the flow of water and becomes a nuisance or gives rise to conditions prejudicial to health (such as blocked drainage ditch);

(4) any tent, shed or similar structure used for habitation which is overcrowded or so deficient in sanitary accommodation as to be a nuisance or prejudicial to health.

It is doubtful whether local authorities nowadays have much need to have recourse to such provisions.

Checklist – does Part III, EPA 1990 apply?

- Does the nuisance fall within one of the s 79 categories:
  — state of premises
  — smoke emissions
  — fumes or gas emissions from private dwellings
  — dust, smell or other effluvia from industrial, trade or business premises
  — accumulations or deposits
  — kept animals
  — noise emissions
  — any statutory nuisance under some other Act.
- Is the nuisance 'prejudicial to health or a nuisance'?
- Is any requirement that the nuisance should be connected with 'premises' satisfied?

3.11 Enforcement by a local authority – introduction

Responsibility for enforcement

3.11.1 Prime responsibility for enforcement rests in the hands of local authorities. These include a London borough council in Greater London, the Common Council of the City of London, district councils, the Council of the Isles of Scilly (ss 79–82 do not apply to Scotland) and unitary authorities.

Duties imposed on local authorities under the EPA 1990 – overview

3.11.2 There are three key duties imposed on a local authority:
  (1) To cause its area to be inspected from time to time to detect any statutory nuisance (s 79(1)).
  (2) To take such steps as are reasonably practicable to investigate any complaints received (s 79(1)).
  (3) To serve an abatement notice if satisfied that a nuisance exists or is likely to occur (s 80(1)).

3.11.3 To assist in the execution of these functions environmental health officers (EHOs) have, on production of authority, extensive rights of entry onto property to investigate, take samples and, if relevant, seize equipment. However, unless it is an emergency the EHO must give 24 hours' notice where entry is required to premises in residential use. If entry is refused, a magistrate's warrant may be obtained (Sched 3, para 2(3) of the 1990 Act).

Presenting a complaint to the local authority

3.11.4 Complaining to your local authority is relatively easy. The first step is to telephone the EHO. All telephone complaints should be followed up in writing. Keep a copy of correspondence and after any telephone or other contact with an EHO always make a note of:
  (1) the person you spoke to and their contact telephone number;
  (2) the date and time of contact;
  (3) the contents of any conversation.

3.11.5 It will be extremely useful for the authority if you keep a running diary of events, especially dates, times, the duration of the nuisance and details of how it affects you. This evidence may be essential to support a case brought by the local authority. The following information should be provided:
  (1) your name, address and contact telephone number, or if not available, times for site inspection, name and address of agent/landlord (if the condition of your property is of concern);
  (2) name and address of source of complaint if caused by a neighbour;
  (3) details of complaint, times, dates, etc;
  (4) a request for an inspection to be made;
  (5) details of attempts to resolve the situation amicably (for instance correspondence, conversations).

3.11.6 The EHO will have to undertake a site visit to establish whether a statutory nuisance exists. If the complaint involves the condition of the property he may need to see the rent book or tenancy agreement to verify the name of the landlord or agent.

3.11.7 Depending on the level of statutory nuisance it may be necessary to write to the EHO after a specific period and ask for an update on what is being done. Eliciting support from the local councillor and MP may also assist in speeding up matters.

3.11.8 Where the condition of a property is involved, it can be extremely helpful if an inspection report from a surveyor can also be provided confirming your allegations. However, as this must be paid for privately, this will depend on the availability of funds.

Checklist – local authority enforcement

- Is there a responsibility on the local authority to pursue the issue?
  — is the authority inspecting its area?
  — is the authority investigating a complaint?
  — if satisfied that a statutory nuisance exists, has the authority served an abatement notice?
  — has the authority made use of any powers to assist in its investigation?
- What should a private individual do to assist with a complaint?
  — take details of all contacts with EHOs
  — keep a careful diary of all details of the nuisance
  — request an inspection
  — seek an amicable resolution
  — obtain a surveyor's report if funds are available.

3.12 Issue and service of abatement notices

3.12.1 Where the local authority is satisfied that a statutory nuisance exists, or is likely to occur or recur, then it is under an obligation to serve an abatement notice on the person responsible. The abatement notice may require the abatement of the nuisance, prohibit or restrict its occurrence or recurrence and require the carrying out of necessary works or other steps for these purposes (EPA 1990, s 80(1)).

3.12.2 The notice is also required to set out the time period within which the nuisance should be abated, the right of appeal to the local Magistrates' Court and the available grounds of appeal against the notice.

3.12.3 Although not specific in the Act, it is reasonable to expect a degree of clarity as to what is required. In *Network Housing Association v Westminster City Council* (1994) *The Times*, 8 November, the court held that it was for the City Council to specify with precision in its abatement notice the work which was to be carried out. The notice in question was held to be defective since it was not practicable for the landlord to determine in advance what would be the effect of the work undertaken. In the light of the criminal penalties for non-compliance, it was held essential for the landlord to be told clearly what work was required to be carried out. The notice was quashed. In *Kirklees MBC v Field* (1997) *The Times*, 26 November the QB held that where an abatement notice required a person to carry out works to abate a nuisance, rather than cease the nuisance, it is necessary to specify what steps or works must be done. See also *Sterling Homes (Midlands) Ltd v Birmingham City Council* [1996] Env LR 121.

3.12.4 The information which should go in the notice needs to be considered carefully. If the notice is too prescriptive in identifying what needs to be undertaken, it might fail. Nevertheless notices have been upheld which have required the use which has caused the statutory nuisance to cease, without specifying what alternative remedies would abate the nuisance (*McGillivray v Stephenson* [1950] 1 All ER 942 – a notice requiring the cessation of the nuisance and cessation of the use of the premises for pig keeping). In *Lowe v South Somerset DC* [1997] EGCS 113 an abatement notice requiring the appellant to abate the statutory nuisance caused by the crowing of cockerels and a chorus of waterfowl was held to be valid.

The 'responsible person'

3.12.5 The abatement notice is required to be served on one of the following:
 (1) the person responsible for the nuisance (s 80(2)(a) EPA 1990);
 (2) where the nuisance arises from a structural defect, the owner of the premises (s 80(2)(b));
 (3) where the person responsible cannot be found or the nuisance has not yet occurred, the owner or occupier of the premises (s 80(2)(c)).

'Owner' is now defined in s 81A(9) of the EPA 1990 (as amended by the Noise and Statutory Nuisance Act 1993). He is:

> a person (other than a mortgagee not in possession) who, whether in his own right or as a trustee for any other person, is entitled to receive the rack rent of the premises or, where the premises are not let at a rack rent, would be so entitled if they were so let.

3.12.6 In relation to a statutory nuisance, the 'person responsible' means the person to whose act, default or sufferance the nuisance is attributable (s 79(7)).
3.12.7 Service of the notice through an occupier's letterbox is adequate (*Lambeth LBC v Mullings* (1990) RVR 259, (1990) *The Times* 16 January).
3.12.8 Although the local authority is subject to a duty to serve the abatement notice, this will not take precedence over other remedies that may be available, for instance any remedies available for unfit housing under the Housing Acts.

3.13 Appealing against an abatement notice

3.13.1 Although no standard form is prescribed, an abatement notice must contain a statement advising of the right of an appeal to magistrates within 21 days from the date of service of the abatement notice. It is therefore important to decide on a course of action as promptly as possible.

3.13.2 The regulations governing appeals against abatement notices are contained in the Statutory Nuisance (Appeals) Regulations 1995 and further provisions can be found in Schedule 3 to the 1990 Act.

3.13.3 The Regulations set out an extensive list of grounds of appeal including the following:

(1) the abatement notice is not justified under the Act;

(2) there has been some informality, defect or error in or in connection with the notice (for instance, the abatement notice does not provide a sufficient explanation of the works required);

(3) the requirements of the notice are unreasonable or unnecessary, or the authority has unreasonably refused to accept alternative requirements;

(4) the times for compliance are not reasonably sufficient;

(5) the best practicable means were used to prevent or to counteract the effects of the nuisance falling within:

(a) s 79(1)(a), (d), (e), (f) or (g) and arises on industrial, trade or business premises, or

(b) s 79(1)(b) and the smoke is emitted from a chimney, or

(c) s 79(1)(ga) and the noise is emitted from or caused by a vehicle, machinery or equipment used for industrial trade or business premises;

(6) where the statutory nuisance is caused by noise falling within s 79(1)(g) or (ga) the requirements of the abatement notice are more onerous than the requirements of any notice served under s 60 or 66 of the Control of Pollution Act 1974 or any consent given under s 61 in relation to noise from construction sites;

(7) where the statutory nuisance is caused by noise emitted from or caused by vehicles, machinery or equipment and falls within s 79(1)(ga) the requirements of the abatement notice are more onerous than the requirements of any condition of a consent given under paragraph 1 of Schedule 2 to the Noise and Statutory Nuisance Act 1993.

Magistrates' powers

3.13.4 After considering the evidence, the magistrates can quash or uphold the notice, or vary it in favour of the appellant. It is within the power of the magistrates to make an order which specifies:

(1) who should carry out work in connection with the notice;

(2) the contribution to be made by any person towards the cost involved;

(3) the proportion in which any costs which may become recoverable by the local authority are to be borne by the appellant or any other person. (An example would be when there is a failure to comply with the notice and the authority uses its powers to abate the nuisance itself);

(4) costs to cover the expenses of the complainant.

(Compensation may also be awarded to the complainant under the Powers of Criminal Courts Act 1973 s 35.)

Suspension of the notice

3.13.5 If an appeal is lodged, the notice normally will be suspended, until either the appeal is abandoned or decided by the court, providing that compliance with it would involve any person in expenditure before the hearing of the appeal or (where the action is for noise) the alleged noise is caused while performing a duty imposed by law on the appellant.

3.13.6 By reg 3 of the 1995 Regulations a notice will not be suspended if in the opinion of the local authority either:

(1) the nuisance concerned is injurious to health;
(2) the nuisance is likely to be of such limited duration that suspension would render it of no practical effect; or
(3) expenditure incurred before the appeal hearing would not be disproportionate to the public benefit.

For one of the above to apply the notice must include a statement that it will have effect notwithstanding an appeal and set out the applicable grounds in support. It is obviously important to check the notice for this.

Costs on a successful appeal

3.13.7 If an appeal is successful costs may be recovered. The case of *R v Southend Stipendiary Magistrates ex parte Rochford District Council* (1994) *The Times*, 10 May, addresses succinctly the issue of costs in the Magistrates' Court.

3.14 Offences in connection with abatement notices

Offences of non-compliance with an abatement notice

3.14.1 If a person on whom an abatement notice is served, without reasonable excuse, contravenes or fails to comply with any requirement or prohibition imposed by the notice, he will be guilty of an offence contrary to s 80(4) of the EPA 1990. At the same time, a failure to comply with an abatement notice allows the local authority to take steps to abate the nuisance whether or not they commence summary proceedings (s 81(3)).

3.14.2 By s 80(5) the maximum penalty which may be imposed under s 80(4) is a fine not exceeding level 5 on the standard scale together with a further fine of an amount equal to one tenth of that level for each day on which the offence continues after the conviction. See *Canterbury City Council v Ferris* [1997] Env LR D14, Part 3 for further information on the level of daily penalties imposed.

3.14.3 Where the offence was committed on industrial, trade or business premises the maximum penalty imposed on summary conviction increases to

£20,000 (s 80(6)). 'Industrial, trade or business premises' are defined under s 79(7) as:

> premises used for any industrial, trade or business purposes or premises not so used on which matter is burnt in connection with any industrial, trade or business process, and premises are used for industrial purposes where they are used for purposes of any treatment or process as well as where they are used for the purpose of manufacturing.

Defences

3.14.4 In any criminal proceedings under Part III of the 1990 Act it is a defence to prove that the best practicable means were used to prevent, or counteract the effects of, the nuisance (s 80(7)). The meaning of 'best practicable means' is set out in s 79(9), which reads:

(a) 'Practicable' means reasonably practicable having regard among other things to local conditions and circumstances, to the current state of technical knowledge and to the financial implications,

(b) the means to be employed include the design, installation, maintenance and manner and periods of operation of plant and machinery, and the design, construction and maintenance of buildings and structures,

(c) the test is to apply only so far as compatible with any duty imposed by law,

(d) the test is to apply only so far as compatible with safety and safe working conditions, and with the exigencies of any emergency or unforeseeable circumstances.

3.14.5 The onus of proof is on the defendant who intends to rely upon a defence under s 80(7) to establish this defence on the balance of probability. That is to say that he must be able to show that it is more likely than not that best practicable means were used (*Chapman v Gosberton Farm Produce Co Ltd* Env Law 1992–1993, 191). However where such a defence is raised it is for the prosecution to satisfy the court that the excuse is not a reasonable one (*Polychronakis v Richards & Jerrom Ltd* (1997) Ind LR, 22 October).

3.14.6 Lack of funds is not a 'reasonable excuse' to justify non-compliance with the abatement notice (*Saddleworth UDC v Aggregate and Sand* (1970) 114 SJ 931). The relevant date for deciding whether the nuisance has been abated is the date the information is laid and not the date of the hearing (*Northern Ireland Trailers v Preston Corporation* [1972] 1 WLR 203 and *Lambeth LBC v Stubbs* [1980] JPL 519).

3.14.7 It may be open to the defendant to defend the prosecution on the grounds that the notice contained no lawful requirement even though an appeal was not lodged (see *Sterling Homes (Midlands) Ltd v Birmingham City Council* (unreported Divisional Court July 5 1995), *Hope Butuyuyu v London Borough of Hammersmith and Fulham* [1997] Env LR D13 Part 3, and the opposite conclusion in a Scottish case: *Stagecoach Ltd v McPhail* [1988] SCCR 289).

3.14.8 By s 80(8) a defence under s 80(7) is not available:

(a) in the case of a nuisance falling within paragraph (a) [the state of premises], (d) [dust, steam, smell or other effluvia], (e) [any accumulation or deposit], (f) [animals], (g) [noise] of section 79(1) . . . except where the nuisance arises on industrial, trade or business premises;

(b) in the case of a nuisance falling within paragraph (ga) of section 79(1) above except where the noise is emitted from or caused by a vehicle, machinery or equipment being used for industrial, trade or business;

(c) in the case of a nuisance falling within paragraph (b) [smoke] except where the smoke is emitted from a chimney; and

(d) in the case of a nuisance falling within paragraph (c) [fumes or gases] or (h) [any other matter declared by any enactment] of section 79(1).

3.14.9 Where the statutory nuisance concerns noise emitted from premises, a further defence is available under s 80(9) where the defendant can prove:

(a) that the alleged offence was covered by a notice served under section 60 or a consent given under section 61 or 65 of the Control of Pollution Act 1974 (construction sites, etc); or

(b) where the alleged offence was committed at a time when the premises were subject to a notice under section 66 of that Act (noise reduction notice), that the level of noise emitted from the premises at that time was not such as to constitute a contravention of the notice under that section; or

(c) where the alleged offence was committed at a time when the premises were not subject to a notice under section 66 of that Act, and when a level fixed under section 67 of that Act (new buildings liable to abatement order) applied to the premises, that the level of noise emitted from the premises at that time did not exceed that level.

Wilful obstruction

3.14.10 It is an offence for anyone wilfully to obstruct any person authorised by a local authority who is seeking to exercise its powers of entry for the purpose of ascertaining whether or not a statutory nuisance exists or for the purpose of taking any action or executing work authorised by the Act. The maximum penalty payable on summary conviction is a fine not exceeding level 3 on the standard scale.

Disclosing trade secrets

3.14.11 It is also an offence for the person authorised by the local authority to disclose any trade secrets obtained in the exercise of its powers of entry unless the disclosure was made in performance of its duty with the consent of the person having the right to disclose the information. Such a person will be liable on summary conviction to a fine not exceeding level 5 on the standard scale. A member of a local authority or any person authorised by a local authority shall not be personally liable providing they have exercised good faith in carrying out their duties under Part 3 of Schedule 3 of the 1990 Act (Sched 3, para 5).

Further breaches of an abatement notice

3.14.12 Unless stated to the contrary, an abatement notice is of unlimited duration, so that if a further breach occurs the local authority can instigate prosecution proceedings without serving another notice (*Wellingborough DC v Gordon* [1991] JPL 874). This also applies to notices served under earlier legislation notwithstanding repeal of that legislation and the lack of transitional provisions (*Aitken v South Hams DC* (1994) *The Times*, 8 July).

Checklist – abatement notices – practice and procedure

- The abatement notice:
  - must specify the works or other steps required to be undertaken, the time period within the works must be carried out and the rights of appeal
  - must be clear and precise without being too prescriptive
  - is required to be served on the 'responsible person' or owner or occupier, as appropriate.
- Appeal provisions
  - 21 days from the date of service are allowed
  - the 1990 Regulations specify the grounds of appeal
  - check the order required from the magistrates (including orders as to compensation and costs)
  - will the notice be suspended pending the appeal?
- What offences might be committed in connection with abatement notices?
  - non-compliance (including a possible daily fine)
  - the fine for industrial, trade or business premises is significantly higher than for other premises or activities
  - is the 'best practicable means' defence available (the onus being on the defendant)?
  - is the statutory noise defence available (Control of Pollution Act notice)?
  - wilful obstruction of a local authority agent
  - disclosing trade secrets.

3.15 Local authority self-help

3.15.1 An abatement notice is a prosecution in itself. In addition to its powers to prosecute, a local authority has the power to take steps to abate the nuisance (s 81(3)). In doing so the local authority is able to recover its reasonable costs (s 81(4)).

Recovering costs by way of a charging order

3.15.2 Where the local authority is looking to recover its costs from the owner it can place a charge over those premises by s 81A (inserted into the Act by s 10 of the Noise and Statutory Nuisance Act 1993). This section enables a local authority to recover its costs reasonably incurred in abating or preventing a statutory nuisance by imposing a charge on the relevant premises where the current owner of those premises is the person responsible for the nuisance. The local authority must first serve a notice on the owner of the premises and on any other person to the knowledge of the authority who has an interest in those premises which might be affected by the charge. The notice must give details of the expenses the local authority seeks to recover and the rate of interest to be charged until the sum is repaid. The charge comes into force 21 days after the service of the notice unless an appeal is made under s 81A(6) of the 1990 Act. The effect of an appeal is to suspend the notice. The notice will only come into force on the final determination of the appeal or on the date the appeal is drawn. Once the charge is made, interest will accrue and the local authority has the same powers and remedies available to it as if it were a mortgagee (s 81A(8) of the 1990 Act).

Instalment payments

3.15.3 Under s 81B (also inserted by s 10 of the 1993 Act) a local authority may decide to recover its costs and interest accruing by instalments under an Order which must state the expense and interest payable providing the repayment period does not exceed 30 years. This section enables the instalments of interest to be recovered from the occupier instead of the owner where the occupier pays rent to the owner.

3.16 Injunctive relief

3.16.1 Furthermore where the Authority believes criminal proceedings for an offence would afford an inadequate remedy, it may proceed directly to the High Court to obtain an injunction to abate, prohibit or restrict this nuisance (s 81(5) EPA 1990 and s 222 Local Government Act 1972). (*Bristol City Council v Higgins* (unreported, High Court 8 September 1994 and referred to in article in *The Times* on 9 September 1994).)

3.17 Private remedies against the local authority

Judicial review

3.17.1 Despite all efforts the local authority officer may not respond to a complaint, or may not act quickly enough. It may be possible to apply for an application for judicial review for an order of *mandamus* requiring a local authority to fulfil its duty. For obvious reasons this is fraught with uncertainties and considerable expense.

Other alternatives

3.17.2   Referral to the local authority ombudsman might be an option in the long term, but only after separate proceedings to stop the statutory nuisance are successful. Embarrassment caused by newspaper reports may also result in a response.

3.18   Instituting private proceedings for an abatement order

3.18.1   Most complainants tend to go through the local authority as a way to resolve a nuisance problem where it is caused by a private individual as it will reduce the costs they have to incur. Local authority EHOs normally have the qualifications and experience to deal with such problems. However, their ability to respond depends on funds allocated to fulfil its duty. The response time and facilities available vary considerably from local authority to local authority.

3.18.2   Part III of the 1990 Act enables individuals to take action without the benefit of the local authority. By s 82(2) a person aggrieved by the existence of a statutory nuisance can apply to magistrates for an abatement order in similar terms to an abatement notice which might be issued by a local authority. Since the nuisance must be in existence at the time of the application an order cannot be made prohibiting or restricting its occurrence or recurrence.

Such statutory proceedings have a particular use where a local authority has failed properly to maintain or repair its own premises and which are now in a state which is prejudicial to health or a statutory nuisance.

3.18.3   In order for an individual to be able to lodge a complaint with the Magistrates' Court for an abatement order, he must be a 'person aggrieved'. That is to say that he must be a person whose reasonable enjoyment of his property, or whose health, is being prejudicially affected. There are probably very few restrictions on who is an aggrieved person for the purposes of s 82.

3.18.4   The correct approach is to look at the statute under which the relevant duties arise and see whether it gives any express or implied rights to the complainant (*Inland Revenue Commissioners v National Federation of Self Employed and Small Businesses Limited* [1982] AC 617). A council tenant in a block of flats who complained of a statutory nuisance affecting the block in general but not his flat was not a 'person aggrieved' (*Birmingham District Council v McMahon* (1987) 151 JP 709).

Procedure

3.18.5   At the same time as making an abatement order the Magistrates may also impose a fine on the defendant not exceeding level 5 on the standard scale (s 82(2)). If satisfied that the alleged nuisance exists and that the premises are rendered unfit for human habitation, they may also prohibit use of the premises for that purpose until they are rendered reasonably fit (s 82(3)).

3.18.6 Proceedings for an abatement order may be brought against the following:

(1) the person responsible for the nuisance (s 80(2)(a))
(2) where the nuisance arises from a structural defect, the owner of the premises (s 80(2)(b))
(3) where the person responsible cannot be found or the nuisance has not yet occurred, the owner or occupier of the premises (s 80(2)(c)).

Before instituting proceedings the person aggrieved by the statutory nuisance must give the relevant person notice in writing of his intention to instigate proceedings and describe the nuisance about which he complains. Where the statutory nuisance concerns noise emanating from a premises, not less than three days' notice is required. Where it is a nuisance of any other description, then the period of notice is 21 days.

3.18.7 According to *Hollis v Dudley MBC* and *Probex v Same* (1997) *Times Law Reports*, 12 December, the courts must award costs to individuals bringing proceedings for statutory nuisance which can include costs incurred in establishing that a statutory nuisance exists. Even where the alleged nuisance no longer exists at the date of the hearing the court may, providing it is satisfied that the alleged nuisance existed at the date of the complaint, order the defendant to pay the complainant's reasonable costs in bringing the proceedings (s 82(12)). Further, as the proceedings are quasi-criminal in nature, the court also has jurisdiction to make an order for compensation (*Botross v Hammersmith and Fulham LBC* (1995) 27 HLR 179).

Offences in connection with an abatement order

3.18.8 Any person who, without reasonable excuse, contravenes an abatement order will be guilty of an offence and liable to a fine on summary conviction not exceeding a level 5 (currently £5,000) on the standard scale together with a further fine of an amount equal to one tenth of that level for each day for which the offence continues after conviction (s 82(8)).

Defences

3.18.9 Defences to private proceedings are similar to those available in proceedings in the case of an abatement notice (see 3.14). It is a defence to prove that the best practicable means were used to prevent, or counteract the effect of, the nuisance (s 82(9)). Similar restrictions on the availability of this defence also apply (s 82(10)) and state that the defence is not available:

> in the case of a nuisance which is such as to render the premises unfit for the circumstances which are prejudicial to health or a nuisance concern the state of the premises (s 82(10)).

3.18.10 The Magistrates' Court also has the power to direct a local authority in whose area the nuisance has occurred, to do any work which the convicted person was ordered to do by the court under s 82(2) (s 82(11)).

3.18.11 Furthermore, if it appears to the Magistrates' Court that neither the person responsible for the nuisance nor the owner or occupier can be found, the Magistrates may direct the local authority to do anything which the court would have ordered that person to do (s 82(13)).

Checklist – enforcement by a private individual

- Judicial review
- Instituting proceedings for an abatement order
- Offences

Chapter 4

The Rule in *Rylands v Fletcher* and Liability for Fire

4.1 Overview

4.1.1 The rule in *Rylands v Fletcher* renders a person who is in control or occupation of land liable for damage caused by the escape of some dangerous object accumulated by him on that land where the use of the land is for some 'non-natural' purpose.

4.1.2 *Rylands v Fletcher* is a tort of strict liability, by which is meant that a defendant is liable for all the foreseeable consequences of the escape, even though he may have exercised all due care to prevent such an escape from occurring (*Cambridge Water Co v Eastern Counties Leather plc* [1994] 2 AC 264 at 302D).

4.1.3 Well before *Rylands v Fletcher* was decided, the common law imposed strict liability for damage caused by fire spreading from an owner's property. *Rylands v Fletcher* and the rise of negligence have meant the old common law rules have been largely superseded, but even where liability for the spread of fire lies in negligence, the relevant principles show something of the recognition by the courts of the extra steps needed to safeguard one's neighbours from damage by fire (notably the liability of a landowner for the acts of an independent contractor).

4.1.4 This chapter will seek to identify the requirements to be satisfied before a plaintiff can recover in an action based on the rule in *Rylands v Fletcher*. It will also examine the nature of an action for damage by fire. The available defences in both categories of case are similar, but will be considered separately.

4.2 Liability in *Rylands v Fletcher*

Rylands v Fletcher and the principle in outline

4.2.1 *Rylands v Fletcher* itself concerned liability for a badly constructed reservoir. The site was properly selected and planned by independent contractors. Incompetent subcontractors failed to ensure that old mine-shafts could withstand the pressure of the water in the reservoir. One of the shafts burst and water flowed through the shaft into a neighbouring mine, rendering it useless. **4.2.2** The court originally found for the defendant (see *Fletcher v Rylands* (1865) 3 H & C 774). This was, however, overturned in the higher court (*Fletcher v Rylands* LR I Ex 265, 159 ER 737) in which Blackburn J delivered his well-known judgment which is often cited in full (at 279–280) and should be repeated:

> We think that the true rule of law is, that the person who, for his own purposes, brings on his lands and collects and keeps there anything likely to do mischief if it escapes, must keep it at his peril and, if he does not do so, is *prima facie* answerable for all the damage which is the natural consequence of its escape. He can excuse himself by shewing that the escape was owing to the Plaintiff's default; or, perhaps that the escape was the consequence of *vis major*, or the act of God; but as nothing of this sort exists here, it is unnecessary to inquire what excuse would be sufficient. The general rule, as above stated, seems on principle just. The person whose grass or corn is eaten down by the escaping cattle of his neighbour, or whose mine is flooded by the water from his neighbour's reservoir, or whose cellar is invaded by the filth of his neighbour's privy, or whose habitation is made unhealthy by the fumes and noisome vapours of his neighbour's alkali works, is damnified without any fault of his own; and it seems but reasonable and just that the neighbour who has brought something on his own property which was not naturally there, harmless to others, so long as it is confined to his own property, but which he knows will be mischievous if it gets on his neighbour's, should be obliged to make good the damage which ensues if he does not succeed in confining it to his own property. But for his act in bringing it there no mischief could have accrued, and it seems but just that he should at his peril keep it there so that no mischief may accrue, or answer for the natural and anticipated consequences. And upon authority, this we think is established to be the law, whether the things so brought be beasts, or water, or filth or stenches

The essential principle was summarised by Lord Cranworth in the House of Lords (*Rylands v Fletcher* LR III HL 330, 340) when approving the judgment of Blackburn J:

> If a man brings, or accumulates, on his land anything which, if it should escape, may cause damage to his neighbour, he does so at his peril. If it does escape, and cause damage, he is responsible, however careful he may have been, and whatever precautions he may have taken to prevent the damage.

The origin of the tort is beyond the remit of this work, but it is commonly recognised as an extension of the law of nuisance to cases of isolated escape (see *The Boundaries of Nuisance*, Newark (1949) 65 LQR 480).

Non-natural user

4.2.3 Under the modern law of the tort a defendant will not be liable for the escape of a potentially dangerous substance from land if the substance was accumulated for some ordinary use. This is the consequence of the speech of Lord Moulton in *Rickards v Lothian* [1913] AC 263 at 280:

> It is not every use to which land is put that brings into play that principle. It must be some special use bringing with it increased danger to others, and must not merely be

the ordinary use of the land or such a use as is proper for the general benefit of the community.

In some cases the question asked is whether the use of land is 'natural' and in some cases whether 'ordinary'. The expression 'non-natural user' as a short-hand method of indicating that the use of the defendant's land must have been neither ordinary nor natural derives from the speech of Lord Cairns in *Rylands v Fletcher* LR III HL 330.

4.2.4 What is meant by the 'ordinary use of the land or such a use as is proper for the general benefit of the community' will vary, within certain limitations. Thus in *Rickards'* case (at 281) the defendant was not liable for the overflow from a wash-hand basin:

> The provision of a proper supply of water to the various parts of a house is not only reasonable, but has become, in accordance with modern sanitary views, an almost necessary feature of town life

The matter is entirely a question of fact for the judge. In *Mason v Levy Auto Parts of England Ltd* [1967] 2 QB 530 the defendant bought and sold motor parts and engines. These were coated in grease and oil and wrapped in greased and oiled paper, and stored in wooden crates, some of which had broken open. They caught fire as a result of someone's smoking on the premises. The judge held the defendant liable, the use of the land being non-natural, having regard to

(1) the quantities of combustible material on the premises,

(2) the way in which they were stored and

(3) the character of the neighbourhood.

4.2.5 In *Cambridge Water v Eastern Counties Leather plc* Lord Goff advised caution against placing too wide an interpretation on the words 'or such a use as is proper for the general benefit of the community'.

> If these words are understood to refer to a local community, they can be given some content as intended to refer to such matters as, for example, the provision of serv-ices; indeed the same idea can, without too much difficulty, be extended to, for example, the provision of services to industrial premises, as in a business park or an industrial estate. But if the words are extended to embrace the wider interests of the local community or the general benefit of the community at large, it is difficult to see how the exception can be kept within reasonable bounds.

The suggestion made by Viscount Simon in *Read v Lyons & Co Ltd* [1947] AC 156 at 169–170 that the manufacture of explosives by the government in time of war might constitute a natural use of land is therefore open to doubt. In the *Cambridge Water* case itself the House of Lords rejected the trial judge's view that the creation of employment in a small industrial complex was sufficient of itself to establish a natural or ordinary use of land (p 309A).

Dangerous substances

4.2.6 The principle of *Rylands v Fletcher* has been applied to damage caused by the following substances or entities:

(1) the discharge of an electric current into the earth (*National Telephone Co v Baker* [1893] 2 Ch 186 at 201);

(2) an explosion and fire in a motor car's carburettor (*Musgrove v Pandelis* [1919] 2 KB 43);

(3) nuisances caused by caravan dwellers allowed to occupy the defendant's land (*A-G v Corke* [1933] Ch 89);

(4) the explosion of high explosives (*Rainham Chemical Works v Belvedere Fish Guano Co Ltd* [1921] 2 AC 465. Cf counsel's submission in *Read v Lyons* [1947] AC 156 at 161: 'the manufacture of explosives, which was formerly particularly dangerous, is now one of the safest industrial processes, with fewer risks than coal mining');

(5) vibrations caused by pile-driving during construction works (*Hoare v McAlpine* [1923] 1 Ch 167);

(6) spare motor parts and engines protected by oil, grease and coated paper and stored in wooden crates which caught fire (*Mason v Levy Auto Parts of England* [1967] 2 QB 530).

Whether a particular substance is dangerous is a question of fact (*Read v Lyons* at 176). The matter must be approached, however, by looking at the item itself in the context of all its relevant nature and functions. Thus a chair-o-plane must be considered as a machine in motion intended to carry children likely to be fooling upon it (*Hale v Jennings* [1938] 1 All ER 579 at 581–582).

Accumulation

4.2.7　In order to fall within the principle the dangerous item must have been accumulated by some act of the defendant. A fall of rock from a natural outcrop cannot render a defendant liable (*Pontardawe RDC v Moore-Gwyn* [1929] 1 Ch 656). So, too, flooding of a watercourse flowing through a defendant's land as a result of siltation thereby obstructing the normal passage of water does not provide a plaintiff with a right of action (*Neath RDC v Williams* [1951] 1 KB 115).

4.2.8　It is important to note that the accumulated substance need not have been accumulated on land belonging to the defendant. It is sufficient if he has some control over the land in question. In *West v Bristol Tramways Co* [1908] 2 KB 14 for instance, the escape was of creosote from wood-blocks laid in the highway. So too in *Charing Cross Electricity Supply Co v Hydraulic Power Co* [1914] 3 KB 772 the plaintiff's electric cables were damaged by the burst of the defendant's hydraulic mains laid under the same street, and in *Northwestern Utilities Ltd v London Guarantee and Accident Co Ltd* [1936] AC 108 gas escaped from the defendant's mains into the plaintiff's adjacent property.

4.2.9　So too in cases other than subterraneous accumulations there is no principle which limits liability to a landowner. Thus in *Hale v Jennings* [1938] 1 All ER 579 the plaintiff tenant of a fairground stall recovered damages as a result of the escape of a chair-o-plane from a stall tenanted by the defendant. In *Shiffman v Order of St John* [1936] 1 All ER 557 it was held (*obiter*) that a defendant who had erected a temporary tent and flagpole on another's land was liable when the flagpole hit a visitor to the tent.

Escape

4.2.10 As well as having to prove an accumulation of some dangerous substance by the defendant, it is of course necessary to demonstrate that the substance escaped from the place of its confinement. The corollary is that where a person claiming to have sustained damage is present at the same place as the confined substance, he is unable to complain about the escape. Thus in *Read's* case the explosion of a munitions shell on the defendant's premises was not actionable because the only damage about which the plaintiff could complain occurred whilst the plaintiff was on the same land. For Viscount Simons at 168:

> 'Escape' for the purpose of applying the proposition in *Rylands v Fletcher*, means escape from a place where the defendant has occupation of or control over land to a place which is outside his occupation or control . . . . The learned judge was right I think in refusing to apply the doctrine of *Rylands v Fletcher* on the ground that the injuries were caused on the premises of the defendants.

So too Lord Porter explained (at 177) that:

> In all cases which have been decided, it has been held necessary, in order to establish liability, that there should have been some form of escape from the place in which the dangerous object has been retained by the defendant to some other place not subject to his control.

In *Perry v Kendricks Transport Ltd* [1956] 1 WLR 85 the fact that both the plaintiff and the defendant were apparently present on land belonging to the defendant was not a matter explored by the court, the action being dismissed on other grounds.

Damage

4.2.11 It is not at all clear whether a plaintiff can recover compensation when he has suffered some injury other than damage to land. In *Read's* case, in which the only damage sustained by the plaintiff was personal injury, the point does not appear to have been pursued at all by counsel for the defendant. The members of the House of Lords left the matter to be decided on another occasion, but Lord Macmillan (amongst others) was sceptical (at 170–171):

> The action is one of damages for personal injuries. Whatever may have been the law of England in early times I am of opinion that as the law now stands an allegation of negligence is in general essential to the relevancy of an action of reparation for personal injuries.

The issue remains definitively to be tested, but there are authorities to support such a claim. Thus in *Hale v Jennings* [1938] 1 All ER 579 the plaintiff recovered compensation solely for personal injuries and in *Shiffman v Order of*

St John [1936] 1 All ER 557 the court indicated that it would be willing to make an award of compensation for personal injuries in a claim brought under the rule in *Rylands v Fletcher*.

4.2.12 As for damage to chattels, compensation has been recovered for damage caused to plants and shrubs in a nursery garden (*West v Bristol Tramways Co* [1908] 2 KB 14) and for damage to a car (*Halsey v Esso Petroleum Co* [1961] 1 WLR 683).

Foreseeability of damage

4.2.13 It is now conclusively settled by *Cambridge Water Co v Eastern Counties Leather plc* [1994] 2 AC 264 that liability under *Rylands v Fletcher* as well as in nuisance depends on foreseeability by the defendant of the relevant type of damage (see 304E).

Defences – (1) Act of God

4.2.14 The courts recognise Act of God as a defence to a case based on *Rylands v Fletcher*. Thus in *Nichols v Marsland* (1876) 2 Ex D 1, a sudden and unprecedented rainfall occurred, giving rise to a flood of the defendant's ornamental pools. The plaintiff was unable to succeed in recovering damages because the rainfall which precipitated the flooding was 'greater and more violent than any within the memory of witnesses':

> A defendant cannot, in our opinion, be properly said to have caused or allowed the water to escape, if the act of God or the Queen's enemies was the real cause of its escaping without any fault on the part of the Defendant.

Although this decision was criticised in *Greenock Corp v Caledonian Railway Co* [1917] AC 556 (in which the House of Lords reached a contrary view on similar facts) it remains good law.

Defences – (2) Trespassers and acts of strangers

4.2.15 In *Rickards v Lothian* [1913] AC 263 the tribunal adopted the passage cited at 4.2.14 above in deciding that an owner of land cannot be liable for an escape occasioned by the 'malicious act of a third person' (see 278). In *Rickards'* case the defendant was not liable because some unidentified stranger had stuffed the overflow pipes of the wash-basin full with various objects and then left the tap running. So too in *Perry v Kendricks Transport Ltd* [1956] 1 WLR 85 the court held that the defendant was not liable for the consequences of an explosion in a petrol tank of a coach abandoned on its land, the explosion having been caused by the dropping of a match into the tank by a child.

4.2.16 *Perry's* case was decided on the basis that:

> if the damage is caused by the mischievous, deliberate and conscious act of a stranger the occupier can escape liability (156).

It is clear, however, that if it can be shown that the defendant should have been aware of, or anticipated, the danger that a stranger might do what in fact he did, then the defendant may be subject to a duty of care and liable in negligence (*Perry's* case at 159 and *Shiffman v Order of St John* [1936] 1 All ER 557).

Checklist – Liability in *Rylands v Fletcher*

- The principle in outline:
    — is the item itself dangerous? It must be examined in the light of its full nature and characteristics.
    — has the item been accumulated?
    — has there been an escape? This rule is tested by the negative corollary: if the entity has not travelled from one place in the control of the defendant to another, there is no liability.
    — the use of the land for the accumulation must have been other than 'natural' or 'ordinary', a matter which can include a consideration of the narrower benefits to the local community (for instance the provision of services).
- Damage
    — query whether damage to chattels or by way of personal injury is recoverable at all.
- Defences
    — it is important to remember that this is a tort of strict liability
    — Act of God is a recognised defence but unlikely
    — a defendant is not liable for the acts of trespassers or strangers, usually characterised as the malicious acts of third parties which a defendant could not have anticipated.

4.3 Fire

4.3.1 Even before the decision in *Rylands v Fletcher* the common law held a defendant strictly liable for damage done by a fire which originated on his own property unless he could prove that it had started or spread by the act of stranger or of God (see *Musgrove v Pandelis* [1919] 2 KB 43 at 46 and *Mason v Levy Auto Parts of England* [1967] 2 QB 530 at 540).

4.3.2 The practice today is for a claim to succeed if the plaintiff can establish liability in either *Rylands v Fletcher* or negligence.

4.3.3 As to establishing liability under the principle of *Rylands v Fletcher*, a good practical guide is set out in *Mason's* case (at 542), rendering a defendant liable if:

> (1) he brought on to his land things likely to catch fire, and kept them there in such conditions that if they did ignite the fire would be likely to spread to the plaintiff's land; (2) he did so in the course of some non-natural use; and (3) the things ignited and the fire spread.

(The facts of the case are briefly set out at 4.2.4 above.) All the necessary ingredients of *Rylands v Fletcher* must be established, so that if, for instance, premises have been used in a natural and ordinary way, the defendant will not be liable (see *Sochacki v Sas* [1947] 1 All ER 344).

4.3.4 So far as establishing liability in negligence is concerned, this may take any number of forms. Examples include:

(1) a fire lit in a pipe to kill a rat within close proximity of a packing-case impregnated with paraffin and full drum of paraffin (*Mulholland & Tedd Ltd v Baker* [1939] 3 All ER 253);

(2) a blow lamp used too close to felt lagging in an effort to unfreeze pipes in a roof (*Balfour v Barty-King* [1957] 1 QB 496);

(3) a demolition contractor's fire from which sparks spread to a neighbouring property (*H & N Emanuel v GLC* [1971] 2 All ER 835).

A landowner who becomes aware (or who should have been aware) of a fire which has started on his land has a duty to prevent it from spreading so as to cause damage (see *Goldman v Hargrave* [1967] 1 AC 645 discussed at 1.10.6 above).

Liability for servants and independent contractors

4.3.5 A defendant will be held liable for the work of his servant if the servant is negligent in causing a fire (*Mason v Levy Auto Parts of England* [1967] 2 QB 530 at 540). So too he will be liable if the fire was negligently caused by an independent contractor (*Hobbs v The Baxendale Chemical Co Ltd* [1992] 1 Lloyd's Rep 54). It does not matter that the contractor was not paid by the defendant and was present on his premises as an invitee (*Balfour v Barty-King* [1957] 1 QB 496).

Defences – (1) Act of God

4.3.6 An occupier of premises is not liable for a fire which causes damage through some unforeseen work of nature. Thus, under the old common law, a defendant will not be liable for a fire used to burn weeds or stubble which spreads by some 'unforeseen wind-storm' (*Turberville v Stampe* (1697) 1 Ld Raym 264, 91 ER 1072).

Defences – (2) Trespassers and acts of strangers

4.3.7 A defendant will not be liable for the act of a trespasser or a stranger (*Turberville's* case and *Beaulieu v Finglam* (1401) YB 2 Hen 4, fo 18, pt 6). The relevant principles are set out at 4.2.15–4.2.16 above. The relevant question appears to be whether the landowner could reasonably have anticipated the acts which led to the fire (*H & N Emanuel v GLC* [1971] 2 All ER 835).

Fires Prevention (Metropolis) Act 1774, s 86

4.3.8 By s 86 of the above Act:

> . . . no action, suit, or process whatever, shall be had, maintained or prosecuted, against any person in whose house, chamber, stable, barn, or other building, or on whose estate any fire shall . . . accidentally begin, nor shall any recompense be made by such person for any damage suffered thereby; any law, usage, or custom to the contrary notwithstanding . . . .

This section applies only to fires which occur by accident. It was therefore relevant in the following circumstances:

(1) a fire which started through an unknown defect in wiring (*Collingwood v Home and Colonial Stores Ltd* [1936] 3 All ER 200);

(2) a spark which jumped out of a grate (*Sochacki v Sas* [1947] 1 All ER 344);

(3) 'spontaneous combustion' (see *Vaughan v Menlove* (1837) 3 Bing NC 468).

(See also *H & N Emanuel v GLC* [1971] 2 All ER 835.)

4.3.9 Where a plaintiff can prove that the fire was started by some negligence on the defendant's part, the Act does not apply (*Mason's* case at 538). To have the protection of the Act the court must be satisfied that the fire was 'produced by mere chance, or incapable of being traced to any cause' (*Filliter v Phippard* (1847) 11 QB 347, 116 ER 506).

4.3.10 If the circumstances of the fire are caught by the principle in *Rylands v Fletcher*, then even though the start of the fire may be caught by the Act (in that it was occasioned by mere chance or incapable of being traced by any cause), a defendant will not escape liability (*Musgrove v Pandelis* [1919] 2 KB 43 and *Mason's* case at 540–542).

Checklist – liability for damage caused by fire

- Liability should now be seen as arising in either *Rylands v Fletcher* or negligence.
- In *Rylands v Fletcher*:
  - has the defendant brought on his land things likely to catch fire?
  - were those things kept in such conditions that if they did ignite the fire would be likely to spread to the plaintiff's land?
  - was the accumulation an accumulation in the course of some non-natural use of land?
- In negligence:
  - can liability be established under *Goldman v Hargrave* (liability for dangerous hazards)?
  - is there some other liability on the facts of the particular case?
- Defences:
  - these are, in essence, as for the rule in *Rylands v Fletcher* (4.2)

— even where liability arises in negligence a defendant is liable for the acts of his independent contractors.

- Section 86 of Fires Prevention (Metropolis) Act 1774:
  — the Act only applies where the fire was 'produced by mere chance'
  — where there is negligence the Act does not assist a defendant
  — where liability can be established under *Rylands v Fletcher* the Act has no application, even though the fire itself may have been produced by mere chance.

Chapter 5

Trespass

5.1 Overview

5.1.1 Trespass is the name given to a variety of distinct torts designed to give a measure of protection against a defendant who has perpetrated some direct physical interference with a plaintiff's land, chattels or person.

5.1.2 This chapter is concerned primarily with trespass to land, a tort which is closely allied to the law of nuisance. Facts that may found a cause of action in trespass may also found an action in nuisance. For example, a tree overhanging a neighbour's property will constitute both a trespass and a nuisance. The distinguishing feature about an action in trespass to land is that it is not necessary to prove any actual damage.

5.1.3 In addition to common law causes of action in trespass, the Criminal Justice and Public Order Act 1994 has introduced a variety of statutory concepts, including 'aggravated trespass' and 'trespassory assembly'. Whereas trespass to land provides individuals with remedies they can pursue by way of self-help and personally in the civil courts, the new provisions of the 1994 Act provide a variety of measures which public bodies (mainly the police and local authorities) can pursue at the instigation of any complainant. These are all powers to be exercised in connection with land and in consequence these statutory powers are dealt with in this chapter.

5.1.4 A trespass to goods involves seizure, removal or damage to goods and may also found other potential causes of action. Trespass to goods is not considered further in this book, save for wheel clamping (see chapter 11).

5.1.5 Trespass to the person at common law results from some intentional or negligent physical interference or wrongful detention. In so far as such issues as assault and battery are relevant as means of obtaining remedies against 'stalkers', they are considered at chapter 10.

5.1.6 This section contains the following material:

Introductory
    (1) Acts capable of amounting to trespass to land
    (2) Trespass where a licence or permission is exceeded
    (3) The scope of the protection afforded to 'land'
    (4) The duration of trespass and intermittence.

The plaintiff
Who can sue?

The defendant
Who can be sued?

Remedies available to the individual
   (1) Injunctions; damages; contribution
   (2) Self-help
   (3) Proceedings under RSC Ord 113
   (4) Proceedings under CCR Ord 24.

Police and local authority powers under Part V of the Criminal Justice and Public Order Act 1994
   (1) Removing trespassers (ss 61, 62)
   (2) Raves (ss 63–66)
   (3) Aggravated trespass (ss 66–69)
   (4) Trespassory assemblies (ss 70–71)
   (5) Unauthorised campers (ss 77–79).

Adverse possession
   (1) The nature of adverse possession
   (2) Making and resisting claims for adverse possession
   (3) The position of the adverse possessor.

Occupiers' duties in relation to trespassers
The Occupiers' Liability Act 1984

5.2 Trespass to land – introductory

Introductory – what constitutes trespass?

5.2.1 Trespass to land constitutes the unlawful interference with, or entry upon, land in the possession of another. There is no requirement of actual physical damage to found a trespass so that it is said to be actionable *per se* (see *Ashby v White* (1703) 2 Ld Raym 938, 92 ER 126). Mere presence on another's land, without the licence or consent of the person entitled to possession, is sufficient.

5.2.2 A trespass may be committed not simply by the presence of another person on land but equally by the presence of articles belonging to a third party. The following have been held to be the proper subjects of actions in trespass:
   (1) a bathing machine placed on the seashore (*Mace v Philcox* (1864) 15 CBNS 600, 143 ER 920);
   (2) animals straying onto another's land (*League Against Cruel Sports v Scott* [1986] QB 240);

(3) an overhanging advertising sign (*Kelsen v Imperial Tobacco Co* [1957] 2 QB 334);

(4) a building or crane (*London & Manchester Assurance Co Ltd v O & H Construction Ltd* [1989] 29 EG 65);

(5) water discharged over another's land (*Brine v Great Western Rly Co* (1862) 2 B & S 402, 121 ER 1123).

5.2.3 The expulsion (or ejectment) of the person entitled to possession may also amount to a trespass, as might the removal of items on the land (*Lavender v Betts* [1942] 2 All ER 72).

Trespass where licence or permission is exceeded

5.2.4 Remaining on land once a licence has expired, or exceeding the terms of a licence, amounts to trespass (*Vaughan v McKenzie* [1969] 1 QB 557). So too it is a trespass to use land without permission even though entry itself may not have been a trespass (an example is straying off a public footpath). To quote Scrutton LJ in *The Carlgarth* [1927] P 93 at 110:

> when you invite a person into your house to use the staircase, you do not invite him to slide down the banisters.

The scope of the protection afforded to 'land'

5.2.5 'Land', whether the interest be freehold or leasehold, in the absence of a contrary intention being shown, is presumed to stretch from below the surface of the earth to the sky and includes any buildings or parts of buildings thereon (see for instance s 205(1)(ix) of the Law of Property Act 1925). Hence, an invasion of the airspace over the land gives rise to a claim in trespass, but only to such a height as is necessary for the ordinary use and enjoyment of the land and buildings on it (*Didow v Alberta Power Ltd* [1988] 5 WWR 606). Special rules apply in respect of aircraft (see Civil Aviation Act 1982, s 76(1)).

Duration of trespass and intermittence

5.2.6 The trespass does not have to last for any period of time, merely crossing the land is sufficient (*Blundell v Catterall* (1821) 5 B & Ald 268, 106 ER 1190).

5.2.7 An owner of land must be cautious where there are acts of short term intermittent trespass, for instance the parking of motor vehicles. If the trespass is allowed to continue there is the danger that an easement by prescription may be created.

5.3 The plaintiff

The plaintiff must be entitled to possession of the land

5.3.1 As in the tort of private nuisance, it is the person who is entitled to possession of the property who can commence proceedings for trespass (see 1.1 and 1.2). It is not always easy to determine who is entitled to possession. A mere licensee (as opposed to a tenant) obtains no right to possession. It is a personal privilege only (*Isaac v Hotel de Paris* [1960] 1 WLR 239). To quote Vaughan CJ in *Thomas v Sorrell* (1673) 124 ER 1098 at 1109, a licence:

> properly passeth no interest nor alters or transfers property in any thing, but only makes an action lawful, which without it had been unlawful.

If in any doubt as to who is entitled to possession, the court will attach possession to the person able to prove title (*Canvey Island Comrs v Preedy* [1922] 1 Ch 179). A defendant may well seek to assert that it is a third party who is entitled to possession and a plaintiff must be prepared to meet such a challenge.

Property held subject to a lease

5.3.2 If a freeholder leases the property it is generally the leaseholder and not the freeholder who is entitled to possession. Hence, it will sometimes be the case that a right of action in respect of a trespass will not lie with the person who is most affected by the trespass. For example, a tenant of a multi-tenanted building is unlikely to hold an interest which extends into the airspace. The structure and the common parts of the building are likely to remain vested in the landlord, or perhaps in a superior landlord. In such a case, the issue for the tenant whose landlord is reluctant to prevent a trespass may be whether the act complained of also constitutes a nuisance, thus giving the tenant a right of action (see 1.2.2).

5.4 The defendant

Former tenants and licensees

5.4.1 This book is not intended to go into any detail in relation to tenancies and licences, and reference should be made to one of the standard text books for a detailed examination of this complicated area of the law (for instance *Woodfall's Law of Landlord and Tenant*). In essence, however, a tenant or licensee will become a trespasser at the termination of his interest and in the absence of any other arrangement or statutory provision (*Coffee v M'Evoy* [1912] 2 IR 95). Obvious exceptions are the provisions of the Housing Act 1988 in relation to residential premises and the Landlord and Tenant Act 1954 regarding tenancies of business premises.

5.4.2 Where a purported trespasser has formerly been in occupation under a lease or a licence, the first question is: Has the lease or licence been effectively terminated? In order to terminate the arrangement, it may be necessary to serve a notice to quit, or to give notification of the termination of a tenancy at will or of a licence. If the former interest has been validly terminated, the question must be asked whether there is any possibility of any new interest having been created in the interim. Acceptance of rent by the landlord due after the expiration of a notice to quit may be evidence by the creation of a new tenancy, but it depends on the real intention of the parties (*Land v Sykes* [1992] 1 EGLR 1).

5.4.3   If the answer to this last question is No, then proceedings for possession may be commenced. The self-help remedy of effecting a peaceable re-entry may be invoked, but not if any person is opposed to the entry (Criminal Law Act 1977) or if any person is residing at the premises (Protection from Eviction Act 1977).

5.4.4   It is important to note that where any premises have been leased as a dwelling and the lease has come to an end but the resident remains in occupation, court proceedings for possession must be commenced. For these very particular proceedings and rules relating to them reference should be made to landlord and tenant text books and the *County Court Practice* (*The Green Book*).

'Squatters'

5.4.5   A 'squatter' may be defined as somebody who, without the licence or consent of the true owner, has entered into or remained in possession of land. To quote Lord Denning in the case of *McPhail v Persons, Names Unknown* [1973] Ch 447, 456:

> What is a squatter? He is one who, without any colour of right, enters on an unoccupied house or land, intending to stay there as long as he can. He may seek to justify or excuse his conduct. He may say that he was homeless and that this house or land was standing empty, doing nothing. But this plea is of no avail in law.

5.4.6   Squatters are most commonly found in vacated residential premises, although so long as there is water available, they do occupy industrial or storage premises too. One fairly recent phenomenon is the 'shop squatter', ie one or more squatters taking over retail premises for the purpose of trading. Very often one of the squatters will be found remaining on the premises throughout the day and night to defeat any peaceable re-entry by the landlord.

Gypsies and travellers

5.4.7   In considering these groups, this book refers to persons who travel about the country in vehicles and caravans in a nomadic way of life. There have been many attempts to describe them. 'Gypsies' were defined by s 16 of the Caravan Sites Act 1968 (now repealed) as:

> persons of nomadic habit of life, whatever their race or origin, but does not include members of an organised group of travelling showmen, or of persons engaged in travelling circuses, travelling together as such.

In *R v South Hams District Council ex parte Gibb* [1995] QB 158, Leggatt LJ stated (at 172) that this definition:

adopts the element of leading a nomadic life, makes no reference to employment, and treats the lack of fixed abode as implicit in the need for a caravan site. It also asserts that the Act applies irrespective of race or origin. Yet the term 'gypsy' is used as the word to be defined. The term might have been 'nomads' or 'travellers', but 'gypsies' was preferred. From this it may be inferred that Parliament intended the Act to apply to persons who behave like gypsies without necessarily being Romanies by race or origin.

Merely adopting a nomadic way of life does not entitle persons to be treated as if they are gypsies (*R v Dorset County Council ex parte Rolls* [1994] EGCS 13).

5.4.8 If, during their travels, these persons trespass, they are treated as any other squatter would be treated by the person entitled to possession of the land on which they are encamped.

5.4.9 It should be noted that the *duty* upon local authorities to provide sites for gypsies and control of unauthorised encampments as introduced by Part II of the Caravan Sites Act 1968 was repealed by s 80 of the Criminal Justice and Public Order Act 1994. However, the *power* to provide sites for caravans pursuant to the Caravan Sites and Control of Development Act 1960 remains.

5.4.10 As for privately owned caravan sites, these will require both a licence (Caravan Sites and Control of Development Act 1960) and planning permission. In *Buckley v United Kingdom* [1995] JPL 633 a landowner who wished to live on her land in a caravan was refused planning permission. She made a successful application to the European Commission on Human Rights, complaining that the refusal was a violation of Article 8 of the European Convention of Human Rights, which provides, *inter alia*, that:

> Everyone has the right to respect for his private and family life, his home and his correspondence.

5.4.11 Persons residing in a vehicle (including a caravan) on land forming a highway, or land which is unoccupied may be directed to leave by the local authority (see Criminal Justice and Public Order Act 1994, ss 77–79 at 5.6.18 below). Additionally, the occupation may constitute a nuisance if the group of occupiers are noisy or create a health hazard (eg by lack of sanitation).

Checklist – identifying a trespass to land

- Is the act capable of amounting to a trespass?
  - actual damage is not required of an act said to constitute a trespass
  - has a person entered onto the plaintiff's land without permission?
  - has an item been deposited on the land?
  - has an individual gone beyond what was permitted under the grant of some licence or permission?
  - NB 'land' includes land below and above the level of the ground
  - check that an easement by prescription has not been created by continuous acts of trespass over the relevant period.

- Is the plaintiff entitled to sue?
  - can the plaintiff establish an entitlement to possession (rather than, for instance, a mere licence to occupy)?
  - if the plaintiff has leased premises it is the leaseholder who will be entitled to possession. Is there an alternative right of action (for instance in nuisance)?
- Can the intended defendant be sued?
  - possession proceedings should be commenced against a tenant or licensee who remains in occupation. Care must be taken of all statutory provisions which restrict the right of entry
  - 'squatters' are people who enter onto or remain on land without the consent of the true owner
  - proceedings may be taken against gypsies and travellers only if they satisfy the usual requirements for commencing proceedings in trespass.

5.5 Remedies available to the individual

5.5.1 As has been said trespass is actionable *per se* without proof of any actual damage. As to the remedies which may ordinarily be available to a plaintiff, a note referring to some of the key principles (including injunctions) will be found in chapter 16. This section will consider some special rules which apply in the case of trespass to land, especially so far as they relate to the right to regain possession of land. It should always be remembered that it may be possible to obtain the effective assistance of the local authority or the police under the statutory provisions set out at 5.6 below.

Damages in outline

5.5.2 Historically the ordinary remedy for a trespass is a claim for damages. In relation to trespass to land, the following principles apply in outline:

(1) The trespasser is not allowed to make use of another's land without being liable for compensation (*Stoke City Council v Wass* [1988] 1 WLR 1406).

(2) The level of compensation is ordinarily based on the letting value of the property in question (*Strand Electric and Engineering Co v Brisford Entertainments* [1952] 2 QB 246).

(3) If the owner of the land would or could not have let the premises it could be said he suffered no loss, so that the court will then consider the value of the occupation to the trespasser (*Ministry of Defence v Thompson* [1993] 2 EGLR 107).

Further assistance will be found in chapter 16 (especially at 16.5).

Damages and tenants or licencees who remain in occupation

5.5.3 If a tenant or licensee has remained after the expiry of his interest in the property and this has given rise to a trespass, the measure of damages will reflect the letting value of the property in the open market. Although the amount of the previous rental is good evidence of this, evidence of comparable lettings may be required if the value of the premises is higher or lower than the rent or licence fee formerly payable.

5.5.4 In the case of a tenant holding over, the following should be considered:

(1) A claim for double the yearly value of the premises if the landlord has demanded possession of the premises in writing (see Landlord and Tenant Act 1730, s 1).

(2) A claim for double rent if the tenant gave notice to quit but fails to give up possession (Distress for Rent Act 1737, s 18).

Contribution

5.5.5 If the claimant has suffered damage partly due to his own fault, the damages are reduced as the court thinks fit (see Law Reform (Contributory Negligence) Act 1945, s 1(1)).

Self help

5.5.6 Self-help remedies may extend to measures to prevent a trespass, for instance the placing of a physical obstruction on land or the use of reasonable force for self-defence or defence of another. However, the use of such remedies may also constitute a civil wrong, for example in placing a trespasser at risk of injury, or in using unreasonable force in ejecting him, or in interfering with another's goods and causing damage to them. Regard should be had to the Occupiers' Liability Act 1957 and the Torts (Interference with Goods) Act 1977.

5.5.7 A squatter may be evicted by the person entitled to possession without recourse to the courts. Is this a remedy which the landowner should realistically consider? Lord Denning in *McPhail v Persons, Names Unknown* [1973] Ch 447, considered first self help:

> Now I would say this at once about squatters. The owner is not obliged to go to the courts to obtain possession. He is entitled, if he so desires, to take the remedy into his own hands. He can go in himself and turn them out without the aid of the courts of law. This is not a course to be recommended because of the disturbance which might follow. But the legality of it is beyond question.

He continued:

> Even though the owner himself should use force, then so long as he uses no more force than is reasonably necessary, he is not himself liable either criminally or civilly.

Lord Denning did not recommend such action, however:

Although the law thus enables the owner to take the remedy into his own hands, that is not a course to be encouraged. In a civilised society, the courts should themselves provide a remedy which is speedy and effective; and thus make self-help unnecessary.

It has been held that self-redress for trespass is a summary remedy justified only in clear and simple cases or in an emergency (*Burton v Winters* [1993] 1 WLR 1077 – trespass by encroachment).

Self help and statutory restrictions

5.5.8 A person using or threatening violence to secure entry into premises, knowing there is someone on the premises opposed to entry, is guilty of an offence under the Criminal Law Act 1977, s 6.

5.5.9 However, the above does not apply to a person who is 'a displaced residential occupier or a protected intending occupier of the premises in question or who is acting on behalf of such an occupier' (s 6(1A), inserted by s 72 of the Criminal Justice and Public Order Act 1994).

5.5.10 A 'displaced residential occupier' is a person who was occupying premises as a residence immediately before being excluded from possession by the offending trespasser (Criminal Law Act 1977, s 12(3)). However, a trespasser cannot himself be a displaced residential occupier (Criminal Law Act 1977, s 12(4)).

5.5.11 A 'protected intending occupier' is defined under s 12A of the 1977 Act (inserted by s 74 of the 1994 Act) as a person who:

(1) has a freehold or leasehold interest with not less than two years to run or is a tenant or licensee of such a person or is a tenant or licensee of a local authority, housing association or corporation; and

(2) requires the premises for his own occupation as a residence; and

(3) is excluded from occupation by the trespasser; and

(4) holds a written statement specifying his interest in the premises, that the premises are required for his occupation and the statement was signed by the protected intending occupier before a justice of the peace or a commissioner for oaths and is signed by them also.

5.5.12 A person who obtains a written statement as above by knowingly or recklessly including false or misleading material is guilty of an offence and is liable to imprisonment for a term not exceeding six months or a fine or both (s 75).

5.5.13 Anyone keen to exercise a right of self-help should also be very well aware of the effect of s 1 of the Protection from Eviction Act 1977 (unlawful eviction and harassment) and of the corresponding liability to pay extensive damages for such acts (Housing Act 1988, ss 27 and 28).

5.5.14 As an alternative to actual self help a landowner should consider seeking the assistance of the police under s 7 of the Criminal Law Act 1977 (as amended by s 73 of the Criminal Justice and Public Order Act 1994), by virtue of which it is a criminal offence for a trespasser to fail to leave premises if requested to do so by a displaced residential occupier or a protected intending occupier. A constable in uniform may arrest without warrant any person whom he reasonably suspects to be guilty of an offence of adverse occupation.

5.5.15 Other provisions under Part V of the Criminal Justice and Public Order Act 1994 should also be considered since these provide the police and local authorities with powers to deal with certain types of trespasser (see 5.6 below).

Court proceedings for the repossession of land

5.5.16 Turning to the courts, squatters may be removed from the land by three main forms of summary proceedings giving a speedy remedy to the plaintiff:

    (1) RSC Ord 113 (in the High Court), or

    (2) CCR Ord 24 Part I (in the County Court)

    (3) CCR Ord 24 Part II (in the County Court).

The third course is wider in its ambit than proceedings under RSC Ord 113 and CCR Ord 24 Part I but has proved less successful in its implementation for a number of reasons.

5.5.17 It should be pointed out that if residential premises are occupied by a former tenant, ordinary possession proceedings must be commenced and the following summary remedies are inappropriate.

Proceedings under RSC Ord 113

5.5.18 In the High Court proceedings may be brought under RSC Ord 113 against any person in possession of land and premises without the licence or consent of the person entitled to possession or the person who has remained without licence or consent. However, Ord 113 may not be used against a tenant who holds over after the termination of his tenancy.

5.5.19 Proceedings in the High Court are commenced by originating summons which must state *inter alia* whether the proceedings concern the recovery of possession of residential property. (See Appendix A5.14 for a precedent in the prescribed form.) No acknowledgment of service form is necessary.

5.5.20 It is not necessary for the names of the trespasser to be known (the defendants being referred to as 'Persons Unknown') but if the plaintiff is aware of the defendant's identity he must name him and that individual must then be personally served with the proceedings (see below).

5.5.21 A fee (of £120) is payable upon issuing the originating summons. It is necessary to file the affidavit in support (see below) at the time of issuing the summons. The summons is issued in either the Queen's or Chancery Division of the High Court.

5.5.22 The supporting affidavit must be sworn and a copy served with a sealed copy of the originating summons. It must state the plaintiff's interest in the land, the circumstances in which it became occupied by the defendants without licence or consent and that the deponent does not know the name of any person in occupation (if a name is known, the defendant must be identified). (A precedent affidavit is reproduced at Appendix A5.15.) It is good practice to exhibit to the supporting affidavit details of the title together with a plan, particularly if the land is open or partially open. (Title will need to be proved at the hearing in any event.) This should ensure that the order for possession is not in doubt as to its extent and assist the bailiff in executing the warrant for possession. An important point to note is that the order for possession bites not against the defendants, but against the land (ie it is an order *in rem*), and, once made, is good against all on the land. A squatter not named in the proceedings can therefore seek to join himself in the proceedings in order to defend them, but should do so before the making of the final possession order.

5.5.23 RSC Ord 113 avoids difficulties over service of proceedings by providing that where the names of the occupiers of the land are unknown all that is necessary to effect good service is to affix a copy of the summons and affidavit in a transparent envelope addressed to 'the occupiers' to the main door or conspicuous part of the premises. If necessary, and as is commonly done where gypsies or travellers are being served, the proceedings and supporting affidavit can be affixed in the same manner to stakes in the ground situated in conspicuous parts of the occupied land. For the most part, process servers well versed in the court rules should be employed to effect service. An affidavit of service must be prepared, sworn and filed at court on time for the hearing.

5.5.24 If the names of any of those in occupation are known then it is necessary to effect service personally, by leaving a copy at the premises or otherwise as the court may direct. Again, it is usual to employ process servers to effect service. In every case an affidavit of service should be sworn as soon as possible after service has been effected verifying the method of service employed. This must be available for the hearing.

5.5.25 The speed with which service can be effected will determine the date of the hearing. Five clear working days must be given between service and the hearing (not counting either day of service or the hearing) if the premises are residential. Two clear working days must be given in all other circumstances. Time for service must be thought about when the summons is issued. If sufficient time is not given, an order for possession will not be made.

5.5.26 The hearing is before a Master in Chambers. The original summons, affidavit in support and affidavit of service must be before him together with the plaintiff's proof of title (ie the title deeds). The practice is to hand the affidavit of service to the Master at the hearing, the principal affidavit having already been filed.

5.5.27 Once the proceedings have been issued and served it is not uncommon to find that the squatters vacate the land or premises without further action and it is rare for such proceedings to be defended. However, where there has been long term trespass the defendants may attend court to claim some kind of licence or title. Hence proceedings should be commenced as soon after the trespassers are found as is possible.

5.5.28 If the trespassers do not vacate voluntarily, a writ of possession has to be issued (see precedent at Appendix A5.17) and executed by the High Court

Sheriff's officer. His fees relate to the rateable value of premises plus any disbursements (eg the renting of towing equipment). In consequence, fees can be high. Leave of the court will be required to issue a writ of possession if this is not issued within three months of the order. This is to discourage the use of Ord 113 otherwise than in cases of emergency.

Proceedings under CCR Ord 24 – introductory

5.5.29   In the County Court, CCR Ord 24 relates to two separate types of proceedings. The first (Part I) is very similar to RSC Ord 113 in the High Court except for the matters set out below. The second (Part II) was introduced as a result of ss 75 and 76 of the Criminal Justice and Public Order Act 1994.

CCR Ord 24, Part I

5.5.30   Part I is very similar to RSC Ord 113 in the High Court. It relates to the obtaining of a summary possession order against any person in possession of land or premises without the licence or consent of the person legally entitled to possession but is not applicable to persons holding over after the termination of a tenancy.
5.5.31   Details of the procedure are set out in the order itself (see CCR Ord 24). It is commenced by originating application (see form at Appendix A5.18) on the payment of the appropriate court fee supported by an affidavit (see precedent at Appendix A5.15).
5.5.32   Service is also as for proceedings under RSC Ord 113 (see 5.5.18) and, similarly an affidavit of service is necessary. However, a defendant actually named may also be served by an officer of the court by either leaving the papers at or sending them to the premises. The time limits are also as for RSC Ord 113 (see 5.5.25).
5.5.33   A warrant of possession to enforce the order obtained may be issued in the County Court at any time after the making of the order but leave of the court is required if the warrant is not issued within three months of the order. The warrant is executed by the County Court bailiff for a fixed fee. Proceedings under CCR Ord 24 Part I are usually cheaper than those commenced under RSC Ord 113 in the High Court. However, it is usually quicker to issue proceedings in the High Court and easier to obtain an early hearing date.

CCR Ord 24, Part II (interim possession orders)

5.5.34   The Criminal Justice and Public Order Act 1994 came into force in August 1995, but has been little used in relation to this procedure. It provides an alternative remedy to the summary procedures available under RSC Ord 113 in the High Court and CCR Ord 24 Part I in the County Court. However, it is unlikely to be faster than the established procedure.
5.5.35   The procedure is set out in CCR Ord 24, Part II which allows the making of interim and final orders on separate hearings. There is the risk of a

breach of the criminal law pursuant to ss 75 and 76 of the 1994 Act by either the applicant or respondent in the procedure. The perceived benefit in this more cumbersome and onerous procedure is that the squatter commits a criminal offence if the premises are not vacated within 24 hours of the order being made and that he commits a criminal offence thereafter if he re-enters within 12 months of the order.

5.5.36 The applicant files at court an originating application (as for a Part I application), a fee, and an affidavit in support and a notice of application. The date for hearing the interim application is fixed, being not less than three days after the date of issue.

5.5.37 Proceedings, once issued, must be served within twenty-four hours. At the first hearing the court may make an interim possession order on the giving of undertakings by the applicant. If such an order is made, the court will then fix a date for the final hearing, which will be not less than seven days after the hearing of the interim application. The interim order must be served within 48 hours of finalising, and once served the respondent must vacate the premises within 24 hours. Failure to obey an interim order is a criminal offence. Once the respondent vacates, he is entitled to apply to have the interim order set aside. At the final hearing, an order for possession may be made or dismissed or the court may continue the interim order.

5.5.38 The new procedure is not as widely available a remedy as the procedure under RSC Ord 113 or CCR Ord 24 Part I since it has a number of qualifications attached to its use:

(1) The applicant must have an immediate right to possession and must have held that right throughout the period of unlawful occupation. (Hence, the remedy is not available to a purchaser who completes a purchase subject to such occupation);

(2) The trespasser must have entered on to and remained on the land without consent and not entered with consent even if that consent is later terminated;

(3) Proceedings must be commenced within 28 days of the date on which the applicant knew, or ought reasonably to have known, of the unlawful occupation.

5.5.39 Given the capacity of the new procedure to make a criminal of the trespasser, the court is also likely to require one or more of a number of undertakings from the applicant (identified in the rules) on the grant of an interim order. Such undertakings, if required, will need to be given on the hearing of the application for an interim possession order and are:

(1) To reinstate the occupier or pay damages if it is subsequently established that the occupier had a right to be in occupation. (Such an undertaking may need to be supported by accounts demonstrating the ability to pay any damages suffered);

(2) Not to damage the premises or grant any right of occupation to any third party pending final determination of the matter, and not to dispose of or damage the occupier's possessions. (Such an undertaking may cause difficulties unless an inventory of the occupier's goods has been

prepared and there is evidence of the state of the premises at the date of the making of the interim order and immediately thereafter.)

5.5.40 Any false or misleading statement in the application or at the hearing can result in the maker being found guilty of a criminal offence and subject to the following penalties: on summary conviction to a fine not exceeding the statutory maximum and/or six months' imprisonment or on indictment to an unlimited fine and/or two years' imprisonment.

Checklist – private remedies

- Damages
  - to be assessed according to the value to the plaintiff or defendant as appropriate
  - prospective economic loss should be claimed
  - damages against a tenant will be assessed according to the open market value. Watch for claims for double value/double rent as appropriate.
- Injunction (see chapter 16).
- Contribution
  - damages may be reduced under the Law Reform (Contributory Negligence) Act 1945.
- Self help
  - the courts do not encourage a plaintiff to eject a trespasser
  - Parliament has extended protection from the effects of the Criminal Law Act 1977 to displaced residential occupiers and protected intending occupiers
  - landowners must beware the statutory restrictions on re-taking possession of premises (especially the Protection from Eviction Act 1977, the Criminal Law Act 1977 and ss 27 and 28 of the Housing Act 1988)
  - it is a criminal offence under s 7 of the Criminal Law Act 1977 for a trespasser to remain on residential premises after being asked to leave by certain owners, and the assistance of the police (who may arrest without a warrant) should be invoked.
- Emergency procedures in the civil courts
  - speedy remedies to remove trespassers exist in the High Court under RSC Ord 113 and in the County Court under CCR Ord 24 (Part I). CCR Ord 24 (Part II) also provides an emergency procedure which should be considered.

5.6 Police and local authority powers

5.6.1 The Criminal Justice and Public Order Act 1994 sets out at Part V ('Public Order: Collective Trespass or Nuisance on Land') a variety of powers available to the police or local authorities intended to allow speedy methods of dealing with individuals thought to pose a nuisance to others by their activities carried out on land. The characteristic framework of the sections available under this part of the Act is a direction, failure to comply with which constitutes a criminal offence.

Police powers to remove trespassers on land – Sections 61 and 62, Criminal Justice and Public Order Act 1994

5.6.2 By s 61, if the senior police officer present at the scene reasonably believes that two or more persons are trespassing on land with the intention of residing there, the officer may direct them to leave and remove any vehicles or other property they have with them on the land if the following criteria are satisfied, namely that the trespassers:

(1) have been asked to leave by or on behalf of the lawful occupier; and
(2) have caused damage to the land or property on the land; or
(3) have used threatening, abusive or insulting words or behaviour towards the occupier (or a member of his family or employee or agent); or
(4) have six or more vehicles (including caravans) on the land.

Once a direction is given a police constable may seize and remove any vehicle if he suspects the direction will not be complied with (s 62).

5.6.3 A person failing to comply with a police direction as above or complying but returning to the land as a trespasser within three months is guilty of an offence and is liable to a term of imprisonment not exceeding three months or a fine (s 61(4)).

5.6.4 These sections relate to open land but can include land on which agricultural buildings (as defined by the Local Government Finance Act 1988) or scheduled monuments (as defined by the Ancient Monuments and Archaeological Areas Act 1979) are situated (s 61(9)).

5.6.5 In practice the police will often refuse to become involved in what they consider to be civil trespass, leaving the lawful occupier or owner of the land to pursue their remedies under RSC Ord 113 in the High Court or CCR Ord 24 in the County Court. It is, however, always worthwhile calling the local police if the situation falls within s 61 of the 1994 Act.

Police powers in relation to raves – ss 63–66 of the Criminal Justice and Public Order Act 1994

5.6.6 Whilst the Criminal Justice and Public Order Act 1994 gives no definition within the body of the Act of 'a rave' (the word is only used in a heading and side note), s 63 states that the section applies to:

> a gathering on land in the open air of 100 or more persons (whether or not trespassers) at which amplified music is played during the night (with or without intermissions) and is such as, by reason of its loudness and duration and the time at which it is played, is likely to cause serious distress to the inhabitants of the locality.

'Music' is defined as including:

> sounds wholly or predominantly characterised by the emission of a succession of repetitive beats.

The section does *not* apply to a gathering licensed by an entertainment licence (ie granted by a local authority pursuant to the London Government Act 1963, Private Places of Entertainment (Licensing) Act 1967, or Local Government (Miscellaneous Provisions) Act 1982).

5.6.7 As can be seen from the above definition, the Act only applies to unlicensed events held on land in the open air (which such phrase includes 'a place partly open to the air' (s 63(10)). Trespass itself is not a necessary ingredient.

5.6.8 Power to stop a 'rave', even before it begins, is vested in the police. Hence, any individual suffering from distress because of such an event should call upon their local police station. Further, if a police officer of at least the rank of superintendent believes that two or more persons are making preparations for the holding of such a gathering, or ten or more are waiting for a rave to commence, he may give a direction that those persons and any other persons who come to prepare or wait to attend such a gathering to leave the land and remove any vehicles or other property which they have with them (s 63(2)). Failure by a person to comply with such a direction commits an offence and is liable to imprisonment for a term not exceeding three months or a fine (s 63(6)). A police constable in uniform (as opposed to a superintendent) may stop a person who he reasonably believes is on his way to a rave and direct him not to proceed to it (s 65). Failure to comply is an offence and a convicted offender is liable to a fine (s 65(4)). Finally, the police may seize sound equipment and/or vehicle from any person who fails to comply with a direction as above, and the courts can subsequently forfeit these items (ss 62, 64 and 66). 'Vehicle' can mean a caravan (s 61(9)).

5.6.9 If such a gathering is licensed by the local authority or is at an indoor venue, the person disturbed by the gathering will very often still contact the police. They can also contact the environmental health department at their local authority (if an officer is available at the time of the disturbance) since a breach of the entertainment licence may have occurred. It should also be remembered that a fire certificate is almost certainly required for an indoor venue together with a liquor licence if alcohol is being sold. Breach of any of these licences may enable the police or local authorities to enter the premises, with or without a warrant.

Police powers and disruptive trespassers – ss 68–69 of the Criminal Justice and Public Order Act 1994

5.6.10 Aggravated trespass is a criminal offence which was introduced primarily to deter anti-hunt saboteurs and animal rights supporters. It is set out under s 68 of the Criminal Justice and Public Order Act 1994 and has effectively two components:

(1) trespass upon land in the open air; and

(2) intimidatory, obstructive or disruptive acts intended to deter partici-
pants from engaging in lawful activities on the same or neighbouring
land.

'Land' is defined so that it does not include a highway or road (s 68(5)) and
activities intended to be protected are 'lawful' so long as the persons undertaking it are themselves not committing an offence or trespassing (s 68(2)).

5.6.11 If the senior police officer present at the scene reasonably believes
either

(1) that a person is committing, has committed or intends to commit the
offence of aggravated trespass, or

(2) that two or more persons are trespassing on land in the open air with the
purpose of committing aggravated trespass, he may direct them to
leave the land (s 69(1)).

5.6.12 A person guilty of aggravated trespass is liable to imprisonment for a
term not exceeding three months or a fine not exceeding level 4 on the standard
scale or both (s 68(3)). A person failing to comply with a police direction to
leave the land is liable to the same (s 69(3)).

Trespassory assemblies – ss 70–71 of the Criminal Justice and Public Order Act 1994

5.6.13 Sections 70 and 71 of the 1994 Act insert into Part II of the Public
Order Act 1986 (that part dealing with processions and assemblies) a power
to prohibit trespassory assemblies and associated offences. The concept of a
'trespassory assembly' is new and was intended to prevent such activities as
mass gatherings at Stonehenge.

5.6.14 The power to make a prohibitory order lies with the local authority at
the request of the chief officer of police. The order prohibits, for a specific
period not exceeding four days, the holding of all trespassory assemblies in the
district or any part of it, not exceeding a circular area of five miles radius. The
chief officer of police must be reasonably satisfied of the following, namely
that:

(1) An assembly (of 20 or more persons) is intended or likely to be held on
land in the open air;

(2) where the public has no right or a limited right of access;

(3) without the permission of the occupier (ie the person entitled to possession) or in a way which exceeds any permission;

(4) which may result in serious disruption to the life of the community or
significant damage to land, building or monument of historical, archi-
tectural, archaeological or scientific importance.

5.6.15 If the assembly is held in the City of London or the Metropolitan
Police district, the application can be made by the Commissioner with the
consent of the Secretary of State (s 14(A)(4) of the 1986 Act).

5.6.16 A person who organises or takes part in or incites another to take
part in an assembly which he knows to be prohibited is guilty of an
offence (s 14(B)). The offence of organising an assembly or of taking part is

punishable by a term of imprisonment for a term not exceeding three months or a fine not exceeding level 4 on the standard scale or both. The offence of incitement is punishable by a fine.

5.6.17 Finally, a uniformed police constable can stop a person he reasonably believes is on his way to a prevented assembly and direct him not to proceed (s 14C(1)). Anyone not obeying such a direction may be liable to a fine not exceeding level 3 on the standard scale (s 14C(5)).

Local authority powers to remove unauthorised campers – ss 77, 78 and 79 of the Criminal Justice and Public Order Act 1994

5.6.18 If persons are residing in a vehicle (including a caravan) on any open land forming part of a highway, or which is unoccupied or on occupied land without the consent of the occupier, the local authority may direct those persons to leave the land and remove the vehicles or other property owned by them (s 77(1)).

5.6.19 Generally notice of the direction must be served on the offenders, although they need not be named (s 77(2)). However, it a person is named but it is impracticable to serve a document on them, it may be fixed in a prominent place to their vehicle (s 79(2)). If the person is unnamed, the document can be fixed in a prominent place to every vehicle on the land in question (s 79(2)). In any case, the local authority shall take reasonable steps to display a copy of any relevant document on the land in question (as well as on the vehicles) in a manner designed to ensure it is likely to be seen by persons camping on the land (s 79(3)). Failure by the occupiers to comply with a notice or re-entry on the same land within three months after complying may lead to a fine (s 77(3)).

5.6.20 Further the local authority may apply to a magistrates' court for authority to take reasonable steps necessary to ensure that a direction is complied with (s 78(1), (2)). In such a case the authority's officers may, on obtaining the court's authority, enter the land and remove any vehicles on the land (s 78(2)(b)). Obstruction of an officer in executing this authority may lead to a further fine (s 78(4)).

5.6.21 It should be noted that the local authority should look at the personal circumstances of the persons residing in a vehicle *before* and not after implementing its powers under these sections of the 1994 Act (*R v Wolverhampton Metropolitan Borough Council ex parte Dunne* (1997) *The Times*, 2 January). Further, it must balance the interests of both local people and travellers (*R v Lincolnshire County Council ex parte Atkinson* [1997] JPL 65).

Checklist – police and local authority powers

- Remedies available under Part V, Criminal Justice and Public Order Act 1994:
  — the police have powers to direct and remove trespassers in certain circumstances (s 61)
  — the police have various powers in relation to 'raves' (ss 63–66)

— the police have powers to deal with animal rights activists, hunt saboteurs and others as 'disruptive trespassers' (ss 68, 69)
— the police have powers to prevent gatherings which may be disruptive or held at ancient monuments as 'trespassory assemblies' (Public Order Act 1986 (as amended by ss 70, 71)) ·
— local authorities have powers in relation to unauthorised campers.

5.7 Adverse possession

The nature of adverse possession

5.7.1 Long possession of land by a person with no formal ownership of it, or the licence of the person entitled to possession to so occupy the land, coupled with the failure of the true owner to secure the eviction of the trespasser, can lead to the extinguishment of the true owner's title and the trespasser's claim of adverse possession can be established.

5.7.2 Adverse possession effectively extinguishes the former title of the freehold ownership in that the former owner is unable to enforce it, and gives rise to a new title of possessory title. It is therefore different from a long user of land which can generate the prescriptive acquisition of easements, for in that case the freehold title remains vested in the original owner but is made subject to the prescriptive rights. What amounts to adverse possession is entirely a matter of fact depending on all the circumstances. There must be some exclusion of the person entitled to possession and an intention to obtain possession of the land by the claimant.

The periods of limitation

5.7.3 Section 15(1) of the Limitation Act 1980 states that:

> no action shall be brought by any person to recover any land after the expiration of twelve years from the date on which the right of action accrued to him.

The 'date on which the right of action accrued' is the date upon which the owner was dispossessed by the trespasser. Ordinarily the limitation period is 12 years. It is 30 years in respect of actions brought by the Crown and 60 years in respect of the foreshore.

Dispossession by a series of trespassers

5.7.4 It should be noted that there may be a series of trespassers. Hence A may dispossess the true owner for a period of time and then pass his rights to B. Provided both A's and B's occupation amount to a *continuous* period of occupation exceeding 12 years, the true owner can no longer enforce his title (s 15(1) Limitation Act 1980; *Mount Carmel Investments Ltd v Peter Thurlow Ltd* [1988] 1 WLR 1078).

Defeating a claim to adverse possession

5.7.5 On a more practical level, the potential adverse possessor has to prove occupation of the land for a period of 12 years or more and the true owner must be ready to show that he has issued proceedings during that period to recover possession or that the possessor was in occupation with his licence or consent (*Mount Carmel Investments Ltd v Peter Thurlow Ltd* [1988] 1 WLR 1078). A true owner cannot be said to have abandoned land when he has persistently asserted his right to re-enter (*Milton v Proctor* (1989) NSW ConvR 450).

The need for evidence

5.7.6 In the absence of persuasive evidence to the contrary, the owner of the paper title is deemed to remain in possession (see for instance *Morrice v Evans* (1989) *The Times*, 27 February). It is therefore imperative for any party involved in a potential adverse possession claim to keep any evidence of either his occupation or his claim to possession.

The relevance of the future plans of the owner

5.7.7 It has been suggested that a true owner's conduct in relation to future plans for the land is relevant and that even if the undisturbed acts of an intruder exceed 12 years, if the true owner has plans to use undeveloped land no adverse possession can be claimed (see *Leigh v Jack* (1879) 5 Ex D 264). However, this was disapproved by the Court of Appeal in *Buckinghamshire CC v Moran* [1990] Ch 623. Slade LJ (at 639) stated:

> on any footing, it must, in my judgment, be too broad a proposition to suggest that an owner who retains a piece of land with a view to its utilisation for a specific purpose in the future can never be treated as dispossessed, however firm and obvious the intention to dispossess, and however drastic the acts of dispossession of the person seeking to dispossess him may be.

In that case a local authority had acquired land some 30 years previously and left it undeveloped. It had the intention of using it for a road diversion in the future. The neighbouring landowner enclosed it and maintained the plot as part of his garden and his successor in title installed a lock and chain rendering the plot accessible from his garden only. The Court of Appeal held that by enclosing the plot and effectively annexing it to the neighbour's property this assertion of 'complete and exclusive physical control' was sufficient to found a plea of adverse possession.

Tenants and their landlords

5.7.8 It must be noted that no tenant can claim adverse possession as against his landlord during the term of his tenancy (see Limitation Act 1980, s 15(1)).

Adverse possession by a trespasser in respect of land let on a lease

5.7.9 For a trespasser to obtain adverse possession of land let on a lease he must prove that for the requisite period of time (see above) he possessed the land against both the landlord and the tenant. In such an instance, the date upon which the owner is dispossessed is the date when the adverse possessor entered the land not as against the leasehold owner but as against the freehold owner. In such a case it will be the date when the lease expires which determines when time begins to run (Limitation Act 1980, Sched 1 para 4).

5.7.10 The owner of a leasehold interest in adverse possession of adjoining land is presumed to acquire any title for the benefit of his freeholder, rather than for himself. Any such rights acquired will then enure for the benefit of the landlord at the end of the term.

The rights of an adverse possessor

5.7.11 It will of course be appreciated that the person claiming adverse possession will have an evidential burden to prove his title. If the land is unregistered, the Limitation Act 1980 does not affect a conveyance. All it does is prevent the true owner showing a better title. If the land is registered, s 75(1) of the Land Registration Act 1925 states that the estate of the extinguished registered proprietor shall be 'deemed to be held by the proprietor for the time being in trust for the person who, by virtue of the [Limitation] Acts, has acquired title against any proprietor'. Subsequently the adverse possessor can apply for registration in his own name (s 75(2) of the 1925 Act) and in the meantime, his rights are an 'overriding interest' (s 70(1)(f) of the 1925 Act).

An adverse possessor takes those equitable interests which bind the land

5.7.12 Because there is no transfer or assignment of title, the adverse possessor cannot be said to be a *bona fide* purchaser without notice and hence takes the land subject to such equitable interests as may bind the land (whether they are registered or protected by the owner of those interests or not) (see for instance *In re Nisbet and Potts' Contract* [1906] 1 Ch 386).

Checklist – adverse possession

- The nature of adverse possession
  - exclusion of the person entitled to possession of the land and an intention by the claimant to possess the land, must be demonstrated
  - where the true owner's title has been extinguished after long possession of land without permission by the possessor, the possessor will obtain a possessory title
  - the true owner will be unable to enforce his title.

- Making and resisting claims for adverse possession
  - the relevant periods of limitation are 12 years, 30 years (as against the Crown) and 60 years (in respect of the foreshore)
  - dispossession may take place after possession by a series of trespassers
  - the true owner must demonstrate that he has taken proceedings during the limitation period to recover possession, or that the possessor was in possession with either licence or consent
  - there is a presumption in favour of the owner with paper title
  - evidence as to the future plans of the owner is irrelevant
  - a tenant cannot claim adverse possession as against his landlord during the term
  - a trespasser must be able to claim adverse possession against both the freeholder and the leaseholder where premises are let on a lease.
- The position of the adverse possessor
  - where land is unregistered, the Limitation Act does not affect title set out in a conveyance
  - in the case of registered land, an adverse possessor can apply for registration and has the rights of an overriding interest in the intervening period
  - an adverse possessor takes the land subject to such equitable interests as may bind the land.

5.8 Occupiers' duties to trespassers on land

The common duty of care

5.8.1 Occupiers owe a duty of care to all visitors to their premises but may extend, modify and, in some cases, exclude those duties (Occupiers' Liability Act, 1957). Trespassers are not, however, classed as 'visitors' and with regard to an occupier's duties to trespassers, it is necessary to consult the Occupiers' Liability Act 1984, which replaces the common law rules.

5.8.2 The duties under the 1984 Act are owed by the *occupier* of the land, that is, the person in whom occupation is vested. Hence, if a landlord leases premises to a tenant, it is the tenant and not the landlord who is entitled to occupation of those premises. However, if the landlord leases part of a building but retains other parts, he retains possession of the parts retained (*Wheat v E Lacon & Co Ltd* [1966] AC 552).

5.8.3 By s 1(3) of the 1984 Act, an occupier owes a duty to a trespasser in respect of any danger of sustaining some injury on the premises due to the state of the premises or to things done or not done upon them if:

(1) the occupier knows of, or has reasonable grounds to know of, the danger;

(2) the occupier knows, or has reasonable grounds to know, that the trespasser is in the vicinity or may come into the vicinity of the danger; and

(3) the risk is one which, in all the circumstances, the occupier may be expected to offer the trespasser some protection.

5.8.4 The duty will have been satisfied if the occupier has taken reasonable steps to warn of the danger or to discourage persons from incurring the risk (s 1(5)). Further, no duty is owed if the trespasser willingly accepted the risk (s 1(6)) or is using a highway (s 1(7)).

Checklist – occupiers' duties to trespassers

- The Occupiers' Liability Act 1984
  - the occupier owes a duty to trespassers under the 1984 Act
  - the duty arises where the occupier (i) knows of the danger (or has reasonable grounds for such knowledge), (ii) knows that a trespasser may venture into the vicinity (or has reasonable grounds for such knowledge) and (iii) the risk is one for which the occupier should have offered the trespasser some protection
  - the effect of adverse possession is that the freehold owner cannot enforce his title and gives rise to possessory title by the trespasser
  - a landlord is unlikely to be the occupier of premises let under a lease
  - more than one person may be an occupier
  - if reasonable steps have been taken to warn the trespasser, the duty will have been satisfied.

Chapter 6

Boundaries

6.1 Overview

6.1.1 Boundary disputes between neighbours usually start with a fairly minor incident, such as the movement of a fence, the trimming back of a hedge or the digging of footings for a house extension. Unless care is taken to defuse the situation matters can quickly escalate into one involving a high degree of hostility and large legal bills.

6.1.2 The aim of this chapter is to describe how such disputes can be avoided or at least contained to sensible proportions. Some of the more commonly encountered boundary problems will also be considered, together with the physical features involved. In many cases the traditional practice in relation to these physical features has been elevated into a legal presumption (for instance that an artificial boundary structure belongs to the owner of the land on which it exists). It must be remembered, however, that all such presumptions are rebuttable, so that care must be taken that all the relevant evidence is considered and produced. A practical approach has been adopted throughout in order to assist the practitioner determine what evidence is necessary.

6.1.3 This chapter is arranged to deal with the following topics:

(1) New boundaries
(2) Fences
(3) Walls
(4) Hedges
(5) Ditches
(6) Trees
(7) Highways
(8) Railways
(9) The seashore
(10) Lakes and rivers
(11) Evidence establishing boundaries (deeds and plans, the Land Registry, photographs).

6.2 New boundaries

6.2.1 The creation of new boundaries (usually where a new housing develop-ment is being built) affords a golden opportunity to ensure that future boundary disputes do not erupt. There are two good methods of ensuring that the bounda-ries can easily be re-established in the future.

6.2.2 The first method is to relate every change of direction by measurement to the house itself. It is very unlikely that a house will disappear or move, although it may be extended, and so the house can be used as a reference for all measurements to the boundary. Even if the house is extended at some future date, it will be a simple matter to plot or calculate that extension if the original 'first' house is measured around its perimeter. It is only necessary to fix the changes of direction of the boundary, but some redundant measurements should be included for gross-error check purposes.

6.2.3 The second method is to co-ordinate the changes of direction of each boundary on the development site survey grid system carried out usually by EDM (Electronic Distance Measurement). This is the method by which all houses, roads and sewers fit together like a jigsaw. The same grid can be used to record the co-ordinates ('Eastings' and 'Northings') of the boundary changes of direction. This can be related to the OS National Grid, but that can raise problems with scale-factor and earth-curvature. A local grid for each development should suffice. The 'outside world' boundary (ie the boundary of the whole development with surrounding existing properties) will still be sub-ject to the General Boundaries Rule, whilst internally the co-ordinates of each property's boundary can be listed on a schedule in the deeds.

6.2.4 In essence this second method is very similar to the cadastral system used in most European countries whereby property boundaries are not only recorded in co-ordinate format but also on the ground by a boundary-marker stone. Her Majesty's Land Registry (HMLR) have already been involved in a cadastral-type experiment, and this system of recording property boundaries by co-ordinates will no doubt increase in the future.

A photographic log book

6.2.5 When moving into a property it is worthwhile taking photographs of all the boundary features, preferably from an upstairs window (for a typical suburban house), and then keep the photographs safely stored in a dated enve-lope. A similar set of photographs should be taken once a year, from the same viewpoint, preferably when there are no leaves on the trees (February is a good month for this). If any alterations are carried out to or near the boundary then a supplemental set of photographs should be taken.

6.2.6 In essence this means that a log-book of the property is being compiled and it will mean that there will be a clear record of what used to exist should a dispute develop. Many court cases take much longer than they should because the parties have difficulty explaining what the boundary features used to look like before the alterations occurred. A regular log of photographs will remove such doubts. It goes without saying that a certain amount of tact is required when taking the photographs because the mere act of photographing the boundary when the neighbours are in their garden may provoke an unnecessary incident.

Initial communication

6.2.7 Another good precaution when erecting a new fence, building wall or planting a hedge is to talk it through with the owner of the neighbouring property. Whilst, within reason and subject to planning regulations, anyone can construct what structure they like on their own property, the most common complaint from those who dispute such structures is 'why didn't they talk it over with us first?'

Checklist – precautions to protect the boundary

- On creation of a new boundary:
  — refer all changes to the house and/or
  — co-ordinate changes with the grid.
- Other precautions:
  — prepare a photographic log of the premises
  — consult with the neighbours.

6.3 Fences

Different types of fencing

6.3.1 There are many types of fence which are erected as boundary features between properties. Some of the most common are:
  (1) Larch-Lap
  (2) Close-Boarded
  (3) Post-and-Rail
  (4) Post-and-Wire
  (5) Iron Railings
  (6) Palisade
  (7) Post-and-Barbed-Wire
  (8) Post-and-Chain-Link.

Erecting new fences – the presumption of ownership

6.3.2 With the exception of Larch-Lap (considered at 6.3.4 below), all the types of fencing listed above have a common and distinctive method of erection which involves the relationship of the posts to the fence itself and give rise to a presumption of ownership by custom. The increase in DIY fencing means that this presumption may well die out because individual householders, who purchase and erect the fencing material themselves are largely unaware of it.

However, the presumption remains and evidence would be needed to rebut it. When erecting a new fence care should be taken to follow the customary practice by ensuring that it sits completely on the owner's land and not cross the boundary. To avoid possible conflict the post holes (with their concrete mix if used) should also not cross the boundary. There is a lot to be said for giving up a few centimetres of land in the process rather than risking a boundary dispute in future.

6.3.3 In erecting a fence the usual practice is to site the posts on the fence-owner's land and the fencing on the far side of those posts, butting up to the boundary itself. The most obvious example of this is where a close-boarded fence has the upright posts and the arris rails on the owner's side, and then the vertical fencing boards nailed to the other side. The face of the vertical boards should mark the boundary (see Diagram A below). This is a strange custom because it means that any repairs to the fences have to be effected from the neighbour's land and not from the fence-owner's side but it remains the normal way to erect a fence.

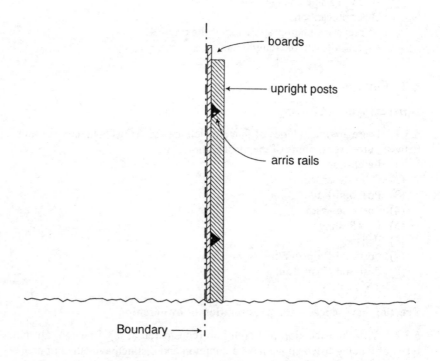

Diagram A

Larch-Lap fences

6.3.4 Increasingly popular, because of the cheapness of the materials, is the Larch-Lap fence. This involves Larch-Lap panels being nailed to vertical wooden posts or slid between vertical (grooved) concrete posts. This method of erection means that it is not possible to deduce ownership from the way in which the panels are attached to the posts (ie the view from one side is the same as from the other). However, even with Larch-Lap fences there is a cosmetic difference. The lapping itself involves horizontal strips being laid 'lapped' over the strip below. The side where the top-strip overlap is visible (ie top-strip over low strip) should face away from the fence-owner (see Diagram B below).

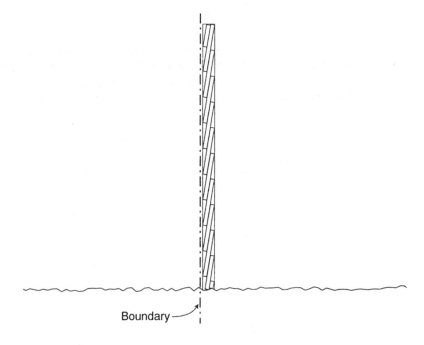

Boundary

Diagram B

Concrete posts

6.3.5 If advising on the erection of fences it should be stressed that concrete posts, although more expensive, tend to last much longer than wooden ones and therefore are less likely to need to be replaced. Every time a fence is replaced the danger of a boundary-dispute incident increases and so a long-life concrete post fence will cut down that likelihood.

Party fences and the boundary line

6.3.6 In urban areas, party fences may be encountered. Theoretically the boundary line should run through the centre of such a fence and the owner on each side of it should be jointly responsible for its maintenance. (See chapter 7 in relation to party walls and structures.)

Presumption of ownership of a fenced enclosure adjoining waste land

6.3.7 A fenced enclosure adjoining waste land gives rise to a presumption that the fence belongs to the owner of the enclosure (*White v Taylor (No 2)* [1969] 1 Ch 160).

T-marks

6.3.8 If a property has dilapidated fences and a property owner is unsure as to who is responsible for the repair and replacement of those fences, then a clue may be found in the deeds where T-marks are shown on the deed-plan (see Diagram C below). The use of T-marks on plans is standard conveyancing

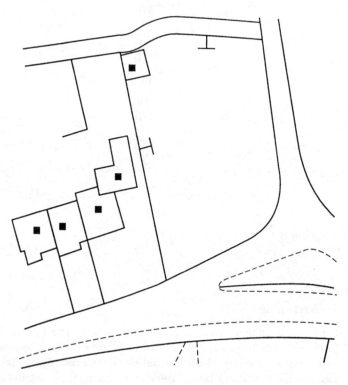

Diagram C

practice. If the T-mark (a capital letter T) is on the inside of any of the boundary lines, then the owner of the property within which those T-marks are situated will normally be responsible for the maintenance of the fences against
those lines. However, care must be taken to read the wording of the deeds
because if the text of the deeds does not mention the T-marks and the plan's
status is for identification only then the T-marks may have little relevance.

The obligation to fence

6.3.9   Whilst there is no general rule obliging a person to erect a fence around
his property, even where it borders a highway, there are situations in which
such a duty does arise. Such a duty exists:
   (1)   Pursuant to a contract, for instance, if the landowner has covenanted to
         do so in a conveyance of part of his property. Being a positive covenant
         (as opposed to a restrictive covenant) the burden does not generally
         pass with the land (*Jones v Price* [1965] 2 QB 618).
   (2)   Pursuant to a lease if either the landlord or tenant has covenanted with
         the other to erect or maintain a fence.
   (3)   On the part of an owner of animals at common law in order to fence
         them in (see 9.5.3). However, if animals are grazing upon common
         land, or waste of the manor, the obligation to fence becomes that of the
         landowner bordering the common land (*Egerton v Harding* [1975] QB
         62).
   (4)   Where there is some artificial structure or excavation on the land which
         could be a nuisance because of its close proximity to the highway.
         (This rule does not relate to a natural feature such as a river (*Attorney-
         General v Roe* [1915] 1 Ch 235).)
   (5)   By statutory provision, for example:
         (a)   The owner of an abandoned mine or one not worked for 12 months
               must provide a device to prevent a person falling down the shaft
               (ss 151 and 181 of the Mines and Quarries Act 1954);
         (b)   The owner of a quarry must provide an adequate, efficient and prop-
               erly maintained barrier to prevent persons falling into the quarry
               (s 151 of the Mines and Quarries Act 1954, Mines and Quarries
               (Tips) Act, 1969);
         (c)   Railway land must be fenced off from adjoining land (unless the
               owner of the adjoining land has accepted compensation in lieu).
               This obligation is an indefinite one and is not affected by cessation
               of the use of the line (see 6.9.5).

Liability for dangerous fencing

6.3.10   A person who has fenced his land (whether under an obligation to do
so or not) may be liable for any damage caused to, for instance the occupiers of
adjoining land or persons lawfully using a highway if the fence is in such a
state as to constitute a danger (*Harrold v Watney* [1898] 2 QB 320).

Checklist – fencing

- Establishing ownership and the duty of maintenance:
  — does the usual presumption of ownership arise?
  — are the fence-posts on the land-owner's land?
  — does the fencing face in the customary direction?
  — is the fence a party fence?
  — where are the T-marks on the deeds?
- Determining whether there is a duty to fence:
  — is there a contractual term?
  — is there a term in the lease?
  — are animals grazed on the land?
  — is there a nuisance on the land which needs to be fenced in?
  — is there a statutory provision (see especially mines, quarries and railways)?

6.4 Walls

6.4.1 Most of the comments on fences (6.3 above) also apply to walls. It is normal practice for buttresses of walls to be an indication that the owner of the land upon which the buttress sits is also the owner of the wall quite simply because the owner of the wall would lay himself open for a claim of trespass if he built the supporting buttress on his neighbour's land. Once again, the advent and spread of DIY is causing that custom to be diluted. The law relating to party walls is set out at chapter 7.

6.4.2 Where any preservation or renewal works are required to be carried out to a wall and the owner of the adjoining land will not give his permission for entry on to his land for the purposes of effecting those works, an appropriate application may be made to the County Court (Access to Neighbouring Land Act 1992). So too the County Court has power to authorise an inspection of the wall (s 1(7) of the 1992 Act).

6.5 Hedges

Keeping modern hedges under control

6.5.1 The most frequently found feature in boundary disputes is the hedge. Traditional hedges, such as privet, present few problems, but the increase in fast growing conifer hedges has led to many boundary disputes. These disputes often arise because the owners of the conifer hedge just cannot cope with the phenomenal growth of the plants. A typical leylandii hedge will grow at 1.2 m a year. If it is kept under control and boxed it can form a very attractive all-year-round green border to a suburban garden. If it is not kept under control, such a hedge can cause mayhem for the neighbours, with its horizontal growing fronds and ever-higher crown. Leylandii hedges need to receive a major cut in July/August and constant trimming between May and October if they are to be kept in a boxed condition.

Beech hedges

6.5.2 Much less dramatic but still potentially troublesome is the beech hedge which can grow into a line of beech trees with huge trunks. Disputes may then arise about where the legal boundary lies and whether (as is often the case) the legal boundary slices through the trunks causing some of the hedge to be on each neighbouring property.

Planting new hedges

6.5.3 Ideally, new hedges should be planted at least 1.2 m inside the boundary line then they are less likely to encroach on to neighbouring land. It is also wise to keep any suburban hedge trimmed to between 2 m and 4 m in height to ensure that neighbourly relationships are not soured. However, the owner of a hedge must always remember that nature does not recognise legal boundaries. Bushes, like all plants, grow towards the light. A hedge may always encroach on neighbouring land however carefully planned.

Rural hedges

6.5.4 In rural areas there may be hedges and ditches (ditches will be described in the next section) and it is normal for a hedge and its typical width to be on one person's land.

Using Ordnance Survey maps to determine a boundary marked by a hedge

6.5.5 A clue to the typical width of a hedge is given by the Ordnance Survey (OS) because although OS maps do not show private property boundaries, they do show civil administrative boundaries such as rural parishes. Where these boundaries (shown by a dotted line) run along the side of a hedge it is usual to see a dimension from the rootline of the hedge to the civil boundary. The most common (although there are variations) is 1.2 m RH, which means 1.2 m from the rootline of the hedge on the side of the hedge where the dotted line is situated.

6.5.6 It should be remembered that the OS (and hence HMLR – see 6.12.11 below) use the centre of the rootline of hedges on their maps. This line may define the registered property but further research will be needed to discover who actually owns the hedge since the legal boundary may be 0.6 m–1.2 m (or more) on one side or other of the centre of its rootline.

Hedge width and County Court practice

6.5.7 It has been accepted in several County Courts (for instance at Bath and at Beverley) that 1.2 m is half the width of a typical rural hedge and 0.6 m is half the width of a typical suburban hedge, but these are just examples and it should not be assumed that this is a standard occurrence.

Returning clippings

6.5.8 If a neighbour's hedge is cut because its fronds overhang the boundary then, strictly speaking, the clippings should be returned to the owner of the hedge. This is a custom which is dying out because most hedge-owners do not want the clippings returned. However, it is still a nicety to make the offer to the hedge-owner.

Checklist – hedges

- Beware hedges which grow out of control, especially leylandii and beech
- Plant new hedges well within the boundary
- Beware special rules which apply to hedges and ditches in rural areas
- Check the rootline dimension on OS maps to establish ownership.
- The provisions of the Access to Neighbouring Land Act 1992 are available where access is needed to adjoining land to deal with a damaged, diseased or dangerous hedge (see s 1(4)(c) of the 1992 Act).

6.6 Ditches

6.6.1 It is rare for a new ditch to be dug in this day and age for boundary purposes. However, many years ago it was normal practice in rural areas to mark the boundary with a ditch.

The 'hedge and ditch' Presumption

6.6.2 One of the most widely known presumptions in boundary law is the hedge and ditch presumption. The origin of this presumption is an original boundary between two properties where the adjacent owners decide that one of them will mark the boundary by way of a ditch. The boundary, at that time, may be marked temporarily by a string line, a row of stakes, a line of tree cuttings, or similar. If A decided to construct a boundary it would be normal practice for him to dig the ditch on his own land, butting up to the boundary. A then tossed the soil excavated from the ditch over his shoulder and on to his own land since he could not throw it on to his neighbour's. A hedge was normally planted on top of the bank. The result was a ditch and soil-bank configuration where the bank as well as the ditch is completely on A's land. The boundary is the far side of the ditch at its top edge. (See Diagram D opposite.)

6.6.3 These hedge-and-ditch features can be seen throughout the countryside. Over the years the ditch will have become shallower and more rounded as debris accumulates in it. Sometimes the ditches are merely shallow depressions. The result will almost certainly be a T-mark at some stage being

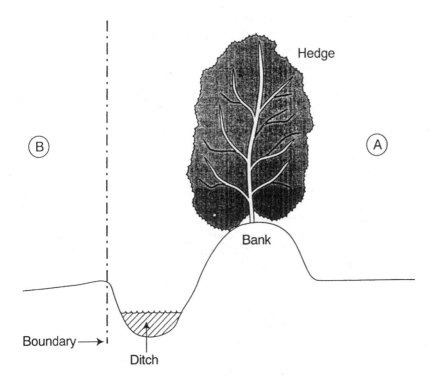

Diagram D

added to A's conveyance and pointing in towards A's land. Nevertheless, in the absence of anything to the contrary the boundary between such properties still lies at the top edge of the ditch furthest away from the hedge so that the hedge and ditch are in the same ownership.

Recognition and rebuttal of the hedge and ditch presumption

6.6.4 The ditch and hedge presumption has received judicial recognition. In *Fisher v Winch* [1939] 1 KB 666, CA, the court observed (at 669):

> [The judge] proceeded upon the footing that a presumption, which is a well known presumption, was to prevail – namely, that where there is nothing else to identify the boundary and there is a ditch and a bank, the presumption is that the person who dug the ditch dug it at the extremity of his land and threw the soil on his own land to make the bank.

However, the presumption is open to some simple rebuttals. These can broadly be classified as follows:

(1) Where the ditch was never part of an original boundary feature. For instance, a more recent ditch may have been dug alongside a hedge or fence so that it cannot have been part of the original boundary arrangement.

(2) Where the hedge and ditch configuration was never part of an original boundary. For example, a farmer may have fields throughout his farm where the internal edges are made up of hedge and ditch configurations. If the farmer then sells off a couple of fields for development purposes using the solid line on the OS map (the OS only show one solid line in a hedge and ditch feature, usually the centre of the rootline of the hedge), then the new boundary will be the centre of the rootline of the hedge (see *Alan Wibberley Building Ltd v Insley*, Law Society Gazette Reports, 26 November 1997). The hedge and ditch presumption cannot be relied upon.

(3) Where the ditch is in fact a stream. The ditch must be man-made and part of a hedge and ditch configuration for the presumption to prevail. When investigating a hedge and ditch it is important therefore to look for signs of running water (sometimes from a spring) which may rebut the presumption.

(4) Where the land is sold by reference to OS field numbers and acreages. The OS shows the centre of the rootline of the hedge in a hedge and ditch configuration and field numbers and acreages are allotted and calculated by the OS using those solid lines. Sometimes a 'tie-mark' (a small snake-like symbol) is used to show that the acreage figure extends into other neighbouring plots (see Diagram E opposite). Despite the existence of a textbook hedge and ditch configuration on the ground, if the land is conveyed by reference to the OS field numbers and acreages (usually, but not always, in the form of a First or Second Schedule in the text of the conveyance) then the land conveyed extends to the OS line and the hedge and ditch presumption is rebutted (*Rouse v Gravelworks Ltd* [1940] 1 KB 489).

(5) Where, on the true construction of the conveyance, the boundary is clearly elsewhere. The hedge and ditch presumption is:

> . . . a very convenient rule of common sense which applies in proper cases in regard to agricultural land where there is no boundary otherwise ascertainable. It also assumes what is not necessarily the fact, that at the time when the ditch was dug there was no common ownership of that piece of land, and the land on the other side of the ditch. The learned judge, thinking that the case was governed entirely by that presumption, decided in favour of the defendant, but the learned judge did not direct his mind to what in this case is the initial question – namely, what, on the true construction of the conveyances to the parties, is the boundary of their respective land. If an examination of those conveyances coupled with any evidence that is admissible for the purpose of construing them shows what the boundary is, there is no room at all for the operation of presumption

(*Fisher v Winch* [1939] 1 KB 666, 669).

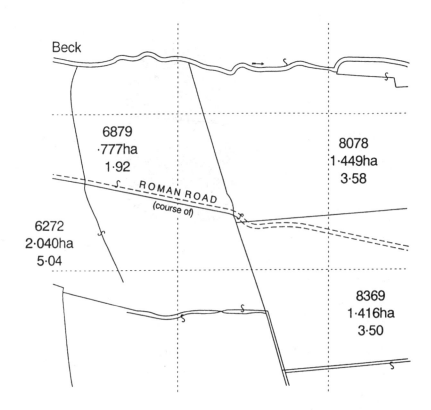

Diagram E

6.6.5 Having described the above situation relating to the conveyance, care must still be taken. For example, one farm (D) may have the land referred to in its conveyance by OS fields and numbers but the neighbouring farm (E) may have no such reference and may just refer to a plan with a red line running along the OS solid line (see Diagram F overleaf). If farm E has a hedge and ditch configuration in its favour (ie the ditch is on farm D's side of the hedge), then obviously there is a clash of theories and it will be a matter of law requiring a historical analysis of the conveyances as to where the boundary lies.

Maintenance of a hedge and ditch

6.6.6 If a hedge and ditch feature exists then the ditch owner would be well advised to clean out and maintain the ditch from time to time to make it clear who is the owner. However, cleaning and maintenance of the ditch by B, A's neighbour, will not rebut the presumption that the hedge and ditch belong to A, particularly if done without the owner's knowledge (*Henniker v Howard*

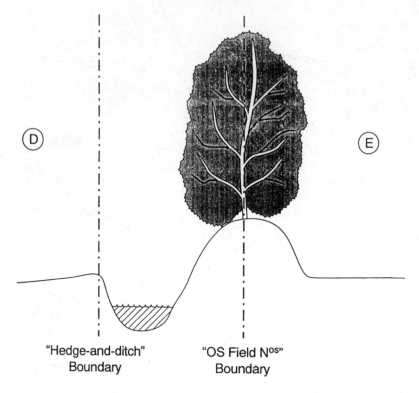

"Hedge-and-ditch"   "OS Field N^os"
Boundary   Boundary

Diagram F

(1904) 90 LT 157). Where the owner of adjacent land refuses to give his consent to a neighbour for purposes of filling in or clearing a ditch, an application may have to be made to the County Court so that the neighbour can enter on to the other's land in order to carry out the works (see s 1 of the Access to Neighbouring Land Act 1992).

Checklist – ditches

- Does the hedge and ditch presumption apply?
- Is the presumption rebuttable?
  - is the ditch a new feature?
  - was the ditch constructed for some purpose other than to mark the boundary?
  - is the ditch in fact a stream?
  - was the land conveyed by reference to OS field numbers and acreages?
  - does the conveyance suggest a different boundary?

- Is an application necessary under the Access to Neighbouring Land Act 1992 for the purposes of filling or clearing a ditch?

6.7 Trees

Introductory – proving ownership

6.7.1 Like hedges, trees tend to grow to a far greater size than the original planter ever envisaged and may breach a nearby boundary. Most boundary disputes involving trees are either about overhanging branches, the trunk itself, or problems in relation to the roots. They may also centre around who owns the tree. In such cases the two sets of neighbours generally do not remember or were not present when the original tree was planted. The trunk of the tree will have crossed the boundary and the tree will therefore be straddling the boundary line. There are few clues to help in such a situation, although a retired gardener or the oldest resident in the area may remember who planted it. Clues may also include tell-tale wire grooves in the tree trunk (sometimes with the wire still in place). If those wire marks are consistently on the same side of the trunk then it is a good indication that the original boundary fence was on that side of the tree.

Choosing and planting a tree

6.7.2 The most important point to remember on planting is not to plant a tree closer to the boundary than half the maximum diameter (at maturity) of the trunk. If this is not done the tree trunk will end up growing over the boundary line. Before purchasing the tree it is advisable to consult someone with arboricultural knowledge (most garden centres will have someone suitable on their staff) and ask what species should be planted. No-one would want a giant redwood in a small suburban garden, but even giant redwoods start off as tiny innocent-looking saplings.

6.7.3 The specification for such a tree should include its maximum height (many flowering cherry trees, for example, do not grow taller than 4 m), the probable overhanging branch spread at maturity and the probable extent of the root system at maturity. Some species are content with dry conditions and other species produce long roots which seek out water many metres from the tree itself.

Overhanging branches

6.7.4 Although an adjoining owner has the right to trim hedges and trees overhanging his land, there is no obligation on him to do so. Any branches of a tree overhanging the boundary may be cut off by the neighbour (*Lemmon v Webb* [1894] 3 Ch 1) without notice, but they must be offered back to the owner (*Mills v Brooker* [1919] 1 KB 555). A point to watch is that a tree with overhanging branches extending for several metres has a considerable weight pulling it in the direction of the neighbouring property. If the neighbour then, with great care and precision, lops off the branches right up to the boundary line, the weight will be lessened and the tree may ease back towards the owner's side. Once steady, it will then appear that the neighbour has lopped off branches on the wrong side of the boundary line. This is one very good reason for consulting with neighbours before carrying out any drastic lopping exercise.

6.7.5 An action in nuisance for an injunction and/or damages lies against the owner or occupier of the land who allows his trees to overhang the boundary and cause damage (*Smith v Giddy* [1904] 2 KB 448) provided the owner of the tree has, or ought to have had, knowledge of the existence of the problem.

Encroaching tree roots

6.7.6 Encroaching roots fall within the same principle as overhanging branches. An action in nuisance for an injunction and/or damages lies against the owner or occupier of land who allows tree roots to burrow under the boundary and cause damage (*McCombe v Read* [1955] 2 QB 429). Whilst there is a right to cut encroaching roots (*Lemmon v Webb* [1894] 3 Ch 1), cutting the roots may cause the tree to die (see 6.7.7 below). Again, there must be foreseeability (*Russell v London Borough of Barnet* (1984) 271 EG 699 – which held risk was foreseeable and action should have been taken when a tree was situated next to a house built on London clay).

Tree preservation orders

6.7.7 Trees may be the subject of a Tree Preservation Order (TPO). If any doubt exists, the local authority should be consulted before a tree is pruned or removed, to ensure that no TPO is breached. An overhanging branch may be lopped to abate a nuisance (s 198 of the Town and Country Planning Act 1990 but it was suggested in an article in the *Law Society Gazette* that there must be proof of actual damage before such action is taken (1978) 75 LSG 1000) (see also Wignall and Stanton (1995) 139 SJ 814–815). If in doubt, obtain consent. (Note the references to statutory controls at Appendix A3.8.)

Trees and the highway authority

6.7.8 A tree privately owned but bordering a highway may be pruned by the highway authority if it overhangs so as to cause a danger or obstruction to the passage of vehicles or pedestrians and the owner or occupier of the land has failed to comply with a notice to carry out the works (ss 154(1)(4) of the Highways Act 1980). The authority may also remove dead, diseased, damaged or insecurely rooted trees if similarly positioned and again, a notice to the

occupier or owner of the land has not been complied with (s 154(2) and
s 154(4)).

6.7.9 A new tree or shrub cannot be planted within 15 feet from the centre of
the made-up highway unless the planter is licensed so to do by the highway
authority (ss 141 and 142(9) of the Highways Act 1980).

6.7.10 The owner of a tree bordering a highway is liable for any nuisance it
causes of which the owner is aware (*British Road Services Ltd v Slater* [1964]
1 WLR 498). He is not exonerated because the highway authority has statutory
duties in relation to the nuisance. A highway authority can also be liable for
damage caused by encroachment because of its statutory powers (*Russell v
London Borough of Barnet* (1984) 271 EG 699).

6.7.11 Finally, a highway authority may itself plant trees in a highway maintainable at public expense (s 96(1) of the Highways Act 1980), but it will be
liable if such a tree becomes a nuisance or is injurious to the owner or occupier
of adjacent premises (s 96(6)). The authority will also be liable for a tree
growing on the highway even if the tree's planting pre-dates adoption (*Hurst
v Hampshire County Council* (1997) LGR 27, (1997) *The Times*, 26 June).
(Further details are set out at Appendix A3.4–A3.7.)

Checklist – trees

- Tree species and ownership
  - — choose a tree carefully – take advice
  - — local residents may help with ownership
  - — are wire marks to be found on the tree?
- Overhanging branches
  - — there is no common law duty to lop
  - — a neighbour may lop overhanging branches or he may take action in
    nuisance
  - — check that if lopped the tree will not have been lopped too much
    when steady.
- Tree roots
  - — actions lie in nuisance and/or trespass
  - — trimming the roots is an option but may result in damage to the tree.
- Tree preservation orders
  - — check if in doubt
  - — abatement of a nuisance is permitted.
- Trees and the highway
  - — the highway authority may lop a tree overhanging the highway or
    causing a danger (after due notice to the owner)
  - — restrictions apply on where a tree can be planted and by whom
  - — take care that the correct defendant is sued – is it the owner or the
    highway authority?
- (See also Appendix A3 – a Note on Disputes Involving Trees.)

6.8 Highways

Introductory

6.8.1 Boundary disputes involving public highways are usually about the ownership of the highway verge. In such cases the dispute is not really a boundary dispute but is an 'extent of highway' dispute. In the absence of a boundary fence or hedge the extent of the highway is only hard surface of the road unless it can be shown that neighbouring strips of land are also used as part of the highway (for instance if they are used by pedestrians or as a bridleway (*Easton v Richmond Highway Board* (1871) LR 7 QB 69). Certain customary rules or presumptions apply in determining the extent of the highway.

The Rule *usque ad medium filum viae*

6.8.2 Firstly, the *usque ad medium filum viae* rule means that the ownership of subsoil extends to the centre of the adjacent highway but that the public have a right over it for highway purposes (*St Edmundsbury and Ipswich Diocesan Board of Finance v Clark (No 2)* [1973] Ch 323).

Ownership of the subsoil passes to a successor in title

6.8.3 Secondly, it is further presumed that ownership of the subsoil passes to a successor in title without express mention (*London and North Western Railway Co v Mayor of Westminster* [1902] 1 Ch 269 – affirmed by the House of Lords [1905] AC 426) unless there is an intention to exclude the road (*Mappin Bros v Liberty & Co Ltd* [1903] 1 Ch 118). However, merely describing land as bounded by a highway, or if the highway is not shown to be within the land on the plan does not rebut the presumption (*City of London Land Tax Commissioners v Central London Railway Co* [1913] AC 364).

Hedges, fences and ditches

6.8.4 Thirdly, if a highway is bounded on each side by fences or hedges, the highway will be assumed to extend from fence to fence or hedge to hedge provided it is apparent from an inspection of the site that the hedge or fence was erected to separate the land from the highway (*AG v Beynon* [1970] Ch 1). This presumption, however, is rebuttable, for instance if it can be shown that a fence or hedge pre-dates the highway (*Minting v Ramage* [1991] EGCS 12). A ditch bordering a road is presumed to belong to the adjacent landowner (it being presumed to have been dug on his own land) unless it can be shown to have been part of the road works, for instance for drainage.

Fencing the highway

6.8.5 A frequent cause of dispute is when a farmer or rural roadside property owner grubs out an old straggly hedge and erects a fence in its place. Unless that fence runs along the centre line of the original hedge it is likely that the local authority will demand its removal. Long, expensive battles can then follow in proving where the hedge used to be.

6.8.6 If any such action of highway fencing is envisaged it is advisable to consult the local highway department before removing the old hedge or fence. Even if the local authority agrees to the replacement, it is advisable to take measurements to the existing feature (from the edge of the metalled surface) with a highway engineer present and then ensure that the engineer signs the measurement sheet. If a dispute then arises it should be a simple matter to show that no encroachment onto the highway has taken place.

Checklist – highways

- Determining the extent of the highway
  - who owns the subsoil?
  - does the rule *'usque ad medium filum viae'* apply?
  - if the highway is bounded by fences or hedges, when and why were they erected?
  - an adjacent landowner is presumed to own a bordering ditch
  - has a bordering hedge been replaced? Did the authority consent?

6.9 Railways

Introductory

6.9.1 Very few new railways are being constructed so that disputes concerning railway land usually involve property which has been owned by the railway companies for a hundred years or more.

Ownership of the subsoil

6.9.2 The subsoil under a railway will belong to the railway company quite simply because land upon which railways were built was compulsorily purchased by the relevant railway company pursuant to a Railway Act of Parliament. The railway company does not simply have a right to run track across another party's land. Compulsory purchase authorised by a private Act of Parliament is still used today for the acquiring of land on which to build a new railway.

Railway history

6.9.3 A typical history of a railway may be as follows:

Mid-1800s	Railway company obtains land through a Railways Act. The land may be for the railway route itself or for accommodation works (see 6.9.6–6.9.9 below).
Mid-late 1800s	The railway is built and fences are erected along the route, around stations, goods-yards, and along the support-slopes of bridge-approaches.
1960s	The railway line is closed and land sold off. Old railway sleepers are even more widely available and used liberally by local farmers as posts. If such posts are seen around properties it does not necessarily mean that the fence was once a railway property boundary.
1996	Railtrack becomes the owner of the railway property. Railtrack should be contacted if any neighbouring landowner has a boundary query. The company has retained many documents.

Railway plans

6.9.4   Whenever a private bill for the construction of a railway was promoted, a plan, together with book of reference, was deposited with the proper officer of the relevant county council(s) through whose land the railway passed. These may be inspected to ascertain what lands were purchased by the railway companies. Contact should initially be made with the archive department at the relevant county council. In addition, some lands were, or are, acquired for temporary purcposes.

The obligation to fence

6.9.5   The railway company has a statutory obligation to fence (s 68 of the Railways Clauses Consolidation Act 1845). The obligation is an obligation owed in perpetuity to the owners or occupiers of the adjoining land. Railway fences are usually constructed from either standard concrete post and chain-link (or strands of wire) or from old railway sleepers. However, use in particular of railway sleepers in the construction of a fence does not always indicate a boundary with railway land (see 6.9.3 above).

Accommodation works

6.9.6   A common problem in relation to railways or land once occupied by a railway relates to 'accommodation works' required by s 68 of the Railway Clauses Consolidation Act 1845. This section obliged railway companies to maintain works for the accommodation of the owners and occupiers of the lands adjoining the railway sufficient to deal with the interruptions to the use of the land and to convey water as clearly as before. An exception was made if the adjoining owner accepted compensation in lieu of the works.

6.9.7 In *Great Northern Railway v McAlister* [1897] 1 IR 605 the function of accommodation works was explained as follows:

> The owner of the adjoining lands was entitled, when the railway was made, to a convenient passage over the railway sufficient to make good, so far as possible, any interruption which the construction of the railway caused by severance in the working of his farm, including, I should say, any alteration or extension of that working which could or ought to have been contemplated by the parties when the accommodation works were made and accepted.

Difficulties have arisen over the extent of the rights to which the adjoining owner or occupier is entitled. As appears from the above quotation the entitlement extended to interruption 'which could or ought to have been contemplated by the parties'. However, in *TRH Sampson Associates Ltd v British Railways Board* [1983] 1 WLR 170, the court held that the accommodation works could be used for a purpose not in the contemplation of the parties provided that the change in use did not impose any added burden on the railway company. Much litigation has followed concerning what does or does not increase the burden, for instance over the safety of the user or additional cost of repair.

6.9.8 Other problems relate to extinguishment of the right particularly by implication. Whilst the rights will be extinguished if the adjoining landowner sells off his land on the other side of the railway and hence his need to keep rights of passage fall away, the fact that the railway is closed down and the lines are removed does not mean the reason to cross the land becomes extinct.

6.9.9 Finally, s 68 also imposed upon the railway company the obligation to fence in perpetuity as part of the accommodation works. This duty now falls upon Railtrack plc and persists even after the land ceases to be used for railway purposes (*R Walker & Sons v British Railways Board* [1984] 1 WLR 805). The fence is merely to mark the boundary of the railway (or previous railway) land – it does not impose a duty to exclude trespassers (*Proffitt v British Railways Board* (1984) *The Times*, 4 February).

Checklist – railways

- Ownership of the land by railway companies
  - has there been compulsory purchase?
  - railway sleepers and fence posts may have been moved if the land has been sold
  - Railtrack has preserved many boundary documents
  - check railway plans issued at the time of the private bill with the county council
  - the railway company has an obligation to fence.
- Accommodation works
  - is an owner of land entitled to the benefit of accommodation works?
  - what was in the contemplation of the parties at the time of the works?
  - is an owner entitled to any alteration or extension of the works?

— has the right been extinguished?

— NB the duty to fence (under s 68).

6.10   The seashore

Ownership of land bounded by the sea

6.10.1   Many properties abut tidal waters. The owner of land bounded by the sea is presumed to own it down to the mean high water mark (the 'mean' being the medium point between the spring and neap high tides). The result is that the landowner will own any cliffs, dunes and a substantial part of the beach. The boundary may move as the high water mark moves. The key points to look for with the help of the current OS map are HWM (High Water Mark) and LWM (Low Water Mark).

Ownership of the seashore

6.10.2   The seashore (also known as 'foreshore') is the area lying below the mean high water mark down to the low water mark. This belongs to the Crown unless it has passed to an individual by grant or prescription (*Fowley Marine (Emsworth) Ltd v Gafford* [1968] 2 QB 618). The freehold of the seashore is also a 'moving freehold', which is to say that it is subject to accretion and erosion. Land described as being 'situate on the seashore' has a fixed boundary and is not subject to variations (*Mellor v Walmesley* [1905] 2 Ch 164).

Ownership of the sea bed

6.10.3   Parliament has established United Kingdom sovereignty over territorial waters surrounding the whole of the United Kingdom. As to ownership, this will ordinarily vest in the Crown. Thus in *Lord Fitzhardinge v Purcell* [1908] 2 Ch 139 the court held (at 166) that:

> Clearly the bed of the sea, at any rate for some distance below low water mark, and beds of tidal navigable rivers, are *prima facie* vested in the Crown, and there seems no good reason why the ownership thereof by the Crown should not also, subject to the rights of the public, be a beneficial ownership.

6.11   Lakes and rivers

Ownership of non-tidal rivers and streams

6.11.1   Where a river or stream abuts a property and that river or stream is non-tidal, the *usque ad medium filum viae* rule applies just as it does with highways (see 6.8.2 above). If it is specifically shown in the deeds, however, that some other configuration applies, then the presumption is rebutted. The 'middle' of the river is established by reference to its width and does not relate to its flow.

6.11.2 It should be noted that it is Land Registry (HMLR) practice to mark the registered property only as far as the river edge, even though ownership may extend to the centre of the river. (A similar practice applies to highways.)

6.11.3 Unlike highways the watercourse may change because of the actions of nature. In this case, as with the seashore, the owner's title may change. If accretion or erosion occurs because of the influence of man (rather than that of nature), there is judicial uncertainty. In *Hindson v Ashby* [1896] 2 Ch 1, the Court of Appeal accepted that gradual accretion, caused by a weir placed upstream accrued to the riparian owner. However, in *A-G for Southern Nigeria v Holt* [1915] AC 599, the Privy Council held that a spread of the seashore, caused by flood prevention works, accrued to the Crown.

6.11.4 The water flowing along a river or stream is not the property of the neighbouring owners (known as riparian owners) but comes under the control of the Environment Agency. The fishing rights do belong to the riparian owners.

Ownership of lakes

6.11.5 Where a lake is part of a river system, ownership will be determined in the same way as the river. In other cases, it will be determined in accordance with the normal rules of title. Hence, a lake entirely within the boundaries of a piece of land will pass without specific reference. If more than one owner's land abuts the lake it is submitted that the question of ownership will be dealt with in the same way as rivers.

Tidal rivers

6.11.6 As with land abutting the seashore, the general rule is that land abutting a tidal river goes down to the mean high water mark (and hence is subject to variation). The presumption is that the Crown owns not only the area between the mean high and low water marks but the whole of the river bed, including estuaries and creeks (*Lord Fitzhardinge v Purcell* [1908] 2 Ch 139). It follows that the riparian owner of a tidal river does not own the fishing rights unless he has acquired ownership of the river bed.

Checklist – lakes and rivers

- Ownership of non-tidal rivers and streams
  — the rule '*usque ad medium filum*' applies (unless rebutted)
  — check the conveyance
  — note HMLR practice
  — the watercourse may change
  — the flowing water is the property of the Environment Agency.
- Ownership of lakes
  — the normal rules of title apply
  — check that the lake is not part of a river system.

- Ownership of tidal streams and rivers
  — the presumption is that land abutting a tidal river goes down to the HWM
  — the presumption is that the Crown owns the land beyond the HWM
  — the riparian owner does not ordinarily own the fishing rights.

6.12 Evidence

Introductory

6.12.1 Although the prime source of evidence as to a boundary is the convey-ance, this will often be unavailable. For many of the issues commonly raised by boundary disputes, such as adverse possession, estoppel, and the rebuttal of legal presumptions, extrinsic evidence will be necessary. This book does not intend to deal specifically with the complex laws of evidence. In this chapter we will seek to give some practical assistance on the evidential questions which may arise in relation to boundary issues.

6.12.2 Three preliminary legal matters are particularly important, that is to say that:

(1) The particular rules of the tribunal hearing the case may contain spe-cific rules concerning the admissibility of, and necessity to produce, evidence;

(2) The 'best evidence' rule prevails, so that in the absence of agreement as to the use of a copy document, an original document must be used (when available);

(3) The Civil Evidence Act 1995 is now in force. This Act enables hearsay evidence to be placed before the court. If a party intends to present such evidence, notice should be given to all other parties to the proceedings and upon request, it should give reasonable and practicable particulars of the evidence. It is for the court to determine the weight to be given to it (see, in particular, s 4(2) of the 1995 Act).

Deeds and plans

6.12.3 The primary source of evidence as to the boundary between any two properties is the conveyance by which the ownership was divided. This may, and very often does, go back well beyond a good root of title (ie 15 years). However, it is always good practice, even if the primary source is located, to compare it with the initial conveyance of the other party since errors can be made. It is the earlier of the two conveyances which will prevail. Once a ven-dor has conveyed land he cannot convey it again even though he may purport to do so.

6.12.4 The deeds are important as a whole and not just for the deed plan (which people often study without reading the text). The parcel clause (that which commences ALL THAT . . .) should first be read and, even if it refers to the plan, studied in detail. It may set out what is included in the conveyance beyond a general description, for instance 'the dwelling house together with its lands, stables and coach-house erected thereon'.

6.12.5 The following points should be noted:
  (1) Dwelling house: This expression includes its 'foundation and service of the earth on which the house stands' (*Grigsby v Melville* [1974] 1 WLR 80).
  (2) Curtilage: defined in *Sinclair-Lockhart's Trustees v Central Land Board* (1950) 1 P & CR 195, 204 as 'ground which is used for the comfortable enjoyment of a house or other building . . . although it has not been marked off or enclosed in any way' (affirmed at (1950) 1 P & CR 320).
  (3) Land: defined by s 205 of Law of Property Act 1925 to include: 'land of any tenure, and mines and minerals, whether or not held apart from the surface, buildings or parts of the buildings (whether the division is horizontal, vertical or made in any other way) and other corporeal hereditaments . . .'.

6.12.6 The parcels clause may also refer to some specific form of occupation which may need investigating. This may mean that some inquiry needs to be made of witnesses in the area as to the occupant and extent of his occupation.

6.12.7 The text in a conveyance may and very often does refer to a plan. However, the context of this reference is important. Some common expressions should be noted:
  (1) 'as shown on the plan attached for identification only' indicates that the plan is purely a picture showing the general location of the property;
  (2) 'more particularly delineated on the plan attached' indicates that the plan is very important because the extent of the property is reliant upon the plan attached to the deed.

6.12.8 A check should be carried out to see whether there are schedules which list the parts of the property with reference to Ordnance Survey field numbers and acreages (or other details). (For discussion on Ordnance Survey see Her Majesty's Land Registry at 6.12.11–6.12.17.)

6.12.9 T-marks may be referred to in the text of the deeds, confirming their importance. If T-marks are shown on the plan but not referred to in the text then they may only be considered by a court to be extrinsic evidence.

6.12.10 Whenever possible it is important that the original deeds are studied. This is because photocopying can have a distorting effect. Both lawyers and surveyors are best engaged on interpretation as a dual exercise. Lawyers will be able to interpret the text of the deeds and confirm the status of the plan, whereas surveyors will be able to measure up the property (using modern electronic equipment and computer plotting) and then compare what exists on the site with what the deeds suggest the true position should be.

Her Majesty's Land Registry (HMLR)

Introductory

6.12.11   There are several excellent leaflets published by Her Majesty's Land Registry (HMLR) which should be obtained by anyone working in the field of boundary disputes. The leaflets explain the workings of HMLR in detail and describe the procedures that need to be followed when applying to HMLR for registration and other matters. They may be obtained from:

> HM Land Registry
> 32 Lincoln's Inn Fields
> London WC2A 3PH
> Tel: 0171 917 8888.

However, it is worth at this stage clarifying some of the points of HMLR practice which are most commonly misunderstood.

The Register; the filed plan

6.12.12   The HMLR Register is divided into two parts. One is the textual part which includes the Proprietorship Register, the Charges Register and describes any covenants which may exist. The other is the filed plan which is the document which most people turn to when a boundary dispute arises. The filed plan is not a 'Land Registry map' but an Ordnance Survey (OS) map which HMLR have adopted for the registration of the property. The OS, however, do not show private property boundaries, they show features which may or may not be boundaries. For example, the OS surveyors may see a hedge and will then map the centre of the rootline of that hedge, but the hedge may in fact be some distance inside the legal boundary. That is of no concern to the OS, who are purely making maps of features.

6.12.13   As a result of the decision of the Court of Appeal in *Fisher v Winch* [1939] 1 KB 666 and *Davey v Harrow Corporation* [1957] 2 WLR 941, courts will accept the OS maps as evidence of what a line on the map indicates. In *Davey's* case the field with which the action was concerned was marked upon the OS map. Lord Goddard CJ, in describing the field, stated:

> The boundary to the south is delineated on the map by a line, and the evidence of an official from the Ordnance Survey Office given before us, but not in the court below, was that the line indicated the centre of the existing hedge. This is in accordance with the invariable practice of the survey as was proved in *Fisher v Winch* and in our opinion, after that case and this, courts in future can take notice of this practice of the Ordnance Survey as at least *prima facie* evidence of what a line on the map indicates.

6.12.14   The OS cannot show features by separate lines on their maps where those features are closer than 1.5–2 m together (at 1 : 2,500 scale). The OS therefore have an order of priority when it comes to, say, a hedge-ditch-fence feature, and in that example they would normally select the rootline of the hedge as the line to be shown on the map. A line on an OS map at 1 : 2,500 scale is plotted to an accuracy of 0.5 m.

6.12.15 HMLR recognise the limitations of OS mapping. Rule 278 of the Land Registration Rules 1925 (LRR) states:

(1) Except in cases in which it is noted in the Property Register that the boundaries have been fixed, the filed plan or General Map shall be deemed to indicate the general boundaries only.
(2) In such cases the exact line of the boundary will be left undetermined – as, for instance, whether it includes a hedge or wall and ditch, or runs along the centre of a wall or fence, or its inner or outer face, or how far it runs within or beyond it; or whether or not the land registered includes the whole or any portion of an adjoining road or stream.
(3) When a general boundary only is desired to be entered into the register, notice to the owners of the adjoining lands need not be given.
(4) This rule shall apply notwithstanding that a part of the whole or a ditch, wall, fence, road, stream, or other boundary is expressly included in or excluded from the title or that it forms the whole of the land comprised in the title.

Thus, when looking at the filed plan it should really be used as a picture of the area showing which property which is registered, and not as a precise boundary demarcation plan. If scaled measurements are taken from such a plan it should be borne in mind that such scaling could be up to 1 m different to on-site measurements. It must also be remembered that the lines being scale-measured may denote just one of several features that exist on the ground.

Rights on first registration; pre-registration deeds
6.12.16 An applicant for registration is entitled to have the precise position of either the whole or part of his boundary indicated on the plan or defined on the register. To do so, the applicant applies to the Registrar who in turn notifies the owners and occupiers of adjoining land (Land Registration Rules 1925 (LRR), r 276). Any dispute arising from such notification is determined by the Registrar (LRR, r 298) with a right of appeal to the High Court (LRR, r 299). Even without such precision, the Register itself is useful because it often contains the dates of earlier pre-registration deeds for which a search can be made.

Obtaining the original deeds
6.12.17 HMLR receives deeds from applicants who wish to register their properties and it is those deeds, and not the HMLR Filed Plan, which provide the legal description of the extent of the property. Wherever possible, deeds must be obtained. Whilst this may sound impractical it is amazing what research can produce. Moreover, the boundary may be a comparatively recent creation.

Photographs

6.12.18 In most court cases involving boundary disputes, photographs play a major part. Although the judge may attend a site-visit it is almost impossible for all the critical features of the site to be recalled without the aid of photographs. Whilst there are three sources of photography which can prove helpful (see below), the producer must be able to give information about the age of the photograph, preferably who took it and the circumstances in which it was taken. Whilst the rules on hearsay evidence may have changed in civil matters (see 6.12.2 above), the judge will give no or little weight to a photograph taken somewhere between uncertain dates by an unknown source.

Old photographs

6.12.19   Old photographs (usually provided by the client) show what used to exist before the incident occurred. Such photography is subject to limitations (angle-of-view, perspective, etc) but can be very helpful in enabling a court to visualise the scene. Other sources of old photography include newspaper cuttings, local historical books and wedding photographs.

Recent photographs

6.12.20   Recent photographs are also very important because they show what exists at the time of trial and may save hours of explanation in the witness box. Most people can picture a feature (such as a kink in a fenceline) but find it very difficult to describe in court without the aid of photographs. Such photographs should always be in colour and all copies should be colour-copied. If a trial is envisaged, then at least five copies of each photograph will be needed (one for the judge, one for each party, one for the witness bundle and one spare).

6.12.21   To ensure that the photographs are helpful either as a record or in a court case, it is important that good clear pictures are obtained. One way of ensuring this (especially as boundary features tend to be in or close to hedges and trees) is to use a photo-flash in every shot. In that way the details lurking in the shadows will be clearly visible. Photographs should be clearly identified in a logical manner with a numbering system and a date attached.

Aerial photographs

6.12.22   Aerial photographs can be useful but it is important to realise that there are two types of aerial photograph.

6.12.23   Firstly there is vertical aerial photography. This is where an aircraft flies in straight lines with a calibrated camera pointing directly downwards and photographs are taken at regular (controlled) intervals so that each photograph includes 60 per cent of the next photograph. When the prints are run off they can then (within the 60 per cent overlap) be viewed in 'stereo', using a hand-stereoscope, or used for intricate mapping using a machine stereoscope attached to a computer system. These are the sorts of photographs used by the OS, the Ministry of Agriculture and Fisheries, the Department of the Environment (for new road/rail route planning), amongst others. Using a hand stereoscope and a 'stereo-pair' of photographs (within the 60 per cent overlap) the area viewed appears to stand up in 3-D (giving dramatic results) and individual fence posts, wall buttresses, etc can be seen easily. If such photographs are to be used as evidence in court then a chartered land surveyor with aerial survey interpretation experience will probably be required to describe the features to the tribunal.

6.12.24 The other type of aerial photography is oblique photography and is most usually taken by speculative photographers taking photographs out of an aircraft with a normal 35 mm camera with the aim of selecting individual properties and selling the photograph to its owner. This is really in the same category as old (or recent) photography (see above) and can be useful for seeing features, but it does not have the accuracy or the 3-D effect of vertical photography. Moreover, the very fact that it is 'oblique' photography can lead to a distortion of angles due to perspective.

6.12.25 Where aerial photography (particularly vertical photography) can be vital is in showing the use of a right of way or the existence of a gate. The OS do not show all tracks and routes across farmland, neither do they show gates, but these features show up clearly on vertical aerial photographs.

6.12.26 Although the most precise form of aerial photography, vertical photography cannot be used as a source of scale measurements because the scale drops away from the centre to the edge of each photograph. Stereo-plotting machines, linked to computers, take care of that scale distortion by comparing the actual viewed area with known control points, but this cannot be done using a hand viewer. Therefore, unless an expensive stereo-plotting exercise is contemplated, aerial photographs are merely photographs taken from very good viewpoints of the area in question.

Existing features

6.12.27 Existing features can also be considered as evidence (often extrinsic evidence) and many boundary disputes are solved by the discovery of the stump of an old fence corner-post or the remains of some building footings. However, such features should be treated with some caution. It is not unknown for instance for a former to move a whole gate (complete with posts) to another location for sound agricultural purposes. The hapless surveyor or solicitor may see that gate and, wrongly, come to the opinion that it is so old that it must have been there for many years. Any old feature should only be accepted as being genuine if its history can be substantiated and, if footings are involved, the brickwork can be compared with other contemporaneous brickwork.

6.12.28 Even where a fence has been removed or a wall demolished, it is often possible with a garden spade to find the stumps of the fence posts or the concrete base of the wall. However, hedges, once removed, leave little trace, and thus the line of a hedge is the most difficult to re-establish. Evidence of an old ditch can be uncovered (even if the ditch has been filled in) by an expert analysis of the soil layers.

Expert witnesses

6.12.29 An expert witness is almost always employed by each party to a boundary dispute in order to assist the court in interpreting the evidence before it. The expert is not there to argue one party's case. He is there to give a true and independent view on the matters about which he is qualified to speak.

6.12.30 Any surveyor acting as an expert witness must be aware of and comply with the Practice Statement entitled *Surveyors Acting as Expert Witnesses* published by the Royal Institute of Chartered Surveyors and available from:

> RICS
> 12 Great George Street
> London
> SW1P 3AD
> Tel: 0171 222 7000.

This Practice Statement reminds surveyors acting as expert witnesses of their duty to the judicial body to whom his evidence is given and 'to be truthful as to fact, honest as to opinion and complete as to coverage of relevant matters'. It underlines the fact that the surveyor's evidence must 'be independent, objective and unbiased. In particular, it must not be biased towards the party who is responsible for paying him'.

6.12.31 In the absence of agreement, the leave of the court is required to call an expert witness. This is usually obtained at the hearing for directions. The calling of experts will usually be dependent upon the prior exchange of their reports and counter-reports at some stage as directed by the court.

6.12.32 It is possible for the court itself to appoint an expert. Whilst this is not a common phenomenon at present, Lord Woolf in his report *Access to Justice* suggests that the court expert will be used more often.

6.12.33 The expert in a boundary dispute should be a boundary surveyor. A surveyor in general practice or employed in valuation or building surveying may not be an appropriate expert.

6.12.34 In order to cope with all measurement requirements and to ensure that a high level of accuracy prevails, a boundary surveyor is likely to need the following equipment (or equivalent alternative):

(1) a set of EDM (Electronic Distance Measurer and theodolite);
(2) a hand-held laser measurer;
(3) a 30 m steel tape (calibrated to a known base);
(4) a 2 m surveyors rod (rigid measuring instrument);
(5) a 4 m survey staff;
(6) a data-logger;
(7) a camera;
(8) tripods, markers, nails, etc.

All measurements taken by the surveyor should be taken in metres (although imperial measurements may be added to the drawing or referred to in brackets). The recorded survey measurements should be stored on a computer disk in DXF format (or an acceptable standard alternative) so that on-screen comparisons can be made and OS digital maps can be imported. Plots can be printed off at any requested scale, the most usual being 1 : 2,500 and 1 : 1,250 (as used by the OS) and 1 : 100 or 1 : 200 (for a more detailed analysis).

Checklist – evidence

- Check legal rules
  - are there any rules specific to the tribunal?
  - the 'best evidence' rule applies
  - does the Civil Evidence Act 1995 apply?
- What to look for in deeds and plans
  - the conveyance is the primary source of evidence
  - compare the initial conveyance
  - read the text of the deed plan
  - consider carefully the contents of the parcels clause
  - check schedules for references to OS maps
  - check for T-marks
  - always check the original deed.
- Photographs
  - what old photographs are available?
  - who can prove photographs?
  - use recent colour photographs
  - take colour copies for the court
  - take photographs with a flash
  - vertical aerial photographs are useful if properly prepared with stereo-plotting machines
  - oblique aerial photographs are useful for seeing features.
- Existing features
  - existing features are useful but caution must be exercised to ensure that they have not been moved and are genuine
  - filled-in ditches can be analysed.
- Expert witnesses
  - expert witnesses must be independent
  - check that directions hearings are complied with
  - what expert is appropriate? A boundary surveyor will be needed for boundary disputes.

Chapter 7

Party Walls

7.1 Overview

7.1.1 It is worth recalling some of the history to the Party Wall etc Act 1996, which is the statute which now governs the rights and liabilities of those affected by party walls in place of the Law of Property Act 1925 and the London Building Acts (Amendment) Act 1939.

7.1.2 Legislation affecting rights over party walls stretches back to the time of the Great Fire of London, when it was considered essential to make provision that the walls between buildings should be made of a material which would provide some protection against the spread of fire. Inevitably provision also had to be made to cover the duties of the owners of these walls.

7.1.3 Over the centuries separate statutory provision came to be made for areas of the country outside and within Inner London. Outside Inner London, the Law of Property Act 1925 held that where two properties are separated by a wall in undivided shares, ownership should be deemed to be severed vertically as between the two owners. This meant that where there was a wall of differing thickness and plan, the dividing line would not necessarily be straight but would be the median line through the wall. Physically determining the position of the boundary line was fraught with difficulties and in practice there was rarely sufficient evidence available.

7.1.4 Under the 1925 Act, each owner had a common right of support and user over the other half. Although in theory each party could do whatever he liked to his half of the wall provided he did not interfere with the other's right of support and user, in practice, this was very difficult to interpret and resulted in many disputes and sometimes in costly litigation.

7.1.5 With the passing into force of the Party Wall etc Act 1996, the London Building Acts (Amendment) Act 1939 has been repealed and its former provisions have been extended to cover the rest of England and Wales. Not only has specific party wall legislation been extended across England and Wales, but so have the rules and procedures governing excavations adjacent to adjoining buildings and structures where there is a risk of undermining stability. Indirectly, this latter change has removed some of the difficulties in establishing rights of support.

7.1.6 Whilst the 1939 Act was on the statute book, surveyors working in Inner London came to understand the way in which the Act worked in everyday practice and established common rules about its interpretation. It remains to be seen whether these rules will be followed throughout the country in respect of some of the more difficult provisions of the 1996 Act which have survived from the 1939 Act.

7.1.7 As a matter of general principle it is of course important that anyone proposing to undertake works to a party structure or excavations adjacent to adjoining buildings is fully aware of the statutory notices and corresponding time constraints and costs that may follow. Failure to make allowance for party wall procedure in the development programme will only expose the developer to the risk of delay and additional costs, and possibly an injunction.

7.1.8 This chapter will consider:
(1) The structures covered by the 1996 Act:
    (a) party walls
    (b) party fence walls
    (c) party structures.
(2) The rights and duties of owners:
    (a) new building on the line of junction (s 1)
    (b) repairs and other works (s 2).
(3) Notification:
    (a) party structure notices
    (b) counter notices.
(4) Dispute resolution.
(5) Security for expenses.

7.2 Structures covered by the 1996 Act – definitions

7.2.1 Three main structures are covered by the 1996 Act. These are the party wall, the party fence wall and the party structure. They are defined under s 20 of the Act.

A. Party wall

Definition
7.2.2 By s 20:

    'party wall' means –
        (a) a wall which forms part of a building and stands on lands of different owners to a greater extent than the projection of any artificially formed support on which the wall rests; and
        (b) so much of a wall not being a wall referred to in paragraph (a) above as separates buildings belonging to different owners.

This definition makes it clear that there are now two possible types of party wall.

The first type of party wall

7.2.3   The first type ((a) above) is a relatively simple concept to grasp. It is a wall which forms part of a building which stands on the land of different owners to any extent. That is to say that the boundary line must run somewhere within the wall itself, essentially the same definition as that set out in the Law of Property Act 1925.

Projections formed to support the wall are not to be taken into consideration

7.2.4   In determining whether a type (a) wall does stand on the land of different owners, (a) goes on to make special division for the support on which the wall rests. If a line could be drawn down each side of wall itself, then anything which projects beyond that line and which has been made to support the wall is not to be taken into consideration. This means, for instance, that any piers or buttresses above ground or any piles or other supports underground cannot turn a wall positioned solely on one person's property into a party wall just because the piers or buttresses or other support project into the adjacent landowner's property.

An example of a wall which is not a party wall for this very reason is illustrated at figure 1 below.

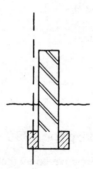

Figure 1

7.2.5   A simple example of a type (a) party wall would be the wall separating two semi-detached houses built at the same time: the wall stands half on one owner's land and half on the other's.

Other examples are illustrated at figures 2 and 3 below.

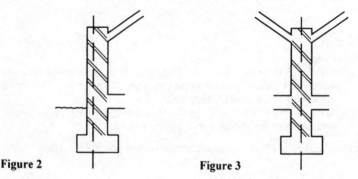

Figure 2   **Figure 3**

The second type of party wall

7.2.6   The second definition (type (b)) is not as straightforward. Whereas a type (a) party wall is defined by its position on lands belonging to different owners, a type (b) party wall has nothing to do with ownership of land but with the ownership of buildings. This means that where a wall stands entirely on the land of A it may still be a party wall to the extent that it separates buildings on A's land from buildings on B's land.

Party walls formed by enclosure

7.2.7   In the absence of any covenants or other contractual arrangements whereby the owners of separate buildings consent to the use by B of a wall built entirely on A's land to form an enclosing wall of B's own property and therefore a party wall, consideration needs to be given to how a situation covered by a type (b) party wall can arise. This requires an examination of the process of enclosure of a wall (or part of a wall) which forms part of a building owned by A as a result of the construction by B of a building against A's wall (or part of that wall), since this is a common cause of the application of the definition set out at (b).

7.2.8   A party who builds on a wall owned by A without A's permission commits a trespass. A will be entitled to an injunction to restrain the trespass. Subsection (b) cannot convert the trespassing wall into a legitimate party wall. Subsection (b) can only safely be relied upon by the party seeking to enclose A's wall after the time has passed for A to be able to enforce his rights. Whether the other party would have to wait the full 20 years to acquire an easement of the right to support is in doubt. It is widely thought that as soon as the six year limitation period has expired then the full rights and liabilities under the Act will apply to the wall in question as a party wall.

The extent to which an enclosing wall is a party wall

7.2.9   It is important to note that only that part of a landowner's wall will be a type (b) party wall which is enclosed by the building of an adjacent owner. This is because the subsection makes it clear that only 'so much of a wall' which separates buildings will be a party wall under type (b). As an illustration, if a single storey lean-to shed is built up against a vast wall, the only part of the wall which becomes a party wall is the amount enclosed by the shed. Examples of party walls are shown at figures 4, 5, 6, 7 overleaf. The bold arrow demonstrates the extent to which the wall built on A's land is a type (b) party wall.

B. Party fence wall

Definition

7.2.10   By s 20:

> 'party fence wall' means a wall (not being part of a building) which stands on lands of different owners and is used or constructed to be used for separating adjoining lands, but does not include a wall constructed on the land of one owner the artificially formed support of which projects into the land of another owner.

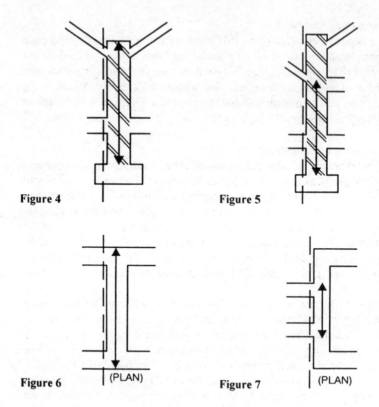

Figure 4

Figure 5

Figure 6   (PLAN)

Figure 7   (PLAN)

Whereas a party wall must have a building attached to it, a party fence wall is a free-standing wall built for the purpose of separating adjoining land. Common examples are a garden wall or boundary wall. The statutory definition requires that a party fence wall does not form part of a building.

Projections

7.2.11   As with party walls, the extent to which the wall's supports project on to an owner's land is excluded from the determination whether the wall stands on the land of different owners (see para 7.2.4 above).

The illustration at figure 8 opposite therefore is a party fence wall whilst figure 9 opposite is not.

7.2.12   Despite the distinction between a party wall and party fence wall, the latter has the benefit of all of the rights granted by section 2 of the Act.

C. Party structure

Definition

7.2.13   An additional definition introduced by s 20 of the Act is that of a party structure:

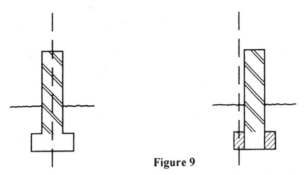

Figure 8   **Figure 9**

'party structure' means a party wall and also a floor partition or other structure separating buildings or parts of buildings approached solely by separate staircases or separate entrances;

This definition is self-explanatory when it comes to 'party wall' and 'floor partition', but exactly what is meant to be included by 'other structure . . .' is not easily envisaged.

What rights can be exercised in relation to floor partitions?
7.2.14 A further problem arises in determining what rights are available under s 2 of the Act to the owner of a floor partition. This is because the various rights set out in subsection 2(2) are contingent on the application of subsection 2(1), which states:

This section applies where lands of different owners adjoin and at the line of junction the said lands are built on or a boundary wall, being a party fence wall or the external wall of a building, has been erected.

It is difficult to picture a case in which it can be said that at the line of junction of a floor partition either
(1) the floor partition has been 'built on' or
(2) any 'boundary wall' has been erected.
The only obvious example is that set out in figure 10 overleaf, where there is a 'flying freehold' interest above the adjoining property.
7.2.15 Surveyors in London as a matter of convention always treated floor partitions as being covered by the similar rights set out in the London Building Acts (Amendment) Act 1939, by reason of a liberal interpretation of the forerunner to s 2(1) (being s 46(1) of the 1939 Act). Whether this practical approach will survive the extension of the old 1939 Act provisions across the country by reason of the introduction of the 1996 Act remains to be seen.

Checklist – structures covered by the 1996 Act

- 'Party wall'
  — a party wall is of two types: (a) it stands on the land of different owners and forms part of a building, (b) it stands entirely on

the land of one owner but separates buildings belonging to two owners

— in determining whether a type (a) wall stands on the land of two owners, supporting foundations, piers, buttresses etc projecting from the wall are not to be taken into account

— a type (b) party wall normally arises after a period of enclosure. The right probably does not arise until the expiry of the six year limitation period

— it is important to note that only that part of a wall which is in fact enclosed will be a party wall.

- 'Party fence wall'
  - — a party fence wall stands on the land of two owners for the purpose of separating land.
- 'Party structure'
  - — a party structure is a party wall or floor partition or other structure separating buildings or parts of buildings approached by separate staircases or separate entrances
  - — floor partitions are not obviously subject to the same rights and obligations set out in s 2(2) as other party structures.

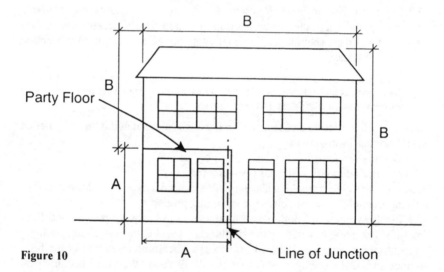

Figure 10

7.3 The rights and duties of owners

A. New building on the line of junction

7.3.1 Section 1 of the 1996 Act lays out rules which are to apply when a building owner wishes to build on any part of a line of junction between his land and neighbouring land. The section only applies where there is a virgin boundary, that is, where nothing has been built on the line of junction or where there is nothing more than a free standing boundary wall which is not a party fence wall or the external wall of a building.

7.3.2 The Act does not grant an express right to build a party wall or party fence wall on the line of junction if the adjoining owner does not agree to it, but it does provide a notification procedure where an owner wishes to erect such a structure (s 1(2)). This allows a notice of an intention to build a wall on the line of junction after a period of more than one month has elapsed. By s 1(3) the adjoining owner can serve a notice indicating his consent to the construction. More discussion of the notification procedure is set out at 7.4 below.

7.3.3 In considering whether to agree to a party wall or a party fence wall being built, an adjoining owner must acknowledge the liabilities which will automatically fall to him once built. Not only will there be the potential loss of a strip of land taken up by up to half the thickness of the wall, but both owners will be able to exercise the full rights granted by the Act for as long as the wall stands. Furthermore, if an adjoining owner agrees to the building of a party wall or party fence wall, he will be liable for a fair proportion of the costs of building the wall, to be determined by the use to which it is to be put by each owner (see s 1(3)). He will also be liable for the future costs of repair and maintenance under a similar mechanism (see ss 2 and 11).

7.3.4 Both s 1(3) (relevant at the time at which a wall is constructed) and s 11 allow for a flexible assessment of the expenses to be borne by the relevant parties. For example, if both owners merely need the wall as a boundary wall, they will derive the same benefit and be liable for equal shares. If, on the other hand, the building owner built a party wall to enclose his new building and the adjoining owner merely needed a boundary wall, it would be clear that the building owner derives the greater benefit and in practice, the adjoining owner would only be liable for nominal costs. Should the adjoining owner make use of the wall at a later date, however, he will be liable to repay a reasonable cost back to the original building owner based on the new use to be made of the wall. This cost will be determined using comparable prevailing costs of labour and materials (s 11(11)).

7.3.5 In the event that an adjoining owner does not consent to the construction of a party wall or a party fence wall, s 1(4)–(6) of the Act provides a building owner with a right to lay such footings or foundations as are necessary to support the wall, even though the adjoining owner may object to its construction. This right extends to access to the adjoining owner's land for the purpose of laying the projecting foundations.

7.3.6 Section 1(7) contains an express provision for the payment of compensation by the building owner to the adjoining owner or occupier for damage caused to the property as a result of the building of the wall or for the placing of any foundations which project on to the adjoining owner's land. This obligation only applies to the building of a boundary wall on the line of junction and separate provisions for compensation will apply where the adjoining owner agrees to the erection of a party wall or party fence wall (s 7).

B. Repairs and other works to party structures

7.3.7 Section 2 of the Act applies to all party structures. Its application to floor partitions is considered at 7.2.14 above. Section 2(2) outlines the 13 rights given to the building owner, which are set out below.

> (a) to underpin, thicken or raise a party structure, a party fence wall, or an external wall which belongs to the building owner and is built against a party structure or party fence wall.

Although this clause is relatively straightforward, it should be noted that it also applies to an independent external wall belonging to the building owner which is built against a party structure or party fence wall. This is often overlooked in the mistaken belief that the Act does not apply to an independent wall in single ownership, not being a party wall or party fence wall.

> (b) to make good, repair, or demolish and rebuild a party structure or party fence wall in a case where such work is necessary on account of defect or want of repair of the structure or wall.

It is important to note that the rights granted by this subsection are for works to make good a defect or want of repair. This distinction is important since if the repair undertaken under this subsection is to the mutual benefit of the owners, the building owner will be entitled to recover a fair proportion of the cost of such repairs from an adjoining owner.

> (c) to demolish a partition which separates buildings belonging to different owners but does not conform with statutory requirements and to build instead a party wall which does so conform;
>
> (d) in the case of buildings connected by arches or structures over public ways or over passages belonging to other persons, to demolish the whole or part of such buildings, arches or structures which do not conform with statutory requirements and to rebuild them so that they do so conform.

On occasion, a party structure may not comply with current statutory requirements (for instance a timber partition in an historic building). Should a building owner be required to upgrade such a component, these subsections would apply.

> (e) to demolish a party structure which is of insufficient strength or height for the purposes of any intended building of the building owner and to rebuild it of sufficient strength or height for the said purposes (including rebuilding to a lesser height or thickness where the rebuilt structure is of sufficient strength and height for the purposes of any adjoining owner).

This subsection grants the far-reaching right to demolish and rebuild a party structure and, in so doing, to lay open the adjoining owner's premises. Although there is provision for compensation at s 11(6), the extent of disruption can be considerable.

> (f) to cut into a party structure for any purpose (which may be or include the purpose of inserting a damp proof course).

The right granted by this clause is self-explanatory but the specific reference to the insertion of a damp proof course is noteworthy and is a result of difficulties encountered with the interpretation of such works in the old 1939 Act.

> (g) to cut away from a party wall, party fence wall, external wall or boundary wall any footing or any projecting chimney breast, jamb or flue, or other projection on or over the land of the building owner to erect, raise or underpin any such wall or for any other purpose.

The rights granted by this subsection should be distinguished from those under s 2(2)(h) below, since it applies to cutting away of projections from a party wall or party fence wall or a wall in the ownership of the building owner, being an external wall of his building or a boundary wall. Since a building owner does not have the right to erect, raise or underpin an adjoining owner's wall, the right to cut off projections under this subsection does not extend to any works to an adjoining owner's wall.

> (h) to cut away or demolish parts of any wall or building of an adjoining owner overhanging the land of the building owner or overhanging a party wall, to the extent that it is necessary to cut away or demolish the parts to enable a vertical wall to be erected or raised against the wall or building of the adjoining owner.

It is common to find features such as gutters, eaves, piers and buttresses which may overhang the land and airspace of the building owner or a party wall. Even where an adjoining owner has acquired possessory title for a trespass, the building owner will have the right to cut away or cut off the projection.

> (j) to cut into the wall of an adjoining owner's building in order to insert a flashing or other weather proofing of a wall erected against that wall.

The simple operation of cutting a flashing detail into an adjoining owner's wall where two buildings abut and are of different height, is frequently necessary as a matter of good building practice. However, it was not a right granted by the 1939 Act and was potentially a problem in many instances. However, although the problem has been overcome by expressly granting the right in s 2(2)(j), it has also placed a specific obligation on the building owner to serve notice for this relatively simple operation, which in the part may have been considered *de minimis* when it was the only work likely to affect an adjoining owner.

> (k) to execute any other necessary works incidental to the connection of a party structure with the premises adjoining it.

It is submitted that this clause has often wrongly been used as a 'catch all' provision under the belief that the words 'any other necessary works' can be construed in their widest meaning. However, the meaning is properly taken to be more literal and simply to cover bonding or tying-in structures to a party wall such as new front, rear and cross walls and for tying back a party wall to an adjoining building following demolition of the building owner's building.

> (l) to raise a party fence wall, or to raise such a wall for use as a party wall, and to demolish a party fence wall and rebuild it as a party fence wall or as a party wall.

This clause is most commonly encountered when an owner wishes to erect a rear extension or conservatory. It gives the building owner the right to raise a party fence wall or to demolish and rebuild it as a party fence wall or as a party wall.

> (m) ... to reduce, or to demolish and rebuild, a party wall or party fence wall to (i) a height of not less than 2 metres where the wall is not used by an adjoining owner to any greater extent than a boundary wall or (ii) a height currently enclosed upon by the building of an adjoining owner.

Before the 1996 Act there was no right to lower a party wall or party fence wall even within the 1939 Act (see *Gyle-Thompson v Wall Street (Properties) Ltd* [1974] 1 WLR 123). This led to many problems, especially where adjoining owners were reluctant to give their consent, even where the height of the wall was of no benefit to either party. It is now lawful to lower the height of a wall down to a minimum height of 2 m where it is used by the adjoining owner as a party fence wall or a boundary wall or; in the case of a party wall, down to the height necessary for enclosure of the adjoining owner's premises and allowing for an appropriate parapet.

> (n) to expose a party wall or party structure hitherto enclosed subject to providing adequate weathering.

No common law right to protection from the weather exists in English law (*Phipps v Pears* [1965] 1 QB 76). Section 2(2)(n) places a statutory obligation on the building owner to provide adequate weather protection to an exposed party wall or structure. Where there is an intention to rebuild immediately after demolition, conventional felt and battens or polythene may be considered adequate, but if it is likely that the wall may be exposed to the elements for some time, it would not be unreasonable to require some form of more permanent protection such as render or cladding.

Repair to an adjoining owner's premises as a result of the works
7.3.8 It should be noted that in exercising the rights granted by s 2(2), the building owner is under a duty to make good any damage caused to the adjoining owner's premises as a result of the works and the extent of this is contained in s 2(3)–(8) as described below.
7.3.9 When raising a party wall under subsection 2(2)(a) or 2(2)(e), there is a duty to raise the chimneys or flues of an adjoining owner to ensure that they continue to operate efficiently (s 2(3),(4)).
7.3.10 Generally, however, the making good of damage to an adjoining owner's premises only applies to subsections 2(2)(a),(e),(f),(g),(h),(j). There is also a further distinction between s 2(2)(a),(e),(f),(g),(h) and (j), in that in the case of the former, the duty is to make good all damage (including damage to furnishings and decorations), whereas in the case of s 2(2)(j), the duty is limited to the wall of the adjoining owner's building.

Checklist – rights and duties of owners

- New building on the line of junction
  - — s 1 sets out a mechanism for consensual agreement to the building of a party wall
  - — a party who agrees to the creation of a party wall must be prepared to pay the costs of future use and maintenance
  - — if an adjoining owner will not consent to the creation of a party wall, s 1 entitles an owner to lay foundations on adjoining land, so long as compensation is paid.
- Repairs and other works
  - — s 2 describes the repairs and other works which can be carried out to a party structure
  - — when exercising rights under s 2, a building owner is under a duty in most cases to make good any damage caused to the adjoining owner's premises.

7.4 Notification

7.4.1 As already indicated, before exercising the rights granted by sections 1 and 2 of the Act, the building owner must give notice to any adjoining owner. Section 3 of the Act prescribes various details to be provided in such 'party structure notices'. Section 4 sets out the details for 'counter notices' which might be served by an adjoining owner.

Notification by party structure notices

7.4.2 There is no prescribed form of notice but a notice must contain three key components (s 3(1)):
(1) the name and address of the building owner
(2) the nature and particulars of the proposed work including, in cases where the building owner proposes to construct special foundations, plans and sections, and details of construction of the special foundations together with any reasonable particulars of the loads to be carried thereby
(3) the date on which the proposed work will begin.

7.4.3 Precedents for different notices are given at A5.20–A5.22. Notices are frequently incomplete or fail to contain sufficient information to allow the adjoining owner to consider the building owner's request. Lack of information has therefore been a common ground for dissension.

7.4.4 It should be noted that plans and sections are required with the notice where 'special foundations' are proposed. 'Special foundations' are any foundation which contains beams or rods for the distribution of load and, essentially, means any foundation with metal reinforcement (s 20).

7.4.5 The period of notice is two months for works to a party fence wall, special foundation or to a party structure (s 3(2)(a)) and one month in the case of a line of junction (s 1(2)).

7.4.6 Notice must be served on all adjoining owners. By reason of the definition of 'owner' set out at s 20, this includes:

(1) a person in receipt of, or entitled to receive, the whole or part of the rent or profits of land;

(2) a person in possession of land, otherwise known as a mortgagee or as a tenant from year to year or for a lesser term or as a tenant at will;

(3) a purchaser of an interest in land under a contract for purchase or under an agreement for a lease, otherwise known under an agreement for a tenancy from year to year or for a lesser term.

The notice provisions must comply with the service provisions set out at s 15. Where the identity of an adjoining owner is not known, it is sufficient to fix a notice onto a conspicuous part of the adjoining owner's premises (s 15(2)).

7.4.7 It should be noted that where works are to be carried out under a Dangerous Structure Notice, there is no obligation to serve a notice under s 3 of the Act.

Counter notices

7.4.8 Having been served with a party structure notice, an adjoining owner may, by s 4(1), serve a counter notice requiring the building owner to:

(1) build in or on the wall or structure to which the notice relates, chimney copings, breasts, jambs or flues, or such piers or recesses or other like works that may reasonably be required for the convenience of the adjoining owner, or;

(2) in respect of special foundations, to place them at a specified greater depth or construct them of greater strength so that they may be used by the adjoining owner.

Section 4(2) requires a counter notice to be served together with plans, sections and particulars and to be served within one month of service of the notice.

Deemed disputes

7.4.9 In the case of both notices and counter notices under ss 3 and 4, an owner has 14 days from the date of service of the notice to indicate his consent to the works, otherwise there shall have been a deemed dissension from the notice and a dispute shall be deemed to have arisen between the parties (s 5).

Checklist – notification

- Party structure notices
  - s 3 of the 1996 Act prescribes a mechanism for giving notice of the intention of a building owner to exercise any rights under ss 1 and 2

— party structure notices must contain proper particulars of the work proposed
— plans and sections are required when special foundations are proposed
— provisions as to time and service must be observed.

* Counter notices
  — s 4 sets out provisions requiring a building owner to build certain additional structures
  — provisions as to time and service must be observed.

7.5 Dispute resolution

7.5.1 Section 10 of the Act contains express provisions for the resolution of disputes between owners. The Act intends to keep warring parties out of the courts although there is a statutory right of appeal to the County Court (see 7.5.12 below).

7.5.2 In the event of a dispute, s 10 allows both parties to agree to the appointment of a single surveyor, referred to as the 'agreed surveyor'. Alternatively each party can appoint his own surveyor and the two surveyors shall appoint a 'third surveyor' who is to resolve any matters between the first two surveyors in the event that they cannot agree (s 10(1)).

7.5.3 If an 'agreed surveyor' refuses or is unable to act within ten days of a written request to do so, the proceedings for settling the dispute must begin again (s 10(3)).

7.5.4 If either owner refuses or neglects to appoint a surveyor within ten days of a written request by the other owner to do so then the other owner, and not his surveyor, may make an appointment on his behalf (s 10(4)).

7.5.5 If an appointed surveyor dies or is unable to act before the difference is settled, the party who appointed him may appoint another surveyor in his place with the same power and authority (s 10(5)).

7.5.6 If an appointed surveyor refuses or neglects to act within ten days of a written request to do so, the surveyor appointed by the other party may proceed *ex parte* as if he were acting in the capacity of an 'agreed surveyor' (s 10(6),(7)).

7.5.7 Where either appointed surveyor refuses to select a third surveyor within ten days of a written request to do so, the other surveyor may request that the appointment be made by the person appointed under the Act by the local authority to act as the 'appointing officer' or, where the local authority is the employer of the 'appointing officer', the request for the appointment of a third surveyor is made to the Secretary of State (s 10(8)).

7.5.8 If a third surveyor neglects, refuses or is incapable of acting within ten days of a written request to do so, the other two of the three surveyors shall select another third surveyor in his place with the same power and authority (s 10(9)).

7.5.9 All appointments and selections must be made in writing.

7.5.10   The agreed surveyor or any two of the three surveyors will settle the dispute by way of an award and the award may determine the right to execute the work and the time and manner of executing any work and any other matter arising out of or incidental to the dispute, including the costs of making the award. The award is an agreement made between the appointed surveyors acting in the capacity of quasi-arbitrators. Their duty is to administer the provision of the Act and to ensure that the works are executed in such a manner as to protect the integrity of the wall. Regardless of the appointing party, the surveyor(s) must act independently. Once appointed under s 10, a surveyor ceases to have a client-consultant relationship with his appointing owner.

7.5.11   In accordance with the provisions for costs and expenses set out in s 11 of the Act, the surveyors may also determine the apportionment of costs incurred in making the award, or inspect the works and any other matters arising out of the dispute.

7.5.12   The award shall be conclusive but either party to an award may within 14 days of service, appeal to the County Court against the award and the court may rescind or modify the award and make such orders as to costs as it thinks fit.

Costs and expenses

7.5.13   The costs to be borne by each party depend on the nature of the works and the appropriate subsection into which it falls. Difficulties generally arise where the works will be to the benefit of both parties and where that benefit is not equal. In such circumstances, it is for the agreed surveyor or two of the three surveyors to determine the respective contributions. As a general guide, the costs will ordinarily be borne by the building owner. The adjoining owner will only be liable for a contribution for costs either in the case of a party struc-ture notice where he makes additional use of a party wall, or where a counter notice is served by an adjoining owner requiring additional works.

Checklist – dispute resolution (s 10)

- Section 10 allows for the resolution of disputes between either an agreed surveyor or a third surveyor appointed by the parties' nominees.
- Section 10 provides for the eventualities of inactivity or death of an agreed or a third solicitor.
- A dispute will be settled by an award which is conclusive, save for a right of appeal to the County Court.

7.6 Security for expenses

7.6.1   An adjoining owner may serve notice on a building owner requiring him to give security for expenses (s 12(1)). In a case where the adjoining owner is liable for certain costs the building owner may also serve notice on the adjoining owner for similar security (s 12(2)).

7.6.2 An example of where security for expenses may be appropriate is in the application of s 2(2)(n) (exposure of a party wall to provide adequate weathering). It is not uncommon for buildings to be demolished so as to expose a party wall to the elements. Where the site is to be immediately redeveloped, simple felt and battens or in some cases polythene, would be considered an adequate form of temporary weather protection. If, however, it is likely that the site may remain as a cleared site, for whatever reason, the temporary protection described above would not be considered adequate as permanent weathering. It would therefore be reasonable for the adjoining owner to require security for the cost of permanent protection.

Chapter 8

Withdrawal of Support and Interference with Light

8.1 Overview

8.1.1 This chapter is concerned with two subjects connected with the use of land which frequently arise in disputes between owners of neighbouring land, the right of support and its withdrawal, and the right to light and interferences with that right. The principal topics to be considered are the following:

(1) Withdrawal of support
   (a) removal of the natural right of support (independent of easements)
   (b) withdrawal of the easement of support to buildings
   (c) the effect of the Party Wall etc Act 1996.
(2) Interference with light
   (a) the nature of the right to light
   (b) measurement
   (c) light from different sources
   (d) unusually good light
   (e) poor light
   (f) alterations to premises
   (g) town planning
   (h) protection against acquisition of the easement.

8.1.2 Since both the withdrawal of support to buildings and interference with the right to light rely on proving the existence of the relevant easements, the substantive material relating to both the right of support and the right to light will be preceded by those rules which govern the establishment of easements. It should be noted that interferences with easements are actionable under the law of private nuisance (the general principles of which are set out in Chapter 1) but that the relevant principles form a set of rules in their own right (see the speech of Lord Macnaghten in *Colls v Home and Colonial Stores Ltd* [1904] AC 179).

8.1.3 The Sweet & Maxwell Practitioner Series contains two related titles relevant to other easements which can be the subject of disputes between neighbours, *Wilkinson's Pipes, Drains and Sewers* and *Garner's Rights of Way*.

8.2 Establishing the existence of an easement

8.2.1 Before turning to the special qualities of the easements of the right of support and the right to light, some brief outline observations will be made on the law relevant to establishing whether an easement exists. It should be noted at the outset that most claims to the right to light are based on s 3 of Prescription Act 1832, set out at 8.2.15–8.2.17 below.

8.2.2 In order to establish the existence of an easement the following four characteristics in a right must be satisfied:

(1) *There must be a dominant and servient tenement*: That is to say that both X who grants the right and Y who is the recipient of the grant must be the freehold or leasehold owners of land.

(2) *The easement must accommodate the dominant tenement*: This means that some benefit must be conferred to the advantage of the dominant land itself.

(3) *The dominant and servient owners must be different persons.*

(4) *The right must be capable of forming the subject matter of a grant*: Although the categories of rights capable of forming easements are considered to be open, an easement is a right which the courts will recognise as being capable of being granted expressly by deed and therefore assignable.

8.2.3 The right in question must also have been acquired in one of the following manners:

(1) by express grant or reservation

(2) by implied grant or reservation

(3) by presumed grant (by 'prescription').

These will be considered in further detail below in so far as they affect the easements which are particularly the subject of this chapter.

Acquisition by express grant or reservation

8.2.4 An express grant can take the form of a specific formal agreement but is most commonly found in the transfer of land as a reservation to the benefit of the retained land. In the case of rights to light, care must be exercised in assessing the scope of an express grant since it can grant more than a simple right to light as measured at common law. In its simplest form there may be theoretically a grant of a straightforward right to light allowing some degree of future development or change in the amount of light which can be received by a building.

Easements acquired by implied grant

8.2.5 Easements may be impliedly granted in a variety of forms, chiefly as:

Easements caught by the rule in Wheeldon v Burrows
Since an owner of land cannot derogate from the grant of land, the rule in *Wheeldon v Burrows* provides that where X owns A and B and grants B to Y, Y will have the benefit of any rights over A which he requires for the necessary enjoyment of B.

Easements existing as a result of s 62 of the Law of Property Act 1925
Section 62 contains a series of general words which, in the absence of any express provision, act to transfer an easement with a conveyance of land.

Easements acquired by prescription

8.2.6 An easement acquired by prescription may be acquired either at common law or by statute or under both. An easement acquired by prescription is an easement in respect of which the courts are willing to presume the existence of a grant of the right enjoyed by the owner of the dominant tenement.

8.2.7 As for prescription at common law, a right enjoyed since 1189 ('time immemorial') ensures that an easement can be claimed by prescription. Should such a claim not be demonstrable, a continuous period of 20 years will do, although it is rebuttable by evidence of some interruption in use of the right at some time since 1189. For modern attempts to apply the principle see *Diment v HN Foot Ltd* [1974] 1 WLR 1427 at 1430 and *Davis v Whitby* [1974] Ch 186.

8.2.8 Where the principle is rebuttable it may be possible to persuade the court to adopt the legal fiction of the 'lost modern grant'. Under the application of this doctrine, a party which can prove continuous user for 20 years can invite the judge to pretend that a right existed on some date arising after 1189 and that this was subsequently recorded in a deed which has now been lost.

8.2.9 Certain additional rules must be satisfied in order for a claim by prescription to be established. This includes the following:

(1) The owner of the servient tenement must be the freehold owner at the time of the beginning of the 20 year period in question

(2) Any right acquired by the owner of the dominant tenement is a right acquired only for the benefit of a freehold owner

(3) The person claiming an easement must show that the right in question has been used continuously for the 20 year period

(4) The exercise of the right must be 'as of right', which is to say that it must not be enjoyed

    (a) by way of force or violence (which may extend to written protests or legal proceedings),

    (b) secretly or hidden from the owner of the servient land,

    (c) with the permission or consent of the servient owner.

Prescription by statute (other than the right to light)

8.2.10 In addition, or in the alternative, to a claim to an easement arising by the operation of the common law rules, a claim may be made on the Prescription Act 1832, which contains different rules for rights to light and for other easements. (The rules dealing with a prescriptive acquisition of the right to light are set out at 8.2.15–8.2.17 below).

8.2.11 Where a party claims the enjoyment of a right for a period of 20 years, that claim raises a rebuttable presumption (at common law) that the right has been enjoyed since 1189 and so gives rise to an easement (8.2.8). Section 2 of the 1832 Act makes this an irreversible presumption which cannot be defeated by evidence. A claim to 20 years uninterrupted use cannot therefore be defeated by showing that user began after 1189. At the same time such a claim can be defeated by any other common law objection, for instance that the dominant and servient tenements were owned by the same person during that period.

8.2.12 When the section requires the right to have been enjoyed 'without interruption' this means uninterrupted by the owner of the servient tenement or some third party. Section 4 requires that an interruption will not be deemed to be an interruption until it has been acquiesced in for at least a year after the owner of the dominant tenement has had notice of it.

8.2.13 Section 2 also provides that where the user has continued for a period of 40 years or more, the right is to be deemed 'absolute and indefeasible unless it shall appear that the same was enjoyed by some consent or agreement expressly given in writing'.

8.2.14 In calculating the 20 and 40 year periods set out in s 2, regard must be had to the deductions set out in ss 7 and 8. Section 7 reduces the appropriate periods by the time during which the owner of the servient tenement was, for instance, an infant or lunatic. Section 8 reduces the 40 year period in certain instances where the servient tenement has been let under the terms of a lease for a period of three years or more.

Prescription by statute – s 3 (the right to light)

8.2.15 The most common basis of a claim to a right to light as an easement is probably by virtue of s 3 of the Prescription Act 1832 which states:

> When the . . . use of light to and for any dwelling-house, workshop, or other building shall have been actually enjoyed therewith for the full period of twenty years without interruption, the right thereto shall be deemed absolute and indefeasible, any local usage or custom to the contrary notwithstanding, unless it shall appear that the same was enjoyed by some consent or agreement expressly made or given for that purpose by deed or writing.

An absolute right is therefore established after 20, rather than 40, years' uninterrupted use.

8.2.16 In order to establish uninterrupted enjoyment for a period of 20 years it does not necessarily matter that the premises were not occupied for the whole period. Whether there has been uninterrupted enjoyment for 20 years is a matter of fact and degree. Thus in *Courtauld v Legh* (1869) LR 4 Exch 126 it was sufficient that a dwelling-house was partially completed and that the windows had been put in and were capable of being opened and shut for part of the period. So too in *Smith v Baxter* [1900] 2 Ch 138 the plaintiffs claimed a prescriptive right going back over a period when a previous building had been on the same site. Shelving placed over windows on the building which had nevertheless admitted light did not interrupt the enjoyment of the right to light. On the other hand the fact that two windows had been boarded over was held to have interrupted the period of enjoyment of a right to light in respect of those windows.

8.2.17 It is important to note that by reason of s 3 of the 1832 Act the common law rules for establishing an easement by prescription do not have to be satisfied. This means for instance that:

(1) Distinctions between freehold and leasehold owners are irrelevant

(2) The exercise of the right need not be 'as of right' (cf 8.2.9 above)

(3) The deductions in ss 7 and 8 do not apply.

Checklist – establishing an easement

- Is the right claimed as an easement accompanied by the following four characteristics?
  — the existence of a dominant and servient tenement
  — a benefit conferred on the dominant tenement by the right
  — separate ownership of the dominant and servient tenements
  — capacity to exist as the subject matter of a grant (ie 'in gross').
- Has the easement been acquired by one of the following means:
  — express grant or reservation
  — implied grant or reservation, meaning:
    — of necessity
    — by the rule in *Wheeldon v Burrows*
    — by the operation of s 62, Law of Property Act 1925
  — presumed grant ('prescription'), meaning:
    — (a) at common law – (i) after continuous use since 1189 (a use being presumed by 20 years of enjoyment unless rebutted by evidence of interruption since 1189), (ii) by the application of the doctrine of the lost modern grant
    — (b) by statute (Prescription Act 1832).
- Establishing the right to light by statute (s 3 of the Prescription Act 1832)
  — the proper construction of s 3 of the Prescription Act 1832 is significant
  — it is important to note that the same requirements are not expected in order to establish a right to light as they are for other easements
  — in particular, an absolute right is established after 20 years' uninterrupted use.

8.3 Withdrawal of support

8.3.1 There are two categories of rights of support. The first is not an easement at all, but a natural right of support to land from neighbouring land. The second is a right of support for buildings and other forms of land which are not in their natural state, for instance man-made earthworks or an embankment. Whereas the former is a natural right attached to land, the latter can only be protected in nuisance if it satisfies the usual requirements as to easements. This section will consider both rights of support.

Natural support to land

8.3.2 The right to the support of land in its natural state is an ordinary right of property. An owner is under an obligation not to act in such a way as to diminish the support to adjoining land so as to cause damage (*Backhouse v Bonomi* (1861) 9 HL Cas 503, 11 ER 825). Damage must be proved in order to establish a cause of action (*Darley Main Colliery Co v Mitchell* (1886) 11 App Cas 127). It is a negative obligation not to remove support rather than a positive obligation to maintain or provide support (*Sack v Jones* [1925] Ch 235; *Bond v Nottingham Corp* [1940] Ch 429 at 438).

8.3.3 Examples of interferences with the natural right of support include:
   (1) Quarrying at the foot of a hill which dislodged the land of a neighbouring fruit farm extending up the adjoining slope (*Redland Bricks Ltd v Morris* [1970] AC 652);
   (2) The removal of an underground wet sand formation by operations which caused the sand to run (*Jordeson v Sutton, Southcoates & Drypool Gas Co* [1898] 2 Ch 614);
   (3) The solution of salt beds under land by pumping in water prior to the extraction of salt (*Lotus Ltd v British Soda Co Ltd* [1972] Ch 123).

8.3.4 It is important to note that there must be some operation or activity on the part of the defendant which causes the damage for the plaintiff to have a right of action. In *Rouse v Gravelworks Ltd* [1940] 1 KB 489 the defendant excavated minerals to the edge of its land bounded by the land of the plaintiff farmer. The plaintiff's land began to erode by reason of the effect of wind on a pool of water which had collected where the minerals had been extracted. The plaintiff was held to have no cause of action. The defendant had a right at common law to extract all the minerals on its land. The erosion of the defendant's land was held to have been caused solely by the operation of natural factors.

Support to buildings

8.3.5 Where a building is erected on the dominant land, it does not have an automatic natural right of support. As in *Lotus'* case, however, where there has been an actionable interference with the natural right to support it may also be possible to recover compensation for damage caused to buildings on the land.

8.3.6 In order to make a successful claim for a remedy in the absence of a claim arising out of the withdrawal of natural support to land, it is necessary to establish the existence of an easement, whether by express or implied grant or by prescription. The general rule in the absence of express or implied grant is that it must be shown that the building has enjoyed over 20 years of support and as of right to the full and reasonable knowledge of the servient owner. The need to be able to prove the existence of an easement is particularly relevant where it is claimed that a building has suffered some interference with its right to support from a neighbouring dwelling although it is important to note the effect of the Party Wall Act 1996 (see 8.3.9–8.3.10 below).

8.3.7 The nature of the easement is succinctly set out in *Bond v Norman* [1940] Ch 429 at 438:

> The nature of the right of support is not open to dispute. The owner of the servient tenement is under no obligation to repair that part of his building which provides support for his neighbour. He can let it fall into decay. If it does so, and support is removed, the owner of the dominant tenement has no cause for complaint. On the other hand, the owner of the dominant tenement is not bound to sit by and watch the gradual deterioration of the support constituted by his neighbour's building. He is entitled to enter and take the necessary steps to ensure that the support continues by effecting repairs, and so forth, to the part of the building which gives the support. But what the owner of the servient tenement is not entitled to do is by an act of his own, to remove the support without providing an equivalent. There is the qualification upon his ownership of his own building that he is bound to deal with it and can only deal with it subject to the rights in it which are vested in his neighbour.

It should be noted therefore that the right of support does not place a positive obligation on a servient owner to keep his property in repair. Where the condition of the servient tenement is so bad that some hazard spreads on to the dominant tenement, it may be possible to make a claim in private nuisance. Thus in *Bradburn v Lindsay* [1983] 2 All ER 408 it was held (applying *Leakey v National Trust* [1980] QB 485) that the defendant was liable because she should have appreciated the danger of dry rot affecting her neighbour's semi-detached dwelling and taken steps to avoid that danger from occurring. The relevant principles relating to dangerous hazards are set out at 1.10 above.

8.3.8 In establishing a nuisance to a right of support, the degree of both damage and interference will be a matter of fact and degree requiring a technical consideration of the structure and ground conditions. An interference with the right to support should not be confused with vibration from the servient land, which in itself may amount to a separate action in nuisance.

Effect of the Party Wall Act 1996

8.3.9 With the passing of the Party Wall Act 1996 many of the problems associated with rights of support will no longer apply. Buildings adjacent to development sites will largely be covered by the new statutory framework, removing many of the difficulties experienced in establishing a right of support and any interference which may affect it. In fact, in a case where the Act applies, it will no longer be necessary to establish that a right of support exists at all, since the Act deems that the adjoining owner's buildings must be reasonably safeguarded regardless of the existence of any common law right of support. In addition, the difficulties and risks in proving causation in an action for the abatement of a nuisance will be reduced by the effect of s 2 of the 1996 Act. This is because s 2 requires that a building owner only need show that there is a defect or want of repair to a party wall to give him the right to enter on to an adjoining owner's land to execute the repair. He will also be able to recover part of the costs involved.

8.3.10 The one main circumstance not covered by the 1996 Act is where two independent buildings separated by two separate walls, not being a party wall, rely on one another for lateral support. In such a case it will be necessary to consider whether or not an easement of support exists, whether there has been an interference with the easement and the remedies available to the dominant owner.

The Party Wall Act 1996 and adjacent excavations and construction

8.3.11 The 1996 Act, by s 6, also governs the rights of a building owner to carry out certain excavations for the purposes of construction on his own land where those excavations are within three or six metres of adjoining premises. The aim of the section is to prevent damage occurring to those adjoining premises.

8.3.12 Section 6 now requires a building owner to notify an adjoining owner where he proposes to carry out excavations or undertake construction work which may affect the support to an adjoining owner's building or structure.

8.3.13 Notification applies to two situations:

Three Metre Notice
(1) (a) [where] a building owner proposes to excavate, or excavate for and erect a building or structure, within a distance of three metres measured horizontally from any part of a building or structure of an adjoining owner; and
(b) any part of the proposed excavation, building or structure will within those three metres extend to a lower level than the level of the bottom of the foundations of the building or structure of the adjoining owner.

This is represented by figure 1 overleaf.

Six Metre Notice
(2) (a) [where] a building owner proposes to excavate, or excavate for and erect a building or structure, within a distance of six metres measured horizontally from any part of a building or structure of an adjoining owner; and
(b) any part of the proposed excavation, building or structure will within those six metres meet a plane drawn downwards in the direction of the excavation, building or structure of the building owner at an angle of forty-five degrees to the horizontal from the line formed by the intersection of the plane of the level of the bottom of the foundations of the building or structure of the adjoining owner with the plane of the external face of the external wall of the building or structure of the adjoining owner.

This is represented by figure 2 overleaf.

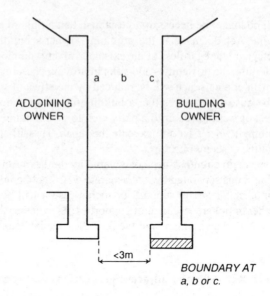

Figure 1

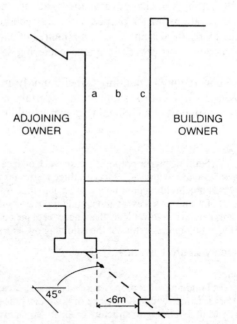

Figure 2

8.3.14 In essence, a six metre notice will apply if the new foundations or excavations of the building owner are deeper than a notional line drawn at 45° from the base of the adjoining owner's foundation (taken from the outside face of the building and not the edge or projection of any footing).

8.3.15 As to the requirements for notification themselves, s 6(5) requires a building owner to serve notice of his intention to excavate and erect a structure one month before the works are carried out. He must state whether it is intended to carry out any underpinning works or otherwise to strengthen or safeguard the foundations of the building or structure of the adjacent owner. Full plans and details are required to be served.

8.3.16 Where no consent is received in response to the notice a dispute will be deemed to have arisen which must be resolved according to the provisions of the Party Walls etc Act 1996 (set out at 7.5).

8.3.17 The remaining provisions of the 1996 Act as to compensation, rights of entry, notification, expenses and so on, also apply to the works covered by s 6 of the Act.

Checklist – the right to support

- Does the plaintiff have a claim for a natural right to support?
  - — this is not an easement and does not have to be acquired as such
  - — try and set out a claim under this head if possible, claiming damages to buildings as consequential damage.
- Is a right of support to a building actionable?
  - — the existence of an easement must be established (see above)
  - — the servient owner has no duty to repair unless there is evidence of knowledge (or presumed knowledge) of the existence of a dangerous hazard (for instance dry rot)
  - — the servient owner may not remove the support
  - — the dominant owner is entitled to enter on to the servient tenement to ensure continued support by effecting repairs, having due regard for the rights of the servient owner
  - — if the right of support is a party wall, regard must be had to the effects of the Party Walls etc Act 1996.
- Adjacent excavations and construction
  - — have any notices required by s 6 of the 1996 Act been served?
  - — has an adjacent owner complied with the provisions of the 1996 Act as to dispute resolution, compensation, expenses, etc?

8.4 Interference with light

Introduction

8.4.1 At common law there is no natural right to light over adjoining land (*Tapling v Jones* (1865) 11 HL Cas 290, 11 ER 1344). In order to protect a right to light enjoyed by an owner of land it is therefore necessary to establish the existence of an easement. Where there has been some interference with such an easement the appropriate cause of action will lie in nuisance.

The nature of the right to light

8.4.2 The right to light which is protected by the courts is a right to have that amount of light through the windows of a property which is sufficient, according to the ordinary notions of mankind, for the comfortable use and enjoyment of that property (*City of London Brewery Co v Tennant* (1873) LR 9 Ch App 212). Inevitably the amount which will be required will vary according to the type of building in question, so that what is appropriate for a residential dwelling may not be appropriate for a warehouse (*Colls v Home and Colonial Stores Ltd* [1904] AC 179).

8.4.3 The extent of the easement is a right to prevent one's neighbour from building upon his land so as to obstruct the access of sufficient light to such an extent as to render the premises substantially less comfortable and enjoyable than they were without the infringement in question. Whether there has been an actionable interference with the right so as to amount to a nuisance is a matter of fact and degree. This means that the court is entitled to take into account the general nature of the locality (*Ough v King* [1967] 1 WLR 1547), although it must not embark on too critical an analysis of the surrounding area (*Horton's Estate Ltd v James Beattie Ltd* [1927] 1 Ch 75). The underlying question is always not how much has been taken away but how much is left, so that it is not every diminution of light which will give rise to the cause of action (*Colls'* case).

Measuring the interference

8.4.4 Although the question whether there has been a material interference is one of fact and degree for the court there are certain conventions which have come to be applied in a right to light case. In the ordinary way an expert will be engaged to advise how much light has been lost. Such an expert will be of great assistance since he will be able to make allowances for seasonal variations in the intensity of light in the sky and for variations caused by the time of day at which a measurement might be taken.

8.4.5 It is important to note that the enjoyment of light must be to an actual building through defined apertures intended for the access and use of light (that is a window, rooflight or similar), and it is the aperture to which the measure of light is taken in any assessment, not necessarily the room it serves.

8.4.6 Accordingly, the measurement is taken as the amount of light that would be received from a standard overcast sky at a given reference point within the room in question. That reference point is taken on a working plane, the height of which will depend on the use of the room. The value of visible sky is expressed as a Sky Factor percentage, and through detailed measurement and calculation, a surveyor will eventually be able to plot a contour within the room representing a line joining points with a value of 0.2 per cent Sky Factor. This value has been taken to equate to the minimum amount of daylight required to undertake tasks requiring a given amount of visual discrimination such as reading or sewing.

8.4.7 By undertaking this exercise using both 'before' and 'after' conditions, the movement of the contour represents the loss of adequately lit space. The surveyor is then able to assess the level of injury by zoning the working plane, since light nearer to the aperture will be more valuable. Once the zonal areas have been weighted to reflect the seriousness of the loss, they can be used to assess the degree of injury. This will be expressed by reference to a generally accepted '50/50' working rule. This means that if 50 per cent of a room remains adequately lit after the erection of the obstruction then there is unlikely to be an actionable injury.

8.4.8 It should also be noted that the appropriateness of the 50/50 working rule set out above must be treated with some caution. Judges can be suspicious of it and in some cases it has been held to be 'wholly unsound' (*Sheffield Masonic Hall Co Ltd v Sheffield Corp* [1932] 2 Ch 17). The ultimate test is always one for the judge, who will ordinarily be expected to view the premises (*Ough v King* [1967] 1 WLR 1547, 1552).

8.4.9 In *Price v Hilditch* [1930] 1 Ch 500 at 504, Maugham J stated that he preferred to decide such a case:

> very largely as depending upon the actual evidence of ordinary members of the public who have used the rooms before and after the alleged obstruction, and who can give positive evidence as to the injury, if any, which they have suffered.

It is always useful to obtain the evidence of such witnesses when presenting a case.

8.4.10 A surveyor should also be engaged to offer a financial assessment of the extent of the interference with the right to light. This will probably be in percentage terms, in which it will be necessary to call evidence as to the value of the property.

Light from different sources

8.4.11 A room may receive light from different sources such as a skylight or two sets of windows on different sides of the building. In such circumstances the question arises whether a plaintiff can object to the obstruction of one set of lights if his premises still receive sufficient light for all reasonable purposes from another servient tenement. The general rule is that both servient tenements have equal rights, so that the same obligation is imposed on each of them not to build so as to cause a nuisance to the plaintiff by their joint action (*Sheffield Masonic Hall Co's* case). This means the owner of either of the servient tenements can only build to such a height as, with a similar building by the owner of the other servient tenement, will still leave sufficient light for the purposes of the owner of the dominant tenement.

Unusually good light

8.4.12 The nature of the use to which the dominant tenement is put is a relevant factor in assessing whether there has been an interference with the right to light. It is therefore possible to acquire a right to a higher level of light provided that the servient owner was, or should have been, fully aware of the exceptional level of light required throughout the prescriptive period (see *Allen v Greenwood* [1980] Ch 119 – actionable interference with the light enjoyed in a greenhouse). The application of *Allen v Greenwood* is questionable in cases when a particular *type* of natural light is required, such as a gallery or artist's studio.

Poor light

8.4.13   There are no clear precedents on rights attached to poorly lit windows. As a general rule it will be a matter of fact and degree in the assessment of which expert opinion will be of great assistance.

8.4.14   It can be argued that where the dominant tenement is poorly lit in the first place, any interference with the present levels of light could amount to an interference with the beneficial use of the premises and so constitute an actionable nuisance. On the other hand, it must be remembered that the underlying question in assessing whether there has been nuisance is the question what light has been left, not the question how much light has been taken away. In *Price v Hilditch* [1930] 1 Ch 500 Maugham J found that a scullery had been deprived of a great deal of light but that 'there is still left sufficient light for the ordinary purposes of such a room'. He asked himself (at 507) whether it was still necessary to decide:

> whether I have got to treat the right of the plaintiff as limited by the use to which this particular room has been put.

The question was answered in the plaintiff's favour and he was awarded damages.

8.4.15   Although the better view is generally that an interference is caused by depriving a poorly lit part of a building of further light, the matter remains a question of fact and degree. It follows that a threshold will exist where the existing light is so poor that any further diminution would have no material effect on the beneficial use of the building. The difficulty will arise in establishing that threshold.

Alterations to premises – has the plaintiff abandoned the right to light?

8.4.16   It is sometimes argued by a defendant that a plaintiff has lost a right to light because of some alteration effected to his premises. Such an argument is based on a proper application of the law of easements and in particular on the question whether by his conduct the owner of the dominant tenement has evinced an intention to abandon the easement (ie an extinguishment by release). In such a case, although the mere lack of evidence of an intention to preserve the ancient lights is not by itself sufficient to prove an intention to abandon them, a plaintiff should ensure that there is some evidence before the court of a clear intention to preserve the privileged windows (*News of the World Ltd v Allen Fairhead & Sons Ltd* [1931] 2 Ch 402).

8.4.17 Where a window is enlarged or replaced by new windows, the owner of the dominant tenement retains the right to light enjoyed through the previous aperture even though he will not be able to extend protection to any new windows (*Tapling v Jones* (1865) 11 HL Cas 290). This is the consequence of s 3 of the Prescription Act 1832 which makes the right to light enjoyed through the previous apertures absolute and indefeasible after a period of 20 years. It follows that even where a building is completely rebuilt the owner of the dominant tenement will have a right to light so long as he can prove the identity of the earlier light (*Scott v Pape* (1886) 31 Ch D 554).

8.4.18 The important issue where there has been an alteration to the previous structure is always whether there is reasonable level of coincidence of the old and new apertures (whether in size or plane). For a plaintiff the difficulty lies in showing that the obstruction would have been a nuisance under the former conditions. Thus in *News of the World v Allen Fairhead & Sons Ltd*, Farwell J summed up the position as follows (at 406):

> The true view is this. If the plaintiff pulls down the building with ancient light windows and erects a new building totally different in every respect, but having windows to some extent in the same position as the old windows, he cannot require the servient owners to do more than see that the ancient lights, if any, to which he is still entitled are not obstructed to the point of nuisance. He cannot require them not to obstruct non-ancient lights merely because a portion of the window through which that non-ancient light enters his premises, also admits of a pencil of ancient light. If the obstruction of the pencil itself causes nuisance the plaintiff is entitled to relief, but if taking the building as it stands the pencil obstruction causes no nuisance at all, the plaintiff is not entitled to relief.

The appropriate measure will therefore need to be taken on the amount of light received by the position of the old aperture, even though most of the light to the altered aperture may have been obstructed.

8.4.19 Where an owner substantially increases the size of his property he may try to retain some of the old windows in an attempt to preserve the easement. The question then arises whether the burden on the servient tenement has been so increased that the court should infer an intention on the part of the dominant owner to abandon the easement. This again is a question of fact. In *Ankerson v Connelly* [1907] 1 Ch 678 the owner of the servient tenement had so extended his premises that the few lights he had retained were not sufficient to demonstrate an intention not to abandon the easement.

Town planning

8.4.20 The town planning system recognises various rights and amenities which cannot be protected as easements. These include a right to sunlight and to a view, a right to overlook adjacent property, and a sense of enclosure as well as a right to daylight. These five considerations are usually contained in the planning authority's Amenity Policy.

8.4.21   There is an important distinction between the planning system and a right to light since the function of the planning system is for the benefit of the public at large and is not to be used to protect private rights.

8.4.22   The Amenity Policy is applied to proposed buildings as much as it is to existing adjoining buildings. Initially the Planning Officer's principal concern will be the availability of sunlight and daylight to the proposed new building and then the impact of the new building on adjoining premises.

8.4.23   Different planning authorities will have different policies and standards but in general they will adopt the guidelines set out in the Building Research Establishment report *Site Layout Planning for Daylight and Sunlight – a Guide to Good Practice* 1991.

8.4.24   Although the target levels of daylight under planning rules are generally considerably higher than a legal entitlement to light, the guidelines are not mandatory and are just one of a number of planning considerations. They sometimes appear to be applied in an arbitrary manner. Experience shows that planning authorities are more inclined to apply the guidelines when seeking to protect listed buildings or buildings in conservation areas.

Protection against acquisition of the easement

8.4.25   Before an easement of the right to light has been acquired it will be possible lawfully to prevent the acquisition by any form of obstruction whether by an actual building or a screen. Unfortunately, the erection of a wall or screen greater than two metres in height requires planning permission so that this will often be impractical.

8.4.26   Under the Rights of Light Act 1959, however, apertures may be obstructed by a notional screen in order to interrupt the prescriptive period by 12 months, so that the time for acquisition will start over again. The application for a notice of notional obstruction is made to the local authority and must identify the servient land and dominant building and specify the position and height of the notional screen to obstruct the servient land. On acceptance, the notice is registered as a Local Land Charge. The servient owner, and anyone likely to be affected by the notice must be given adequate notice of the proposed registration.

Checklist – the right to light

- Is an interference with light actionable?
  — the existence of the easement must be established
  — a plaintiff is entitled to an amount of light through his windows which is sufficient according to the ordinary notions of mankind for the comfortable use and enjoyment of that property
  — the nature of the building in question is relevant
  — whether the interference is actionable is a matter of fact and degree

- — the important issue is always 'how much light is left?', not 'how much light has been taken away?'. Not every interference is therefore actionable
- — the use of an expert is beneficial, although the ultimate decision will be taken by an assessment by the judge, normally after a site visit
- — witnesses of fact should be called to give their impressions of the standard of light before as well as after the defendant's obstruction
- — a defendant will not defeat a claim by demonstrating that there is still sufficient light from another source
- — unusually good light will be protected by the courts
- — a defendant will not defeat a claim because the light enjoyed by the dominant tenement was poor
- — whether alterations to premises amounts to an abandonment of the easement is a matter of fact and degree
- — the effects of the town planning system should be noted.
- The owner of a servient tenement is entitled to take steps to prevent the acquisition of the easement
  - — since the planning rules prevent the most efficacious means of preventing the acquisition of the easement, use should be made of the procedure set out in the Rights of Light Act 1959.

Chapter 9

Animals

9.1 Overview

9.1.1 This chapter is mainly concerned with the liability for damage caused by animals. The relevant law is now largely codified by the Animals Act 1971 so that the scope of the following sections dealing with animal damage is almost exclusively the 1971 Act. In some circumstances, however, there may also be a liability at common law, for instance, where it can be said that the keeper of an animal acted negligently. Some observations about framing an action at common law are set out in 9.2 below.

9.1.2 This chapter is organised into the following topics of general application:

(1) Liability for damage caused by animals at common law
(2) Liability under the Animals Act 1971
(3) Rights and liabilities in respect of trespassing livestock
(4) Liability for damage caused by animals which stray on to the highway.

9.1.3 Specific rules also exist in relation to dogs and these will be considered separately under the following headings:

(1) Dangerous dogs
(2) Pit bull terriers and dogs bred for fighting
(3) Liabilities of owners of dogs which worry livestock
(4) Rights to deal with dogs which worry livestock
(5) Strays.

9.2 Common law liability for damage caused by animals

9.2.1 Although the focus for establishing liability for damage caused by animals is the Animals Act 1971, the common law may well be applicable. A person has a duty to take care that his neighbour is not likely to be injured by his animals. The proposition of law most frequently relied on is that set out in *Fardon v Harcout-Rivington* (1932) 146 LT 391 (HL):

> Quite apart from the liability imposed upon the owner of animals or the person having control of them by reason of knowledge of their propensities, there is the ordinary duty of a person to take care either that his animal or chattel is not put to

such use as is likely to injure his neighbour – the ordinary duty to take care in the cases upon negligence.

Thus in the following examples the defendants were found liable at common law in negligence:

(1) The licensee of a public-house who had a dangerous dog owed a duty to his customers to take steps to see that the dog was kept away from them. When a customer therefore walked unwittingly into a private yard through an open gate from the public-house garden and was savaged, it was held that the defendant was in breach of this duty of care (*Gould v McAuliffe* [1941] 1 All ER 515).

(2) A riding school proprietor who organised a gymkhana was liable for a pony which bolted during a 'saddle-up' race and collided with a passing car after running through gates which had been left open (*Bativala v West* [1970] 1 QB 716).

(3) A breeder of Jack Russell terriers was held liable when the pack savaged a small boy, even though his dogs had entered on to the land occupied by the boy and his family for eight years without incident. The court held that it was reasonably foreseeable that since the pack might get into the adjacent land some harm might be caused to the boy (*Draper v Hodder* [1972] 2 QB 556).

(4) The owner of an unbroken colt was held liable for driving the animal along the highway in the dark where it became frightened by the light of an oncoming cyclist, careered about and injured the cyclist (*Turner v Coates* [1917] 1 KB 670).

(5) The owner of a large dog who took it into a busy urban street and then lost control of it was liable for the damage caused to the plaintiff's van when the van and the dog collided (*Gomberg v Smith* [1963] 1 QB 25).

Foreseeability

9.2.2 Special problems arise when trying to allege negligence as a result of the ownership or management of an animal. The main difficulty stems from the question whether the owner or keeper should have foreseen the incident or damage in question. The special circumstances relevant to an action in negligence involving animals are well set out in *Aldham v United Dairies (London) Ltd* [1940] 1 KB 507 at 514 (Du Parcq LJ):

Where it is sought to impute liability to a defendant for the conduct of a living creature, capable of spontaneous action, it has been found necessary to lay down rules which prevent a jury from attributing to the reasonable man a degree of foresight which would anticipate every mischievous act of which an animal, hitherto docile, might conceivably be guilty, or from regarding the release of such an animal from custody or control, without more, as the direct cause of any violent departure from its accustomed docility which may ensue. Everyone knows that even a well-behaved animal may conceivably be guilty of such a sudden lapse, but if everyone was obliged to be constantly vigilant through his fear of such a misfortune, which the experience of mankind shows to be most improbable, it would hardly be safe ever to let a horse out of its stable.

The relevant question is whether the particular harm suffered was within the range of likely consequences, and not whether the particular type of physical harm actually suffered ought reasonably to have been anticipated (*Draper v Hodder* [1972] 2 QB 556). If, therefore, a farm servant were negligently to allow a herd of horses to enter a field where a school picnic was being held, it would be no defence to say that it was to be anticipated that a child might be trampled but not bitten (the example given by Edmund Davies LJ in *Draper's* case at 573D).

Other common law causes of action

9.2.3   Other causes of action which may be appropriate are private nuisance, trespass and *Rylands v Fletcher*. A person who intends to sue under common law rules must make sure that the requirements of the common law are satisfied. An action based on *Rylands v Fletcher*, for instance, must of course correspond with the appropriate common law rules, so that foreseeability of harm on the part of the defendant must be established as well the escape of some inherently dangerous entity. An action for damage done by a dangerous animal (now under the Animals Act 1971) is an action based purely on the possession of the animal. The distinction between the two is drawn in *Behrens v Bertram Mills Circus Ltd* [1957] 2 QB 1.

Checklist – liability at common law

- Check what cause of action may be appropriate, especially:
  — negligence
  — nuisance
  — trespass
  — *Rylands v Fletcher*.
- Are all the elements of the tort present?
- Was the damage foreseeable?

9.3   Liability for animals under the Animals Act 1971

A. Introduction

9.3.1   The 1971 Act makes provision for the liability for damage done by dangerous animals according to the type of animal. These are:
  (1) Animals which are dangerous by nature;
  (2) Animals which become dangerous by reason of their unusual characteristics.
The provisions of the Act reformulate the common law distinction between damage done by animals:

(1) formerly described as *ferae naturae* (animals which are dangerous by nature) and

(2) those whose vicious or mischievous propensities are known or presumed to be known by the keeper (the old *scienter* rule) (s 1(1)(a)).

In this chapter the two types of animal will be distinguished by the expressions 'animals dangerous by nature' and 'animals with abnormally dangerous characteristics'.

The defendant

9.3.2 Liability for damage under the 1971 Act is imposed on the 'keeper' of an animal. Section 6(3) defines the 'keeper' of an animal as the person who owns the animal or otherwise has it in his possession (s 6(3)(a)). If the true keeper is under the age of 16, then the head of the household becomes the 'keeper' for the purposes of the Act (s 6(3)(b)).

9.3.3 Under s 6(3) of the Act a person who owns or possesses an animal is deemed to remain its keeper until such time as somebody else can be properly identified as its keeper. This means that responsibility for any damage caused by an animal under the Act lies with the original keeper even when the animal has run away or otherwise become lost.

9.3.4 By s 6(4), the fact that a person has taken an animal into his possession either in order to prevent it causing damage or in order to restore it to its owner does not by itself make that person a keeper within the meaning of the Act.

B. Liability for animals which are dangerous by nature

9.3.5 Section 2(1) of the 1971 Act imposes a strict statutory liability on the keeper of an animal which 'belongs to a dangerous species':

> Where any damage is caused by an animal which belongs to a dangerous species, any person who is a keeper of the animal is liable for the damage, except as otherwise provided by this Act.

9.3.6 By s 6(2) an animal is dangerous by nature so long as it is of a species which satisfies both of the following criteria, that is to say that:

(1) It is not commonly domesticated in the United Kingdom (s 6(2)(a));

(2) Its adult member would normally be expected to cause 'severe' damage if not kept under restraint (s 6(2)(b)).

Accordingly, elephants have been held to belong to a dangerous species (*Filburn v People's Palace & Aquarium Co Ltd* (1890) 25 QBD 258). This is the case whatever their nationality (*Behrens v Bertram Mills Circus Ltd* [1957] 2 QB 1). Camels too are as a matter of law 'savage' within the meaning of s 2 (*McQuaker v Goddard* [1940] 1 KB 687).

9.3.7 It is important to note that once identified as a dangerous species the law knows of no individual exceptions, so that any elephant, however tame, will always be dangerous by nature.

Establishing that an animal is dangerous by nature – the need for evidence
9.3.8 Under the old law the question whether an animal is dangerous by nature was a matter of law. The judge needed only to take judicial notice of what is tame and what is savage (*Behrens's* case). This meant that a plaintiff did not have to call any evidence to prove the question, although the judge used to call for the production of evidence if not satisfied in his own mind as to whether an animal was considered to be savage or tame. A plaintiff who seeks to bring his claim under the statutory definition would be wise to have expert evidence to prove that both limbs of the statute are established.

C. Liability for animals with abnormally dangerous characteristics

Introduction – the statutory requirements
9.3.9 Where damage has been caused by an animal which cannot be described as dangerous by nature for the purposes of s 2(1), a plaintiff must bring his action within s 2(2). This section requires proof that the defendant (the keeper of the animal) knew that the animal was capable of causing damage by reason of its abnormal characteristics. The court will conduct an inquiry into the following topics set out in the statute. In summary, they are:

(1) The nature of the damage the animal was likely to cause (s 2(2)(a));
(2) Special characteristics in the animal likely to give rise to damage (s 2(2)(b));
(3) Knowledge by the keeper of the animal's special characteristics (s 2(2)(c)).

Section 2(2) reads as follows:

(2) Where damage is caused by an animal which does not belong to a dangerous species, a keeper of the animal is liable for the damage, except as otherwise provided by this Act, if –
   (a) the damage is of a kind which the animal, unless restrained, was likely to cause or which, if caused by the animal was likely to be severe; and
   (b) the likelihood of the damage or if its being severe was due to characteristics of the animal which are not normally found in animals of the same species or are not normally so found except at particular times or in particular circumstances; and
   (c) those characteristics were known to that keeper or were at any time known to a person who at that time had charge of the animal as that keeper's servant or, where that keeper is the head of the household, were known to another keeper of the animal who is a member of that household and under the age of sixteen.

9.3.10 In practice the first two requirements are so closely linked that it is very difficult to separate them. The correct approach therefore becomes a two-stage inquiry, the state of the defendant's knowledge being distinct from the objective consideration whether the animal was an animal which was likely to cause damage by reason of its abnormal characteristics. These topics are set out in more detail below.

The nature of damage likely to be caused by the animal
9.3.11 Under s 2(2)(a), the statute is concerned with the question whether, if not restrained, the animal was likely either to cause damage of the type in fact sustained or some other severe damage. If it is demonstrated that the animal was likely to cause the type of damage actually sustained, the plaintiff does not have to prove that that damage was likely to be 'severe' (*Curtis v Betts* [1990] 1 WLR 459).

Abnormal characteristics
9.3.12 The mischief which the statute seeks to prevent in the case of animals not normally dangerous is the failure of a keeper to restrain an animal which is, unusually for its type, likely to cause injury (s 2(2)(b)). An animal falls within this category where the likelihood of the damage or of its being severe was due to some special characteristics in the animal in question. These will be characteristics either not normally found in animals of the same species or not normally so found except at particular times or in particular circumstances.
9.3.13 For the purposes of s 2(2)(b) it is not necessary to prove that the likelihood of damage is 'caused by' the abnormal characteristics of the animal but only that they are 'attributable to' its characteristics (*Curtis v Betts* [1990] 1 WLR 459). Moreover there is no underlying need to show that the characteristics themselves must necessarily be of a vicious sort. A nervous and temperamental horse therefore might fall within the section (*Wallace v Newton* [1982] 1 WLR 375).
9.3.14 Where a keeper can demonstrate that the damage caused by an animal which does not belong to a dangerous species is attributable to characteristics normally found in such an animal, then no liability attaches. Thus in *Fitzgerald v ED and AD Cooke Bourne (Farms) Ltd and Another* [1964] 1 QB 249 it was held that since a filly was only dangerous because she was playful in the very manner in which all such animals were playful the defendant was not liable.
9.3.15 There is an exception to the rule that a keeper will escape liability if on the particular facts the likelihood of damage was attributable to characteristics of the animal which are normally found in animals of the same species. This exception applies if the characteristics of the animal which give rise to the likelihood of such damage are normally found in the species only at certain times or in certain circumstances (s 2(2)(b)). Thus in *Curtis v Betts* [1990] 1 WLR 459, although the 12 stone bull mastiff Max was 'in general . . . a docile and lazy dog', when he was transferred into his owner's Land Rover Max considered himself to be within the boundaries of his territory and would react fiercely in order to defend it.

Proving abnormal characteristics – expert evidence
9.3.16 When it comes to proving that an animal is dangerous by reason of its abnormal characteristics, expert evidence will be required. This is generally because the courts will go into great detail to see if liability can be established on the basis that the animal only exhibited its dangerous characteristics at

particular times or in particular circumstances. (See *Curtis'* case and *Cummings v Granger* [1977] QB 397.)

The need to identify the particular animal

9.3.17   It must also be established that a specific animal caused the damage which is the subject of the action. This is so that the abnormal characteristics can be identified. In *Draper v Hodder* [1972] 2 QB 556 (CA) D had kept a pack of Jack Russell terrier puppies next door to premises occupied by the infant plaintiff P and his family. It was impossible to identify the dogs responsible for the injuries so that it was impossible to identify any abnormally dangerous characteristics for which D could be held liable.

Knowledge on the part of the keeper

9.3.18   As to the state of knowledge of the keeper, this must be a real understanding on his part that the animal has abnormally dangerous characteristics (s 2(2)(c)). The fact that the matter was obvious to others, such as neighbours, cannot help the plaintiff if the keeper himself did not appreciate the fact.

9.3.19   If the keeper's servant had charge of the animal and knew of the abnormally dangerous characteristics of the animal, then knowledge will be imputed to the keeper (s 2(2)(c)). The same is true if the keeper is the head of a household and the abnormally dangerous characteristics of the animal were known to another keeper of the animal under the age of 16 (s 2(2)(c)).

Proving knowledge

9.3.20   Evidence that at any stage the keeper knew of the potentially savage characteristics of the animal is admissible. The issue must, however, be properly proved. It should be clearly pleaded and if there is no admission by the defendant then expert evidence will, again, be required.

D. Defences

9.3.21   The 1971 Act sets out various defences. These are:
  (1) Fault of the defendant;
  (2) Voluntary acceptance of risk;
  (3) Trespassers.
The Act does not provide for the defences of intervention by third party or Act of God which are nevertheless available (see *Behrens v Bertram Mills Circus* [1957] 2 QB 1).

Fault of the defendant

9.3.22   A person is expressly not to be held liable for any damage which is wholly the fault of the injured party (s 5(1)). By s 11 'fault' has the same meaning as the definition set out in Law Reform (Contributory Negligence) Act 1945, s 4, that is:

negligence, breach of statutory duty or other act or omission which gives rise to liability in tort . . . .

The 1945 Act therefore allows damages to be reduced in the ordinary way where the damage sustained is partly the fault of the keeper of an animal and partly the fault of the plaintiff.

Voluntary acceptance of risk by the defendant

9.3.23 By s 5(2) of the 1971 Act a person will not be liable for any damage suffered by a person who has voluntarily accepted the risk of such damage. In *Cummings v Granger* [1977] QB 397 Ormrod LJ stated that the expression must be interpreted according to its ordinary English meaning with regard to the specific facts of the case. In that case, a lady savagely mauled by an Alsatian at a scrap metal works was held voluntarily to have accepted the risk. She worked next to the works and knew about the animal's fierce nature.

9.3.24 This rule does not automatically apply to a person who is employed by the keeper of an animal. By s 6(5) someone engaged as the servant of the keeper of an animal shall not be treated as voluntarily accepting a risk of injury if such a risk is incidental to his employment.

Trespassers

9.3.25 The 1971 Act further provides (s 5(3)) that the keeper of an animal is not liable for any injury suffered by a person who is a trespasser on the premises where the animal is kept. If the animal is kept there for the protection of persons or property, then the keeper of the animal must also prove that the keeping of the animal there for that purpose was not unreasonable. It is quite reasonable therefore to keep a vicious Alsatian in a closed scrap yard in the East End of London where bits of car were considered fair game by thieves (*Cummings v Granger* [1977] QB 397).

Checklist – liability for dangerous animals under the Animals Act 1971

- Identify the correct defendant (a keeper)
  — the owner/possessor is a keeper
  — where the animal is owned by a child under 16, the head of the household is a keeper
  — if the animal is abandoned the previous owner/possessor remains a keeper
  — a possessor who has an animal in order to prevent it doing damage or to restore it to its owner is not necessarily a keeper.
- Is the animal dangerous by nature?
  — It is to the advantage of the plaintiff to bring the animal within this category since liability is strict (subject only to the statutory defences). The following must be proved:

— Is the animal commonly domesticated in the United Kingdom (s 6(2)(a))?

— Would the adult members of the species normally be expected to cause 'severe' damage if not kept under restraint (s 6(2)(b))?

— If there is case law available about the animal in question, then this may establish whether the animal is dangerous by nature.

- Is the animal dangerous by reason of its abnormally dangerous characteristics?

— Was the damage of a kind which (i) the animal was likely to cause if not restrained, or (ii) if caused by the animal, was likely to be severe (s 2(2)(a))?
and

— Did the animal have characteristics either (i) not normally found in animals of the same species or (ii) only normally found in animals of the same species at certain times or in certain circumstances (s 2(2)(b))?
and

— Was the likelihood of the damage actually sustained or of its being severe attributable to the animal's abnormal characteristics (s 2(2)(b))?
and

— Were the animal's abnormal characteristics known to the animal's keeper or keeper's servant or the head of the household (s 2(2)(c))?

— Expert evidence of abnormal characteristics will always be necessary

— A plaintiff must be careful to identify exactly when and where an animal's abnormal characteristics manifest themselves. This must be properly pleaded as well as proved

— Evidence of the defendant's knowledge must be available. For instance, was the defendant warned about the animal's characteristics? Did he know of other occasions when the animal's abnormal behaviour manifested themselves?

- What defences are available?
— fault of the defendant
— voluntary acceptance of risk
— trespassers
— Act of God
— acts of strangers.

9.4 Trespassing livestock

Introduction

9.4.1 The Animals Act 1971 contains a regulatory framework governing liability for damage caused by livestock which strays on to others' premises. It also sets out the rights of those on to whose property such animals have strayed to detain and sell them. Then common law rules on cattle trespass were abolished by s 1(1)(c) of the 1971 Act.

The defendant

9.4.2 The correct defendant where damage is caused by straying livestock is the person who is in possession of the animals. He is deemed to be the person to whom the livestock belongs (s 4(1)).

'Livestock'

9.4.3 Section 11 defines livestock as 'cattle, horses, asses, mules, hinnies, sheep, pigs, goats and poultry'. It also encompasses 'deer not in the wild state'.

The plaintiff

9.4.4 By s 4(1)(a) compensation is recoverable by anyone on to whose land livestock has trespassed, save that there is no liability if the livestock was lawfully on the highway and it strayed from the highway on to the complainant's land. Possession as well as ownership of the land is sufficient.

9.4.5 If damage has been caused to the chattels of the person on to whose land livestock has strayed, then compensation is also recoverable, whether or not there has been damage to the land. It is important to note that damages are not recoverable under s 4(1) for damaged goods if the person to whom the goods belong is not also the owner of, or otherwise holds, the land on to which the cattle have strayed. Possession (or ownership) of the land is the *sine qua non* of recoupment under the section.

9.4.6 In *Crow v Wood* [1971] 1 QB 77, P bought one of a number of the farms which adjoined a moor. The local farmers had customarily maintained their walls and fences in order to keep out their neighbours' straying sheep. P did not observe the custom but allowed her walls and fences to fall into disrepair. She claimed damages and an injunction from D, a neighbouring farmer, whose sheep had frequently trespassed on to her premises. The court held that the right to have one's neighbours keep up their fences was an easement which ran with the land and passed to P under s 62, Law of Property Act 1925. P was therefore unable to complain of the sheep trespassing on to her property.

Detaining trespassing livestock

9.4.7 Assuming that the occupier of land on to which livestock has strayed intends to detain it (whether or not his property is at risk), he has a right to do so by s 7 of the Act. If no damage has been caused to his property he must return the animals on demand to their rightful owner (s 7(3)(c)). If they have not been claimed by the rightful owner within 48 hours then notice must be given to the officer in charge of a police station within the same 48 hour period in order to make their further detention lawful. If the identity of the lawful owner is known then he must also be given notice (s 7(3)(a)). Where damage has been occasioned to the property of an occupier which gives rise to a claim under s 4 of the Act, the owner of the livestock does not have a right to the return of his animals unless sufficient compensation has been handed over to the detainer of the animals (s 7(3)(b)). So too, the keeper of the animals is entitled to demand his reasonable expenses incurred in providing for their upkeep (ss 4(1)(b) and 7(3)(b)).

9.4.8   The person who has detained livestock under s 7 has a further right to sell it at a market or by public auction after the expiry of 14 days. If a claim is pending either for the return of the livestock or under s 4 of the Act in respect of the livestock, then such a sale is prohibited (s 7(4)). If the sale goes ahead then the person to whom the livestock belongs is entitled to the proceeds of sale to the extent to which they exceed any claim for damage sustained by the vendor. He is also entitled to his costs (s 7(5)).

9.4.9   The occupier of premises who has incurred any expenditure in looking after livestock which have strayed from their owner on to his premises is entitled to be paid his expenses (s 4(1)(b)). These are also recoverable from any proceeds of sale.

Proving a claim for expenses

9.4.10   In *Morris v Blaenau Gwent DC* (1982) 80 LGR 793 (CA), the County Court judge sitting at Blackwood heard evidence about the wages of workmen engaged to look after straying animals at the plaintiff local authority's pound. He sought to make an award suggested by the defendant which was based on the actual time spent by the staff in looking after the plaintiff's five ponies, the cost of bales of hay, mucking out and so on, having allowed cross-examination by the plaintiff. The plaintiff had claimed a standard fee of £13.50 per pony in rounding up and £4 per day for care. The Court of Appeal decided that this was the best way to approach the question of what expenses had been reasonably incurred by the authority since there was great merit in avoiding complaints that one owner had been charged more than another. Moreover it was desirable that owners should know what they would have to pay to obtain the release of their animals.

The duty to take reasonable care of detained livestock

9.4.11   By s 7(6) a person who detains livestock in pursuance of s 4 is required to treat it with reasonable care and will be liable for any damage he causes by his failure to do so. The subsection specifically requires that the livestock is supplied with adequate food and water during the period of its detention.

Checklist – liability for trespassing livestock

- Who can sue?

— the owner/possessor of land. He can sue for damage either to his land or to his chattels.
— the owner of chattels cannot sue if he does not own or possess the land.
- Who can be sued?
    — the person who possesses the animal is deemed to be the owner
    — the animal must be 'livestock', ie cattle, horses, asses, mules, hinnies, sheep, pigs, goats, poultry and deer 'not in the wild state'.
- Detaining and disposing of trespassing livestock
    — where no damage is caused, animals must be returned on demand
    — if they are not claimed in 48 hours the police and the owner must be informed
    — if damage has been caused the owner must pay compensation before he has the right to the return of his animals
    — after 14 days livestock can be sold unless a claim is pending for the animals' return
    — a person who is entitled to detain livestock is entitled to his expenses. These can be recovered from the proceeds of sale.
- The duty to take reasonable care of detained livestock
    — a person who detains livestock has a duty to take reasonable care of it. In particular he must supply it with adequate food and water.

9.5 Animals straying on to the highway

9.5.1 A person who keeps animals on land owes a duty to take reasonable care to ensure that they do not stray on to the highway and cause damage. That is the effect of s 8(1), Animals Act 1971, which reverses the decision of the House of Lords in *Searle v Wallbank* [1947] AC 341 (see *Davies v Davies* [1975] QB 172). In *Searle v Wallbank* the House of Lords had decided that it was too onerous to impose such a duty on farmers since it was only since the comparatively recent introduction of bicycles and motor cars that serious collisions involving straying animals had started to take place. The rule was unsatisfactorily extended so that in, for instance, *Ellis v Johnstone* [1963] 2 QB 8, the owner of a large dog was not liable when the dog dashed out of D's premises and ran into P's car. The dog habitually crossed the road unaccompanied whenever it liked in order to sport on the common directly opposite. The gate to D's property was rarely closed.

9.5.2 'Straying' is not defined but it includes cattle which break through an extra-strong fence by the use of exceptional force 'because they are subjected to some peculiar inducement or temptation to get across', for instance calves separated from, and determined to join, their dams (*Cooper v Railway Executive* [1953] 1 WLR 223).

9.5.3 The effect of s 8 is that a keeper will generally have to ensure that he has taken steps to ensure that an animal cannot get on to the highway (such as, for instance, the riding school proprietor in *Bativala v West* [1970] 1 QB 716). In the case of herds or flocks of animals this will mean that a landowner will have to ensure that land is fenced and that such fences are adequately maintained. This is, however, a matter of evidence.

9.5.4   In some circumstances a breach of the duty to take care will not be established if the land has not been fenced. If land is common land or situated in a town or village green or on land 'where fencing is not customary', a keeper of animals is not liable for damage caused by a beast which strays on to the highway, so long as he can demonstrate a right to keep them on the land (s 8(2)(a), (b)). In *Davies v Davies* [1975] QB 172 this defence was extended to the farmer's son who actually worked the farm and who had placed the sheep on unfenced land, even though it was his mother as the owner of the farm who had registered the right of pasture. The court pointed out that the registered right was a right 'to graze 10 head of cattle and 100 sheep' and the defendant would not have succeeded if that number had been exceeded.

9.6   Dangerous dogs

A. Dogs Act 1871 and the Dangerous Dogs Acts 1989 and 1991

Introduction – s 2, Dogs Act 1871
9.6.1   The cheapest and most effective way of obtaining a remedy against a dangerous dog is by laying a complaint before magistrates under s 2, Dogs Act 1871. This is a civil procedure and it does not involve a criminal finding against the owner of the animal (*R v Nottingham Justices, ex p Brown* [1960] 1 WLR 1315). Remedies under the Act, however, are restricted either to an order for the dog's destruction (with or without an order under s 1(1)(b), Dangerous Dogs Act 1989 which disqualifies the owner from keeping a dog for some period) or a direction to the owner to keep it under proper control.

Ingredients of a complaint
9.6.2   In order to be able to establish a proper complaint the complainant must prove that:

(1)   The nature and disposition of the dog is savage, ferocious or dangerous (*Henderson v M'Kenzie* (1876) 3 R (SC) 623 at 626 approved in *Keddle v Payn* [1964] 1 WLR 262). It does not matter whether the dog has demonstrated its savage nature towards humans or towards animals.

(2)   The dog was not kept under proper control. This is a question of fact, but in the absence of evidence to the contrary, a dog which is neither muzzled nor led may be considered not to be under proper control (*Ex p Hay* (1886) 3 TLR 24). Section 1(4), Dogs Act 1906 expressly states that a dog which is proved to have injured cattle or poultry or chased sheep, 'may be dealt with under section two of the Dogs Act 1871, as a dangerous dog'.

Identifying the correct owner
9.6.3   It is important to ensure that the correct person is named in the complaint. It is the owner of the dog who is the proper defendant in proceedings.

This can cause difficulties for the informant since the relevant date for determining who is the owner of the dog is the date of the hearing of the complaint (*R v Jones, ex p Daunton* [1963] 1 WLR 270). If evidence is accepted that property in the dog has been transferred to another since the date of the relevant incident, then no order can be made against the original owner of the animal. The complainant will have to begin separate proceedings against the new owner of the animal, although he may rely on the same facts as those which were contested at the previous hearing (*R v Leicester Justices, ex p Workman* [1964] 1 WLR 707).

Who can bring a complaint?

9.6.4 Anyone can bring a complaint under the 1871 Act, although it has been said that in the majority of cases it is a police officer who is the best person to commence proceedings, since the statute exists for the public interest and for the protection of the public (*Smith v Baker* [1961] 1 WLR 38). Proceedings are sometimes taken under both the civil and criminal jurisdiction of the magistrates' courts at the same time. In this event the correct course is for the criminal proceedings to be heard before the civil complaint because of the danger of the magistrates hearing evidence on the civil matter which is not admissible on the hearing of an information (*R v Dunmow Justices, ex p Anderson* [1964] 1 WLR 1039).

Further remedies under Dangerous Dogs Acts 1989 and 1991

9.6.5 Although the 1871 Act provides a speedy method of obtaining a remedy against a dangerous dog by way of summary civil proceedings, additional criminal penalties can lie against the respondent in the event of non-compliance with any order made by the court. Where a person does not comply with an order for a dog's destruction under s 2 of the 1871 Act, s 1(1)(a), Dangerous Dogs Act 1989 allows justices to make an order appointing a person to undertake a dog's destruction and requiring anyone who has custody of the dog to hand it over for its destruction. Magistrates may also disqualify a person from having custody of a dog (s 1(1)(b)). It is an offence by s 1(3) of the 1989 Act for a person against whom an order was made under either s 2 of the 1871 Act or s 1(3) of the 1989 Act not to comply with the justices' order. The penalty is a fine not exceeding level 3 on the standard scale.

9.6.6 By s 1(2) of the 1989 Act a person may appeal against a justices' order. By s 1(4) he may further apply for a direction terminating his disqualification on grounds set out in s 1(5) (the character and conduct of the applicant and all the circumstances of the case).

9.6.7 By s 3(5) of the 1991 Act it is declared that magistrates may specify measures appropriate to keep a dog under control, including the use of a muzzle or lead (s 3(5)(b)). Alternatively by s 3(6) they may order a dog to be neutered if that would render it less dangerous.

B. Section 3, Dangerous Dogs Act 1991

The offence of having a dog dangerously out of control in a public place
9.6.8 By s 3(1) of the Dangerous Dogs Act 1991 the owner of a dog may be prosecuted if his dog is dangerously out of control in a public place. If the dog injures a person whilst dangerously out of control a further offence is committed (an aggravated offence). The dog shall be regarded as dangerously out of control on any occasion on which there are grounds for reasonable apprehension that it will injure any person, whether or not it actually does so (s 10(3)). The penalty for the offence is six months' imprisonment and/or a fine not exceeding level 5 on the standard scale. The penalty for the aggravated offence is six months' imprisonment and/or a fine not exceeding the statutory maximum, whilst on indictment the offence is punishable with a prison term not exceeding two years and/or a fine. If the owner is not in charge of the dog at the time then the person in charge may be prosecuted.
9.6.9 This is an offence of strict liability, allowing for the defence that at the material time the dog was in the charge of someone whom the owner believed was a fit and proper person to look after the dog (s 3(2)).

The offence of allowing a dog to enter a prohibited place and cause injuries
9.6.10 By s 3(3) an owner or person in charge of a dog is guilty of an offence if he allows the dog to enter a place which is not a public place but also a place where the dog is not permitted to be, and the dog either injures someone or causes reasonable apprehension that it may do so. If an injury takes place then an aggravated offence is committed. The penalties are as set out at 9.6.8 above.

C. Section 54 of the Metropolitan Police Act 1839; section 28 of the Town Police Clauses Act 1847

9.6.11 Two other criminal liabilities are worth noting. First, it is a criminal offence 'to suffer to be at large any unmuzzled ferocious dog, or set on or urge any dog or other animal to attack, worry, or put in fear any person, horse or other animal' within the limits of the metropolitan police district (s 54 of the Metropolitan Police Act 1839). The penalty is a fine limited to level 2 on the standard scale.
9.6.12 Secondly, any person who suffers to be at large any unmuzzled ferocious dog or other animal to attack, worry or put in fear any person or animal is guilty of an offence under s 28, Town Police Clauses Act 1847. Where a ferocious unmuzzled dog is on a lead, the keeper has the physical means of controlling it so that it cannot be said to be 'at large' within the meaning of the statute, even if the dog bites a passer-by (*Ross v Evans* [1959] 2 QB 79). The penalty is 14 days' imprisonment or a fine limited to level 3 on the standard scale.

D. Guard Dogs Act 1975

9.6.13 Under s 1(1) of the Guard Dogs Act 1975 it is an offence to:

use or permit the use of a guard dog at any premises unless a person ('the handler') who is capable of controlling the dog is present on the premises and the dog is under the control of the handler at all times while it is being so used except whilst it is secured so that it is not at liberty to go freely about the premises.

This has been interpreted to mean that if the dog is secured the handler of the dog need not be on the premises (*Hobson v Gledhill* [1978] 1 WLR 215).

9.7 Pit bull terriers and dogs bred for fighting

9.7.1 The Dangerous Dogs Act 1991 was intended:

to prohibit persons from having in their possession or custody dogs belonging to types bred for fighting; to impose restrictions in respect of such dogs pending the coming into force of the prohibition; to enable restrictions to be imposed in relation to other types of dog which present a serious danger to the public; to make further provision for securing that dogs are kept under proper control; and for connected purposes.

The Act was brought into force following public concern about attacks carried out by pit bull terriers, a dog re-introduced from the United States of America in 1976. It has now been amended by the Dangerous Dogs (Amendment) Act 1997 to ameliorate the provisions dealing with mandatory destruction.

9.7.2 By s 1(2) of the 1991 Act no-one is allowed to breed, sell, give or abandon a dog of the type known as the pit bull terrier or Japanese Tosa. By s 1(2)(d) a person who owns or is in charge of a pit bull terrier may not have it in a public place if it is not muzzled and kept on a lead. Anyone who treats or deals with a dog contrary to these provisions will be liable to imprisonment for six months or to a fine not exceeding level 5 on the standard scale. Further provisions allow for the destruction of dogs and the disqualification of offenders (see 9.7.5 below).

9.7.3 The 1991 Act provided a system of registration of dogs covered by the Act. The dog must be micro-chipped, neutered/spayed, and insured as well as muzzled and kept on a lead at all times.

9.7.4 The burden is on the defendant to prove on the balance of probabilities that a dog is not a pit bull terrier if this is alleged by the prosecution. The question for the court is not whether the dog for consideration is of the pit bull terrier breed as recognised by breeding associations. The statute was framed in deliberately wide terms so that a court can conclude that a dog is of the type known as the pit bull terrier if the dog approximately amounted to, or had a substantial number of the characteristics of, the pit bull terrier (*R v Knightsbridge Crown Court, ex p Dunne* [1994] 1 WLR 296). It is relevant to consider whether or not a dog exhibits the behavioural characteristics of a pit bull terrier, and evidence about the dog's behaviour cannot be irrelevant but will not be conclusive (*Ex p Dunne*).

9.7.5 Under the unamended Act a dog found in public in breach of the regulations set out in the Act was bound to be destroyed. In *R v Ealing Justices, ex p Fanneran, The Times*, 9 December 1995, 'Dempsey' escaped destruction after his muzzle had been removed when the dog was retching. Dempsey's case led to the amendments of the 1997 Act, so that a dog which faces destruction under s 4 of the 1991 Act will now escape if the court is satisfied that it would not constitute a danger to public safety.

9.7.6 By s 4A of the 1991 Act (as amended) a contingent destruction order can be made where a person is convicted of an offence under s 1 or an aggravated offence.

9.7.7 By s 4B of the 1991 Act (as amended) a destruction order can be made otherwise than on a conviction where no person is to be prosecuted for an offence under the 1991 Act or the dog cannot be released to the owner without a contravention of the prohibition in s 1(3).

9.8 Liability for injury caused by dogs to livestock

Civil liability

9.8.1 By s 3 of the Animals Act 1971 the keeper of a dog is liable for any damage caused to livestock. The exception is in the case of damage caused by a dog to livestock which has strayed on to land and either

(1) the land is occupied by the dog owner or
(2) the dog's presence on the land has been authorised by the occupier of the land (s 5(4)).

The rule is subject to the ordinary rules as to contribution under the Law Reform (Contributory Negligence) Act 1945, s 1. Moreover if the damage is due entirely to the fault of the owner of the livestock then he will have no recourse against the owner of the dog (s 5(1)).

9.8.2 A police officer may seize a dog worrying livestock by virtue of s 2 of the Dogs (Protection of Livestock) Act 1953 and then deal with it under s 2 of the Dogs Act 1871 (see 9.6.1–9.6.4).

Criminal penalties

9.8.3 The owner, or person in charge of a dog, at the time when it was worrying sheep, also faces prosecution under the Dogs (Protection of Livestock) Act 1953. 'Worrying livestock' is defined by s 1(2) to mean:

(a) attacking livestock, or
(b) chasing livestock in such a way as may reasonably be expected to cause injury or suffering to the livestock, or, in the case of females, abortion, or loss of or diminution in their produce
(c) being at large in a field or enclosure in which there are sheep.

An owner, or alternatively a person in charge of a dog, is liable on summary conviction to a fine on level 3 of the standard scale if the dog worries sheep.

9.8.4 If the livestock are trespassing, then the occupier or owner of the field or enclosure or anyone acting with his authority will not be guilty of an offence (save where he deliberately sets the dog at the livestock). Neither, by s 1(2A)(b) does the offence apply to a police dog, a guide dog, a trained sheep dog, a working gun dog or a pack of hounds.

9.9 Liability for the killing of or injury to dogs worrying livestock

9.9.1 The owner of livestock does not have to wait until his livestock has been destroyed. He has a right to take steps to preserve his property. This right, however, is circumscribed by the statutory provisions of the Animals Act 1971. The statute lays down certain rules which will apply if the person who has shot the dog is sued by its owner (the burden of proof being on the defendant). Section 9(1)(a) specifies that the dog must have been shot whilst the defendant was acting for the protection of livestock. That is to say that the dog was shot because the defendant had reasonable grounds for believing that the dog

(1) was worrying or about to worry livestock and there were no other means of preventing or ending the worrying (s 9(3)(a), (4)) or

(2) had been worrying livestock, was still in the vicinity without any control and in circumstances in which there were no practicable means for identifying the owner (s 9(3)(b), (4)).

9.9.2 The 1971 Act only gives protection to a person who can demonstrate that he is entitled to act for the protection of any livestock, either because he is the owner either of the livestock or of the land on which it was found (s 9(2)(a)). In any event notice of the shooting must be given to the officer in charge of a police station within 48 hours (s 9(1)(b)). By s 9(2)(b) a person who shoots a dog must also be satisfied that the owner of the dog cannot rely on s 5(3) of the 1971 Act (straying livestock killed by a dog authorised to be on the land in question).

9.10 Strays

9.10.1 Express powers to deal with stray dogs are reserved to police officers by s 3 of the Dogs Act 1906. Very similar powers are reserved to local authority officers specifically appointed to the task under s 149 of the Environmental Protection Act 1990.

9.10.2 It is the duty of an officer of a local authority to seize and detain dogs which he has reasonable grounds for suspecting are stray (s 149(3) EPA 1990). A police officer is entitled to seize a dog on the same basis (s 3(1) of the 1906 Act), but there is no obligation on him to do so. Dogs can only be seized from private property if the officer in question has obtained permission from the property owner (ss 149(3) and 3(1A)). If the dog is wearing a collar then the chief officer of police or local authority officer as appropriate must serve a written notice on the owner (if known) stating that unless the dog is removed within seven days it will be disposed of (ss 149(4) and 3(2)). In order to recover the dog the owner must pay all the expenses incurred by reason of its detention and a sum prescribed by statutory instrument (ss 149(5) and 3(1)). (The prescribed sum for the purposes of s 149(5) is currently £25 (reg 2, The Environmental Protection (Stray Dogs) Regulations 1992)). After seven days, if a dog is not recovered it can be sold or given away or destroyed (ss 149(6) and 3(4)). The recipient of a dog will get good title to it (s 149(7)).

9.10.3 Both the chief officer of police and local authorities must keep registers of dogs seized pursuant to their statutory powers (ss 149(8) and 3(6)). The police register must include brief descriptions of dogs and their seizure and the manner of disposal and can be inspected for 5p (s 3(6)). The local authority register must set out details of the dog, its seizure and details of any notices served on its owner (The Environmental Protection (Stray Dogs) Regulations 1992). The local authority register is open to inspection at no cost (s 149(8)).

9.10.4 Under s 150 of the EPA 1990, a person who 'takes possession of a stray dog' (described as a 'finder') must either return it to its owner or take it to the nearest police station or relevant officer appointed by the local authority (see above) (s 150(1)). It is a criminal offence for a finder not to comply with s 150(1). If a finder wishes to keep a dog which he has delivered to a local authority, then he may do so once the officer has recorded the particulars in his records and given any known owner an opportunity to collect it (The Environmental Protection (Stray Dogs) Regulations 1992). If the dog has been handed in to the nearest police station then the police are obliged to allow the finder to keep it once identical particulars have been recorded (s 4(2)). It is a criminal offence for the finder of a stray dog who arranged to keep it not to keep it for less than one month (ss 150(5) and 4(3)).

Chapter 10

Stalkers and Nuisance Telephone Calls

10.1 Overview

10.1.1 This chapter is concerned in particular with two peculiarly modern species of anti-social behaviour, stalking and nuisance telephone calls.

10.1.2 Stalking has been widely documented in the press and by other media over recent years. The perpetrators come in a wide variety of shapes and forms. They may be the deluded admirers of media or sports personalities, the obsessed admirers of total strangers, or jilted lovers or spouses determined to ruin the lives of their former partners. Some stalkers pester their victims by staying persistently in their sight. Others will resort to abusive and threatening phone calls, malicious letters and even serious physical assaults.

10.1.3 Nuisance telephone calling has become a common peril. Although the introduction of the 1471 callback service by BT is thought to have reduced the number of such calls, in 1996 no fewer than 663,312 people complained to BT's Nuisance Call Bureau. As a result, 264,116 telephone numbers were changed and 68,845 had a police trace put on their lines. A significant proportion of these calls were by electronic machines incorrectly programmed to phone defects back to their maintenance engineers. The results can be profoundly irritating. In an American case a lady received calls every 90 minutes from an empty oil tank which had been misprogrammed.

10.1.4 Most nuisance callers, however, are either jealous lovers or individuals who bear some unwarranted grievance. They may take pleasure in making obscene telephone calls to women totally unknown to them, or engage in campaigns of hate against specific individuals.

10.1.5 A particular variant of the stalker/nuisance caller is the disgruntled individual who bears a grudge. He may have some resentment against a local authority, insurance company or other institution. Attempts by such a person to interfere with the peace and comfort of its employees need to be taken seriously.

10.1.6 Until the coming into force of the Protection from Harassment Act 1997 it was sometimes difficult to identify an appropriate civil remedy. An anticipatory (*quia timet*) injunction was the obvious form of protection required by a complainant, but in the absence of a threat of assault or a continuing nuisance or some other anticipated cause of action, there was little a court could do to restrain stalkers or nuisance callers. The old forms of action did not mould themselves well to contemporary life. Section 3 of the 1997 Act provides civil remedies for harassment and is likely to provide the best forms of protection against stalkers and nuisance callers.

10.1.7 The criminal law adapted somewhat better in its treatment of both stalkers and nuisance callers. Specific enactments set out penalties for obscene calls, malicious letters and abusive behaviour. Success in criminal cases, however, especially in serious examples where a lengthy prison term may be justified, generally depends on proof of assault (which includes clinical nervous shock). Although an assault may be perpetrated by the use of repeated silent phone calls, the prospect of a criminal trial conditional on proof of actual injury will not be a comfort to a potential victim.

10.1.8 The focus of this chapter is inevitably the Protection from Harassment Act 1997. The Act was prepared specifically with stalkers in mind. Some account will first be given of the relevant criminal law and the main offences which a stalker or nuisance caller may have committed. Appropriate civil remedies apart from the 1997 Act will be considered. These will include an outline of the orders made available under the Family Law Act 1996, since many of the worse forms of stalking are perpetrated by people who have been intimate with their victims. 'Domestic hooliganism' (the expression of Sir George Baker P in *Davis v Johnson* [1978] 1 All ER 841 at 860) is not confined to physical attacks, so that an adviser must be alert to the possibility of an appropriate remedy under these Acts.

10.1.9 This chapter therefore will outline the following:

(1) 10.2 Criminal offences apart from the Protection from Harassment Act 1997
  (a) the advantages of criminal proceedings
  (b) some possible criminal offences
  (c) assaults by stalkers and nuisance callers (including nervous shock)
  (d) obscene telephone calls
  (e) telephone calls and public nuisance
  (f) some miscellaneous offences (threats to kill, rogues and vagabonds, bomb hoaxes, indecent or obscene letters, offences against public order).

(2) 10.3 Civil remedies apart from s 3 Protection from Harassment Act 1997
  (a) recognised torts (assault, trespass, private nuisance, intentionally causing nervous shock)
  (b) the disgruntled individual – using the economic torts
  (c) the 'tort of harassment' at common law
  (d) interlocutory injunctions against stalkers and nuisance callers
  (e) exclusion zones.

(3) 10.4 The Protection from Harassment Act 1997
  (a) civil and criminal remedies under the new Act.

(4) 10.5 Possible Family Law Remedies

(a) remedies available before magistrates
(b) remedies available in the County Court
(c) remedies available in the High Court
(d) Part IV of the Family Law Act 1996.

10.2 Criminal offences

Introductory

10.2.1 This section is not intended to set out a compendious account of the nature of all the criminal offences which a stalker or nuisance caller may have committed. Neither is it designed to assist in how to run a criminal trial. For the victim of a stalker who may be contemplating a private prosecution and others, the following paragraphs are meant to outline in summary form the substantive offences which exist and their likely penalties.

The advantages of criminal proceedings to the victims

10.2.2 Individuals who pester and harass others will bring themselves to the attention of the police. At first blush the use of a criminal remedy would not seem to be a great deal of assistance to the victim, since a criminal trial can only take place after the offence has occurred. In practice, however, a first prosecution will usually be dealt with by way of an order that the stalker (or caller) be bound over to keep the peace or sentenced to some modest penalty, such as a conditional discharge. Criminal prosecutions for such offences, however, are popular with the local press and may be very humiliating experiences. On a second offence the offender is not likely to be treated so leniently. In *R v Burstow* [1997] 1 Cr App R 144 the appellant received three years' imprisonment for a three year campaign of harassment against his victim. He had previously been bound over. In *R v Smith* [1997] Crim LR 614 the appellant received 21 months for pestering his former girlfriend over a four-year period. He had also been the subject of a bind-over by magistrates.

Relevant criminal offences – a summary

10.2.3 It is now clear that a person can properly be convicted of an offence of violence even though no physical act is involved. Grievous or actual bodily harm is no less bodily harm because the consequences are suffered in the nervous system, including the brain. Moreover the use of an indirect implement such as the telephone with which to conduct a campaign of harassment is no different from the use of a stick or knife in more orthodox cases of physical violence. A series of silent telephone calls which results in a nervous disorder amounts to the offence of occasioning actual bodily harm. The most appropriate criminal penalties in serious cases therefore are probably the offences alleging bodily injury set out in the Offences Against the Person Act 1861.

10.2.4 The Protection from Harassment Act 1997 itself creates various new offences. These are:

(1) harassment (s 2)

(2) putting people in fear of violence (s 4).

When s 3(6) comes into force the 1997 Act will create a further offence of being in breach of a civil court injunction. Offences under the 1997 Act are dealt with in the section on the 1997 Act set out below (see 10.4).

10.2.5 In other cases not involving an assault, the following statutory offences will also need to be considered:

(1) s 39 of the Criminal Justice Act 1988 (CJA) (common assault and battery)

(2) s 16 of the Offences Against the Person Act 1861 (OAPA) (threats to kill)

(3) s 4 of the Vagrancy Act 1824 (offering possibilities if a stalker sleeps rough near his victim's house or is found nearby 'for any unlawful purpose')

(4) the Public Order Act 1986

(5) s 43 of the Telecommunications Act 1984 (obscene or menacing telephone calls)

(6) s 51 of the Criminal Law Act 1977 (bomb hoaxes).

Assaults

10.2.6 Assaults are criminal offences under the following statutes:

OFFENCE	STATUTE	PENALTY
common assault	CJA 1988, s 39	Summary only – fine (level 5) and/or imprisonment (six months)
assault occasioning actual bodily harm	OAPA 1861, s 47	Summary – statutory maximum fine and/or imprisonment (six months) Crown Court – imprisonment (five years)
inflicting bodily harm	OAPA 1861, s 20	Crown Court – imprisonment (five years)
wounding with intent to do grievous bodily harm	OAPA 1861, s 18	Crown Court – imprisonment (life)

Psychiatric injuries can constitute assault

10.2.7 An assault is any act by which a person intentionally or recklessly causes another to apprehend immediate and unlawful violence (*R v Venna* [1976] QB 421). It was held in *R v Chan-Fook* [1994] 1 WLR 689 that actual bodily harm may include injury to any part of the body, including internal organs, the nervous system and the brain. It is therefore capable of including psychiatric injury, but not temporary emotions such as fear, distress or panic.

Moreover psychiatric injury can be 'inflicted' for the purposes of s 20 of the 1861 Act (*R v Burstow* [1997] Crim LR 452).

The need for expert evidence to prove psychiatric damage

10.2.8   The Court of Appeal has decided that in order to prove psychiatric injury some evidence must be adduced to demonstrate an identifiable clinical condition. This must be done by calling expert evidence. It cannot be inferred from the facts by a jury (*Chan-Fook's* case).

'Immediate physical violence' – stalkers and nuisance telephone callers

10.2.9   Stalkers and nuisance callers frequently suggest that their victims cannot possibly have thought that they were likely to suffer the infliction of immediate unlawful violence. They argue that this can be shown because they have never actually attacked their victims over the protracted period over which they have harassed them, or because the use of the telephone makes a physical attack impossible. This is not an attractive submission and the higher courts will go to some length to assist a complainant.

10.2.10   In *Smith v Chief-Superintendent, Woking Police Station* (1983) 76 Cr App R 234 the defendant was charged under s 4 of the Vagrancy Act 1824. This Act provides *inter alia* that:

> every person being found . . . in any enclosed . . . garden . . . for any unlawful purpose; . . . shall be deemed a rogue and a vagabond.

The defendant entered the grounds of a private house and looked through the windows of the house occupied by the victim. She was terrified, giving evidence that she was 'very nervous and jumpy for a few days afterwards'. The justices were of the opinion that the defendant had deliberately frightened the victim, and that that constituted an assault. Accordingly they found him guilty of the offence charged, ie being in an enclosed garden for an unlawful purpose, namely to assault the victim thereby causing her fear and shock. The Divisional Court upheld the decision of the magistrates, deciding that the victim had thought that the defendant might immediately use violence against her so that this amounted to an assault. Such a fear was justified since she had no idea what he might do next and she might well have supposed that he was likely to use violence.

10.2.11   Since an assault can be committed by the use of words, it follows that an assault can be perpetrated by the use of a telephone. However, this left the question: how could the receiver of a call think that he could apprehend the infliction of immediate unlawful violence? In the Australian case of *Barton v Armstrong* [1969] 2 NSWR 451, B sued A in civil proceedings alleging assault where B had made many telephone calls in the early hours of the morning 'in an atmosphere of drama and suspense'. A argued that B could not have been in fear of the infliction of immediate violence. The court held (at 455) that such telephone calls can constitute an assault:

If, when threats in this manner are conveyed over the telephone, the recipient has been led to believe that he is being followed, kept under surveillance by persons hired to do him physical harm to the extent of killing him, then why is this not something to put him in fear or apprehension of immediate violence? In the age in which we live, threats may be made and communicated by persons remote from the person threatened. Physical violence and death can be produced by acts done at a distance by people who are out of sight and by agents hired for that purpose. I do not think that these, if they result in apprehension of physical violence in the mind of a reasonable person, are outside the protection afforded by the civil and criminal law as to assault.

The court decided that the necessary fear of violence which formed part of an assault need not be a fear of violence from the actual caller.

Assaults – silence over the telephone

10.2.12   In the United Kingdom silent telephone calls have been held to amount to an assault. In *R v Ireland* [1996] 3 WLR 650 the defendant made frequent telephone calls followed by silence. He would, for instance, make 14 short phone calls in one hour, or make calls of up to several minutes in duration. All were followed by silence. These occurred over about 15 weeks and were directed at three different women. The women suffered cold sweats, dizziness, palpitations and other significant psychological consequences. The Court of Appeal decided that:

> the fact that the violence is inflicted indirectly, causing psychological harm, does not render the act to be any less an act of violence. Nor, in our judgment, is it necessary that there should be an immediate proximity between defendant and victim. Fear can be instilled as readily over the telephone as it can through the window. In our judgment repetitious telephone calls of this nature are likely to cause the victims to apprehend immediate and unlawful violence (656F).

Accordingly the court held that the making of a telephone call followed by silence is capable of amounting to an offence contrary to s 47 of the 1861 Act. Whether the calls were followed by words or silence was immaterial.

Obscene or menacing telephone calls

10.2.13   In the absence of evidence of assault caused by a nuisance caller, a prosecution under s 43 of the Telecommunications Act 1984 (as amended) may be appropriate. This is a specific offence designed to punish the nuisance caller. By s 43:

Improper use of a public telecommunication system
(1) A person who –
   (a) sends, by means of a public telecommunication system, a message or other matter that is grossly offensive or of an indecent, obscene or menacing character; or
   (b) sends by those means, for the purpose of causing annoyance, inconvenience or needless anxiety to another, a message that he knows to be false or persistently makes use for that purpose of a public telecommunication system, shall be guilty of an offence.

This offence is punishable by magistrates by a fine not exceeding level 5 on the standard scale and/or imprisonment for a maximum of six months.

Nuisance telephone calls as a public nuisance

10.2.14 In more serious cases where evidence of assault is unavailable, the prosecution may be able to contemplate a prosecution for public nuisance. This is a practical consideration only where there has been a nuisance which materially affects the reasonable comfort and convenience of life of a class of Her Majesty's subjects (see chapter 2). It is available therefore only against a nuisance caller who is a pest to a significant number of people. The ordinary rules of public nuisance apply, so that the prosecution will have to prove actual (rather than potential) interference with the reasonable comfort and convenience of the relevant section of the public (*R v Madden* [1975] 1 WLR 1379).

10.2.15 A wide variety of forms of telephone calls can constitute a public nuisance. Obscene calls are the most common. In *R v Norbury* [1978] Crim LR 435 the defendant made 605 obscene telephone calls to 494 women resident in Norfolk over about a four-year period. The defendant was a police officer who would select names at random and make obscene calls 'adopting a Pakistani voice'. If his victim put down the receiver he would hold the line open so that should the victim then make a 999 call he could pretend to be an emergency service operator and then a police officer. He would advise the recipient to continue listening to the obscene language and continue as he had done before.

10.2.16 It is generally important that there should be a sufficient number of complainants for the offence of public nuisance to have been committed. This is a question for the jury and was satisfied, for instance, by persistent calls to 13 ladies in the South Cumbria area (*R v Johnson* [1997] 1 WLR 367). In *R v Madden* [1975] 1 WLR 1379 it was held that a hoax bomb warning could constitute a public nuisance so long as there was evidence before the court to show that a considerable number of persons had been affected. The situation was slightly different in the case of *R v Millward* (1986) 8 Cr App R (S) 209. In that case the defendant pleaded guilty to making thousands of phone calls to a police officer with whom he was infatuated. The phone calls were made to police stations where she worked – 636 calls were received on one day. The evidence was that the whole operation of the police station was disrupted so that members of the public could not make calls or were delayed in doing so.

Miscellaneous offences

10.2.17 A significant number of other statutes may be used to obtain a criminal sanction against the stalker or nuisance caller. These are set out below in summary form only to remind the practitioner of the relevant offences which exist. A criminal textbook should be consulted to consider all the implications of the statutes, especially so far as they relate to complex issues such as those raised under the Public Order Act 1986.

Threats to kill

10.2.18 By s 16 of the Offences Against the Person Act 1861:

> A person who without lawful excuse makes to another a threat, intending that that
> other would fear it would be carried out, to kill that other or a third person shall be
> guilty of an offence and liable on conviction on indictment to imprisonment for a
> term not exceeding ten years.

This offence is triable either way. The penalty in magistrates' court is a maximum of six months' imprisonment and/or the statutory maximum fine. The maximum penalty in the Crown Court is five years' imprisonment.

Vagrancy Act

10.2.19 By s 4 of the Vagrancy Act 1824 a variety of offences is created, of which two may be of relevance in the case of stalkers. Where the defendant falls within the following categories, he is liable to conviction as a 'rogue and vagabond'. They apply to:

- every person wandering abroad and lodging in any barn or outhouse, or in any deserted or unoccupied building, or in the open air, or under tent, or in any cart or waggon and not giving good account of himself or herself;
- every person being found in or upon any dwelling house, warehouse, coach-house, stable, or outhouse, or in any enclosed yard, garden, or area, for any unlawful purpose

The penalty for sleeping rough is a fine on level 1 (s 70 of the Criminal Justice Act 1982). There is no power to commit an offender to the Crown Court for this offence alone. For the more serious of the two the maximum penalty before justices is three months' imprisonment or a fine not exceeding level 3 on the standard scale (ss 34(3) and 121(5) of the Magistrates' Courts Act 1980). Where a single justice is sitting the maximum sentence is 14 days' imprisonment or a fine of £1 (s 121(5)).

Bomb hoaxes

10.2.20 The Criminal Law Act 1977 (as amended) creates a specific offence designed to punish the bomb hoaxer. Under s 51:

> **Bomb Hoaxes**
> . . .
> (2) A person who communicates any information which he knows or believes to be false to another person with the intention of inducing in him or any other person a false belief that a bomb or other thing liable to explode or ignite is present in any place or location whatever is guilty of an offence.
> (3) For a person to be guilty of an offence under subsection . . . (2) above it is not necessary for him to have any particular person in mind as the person in whom he intends to induce the belief mentioned in that subsection.

This offence is punishable by magistrates by a fine not exceeding the statutory maximum and/or imprisonment for a maximum of six months. If tried in the Crown Court an offender can receive a maximum of seven years' imprisonment.

Sending indecent or obscene letters

10.2.21   The Malicious Communications Act 1988 makes it an offence to send indecent or obscene material in the post. The maximum sentence on conviction before magistrates is six months' imprisonment or a fine not exceeding the statutory maximum. After conviction on indictment the maximum sentence is one of 12 months' imprisonment.

Public Order Act offences

10.2.22   The Public Order Act 1986 sets out a variety of summary offences which a stalker may have committed. These offences are set out below in outline only.

Fear or provocation of violence

10.2.23   By s 4(1) of the Public Order Act 1986:

Fear or provocation of violence
A person is guilty of an offence if he –
> (a)   uses towards another person threatening, abusive or insulting words or behaviour, or
> (b)   distributes or displays to another person any writing, sign or other visible representation which is threatening or insulting

with intent to cause that person to believe that immediate unlawful violence will be used against him or another by any person, or to provoke the immediate use of unlawful violence by that person or another, or whereby that person is likely to believe that such violence will be used or it is likely that such violence will be provoked.

The offence is summary only and is punishable by imprisonment not exceeding six months and/or a fine at level 5 on the standard scale.

Intentional harassment, alarm or distress

10.2.24   By s 4A(1) of the Public Order Act 1986 (inserted by s 154 of the Criminal Justice and Public Order Act 1994):

Intentional harassment, alarm or distress
A person is guilty of an offence if, with intent to cause a person harassment, alarm or distress, he –
> (a)   uses threatening, abusive or insulting words or behaviour, or disorderly behaviour, or
> (b)   displays any writing, sign or other visible representation which is threatening, abusive or insulting,

thereby causing that or another person harassment, alarm or distress.

The offence is summary only and is punishable by imprisonment not exceeding six months and/or a fine at level 5 on the standard scale.

Harassment, alarm or distress

10.2.25 By s 5(1) of the Public Order Act 1986:

Harassment, alarm or distress
A person is guilty if he –
  (a) uses towards another person threatening, abusive or insulting words or disorderly behaviour, or
  (b) displays to another person any writing, sign or other visible representation which is threatening abusive or insulting.

The offence is summary only and is punishable by a fine at level 5 on the standard scale.

10.3 Civil remedies apart from s 3 Protection from Harassment Act 1997

10.3.1 Although in practice the activities of a stalker or nuisance caller may ultimately be curtailed by a criminal prosecution, this prospect is not of much immediate comfort to the victim, especially since proof of clinical injury is necessary to prove an assault (being the most appropriate criminal charge in a serious case). Where an injury is anticipated which can be classified under a common law cause of action (such as trespass to the person or nuisance) then the courts will readily come to the assistance of the victim by way of a *quia timet* injunction. Although s 3 of the Protection from Harassment Act 1997 is likely to be the main source of a remedy in civil proceedings, a brief account of other relevant causes of action will be provided before turning to s 3.

Actionable torts

10.3.2 The following torts are the most likely causes of action to give proper grounds for an injunction against a stalker or (when appropriate) a nuisance caller:

  (1) **Trespass to the person**: This tort is appropriate where there is some real fear of the likelihood of an assault culminating in clinical injury (of either a physical or mental state).
  (2) **Trespass to chattels**: It is characteristic of the stalker that he resorts to damaging his victim's property. This may include, for instance, graffiti or scratches to a car, shredding a garment, or giving poisoned meat to an animal. The better remedy is by way of an action under the Torts (Interference with Goods) Act 1977 (wrongful interference with goods). This covers any unwanted physical interference with the victim's belongings. To found the full cause of action some damage must

have been caused (*Letang v Cooper* [1965] 1 QB 232 at 239), although only an anticipated fear of such damage will be required to found a *quia timet* injunction.

(3) **Trespass to land**: Trespass to land may encompass graffiti to a house or any unwarranted attempt to get into the plaintiff's building. The principles are set out at 5.2.

(4) **Intentionally causing emotional distress**: This is a useful tort in its own right which should not be forgotten when looking for a remedy against a stalker or nuisance caller. It arises from *Wilkinson v Downton* [1897] 2 QB 57 (approved in *Janvier v Sweeney* [1919] 2 KB 316) and provides a remedy where a defendant wilfully does any act calculated to cause injury (including clinical nervous shock). In *Wilkinson's* case D told W that W's husband had met with a serious accident in which he had broken both legs. These statements were untrue and W suffered nervous shock as a result. The court readily inferred that D must have realised that his words would have had the effect they in fact had on W. It imputed an intention on the part of D to produce the injury that W sustained.

The disgruntled individual and the economic torts

10.3.3 Individuals can develop a grievance or grudge against a firm or organisation for any number of reasons. The underlying reason may be a complaint about a judicial judgment, a dismissal at work or a decision not to grant some form of payment. In these cases it has been known for the defendant to make threats which would affect the employees of the organisation involved. An injunction can properly be applied for by the employer on the following grounds:

(1) **Intimidation**: Intimidation is recognised as a tort in a variety of guises. Where D intimidates P by threatening to carry out some illegal act which causes P to act to the detriment of his business or trade, then P has a direct cause of action against D. So too if D threatens to carry out some unlawful act on X, the result of which is to intimidate X from carrying out some lawful act to the detriment of P, then P has a right of action against D. (See *Rookes v Barnard* [1964] AC 1129 and *Morgan v Fry* [1968] 2 QB 710). So in a case in the County Court where a disgruntled individual threatened to send sputum infected with tuberculosis in the post to a local authority's employees, an injunction was granted in the local authority's favour.

(2) **Unlawful interference**: The same facts as those set out above would give rise to a cause of action for causing loss by unlawful means. This is another form of economic tort where D uses some unlawful means to cause harm to an economic entity such as a business. Intention does not have to be proved (*Lonrho Plc v Fayed (No 2)* [1992] 1 WLR 1).

The boundaries between these different causes of action are not clearly marked but are probably the best means which an employer will have to protect his interests against an individual determined to cause trouble to his business.

The 'tort of harassment' at common law

10.3.4   In *Khorasandjian v Bush* [1993] QB 727 (CA), a County Court judge made an order forbidding the defendant *inter alia* from harassing, pestering or communicating with the plaintiff. At the time the plaintiff was living with her mother as her licensee. This decision was widely supposed to have invented the tort of harassment. In *Hunter v Canary Wharf Ltd* [1997] AC 655 Lord Goff said (at 691H):

> In truth, what the Court of Appeal appears to have been doing was to exploit the law of private nuisance in order to create by the back door a tort of harassment which was only partially effective in that it was artificially limited to harassment which takes place in [the plaintiff's] home.

Hunter's case reiterates the primacy of a proprietary interest in land as the foundation of the tort of private nuisance (see chapter 1). It means that *Khorasandjian* was wrongly decided on the point and is conclusive that there is no common law tort of harassment.

Interlocutory injunctions

10.3.5   The jurisdiction to grant injunctions, whether interlocutory or final, is granted in the High Court by reason of s 37(1) of the Supreme Court Act 1981. This provides that the High Court may by order grant an injunction 'in all cases in which it appears to the court to be just and convenient to do so'. The County Court's jurisdiction arises by reason of s 38 of the County Courts Act 1984, allowing the county court to make any order (with certain exceptions), including an interlocutory order, which could be made by the High Court if the proceedings were in the High Court.

10.3.6   The power to make interlocutory orders is not unlimited. As Lord Diplock pointed out in *The Siskina* [1979] AC 210 at 254:

> [Section 37(1) of the 1981 Act], speaking as it does of interlocutory orders, presupposes the existence of an action, actual or potential, claiming substantive relief which the High Court has jurisdiction to grant and to which the interlocutory orders referred to are but ancillary.

It is therefore always necessary to consider what claims for substantive relief (or causes of action) exist, since the court will not grant an interlocutory order if the plaintiff will be unable to complain of an infringement of a right which the court does not recognise. In *Patel v Patel* [1988] 2 FLR 179 a series of allegations by a man complaining of a feud against him by his son-in-law resulted in a limited injunction that the defendant was not to assault or molest the plaintiff. The plaintiff appealed, arguing that the terms of the injunction should be wider. The Court of Appeal refused, pointing out that many of the actions relied upon did not constitute any recognised form of tort.

10.3.7 So long as there is some right of action to protect, the courts will not stand idly by. The purpose of an order at the interlocutory stage is to protect the parties' positions pending a final determination and the terms of an interlocutory order may be very wide. So in *Fresh Fruit Wales Ltd v Halbert* (1991), *The Times*, 29 January the Court of Appeal held that:

> if the situation which arises at the date when the interlocutory order is sought is such that the interest of the parties can in justice be guarded by some order which would not be appropriate at the end of the trial, there is no reason whatever why the judge should not do so.

The means that the courts will act with a wide measure of discretion to grant an effective form of relief.

10.3.8 Various examples of the courts' approach to the wording of injunctions against stalkers and nuisance callers are worth considering:

(1) In *Burnett v George* [1992] 1 FLR 525 the plaintiff's resentment against his former girlfriend led him to pursue a campaign against her, consisting of assaults, attacks on her home, unwanted visits and 'heavy breathing' telephone calls. The order made in the County Court was one prohibiting the defendant from 'assaulting, molesting or otherwise interfering with the defendant'. The Court of Appeal held that molestation and interference did not amount to recognised torts. The injunction was varied so that it prohibited the defendant from 'assaulting, molesting or otherwise interfering with the defendant by doing acts calculated to cause her harm' (see also *Wilkinson v Downton* and *Janvier v Sweeney* at 10.3.2 above). This formula was approved by Peter Gibson J in *Khorasandjian's* case, who also accepted that the words 'harassing', 'pestering' and 'communicating with' were quite acceptable.

(2) In *Pidduck v Molloy* [1992] 2 FLR 202 an order forbidding the defendant *inter alia* from speaking to the plaintiff was justified given the past conduct of the defendant in intimidating, threatening and abusing the plaintiff.

10.3.9 It must be remembered that where an injunction or undertaking is given, the injunction or undertaking operates until it is revoked. It has to be obeyed whether or not it should have been granted or accepted in the first place (*Johnson v Walton* [1990] 1 FLR 350 at 352; *M v Home Office* [1992] QB 270 at 298–299):

> It cannot be too clearly stated that, when an injunctive order is made or when an undertaking is given, it operates until it is revoked on appeal or by the court itself, and it has to be obeyed whether or not it should have been granted or accepted in the first place (*Johnson's* case at p 352D)

Exclusion zones

10.3.10   Where a stalker's activities lead him to make his presence felt, an obvious advantage is an order prohibiting the defendant from coming near the plaintiff. Such an order will be granted in an appropriate case. In *Burris v Azadani* [1995] 1 WLR 1372 the defendant sought a close and intimate relationship with the plaintiff. She did her best to resist. The defendant made a number of visits to her house, often in the middle of the night, and refused to leave. He made nuisance calls and threatened to kill the plaintiff and himself. The defendant was restrained in the following terms (see 1374H–1375B):

> whether by himself, his servants or agents or any of them, or otherwise howsoever from:- (a) Assaulting, molesting, harassing, threatening, pestering or otherwise interfering with the plaintiff whether directly or indirectly to the [plaintiff, the plaintiff's children and the plaintiff's friend]. (b) Making any communication to the plaintiff, the plaintiff's [children and the plaintiff's friend] whether in writing or orally, whether by telephone or otherwise howsoever save that he may send written communication to her solicitors. (c) From coming or remaining with[in] 250 yards of the plaintiff's home address... until after the trial of this action or further order.

The defendant did not seek to appeal any of the rest of the order, but appealed against the exclusion order. The appeal was dismissed.

10.3.11   Where it is clear on the facts that a defendant who approached the vicinity of the plaintiff's home would then commit a tort, whether by assault or abuse or 'watching and besetting it', an exclusion zone would be appropriate. In *Pidduck v Molloy* [1992] 2 FLR 202 an order was approved that the defendant should not 'visit or enter the curtilage of the plaintiff's home' with the added words 'without her consent or loitering within the vicinity thereof'.

10.4   The Protection from Harassment Act 1997

10.4.1   The most likely avenue for obtaining an interlocutory remedy against a stalker arises from the provisions of the Protection from Harassment Act 1997. This sets out a new cause of action (the prohibition from harassment) at civil law. A breach of the prohibition of harassment under s 1 also gives rise to a concurrent sanction punishable by the criminal courts.

Harassment defined

10.4.2   Section 1 of the 1997 Act prohibits harassment in the following terms:

> (1) A person must not pursue a course of conduct –
>   (a) which amounts to harassment of another, and
>   (b) which he knows or ought to know amounts to harassment of the other.
> (2) For the purposes of this section, the person whose course of conduct is in question ought to know that it amounts to harassment of another if a reasonable person in possession of the same information would think the course of conduct amounted to harassment of the other.

'Harassment' is not statutorily defined but it includes alarming the person or causing him distress (s 7(2)). It has been stated to include 'an element of intent, intent to cause distress or alarm' (*Johnson v Walton* [1990] 1 FLR 350 at 352H). A 'course of conduct' must involve conduct on at least two occasions (s 7(3)) and may include speech (s 7(4)). By s 1(2), the relevant question (whether a person ought to know that his conduct amounts to harassment) is to be determined according to an objective test: would a reasonable person in possession of 'the same information' have thought that the course of conduct amounted to harassment of the other?

10.4.3 Section 1(3) excludes a course of conduct from the application of s 1(1) if it was pursued either for the purpose of preventing or detecting crime (s 1(3)(a)) or under any enactment or rule of law or to comply with any condition or requirement imposed by any person under an enactment (s 1(3)(b)). Section 1(3)(c) also excludes a course of conduct from the application of s 1(1) if 'in the particular circumstances the pursuit of the course of conduct was reasonable'.

10.4.4 A breach of the prohibition of harassment under s 1 gives rise to both a criminal and a civil liability.

The offence of harassment

10.4.5 A person who pursues a course of conduct contrary to s 1 is liable on summary conviction for the offence of harassment contrary to s 2 of the Act to a maximum of six months' imprisonment or a fine not exceeding level 5 on the standard scale. The offence of harassment is an arrestable offence by virtue of s 2(3), which amends s 24(2) of the Police and Criminal Evidence Act 1984.

Restraining orders

10.4.6 In addition to making any of the orders usually available to a criminal court, magistrates may also make a restraining order (s 5(1)). By s 5(2)):

> The order may, for the purpose of protecting the victim of the offence, or any other person mentioned in the order, from further conduct which –
> (a) amounts to harassment, or
> (b) will cause a fear of violence,
> prohibit the defendant from doing anything described in the order.

By s 5(3), the order may have effect for a specified period or until further order. Either the prosecutor, the defendant 'or any other person mentioned in the order' may apply to the court which made the order to have it varied or discharged by further order (s 5(4)).

The criminal offence of breach of a restraining order

10.4.7 A restraining order therefore has all the characteristics of an injunction in the civil courts. Moreover if, without reasonable excuse, there is a breach of a restraining order, a further offence is committed contrary to s 5(5). The offender may be committed to the Crown Court where he will face a maximum term of imprisonment of five years (s 5(6)(a)). If convicted before justices he may be imprisoned for a maximum of six months or be fined the statutory maximum.

The statutory tort of harassment – remedies

10.4.8   As well as giving rise to a criminal liability, a breach of s 1 of the 1997 Act provides an aggrieved party with a claim in civil proceedings (s 3(1)). On such a claim the question of damages is at large, but they may expressly include damages for anxiety caused by the harassment inflicted by the defendant and 'any financial loss resulting from the harassment' (s 3(2)). The Act envisages that an application will be made for an interlocutory injunction, whether in the High Court or county court, and the qualifications made at 10.3.6 above in relation to interlocutory remedies at common law apply equally to the statutory cause of action set out at s 3.

Power of arrest

10.4.9   Where an injunction has been granted, a plaintiff who considers that the terms of the injunction have been breached will be able to apply to the court for a warrant for the defendant's arrest under s 3(3) when it comes into force. If the injunction is granted in the High Court then the application should be made to a High Court judge (s 3(4)(a)). In the County Court either the circuit judge or district judge will have power to grant the application (s 3(4)(b)). The application for a warrant of arrest must be substantiated on oath (s 3(5)(a)). It may be granted if the judge has reasonable grounds for believing that the defendant has done anything which is prohibited by the injunction.

Contempt of court

10.4.10   If there has in fact been a breach of the terms of an injunction then an option will be to seek the committal of the defendant as a contempt of court (implicit in s 3(8) when in force).

The criminal offence of breaching an injunction restraining a person from pursuing a course of conduct amounting to harassment

10.4.11   An alternative, however, is provided by s 3(6). When in force this will permit a plaintiff to seek the prosecution of a defendant who, without reasonable excuse, does an act prohibited by the terms of the injunction. The criminal offence of breaching the terms of an injunction without reasonable excuse is punishable on conviction on indictment by a maximum of five years' imprisonment and/or a fine. On summary conviction the defendant faces imprisonment for a term not exceeding six months and/or a fine not exceeding the statutory maximum.

Avoidance of double jeopardy

10.4.12 Remedies by way of committal or prosecution under s 3(6) are alternatives, so that a defendant will not be liable to punishment twice for the same conduct (s 3(7) and (8)).

10.5 Family law remedies

Introduction

10.5.1 Some account needs to be given of the remedies available under matrimonial law. This is because many people who can properly be described as stalkers are people who remain obsessed with their former partners after the break-up of a relationship. Their objectionable conduct will often include a whole range of activities, not the least of which is likely to be the use of physical violence. The fact that a power of arrest under s 3(3) of the 1997 Act is still not available means that many practitioners prefer to make use of the relevant provisions of the Family Law Act 1996 when possible. Another reason for preferring the 1996 Act is the evidential difficulty required to prove a course of conduct.

10.5.2 Reported examples of orders made under the old law involving those who might be described as stalkers include:

    (1) *Horner v Horner* [1982] 2 WLR 914, in which the husband had been handing his wife threatening letters, intercepting her on the way to the station and making offensive telephone calls.

    (2) *Johnson v Walton* [1990] 1 FLR 350, in which the complainant and the defendant had a sexual relationship. They fell out. The defendant was said to have trespassed in the plaintiff's house, struck her, made persistent telephone calls and gone to the public house where she worked to create a scene. He gave an undertaking *inter alia* not to molest her. Articles then began to appear in the national press about the relationship between the two. They included photographs of the plaintiff in a partially nude state. This was held to be a breach of the undertaking by the Court of Appeal.

10.5.3 This section will consider those orders designed to protect a complainant from ill-treatment by a respondent:

    (1) wherever the complainant might be ('non-molestation orders') and

    (2) in the occupation of his home ('occupation orders').

Occupation orders in this context include the power of the court to make an order excluding the respondent from a zone within a certain range of the home.

Family Law Act 1996 – introduction

10.5.4 Prior to the coming into force of Part IV of the Family Law Act 1996, the jurisdiction of the courts to make non-molestation and occupation orders was governed by the Domestic Proceedings and Magistrates' Courts Act 1978, the Domestic Violence and Matrimonial Proceedings Act 1976 and the Matrimonial Homes Act 1983. These have now been repealed and replaced by a single coherent set of provisions.

10.5.5 The Law Commission report which preceded the 1996 Act (*Domestic Violence and the Occupation of the Family Home*) recommended that the categories of person against whom non-molestation orders should be available should include any couple who have or have had a sexual relationship with each other (not necessarily amounting to sexual intercourse). Although this category has not been included in the Act, the Act does extend the range of persons against whom such an order can be made (for instance couples who have agreed to marry, even though their engagement may have been terminated up to three years beforehand). Like the Protection from Harassment Act 1997 the non-molestation order provisions of the 1996 Act are attractive because it is not necessary to make allegations of assault.

'Molestation'

10.5.6 'Molestation' is not given a statutory definition. The following quotations may be useful in attempting to understand what is meant by the term:

(1) 'Violence is a form of molestation but molestation may take place without the threat or use of violence' *Davis v Johnson* [1979] AC 264 at 334A.

(2) 'There are two different definitions respectively in the Concise Oxford Dictionary and in the Shorter Oxford Dictionary. The former gives the meaning for "molest" as: "meddle hostilely or injuriously". The Shorter Oxford Dictionary gives a much wider definition in these terms: "to cause trouble; to vex; to annoy; to put to inconvenience" (*Vaughan v Vaughan* [1973] 1 WLR 1159 at 1162–1163A).

(3) 'For my part I have no doubt that the word "molesting" in s 1(1)(a) of the 1976 Act does not imply necessarily either violence or threats of violence. It applies to any conduct which can properly be regarded as such a degree of harassment as to call for the intervention of the court' (*Horner v Horner* [1982] 2 WLR 914 at 916G).

(4) 'Harassment, it has to be said, of course, includes within it an element of intent, intent to cause distress or alarm. For my part, I think that 'molestation' has that meaning whenever it is used, regardless of whether the particular proceedings are or are not brought under the Domestic Violence Act' (*Johnson v Walton* [1990] 1 FLR 350 at 352H).

(5) '"Molestation" [for the purposes of the Domestic Violence and Matri-monial Act 1976] is deliberate conduct which substantially interferes with the applicant or child, whether by violence or by intimidation, har-assment, pestering or interference that is sufficiently serious to warrant intervention by the court. "Molestation" includes the forcing by the other party of his or her society on the unwilling suffering party, whether the purpose of the molester is seeking to resume affectionate relations or to harm or annoy the suffering party' (*F v F (Protection from Violence: Continuing Cohabitation*) [1989] 2 FLR 451).

(6) 'Molestation implies some quite deliberate conduct which is aimed at a high degree of harassment of the other party so as to justify the inter-vention of the court' (*C v C* [1998] 1 FLR 554, an important recent decision by Sir Stephen Brown P). In this case the applicant had obtained an *ex parte* order in the County Court preventing his wife from distributing details about his treatment of her to the press. The President of the Family Division discharged the order. In his judgment the facts came nowhere near what was required by s 42 of the 1996 Act (*Johnson v Walton* [1990] 1 FLR 350 applied).

It will be seen that the scope of activities likely to be covered by a non-molestation order is very wide.

Non-molestation orders: the categories of person protected

10.5.7 Section 42 of the 1996 Act gives courts the power to make non-molestation orders.

10.5.8 By s 42(1)(a) such an order can be made prohibiting the respondent from molesting another person who is 'associated with' the respondent. By s 62(3) a person is associated with another if:

(1) they are or have been married to each other (s 62(3)(a))
(2) they are cohabitants or former cohabitants (s 62(3)(b))
(3) they live or have lived in the same household, otherwise than merely by reason of one of them being the other's employee, tenant, lodger or boarder (s 62(3)(c))
(4) they are relatives (s 62(3)(d))
(5) they have agreed to marry one another (whether or not that agreement has been terminated) (s 62(3)(e))
(6) they are parties to the same family proceedings.

By s 42(4) a non-molestation order cannot be made in the case of a couple who have terminated an agreement to marry after the end of the period of three years beginning with the day on which it was terminated.

10.5.9 A molestation order can also be made in certain circumstances prohib-iting a party from molesting a child (s 42(1)(b)), but such provisions are unlikely to be relevant in relation to stalkers.

Non-molestation orders: the applicant

10.5.10 A non-molestation order can be made on an application by any person associated with the respondent (s 42(2)(a)). It can also be made by the court of its own motion during any family proceedings (s 42(2)(b)). Where the court is satisfied that a child under 16 has sufficient understanding to make an application (s 43(2)), the application can be made by the child with the leave of the court (s 43(1)).

The grounds for making a non-molestation order

10.5.11 Orders prohibiting a party from molesting another can clearly only be made where there has been some act of molestation by the respondent. The court is expressly required to have regard to all the circumstances, including the need to secure the health, safety and well-being of the person for whose benefit the order is to be made and any relevant child (s 42(5)).

The order

10.5.12 A non-molestation order may be made for a specified period or until further order (s 42(7)). If it is made in other family proceedings it will cease to have effect if those proceedings are withdrawn or dismissed (s 42(8)).

Occupation orders

10.5.13 Orders regulating the occupancy of the home are set out in ss 33–41 of the 1996 Act. These are determined according to the following categories:
  (1) where an applicant has an estate or other interest or matrimonial home rights under s 30 of the Act (s 33)
  (2) where one former spouse has no existing right of occupation (s 35)
  (3) where a cohabitant or former cohabitant has no existing right of occupation (s 36)
  (4) where neither spouse is entitled to occupy (s 37).
The orders which may be made by the court under these provisions grant the court a wide range of powers to determine the rights of each party to enter and remain in the home. The orders which may be made include an order requiring a party to leave the home.

The grounds for making an occupation order

10.5.14 The circumstances to be taken into consideration when making an occupation order vary according to the categories of occupancy set out above. They are based largely on the four matters set out under s 1(3) of the Matrimonial Homes Act 1983, and in each case include:
  (1) the housing needs and resources of the parties and of the children
  (2) the parties' financial resources

(3) the likely effect of the order on the health, safety or well-being of the parties or the children

(4) the conduct of the parties.

The court is also required to consider

(1) the degree of 'significant harm' likely to be sustained by the conduct of the respondent and

(2) the extent to which the respondent himself (and any relevant child) will suffer harm as a result of any order made by the court.

10.5.15 In a s 35 case (one former spouse with no existing right of occupation) the court is also required to consider:

(1) the length of time which has elapsed since the parties ceased to live together (s 35(6)(e))

(2) the length of time which has elapsed since the marriage was annulled or dissolved (s 35(6)(f)).

10.5.16 In a s 36 case (a cohabitant or former cohabitant with no existing right of occupation) the court is required to consider:

(1) the nature of the parties' relationship (s 36(6)(e))

(2) the length of time during which they have lived together as husband and wife (s 36(6)(f))

(3) whether there are any children (s 36(6)(g))

(4) the length of time which has elapsed since the parties ceased to live together (s 36(6)(h)).

10.5.17 Section 41 obliges the court, if the parties are cohabitants or former cohabitants, 'to have regard to the fact that they have not given each other the commitment involved in marriage'.

10.5.18 Under s 33(2) an application for an occupation order cannot be made by a person who has terminated an agreement to marry after the end of the period of three years beginning with the day on which the agreement was terminated.

Exclusion zones

10.5.19 Importantly, the court can in each case 'exclude the respondent from a defined area in which the dwelling-house is included' (ss 33(3)(g), 35(5)(d), 36(4)(d), and 37(3)(d)).

Additional financial provisions in certain occupation orders

10.5.20 It should be remembered that s 40 allows the court to make ancillary financial orders, for instance that the evicted or excluded party continues to pay part of a mortgage. If no such order is made then the other party is unable to complain at a later stage to the court.

Ex parte non-molestation and occupation orders

10.5.21 An application will be made by originating application with an affidavit in support. A draft order should be before the court. An affidavit of service is usually required. Non-molestation orders can be made on an *ex parte* basis in urgent cases where there is no time for notice to be given or it is likely that the defendant will take action to defeat the order (see *Loseby v Newman* [1996] 1 FCR 647). *Ex parte* ouster and exclusion orders can be made but they are available only in cases of real immediate danger of serious injury or irreparable damage (see *Practice Note* [1978] 2 All ER 919).

Undertakings

10.5.22 The 1996 Act makes express provisions for undertakings to be accepted by the court. These provisions are set out at s 46, which grants a court a power to accept an undertaking in place of an occupation or non-molestation order (s 46(1)). Such an undertaking cannot be accepted where a power of arrest would be attached to an order which the court would otherwise grant (s 46(3)). Section 46(2) makes it clear that a power of arrest cannot be attached to an undertaking, and by s 46(4) an undertaking is enforceable as thought it were a full order of the court.

Powers of arrest

10.5.23 Section 47 of the 1996 Act makes detailed provisions for attaching a power of arrest to either an occupation or a non-molestation order. By s 47(2) the court is obliged to attach a power of arrest to an order if satisfied that the respondent has either used or threatened violence against the applicant or a relevant child. The court has a discretion not to attach such a power if satisfied that without it the applicant or child will be adequately protected. It is widely thought that more applications are contested today than they were since the threshold for obtaining a power of arrest (now only 'threatened violence') is lower than it was.

10.5.24 Where an occupation or non-molestation order is made *ex parte*, a power of arrest can only be attached if the court is further satisfied that there is a risk of serious harm if no such power were to be attached to the order (s 47(3)(b)).

10.5.25 A power of arrest enables a police officer to arrest a person whom he has reasonable grounds for suspecting to be in breach of an order (s 47(6)). A respondent who is arrested under such a power must be brought before a judge within 24 hours (s 47(7)(a)) and may be dealt with then and there or be remanded (s 47(7)(b)).

10.5.26 If a power of arrest has not been attached to an order or has only been attached to part of it, the applicant can make an application on oath for a warrant to be issued (s 47(8),(9)(a)). The court must first be satisfied that there are reasonable grounds for supposing that the respondent has failed to comply with the order (s 47(9)(b)).

10.5.27 Any court before which a respondent is brought on a warrant has a power to grant bail or to remand in custody. Further, a remand can be made for the purposes of preparing a medical report (s 48).

Committal

10.5.28 A respondent can be committed for contempt of court only when it can be established that
(1) he clearly knew of the terms of the injunction and
(2) the incident giving rise to the breach was deliberately or wilfully committed.

No formal documents are required if the defendant is brought before the judge under a power of arrest. If the applicant wishes to bring separate contempt proceedings then the appropriate form compelling the respondent to show cause must be served together with any affidavit in support. Since the liberty of the subject is at stake, the highest standards of fairness will be expected of the court. The respondent must be able to tell from the committal application exactly what it is that is said to have been done which was in breach of the order. By s 50 of the 1996 Act, magistrates are expressly given the power to suspend the execution of a committal order under s 63(3) of the Magistrates' Courts Act 1980.

Checklist – determining an appropriate remedy

- Have the respondent's activities recently started?
  - — if yes, then an order from the civil courts may be granted to ensure that this conduct does not continue
  - — if no, then consideration must be given to reporting the matter to the police with a view to a criminal prosecution.
- Is there an available interlocutory remedy under the Family Law Act 1996?
  - — Part IV of the 1996 Act came into force in October 1997 and substantially extended the categories of person between whom the courts have jurisdiction to grant orders. These include children and people who were engaged at any time up to three years prior to the incident in question
  - — Part IV proceedings are advisable for a number of reasons:
    - — it is not necessary to show an assault or a course of conduct (as required by the Protection from Harassment Act 1997)
    - — a power of arrest can be attached and this power is not yet in force under the 1997 Act
    - — the courts (especially the County Courts) are well used to this jurisdiction

— the intricacies of the old forms of action do not have to be considered

— in addition to a non-molestation order, is an occupation order appropriate?

— there is a power to make an exclusion zone which the respondent cannot enter – does this apply?

— a power of arrest should be obtained if possible

— an applicant should not hesitate to apply for a committal order.

- If no Family Act remedy is available, is an interlocutory remedy available by some other means?

  — possibilities to be considered by the individual plaintiff are:
    — trespass to the person (assault)
    — wrongful interference with goods
    — trespass to land
    — nuisance (relevant only if the use and enjoyment of the land owned or occupied by the plaintiff is in issue)
    — intentionally causing emotional distress (*Wilkinson v Downton*)
    — harassment (under s 3 of the Protection from Harassment Act 1997)

  — possibilities to be considered by the employer also include:
    — intimidation
    — unlawful interference

  — an interlocutory injunction should be speedily applied for. Is the case so urgent that the applicant should seek an *ex parte* order?

  — an applicant should not hesitate to institute committal proceedings.

- What criminal penalties are appropriate after the event?

  — if there is medical evidence of assault, which includes nervous shock, then an assault charge is appropriate. A very serious case would merit proceedings under s 20 of the Offences Against the Person Act 1861 in the Crown Court. Less serious offences are appropriately dealt with in the magistrates' court under s 39 of the Criminal Justice Act 1988. There is a range of offences in between

  — a persistent pest to a number of victims, especially by phone, may properly be prosecuted as a public nuisance.

Chapter 11

Wheel Clamping

11.1 Overview

11.1.1 This chapter considers briefly the modern phenomenon of the immobilisation of motor vehicles, in particular 'wheel clamping'. The police have certain statutory powers which are summarised at 11.2. Immobilisation on private land, however, is a particular irritation for the motorist and has led to attempts by drivers to take steps to remove the immobilising device. Section 11.3 below considers whether the destruction of a device is a defence to a prosecution for criminal damage and also what cause of action is available to a driver who believes that his vehicle has been improperly impounded (distress damage feasant). The important factor in both criminal and civil actions is the question whether the motorist has impliedly consented to the risk of being clamped.

11.2 Police powers

11.2.1 A constable may fix an immobilisation device (generally known as a 'wheel clamp') to a vehicle parked on a public road in contravention of any prohibition or restriction, or authorise another person to do so under his direction (s 104 of the Road Traffic Regulation Act 1984). The Secretary of State is required to designate such areas (s 106 of the 1984 Act).

11.2.2 Section 104 does not apply if the vehicle is displaying a disabled person's badge or is in a meter bay designated as a parking place. However, the exemption does not apply if the meter bay is not authorised for use, or if the parking is in contravention of a designation order at the time at which the vehicle was left, or if an initial charge was not paid or more than two hours have passed since expiry of the initial charge (s 105 of the 1984 Act).

11.3 Wheel clamping on private land

11.3.1 There has been much public debate concerning whether or not a private individual may clamp vehicles parked on private property (as opposed to a public roadway) including a Home Office consultation paper (issued in 1993), but no statutory guidelines have been produced.

11.3.2 The courts, however, have considered the point. In *Lloyd v Director of Public Prosecutions* [1992] 1 All ER 982, the Queen's Bench Division, in exercising its criminal jurisdiction, had the following facts put before it. The appellant parked his car in a private car park which he had no entitlement to use. At the entrance and exit to the car park, large notices (admittedly seen by the appellant) stated that unauthorised or unlawfully parked vehicles would be immobilised and a £25 fee charged for the release. A wheel clamp was attached to the appellant's car by the car park owner's agents and notices were displayed on the car informing the appellant how to have the vehicle released. He cut through the wheel clamp padlocks and removed his vehicle. Nolan LJ, giving judgment, stated (at 992G):

> Situations like those which have arisen in the present case are becoming increasingly common. They can cause intense irritation both to the motorist deprived of the use of his car, as he thinks, unreasonably, and to the landowner or other victim of the motorist's unauthorised parking. That makes it all the more necessary for it to be clearly stated that, at any rate as a general rule, if a motorist parks his car without permission on another person's property knowing that by doing so he runs the risk of it being clamped, he has no right to damage or destroy the clamp. If he does so he will be guilty of a criminal offence.

11.3.3 The above case was brought in the criminal and not the civil courts. All that *Lloyd* can be said to have decided is that where a motorist consents to the risk of having a clamp attached to his vehicle it cannot be argued that the destruction of the clamp amounts to a lawful excuse in a prosecution under s 1(1) of the Criminal Damage Act 1971.

11.3.4 In *Lloyd*, the appellant sought to argue that he had a self-help right of recaption of his vehicle since the vehicle was unlawfully held by the impounder. The ancient right of recaption has not been reconsidered by the courts and cannot be said to be a live issue. In the subsequent case of *Arthur and Another v Anker and Another* [1996] 2 WLR 602, the landowner who placed a clamp on the appellant's vehicle sought to justify his actions by reference to another legal right with medieval origins, distress damage feasant.

11.3.5 Distress damage feasant is a means of preventing a chattel from continuing to cause damage to property. In the case of animals it has received statutory force by s 7(1) of the Animals Act 1971 (detention of trespassing livestock) (see 9.4.7). In *Arthur's* case the Court of Appeal held that the act could not be justified by reference to distress damage feasant since the purpose of the detention was not to put an end to any damage caused by the presence of the vehicle but to prolong it until the plaintiff paid the release fee. Moreover, although an action in trespass is actionable *per se* (without proof of damage) in order to succeed in a claim of distress damage feasant there had to be more than nominal damage. In *Arthur's* case the respondent had not suffered so much as an inconvenience, so that it could not be said that the damage was other than nominal.

11.3.6 The Court of Appeal preferred to dismiss the appellant's claim that the respondent had committed a tortious interference with his car by reference to the principle *volenti non fit injuria* (drawing no distinction between that defence and the defence of consent).

11.3.7 The principle has good authority. In *Smith v Baker & Sons* [1891] AC 325 at 360 it was said by Lord Herschell that:

> The maxim is founded on good sense and justice. One who has invited or assented to an act being done towards him cannot, when he suffers from it, complain of it as a wrong.

So too in *Cummings v Granger* [1977] QB 397 it was held that a plaintiff who entered a closed yard at night knowing of the existence of an Alsatian dog loose in the premises accepted the risk of injury.

11.3.8 The only relevant question therefore in seeking to establish a liability for the imposition of a wheel clamp is the question whether the driver realised that there was a risk of being clamped. The situation is very different in Scotland, where private clamping of vehicles has been held to be theft by appropriation (*Black and Another v Carmichael* (1992) *The Times* 25 June).

11.3.9 Just as there can be no objection to the imposition of a clamp it should also be noted that a motorist cannot object to having to pay a reasonable release fee (see Hirst LJ in *Arthur v Anker* [1996] 2 WLR 602).

11.3.10 Where a vehicle has been clamped without notice of the danger of clamping, the appropriate remedy is under the Torts (Interference with Goods) Act 1977 and an injunction for its removal.

Chapter 12

Noise

12.1 Overview

12.1.1 Published studies and reports have confirmed that noise is undoubtedly the major source of complaint received by local authorities. Whilst earlier chapters of this book seek to set out the relevant law in relation to remedies at common law and in statutory nuisance, this chapter will seek to give a practical account of the special statutory rules which relate in particular to the following:

(1) Street noises as statutory nuisances (the Environmental Protection Act 1990) (see 12.2)
(2) Construction works (see 12.3)
(3) Loudspeakers (see 12.6)
(4) Burglar alarms (see 12.7)
(5) Road vehicles (see 12.8)
(6) Aircraft noise (see 12.9)
(7) Night-time neighbour noise (see 12.10)
(8) Entertainment licences (see 12.11)
(9) Noise abatement zones (see 12.13)
(10) Plant and machinery (see 12.5)
(11) Waste management (see 12.12)
(12) Planning control (see 12.14)
(13) Compensation and major projects (see 12.15).

12.1.2 Success in obtaining a remedy depends on the strength of the evidence available. The keeping of detailed diaries describing the duration and frequency of occurrence of a noise and how a complainant is affected by the loudness and any tonal qualities, can be essential, whether by assisting a local authority to take action, or in using a self-help remedy in the magistrates' court under s 82 of the Environmental Protection Act 1990 (EPA 1990), or in seeking an injunction to restrain a nuisance.

12.2 Street noise as statutory nuisances

Statutory nuisances

12.2.1 The principles relevant to statutory nuisances, in particular the remedies which are available to both local authorities and individuals and the correct procedures to be followed are set out in chapter 3. This section is intended to look a little more closely at statutory nuisances created in the street by way of emissions of noise from vehicles, machinery or equipment. In particular, it will examine the abatement procedure appropriate to such a statutory nuisance.

Emissions of noise by a vehicle, machinery or equipment (VME)

12.2.2 Under ss 2–5 of the Noise and Statutory Nuisance Act 1993 (the 1993 Act), s 79 of the EPA 1990 has been amended by the addition of a new category to s 79(1):

(ga) noise emitted from or caused by a vehicle, machinery or equipment in a street

Such an emission (by a 'VME') must, of course, be 'prejudicial to health or a nuisance' in order to fall within the ambit of s 79 of the Act.

12.2.3 The effect of s 79(1)(ga) of the EPA 1990 is to extend the statutory duties of a local authority in relation to noise. The amendment plugged a gap since the original subsection only dealt with problems occurring in a driveway, but not on the road. 'Equipment' includes musical equipment and will therefore include loudspeakers, tannoys, loud hailers, radios and hi-fi equipment.

Political demonstrations and employment disputes

12.2.4 A noise emitted or caused by a VME in a street in connection with a political demonstration is exempt under s 79(6A) of the EPA 1990. However, this exemption does not apply to noise or disturbance made by pickets in an employment dispute as this is not considered to be a political demonstration under the Act.

'Street'

12.2.5 The noise must come from a street, which has the same meaning as that in s 62 of the Control of Pollution Act 1974, namely:

a highway or any other road, footway, square or court that is for the time being open to the public.

Therefore noise from vehicles in a public car park could be covered by this subsection.

The special abatement procedure

12.2.6   The 1993 Act introduces a special abatement procedure to deal with a statutory noise nuisance coming from a VME in a street which is unattended and where the owner or person responsible cannot be easily found and served with an abatement notice. These provisions, introduced by a new s 80A inserted into the EPA 1990, are designed to balance the rights of the owners against the needs of those who are suffering the noise nuisance. In common with other abatement notices served under s 80 of the EPA, the abatement notice may be served on the basis either that a statutory nuisance is anticipated or is already in existence. Environment Circular 9/97 (WO Circular 42/97) contains advice to local authorities who wish to implement the provisions in the 1993 Act, and is a useful reference point for complainants to check whether the local authority is doing its job properly.

Serving the abatement notice

12.2.7   Where the person responsible for the VME can be found then the abatement notice must be served on that person (s 80A(2)(a)). The main types of noise from vehicles in the street are likely to arise from vehicle repairs, tuning, and car alarms. In these cases the identity of the responsible person is not normally a problem and the Environment Circular advises that in such cases they should be served with an abatement notice. The local authority may seek further information from the local police on the identity of the responsible person through a vehicle licence check.

12.2.8   Where the person responsible for the VME cannot be found, the local authority must fix the notice to the VME (s 80A(2)(b)). If the local authority can locate the responsible person within an hour of fixing the notice to the VME, it must also serve a copy of the notice on that person. In that situation a notice must state if the person responsible for the VME is subsequently served with a copy of the notice under s 80A(3) and it must also specify whether the time for complying with the notice is extended (s 80A(4)).

12.2.9   If the person responsible for the VME is not found and the abatement notice has been fixed to the VME the one hour requirement will not apply and the local authority can, as soon as the time for compliance with the abatement notice has expired, take immediate action to abate the noise nuisance.

Local authority powers under a VME abatement notice

12.2.10   The provisions of para 2A of Schedule 3 to the EPA 1990 enable a local authority officer to enter or open a VME. If necessary, force may be used and the VME removed from the street to a secure place. If the local authority officer is unable to secure the VME after entering or opening it he may, for the purpose of securing the unattended VME, either immobilise it (eg by way of a vehicle clamp) or remove it from the street to a secure place (para 2A(3) of Schedule 3 to the EPA). The second option would be appropriate if merely immobilising the VME would not provide adequate security from theft, for example where the vehicle contains personal possessions or a radio/cassette which could be stolen even if the vehicle was clamped. Before entering, opening or removing a VME, the local authority officer must notify the police of its intention to take this action.

Right of appeal

12.2.11   There is a right of appeal against the service of the abatement notice to the Magistrates' Court within 21 days (beginning with the date on which the notice is served or fixed on the VME (s 80(3)). The notice must include a statement confirming that there is a right of appeal and specify the time in which the appeal must be brought (para 6 of Schedule 3 to the EPA 1990). The grounds of appeal are set out in the Statutory Nuisance (Appeals) Regulations 1995. The effect of an appeal is to suspend the notice unless the local authority has included a statement in accordance with regulation 3 (see 3.13.6).

Removing or interfering with an abatement notice

12.2.12   It is an offence for a person to remove or interfere with an abatement notice fixed to a VME and the maximum penalty imposed on summary conviction is a fine not exceeding level 3 on the standard scale (s 80A(7),(8)).

Non-compliance with an abatement notice

12.2.13   It is also an offence not to comply with the abatement notice under s 80(4).

Defences

12.2.14   In common with other provisions relating to statutory notices, there is a defence of using the best practicable means to prevent, or counteract the effects of the noise nuisance, except where the noise is emitted or caused by a VME being used for industrial, trade or business premises (s 80A(7),(8)).

12.2.15   This means that the test of 'best, practicable means' will only apply in so far as the activity complained of is compatible with a duty imposed by law, or is a specific statutory duty, or relates to matters of safety or an emergency. These matters should be taken into account by a local authority when deciding whether it is appropriate to serve an abatement notice.

12.2.16   It is also a defence to prosecution proceedings if the noise was authorised by a notice served under s 60 or a consent given under s 61 of the Control of Pollution Act 1974 (relating to the noise from construction sites) (s 80(9)).

Checklist – street noise as a statutory nuisance

- Does s 79 apply (as amended)?
  — has a noise been emitted by a vehicle, machinery or equipment (VME) in a street?
  — (NB the wide meaning of 'equipment')
  — is the emission prejudicial to health or a nuisance?
  — political and employment disputes are exempt
  — 'street' includes any public place.
- Can the special abatement procedure be utilised by the local authority?
  — serve on the person responsible or attach to the VME
  — the VME can be opened, removed or immobilised
  — the VME must be made secure
  — the police must be notified
  — it is an offence either to remove or interfere with an abatement notice or to fail to comply
  — check whether any special defences are available.

12.3 Construction works

12.3.1 A local authority has a choice when dealing with noise emanating from a street or roadworks. It may rely on the new provisions introduced by the 1993 Act referred to above (where the noise is emitted from or caused by VMEs associated with street or roadworks) or it may choose to control noise emitted from construction sites by using the powers found in ss 60 and 61 of the Control of Pollution Act 1974 (the 1974 Act). Where noise or vibration is being caused by a construction site and is causing a nuisance which is not on the street then the normal statutory nuisance provisions may also apply (s 79(7) EPA 1990) (see chapter 3).

12.3.2 The types of construction work that are subject to the provisions are set out in s 60(1) of the 1974 Act including:

(1) the erection, construction, alteration, repair or maintenance of buildings, structures and roads;

(2) the breaking up, opening, or boring under any road or adjacent land in connection with the construction, inspection, maintenance or removal of works;

(3) demolition or dredging work;

(4) any work of engineering construction.

Persuading the local authority to pursue a complaint

12.3.3 The keeping of a diary to record the duration, loudness, frequency of occurrence and efforts taken to persuade the construction workers to take action can be extremely helpful in persuading a local authority to investigate the case in the first place. Do not stop recording this information just in case the EHO does nothing as it can be used to support your own proceedings.

Section 60 notice

12.3.4 The local authority may serve a notice on any person who appears to the local authority to be or about to be carrying out the works or has control over carrying out the works which will govern the manner in which the works are to be carried out (s 60(2)). The notice must be limited to specific identifiable works in contemplation at the time of serving the notice and cannot extend to other uncontemplated works (which will require a fresh notice) (*Walter Lilly & Co Ltd v Westminster City Council* (1994) *The Times*, 1 March). The local authority may decide to publish details of the notice describing the requirements it seeks to impose.

12.3.5 When considering whether to serve a notice the local authority is required to have regard to the provisions of any relevant Code of Practice issued under this section (s 60(4)). For example, the Control of Noise (Code of Practice for Construction and Open Sites) Order 1987 could apply. The local authority must have regard to the need for ensuring that the best practicable means are employed to minimise any noise. The notice may specify the plant or machinery which is or is not to be used, the hours of work, the level of noise which may be emitted from the premises and provide for any change in circumstances.

Right of appeal

12.3.6 A person served with a notice under this section may appeal against the notice to a Magistrates' Court within 21 days of the date of service of the notice (s 60(7)).

12.3.7 The grounds of appeal and the appeal procedure are contained in the Control of Noise (Appeals) Regulations 1975 (SI 1975 No 2116). These grounds of appeal may include any of the following, namely that:

(1) s 60 does not justify the service of the notice;

(2) there has been some informality, defect or error in the notice;

(3) the local authority has refused unreasonably to accept compliance with alternative arrangements, or that the requirements with the notice are otherwise unreasonable in character or extent, or are unnecessary;

(4) the time or times given for compliance with a notice is or are not reasonably sufficient;

(5) the notice should not have been served on the appellant but on someone else who is carrying out or is proposing to carry out the works or who is responsible for or who has control over the carrying out of works;

(6) the notice might lawfully have been served not only on the appellant but also on someone else falling within category (5) above and it would have been equitable for that person to also be served;

(7) the local authority has not had regard to some or all of the requirements of s 60(4) (ie a Code of Practice, the use of 'best practicable means', a

failure to specify other methods of plant or machinery which would be as effective, and the need to protect persons in the locality).

12.3.8   Where an appeal is based on grounds (5) or (6) above, the appellant must serve a copy of his appeal on the other person to whom the appeal notice refers. The magistrate who considers the appeal has the power to quash the notice, vary or dismiss it.

12.3.9   The effect of the appeal is to suspend the notice until the appeal has either been determined or abandoned. In practice such a notice contains a statement that it will have effect notwithstanding any appeal (reg 10(2), Control of Notice (Appeals) Regulations 1975). This statement can be added to the notice if, in the opinion of the local authority:

(1)   The noise concerned is injurious to health or is likely to last for so short a time that suspension of a notice would make it ineffective in practice;

(2)   Any expenditure which would be incurred before determination of any appeal would not be disproportionate to the public benefit which would accrue from compliance with the notice.

Interrelationship with statutory nuisance proceedings

12.3.10   Where a s 60 notice has been served and complied with, this will constitute a defence to any proceedings brought by the local authority under ss 80 and 81 of the EPA 1990 (statutory nuisance provisions), but not to proceedings brought by individuals under s 82 of the EPA 1990. However, the service of a notice under s 60 does not create a defence against proceedings for an injunction to restrain a nuisance, notwithstanding compliance with the conditions of the s 60 notice (*Lloyds Bank v Guardian Assurance Plc* 17 October 1986 unreported).

Failing to comply with a s 60 notice

12.3.11   Failure to comply with the s 60 notice is a criminal offence. A person found guilty will be liable on summary conviction to a fine not exceeding level 5 on the standard scale and a daily penalty may be imposed not exceeding £50 for each day on which the offence continues after conviction (s 74(1)).

Personal liabilities

12.3.12   In addition, s 87 of the 1974 Act also imposes personal liability on any director, manager, secretary or similar officer of a corporate body or any person who is purporting to act in such capacity (for instance a shadow director) for any offence committed by the company which is proved to have been committed with their consent, connivance or neglect.

Injunctive relief

12.3.13   Nevertheless, experience has shown that the threat of criminal proceedings under s 60 may not deter a company which is under a contractual obligation to meet a deadline to complete the works, since the failure to meet the deadline will impose considerably higher financial penalties. In that situation a local authority may have no alternative but to apply for an injunction to prevent or restrict a nuisance under s 81(5) of the EPA and s 222 of the Local Government Act 1972. In *City of London Corporation v Bovis Construction Limited* [1992] 3 All ER 697, it was held that an injunction could be granted to prevent a breach of criminal law (the failure to comply with a s 60 notice).

Prior consent for work on construction sites

12.3.14   Where a person intends to carry out works on a construction site, he has the option to apply to the local authority for consent under s 61 of the 1974 Act. In practice very few applications are made. The consent may involve approval of the hours of work, details of the nature of the works to be carried out and any steps to be taken to minimise any noise. This is known as a s 61 consent. The application for consent must be made at the same time as, or after, the request for building regulation approval. The local authority must give its consent to the application if it considers that if the works were carried out in accordance with the particulars given, it would not serve a s 60 notice. The local authority may grant consent subject to conditions, it may limit or qualify a consent to allow for any change in circumstances and may limit the duration of the consent. A consent given under s 61 must contain a statement to the effect that it does not of itself constitute grounds of defence against any proceedings under s 82 of the EPA 1990.

Breaching a s 61 consent

12.3.15   Any person who knowingly carries out works or permits works to be carried out in contravention of any conditions attached to a s 61 consent will be guilty of an offence and liable on summary conviction to a penalty not exceeding level 5 (s 74 of the 1974 Act). A daily penalty not exceeding £50 per day may also be imposed for each day the works continue in breach of the consent.

Appeal

12.3.16   The local authority is required under s 61(6) to inform the applicants of its decision within 28 days from the date of receipt of the application. If it does not give consent within this period or if it grants consent subject to any conditions or limitations, the applicant may appeal to magistrates within 21 days from the end of that period in accordance with the provisions of the Control of Noise (Appeal) Regulations 1975 (as amended). Alternatively, the local authority and appellant may agree within seven days of giving the notice of appeal that the matter will be determined by the Secretary of State instead of the magistrates.

Checklist – noise from construction works

- Check whether a remedy lies under s 79 (12.2 above).
- Use the powers available under ss 60 and 61, Control of Pollution Act 1974:
  - does the type of construction work fall within the ambit of s 60(1)?
  - serve a notice identifying the specific works in question and clarifying what is required to be done or discontinued
  - the local authority must have regard to codes of practice
  - NB the extensive grounds of appeal (which give an idea as to the requirements with which the authority must comply)
  - does the notice contain a statement overriding the suspension powers of a notice of appeal?
  - NB the interrelationship with statutory nuisance proceedings
  - it is an offence to fail to comply with a notice
  - the directors and managers of a body may face personal liabilities
  - has a s 61 authorisation (prior consent) been granted and complied with?
- An injunction may be necessary if a s 60 notice does not deter a contractor.

12.4   Building control under the Building Regulations 1991

12.4.1   Building work carried out after 1 June 1992 is subject to the Building Regulations 1991, which contain technical requirements concerning the passage of sound where a new building is being constructed or a conversion is taking place. In such cases, building work must be carried out in compliance with Part E of Sched 1 to the Regulations. The main problem in England and Wales (unlike Scotland) is that there is no requirement to test the noise insulation following completion of construction, so that it is difficult to assess whether the right insulation has been used.

12.5   Noise from plant or machinery

12.5.1   By s 68 of the Control of Pollution Act 1974, the Secretary of State is empowered to make regulations requiring the use of silencing devices on plant or machinery in order to reduce the noise levels they cause. Failure to comply with the regulations is a criminal offence (ss 68(3) and 74) and a person found guilty would be liable on summary conviction to a fine not exceeding level 5 on the standard scale and a daily penalty not exceeding £50 for each day the offence continues after conviction.

12.6 Loudspeakers

12.6.1 Section 62(1) of the Control of Pollution Act 1974 prevents the use of loudspeakers in a street between 9.00 pm to 8.00 am the following day, or at any time for the purpose of advertising any entertainment, trade or business. Although the section as originally drafted had worked well, it was considered to be unduly restrictive. It was amended by s 7 of the Noise and Statutory Nuisance Act 1993 (the 1993 Act), enabling the Secretary of State to amend the times specified above by Order.

12.6.2 These restrictions do not apply to the exercise of functions by the police, fire brigade, ambulance, Environment Agency, water or sewerage undertaker, local authority, or by someone directing persons on a vessel, or where the loudspeaker forms part of a public telephone system, or in certain specified cases where it is fixed to a vehicle or is operated by a travelling showman at a pleasure fair, or in cases of emergency.

12.6.3 By s 8 of the 1993 Act local authorities have the power to resolve that Sched 2 to the 1993 Act ('consent to the operation of loudspeakers in streets or roads') will apply to its area. This means that the provisions will not automatically apply in every local authority area because of the cost implications. The first matter to establish therefore will be whether the authority has taken the appropriate decision. This can be done by asking the Environmental Health Officer or by asking the relevant committee clerk to produce a copy of the relevant minutes and committee reports, or alternatively by asking someone in the legal department for the information. Sched 2 enables local authorities to grant consents to the operation of loudspeakers in the street outside the restriction period of 9.00 pm to 8.00 am, provided that consent shall not be given to the use of a loudspeaker for any election or for the purpose of advertising any entertainment, trade or business.

12.6.4 A local authority in this case includes a district council, a London borough council or unitary authority or a district or island Council of Scotland. The consent granted under Sched 2 may be granted subject to such conditions as the local authority considers appropriate following receipt of a written application. The local authority has 21 days beginning with the day on which the application is received by the local authority to determine the application on the payment of a fee. Details of the consent may be published in a local newspaper circulating in the local authority area.

Ice cream and burger vans

12.6.5 There is one important exception. The restrictions referred to above do not apply to the operation of a loudspeaker between the hours of 12.00 pm and 7.00 pm on the same day providing the loudspeaker is fixed to a vehicle which is being used for the conveyance of perishable commodities for human consumption, is operated solely for informing the members of the public and does not give reasonable cause for annoyance.

The interrelation between a Sched 2 consent and proceedings for statutory nuisance

12.6.6 The grant of consent under Sched 2 to the 1993 Act does not in itself provide an exemption from the statutory nuisance proceedings. If complaints are received about noise levels in the street, the local authority is subject to a duty to take such steps as are reasonably practical to investigate those complaints and serve an abatement notice if the noise constitutes a statutory nuisance. (Further advice can be found in the Code of Practice on Noise from Ice Cream Van Chimes Etc 1982.)

Checklist – loudspeakers

- Section 62(1) (as amended) prohibits the use of loudspeakers:
  - this section does not affect the emergency services, Environment Agency, water or sewage undertakers, local authorities or in certain other circumstances
  - has the local authority passed a resolution consenting to the operation of loudspeakers and has it granted a specific consent?
  - (NB a consent does not mean that there will be an exemption from statutory nuisance proceedings in an appropriate case)
  - the restrictions do not apply to ice cream and burger vans (see also the relevant code of practice).

12.7 Burglar alarms

12.7.1 The operation of burglar alarms is controlled outside London by the use of the statutory nuisance abatement procedures under ss 79–82 of the EPA 1990. In addition, a 1982 Code of Practice From Noise of Audible Intruder Alarms provides guidance on the installation or preparation of intruder burglar alarms and in particular suggests that all alarms should be fitted with a 20-minute cut-off device. BS 4737 also includes a requirement to comply with the Code of Practice.

12.7.2 In London, s 23 of the London Local Authorities Act 1991 (as amended by s 25 of the London Local Authorities Act 1996) enables London borough councils to adopt a free-standing set of provisions (these primarily mirror the 1982 Code of Practice) and govern both the technical specification of the alarm (for instance the 20-minute cut-off period), and the procedure for notifying the local authority and the police of the installation and identity of nominated key holders. In addition, s 23 enables an authorised local authority officer to request a warrant from magistrates to enable him to gain access and entry to property for the purpose of deactivating the alarm where it can be demonstrated that the alarm is causing annoyance to persons living or working near the premises and the alarm has been ringing for more than one hour.

12.7.3   Section 9 of the Noise and Statutory Nuisance Act 1993 enables local authorities, after consulting the chief officer of police, to resolve that Sched 3 to the Act will apply to its area. The provisions in s 9 and Sched 3 have yet to be brought into force by Order. Until the provisions are brought into force, local authorities can only resort to the powers under ss 79 and 81(3) of and Sched 3 to the EPA to serve an abatement notice and on s 23 of the London Local Authorities Act 1991 if relevant. Schedule 3 to the EPA 1990 contains detailed provisions which local authorities may rely on which govern powers of entry and recovery of expenses. These mirror the provisions under s 23 of the London Local Authorities Act 1991.

Checklist – burglar alarms

- Control outside London is under ss 79–82 of the Environmental Protection Act 1990.
- Control in London is by way of s 23 of the London Local Authority Act 1991 (as amended).
- NB the Code of Practice from Noise of Audible Intruder Alarms.
- Section 9 of and Schedule 3 to the Noise and Statutory Nuisance Act 1993 will be relevant when in force.

12.8   Road vehicle noise

12.8.1   A plethora of European legislation exists which seeks to control the amount of noise emitted from four wheeled vehicles, motorcycles and tractors which is outside the remit of this book. In addition the Road Traffic Regulation Act 1984 contains provisions enabling a local authority to make a traffic regulation order if it appears to be expedient for a variety of purposes, including the need to preserve or improve the amenities of an area through which the road runs (see ss 1(1)(f) and 2(4)). In *R v London Boroughs Transport Committee, ex p Freight Transport Association Ltd* [1991] 1 WLR 828, an order to require lorries of a certain size to fit airbrake silencers was held to be lawful. For noise created by vehicles in a street, see the section on street noise at 12.2.

12.9   Aircraft noise

12.9.1   The principal legislation governing aircraft noise is the Civil Aviation Act 1982. Section 76 stipulates that there can be no action in trespass or nuisance to prevent aircraft flying over any property at the appropriate height having regard to wind, weather and all circumstances so long as the rules of the Rules of the Air, Air Traffic Control Regulations and any relevant air navigation order and normal aviation practice are observed. Section 77 enables an Air Navigation Order to be made to regulate conditions under which noise and vibration may be caused by aircraft on aerodromes. No action in nuisance is available so long as the provisions of the Order are complied with (including ground running and taxiing).

12.9.2 Under s 78 of the Civil Aviation Act 1982 the Secretary of State for Transport has the power to prescribe noise abatement measures for aircraft taking off and landing at designated airports. Responsibility for compliance will lie with the aircraft operator. The Secretary of State is also empowered to make noise insulation grant schemes if it appears that buildings near a designated aerodrome require protection from noise and vibration (s 79).

12.9.3 Furthermore, most types of aircraft may only take off or land in the UK if they possess a noise certificate appropriate to the aircraft type. The standards that must be met to obtain a noise certificate are set out in the Air Navigation (Noise Certification) Order 1990, made pursuant to the Civil Aviation Act 1982.

12.9.4 Restrictions on the movement of aircraft are based on international agreements under the jurisdiction of the International Civil Aviation Organisations. Controls over the height at which aircraft may fly are contained in the Rules of the Air Regulations 1991. For example, reg 5 stipulates that subject to a number of exceptions, aircraft should not fly at below 1,500 feet over heavily populated areas.

12.10   Late night revellers and night time neighbour noise

Introduction

12.10.1 The Noise Act 1996 (the 1996 Act) introduces a new night noise offence and complements the existing statutory nuisance controls by providing a swift remedy to deal with these problems. The noise nuisance offence is based on exceeding an objective value (permitted level), so that it is possible that a noise which is not an offence under the 1996 Act may still be a statutory or common law nuisance.

12.10.2 The 1996 Act does not automatically apply in every local authority area. Each local authority must first resolve to apply the noise nuisance offence in its area so it is necessary to ask the relevant local authority environmental health officer if the Act applies. A local authority for this purpose will be a London borough council, district council, unitary authority and, where there are no district councils, a county council in Wales and the Council of the Isles of Scilly. The local authority cannot rely on the 1996 Act unless at least three months have passed following the resolution and has advertised its intention in the local press in accordance with the provisions in the 1996 Act. Many local authorities have resolved not to rely on the 1996 Act mainly due to lack of manpower and the costs involved.

12.10.3 The Secretary of State has retained the power to apply the night noise offence to a local authority's area.

Investigating a complaint

12.10.4 Where the requisite resolution has been made, the local authority is required to take reasonable steps to investigate a complaint made by any individual present in a dwelling during night hours (ie the period between 11 pm and 7 am) that an excessive noise is being emitted from another dwelling (the offending dwelling). Section 11 defines dwelling as 'any building, or part of a building, used or intended to be used as a dwelling'. The noise must be emitted from a dwelling, and this will include the garden, yard and other buildings belonging to this.

12.10.5 If the local authority officer is satisfied following the investigation that:

(1) noise is being emitted from the offending dwelling during night hours; and

(2) the noise if it were measured from within the complainant's dwelling would or might exceed the permitted level,

he may serve a warning notice about the noise under s 3 (s 2(4)).

12.10.6 Advice to local authorities on how to comply with the provisions of the 1996 Act is contained within Environment Circular 8/97 (WO Circular 41/97). The advice states that an officer can decide by using his judgment or by taking noise measurements whether or not the noise complained of exceeds the permitted level (s 5). The permitted level is set out in Directions made by the Secretary of State, who also has the power to approve the appropriate use of measuring devices. The noise complained of must be measured using an approved device in accordance with any conditions in the approval. The Directions are contained in an Annex to the Circular and if the approved procedure is not followed, the measurement made will not be admissible as evidence in any court proceedings for the night noise offence.

12.10.7 For example, the permitted level shall be determined in accordance with the following:

(1) in any case where the underlying level of noise does not exceed 25dB, a permitted level shall be 35dB; and

(2) in any case where the underlying level of noise exceeds 25dB, the permitted level shall be 10dB in excess of that.

Therefore the permitted level is determined by reference to the underlying noise level and the Circular goes into great detail on how this should be properly measured.

Warning notice

12.10.8 Where the local authority officer is satisfied that a night noise offence exists, he may serve a warning notice under s 3. The notice will state that the officer considers that:

(1) the noise is being emitted from the offending dwelling during night hours;

(2) the noise exceeds, or may exceed, the permitted level, as measured from within the complainant's dwelling.

The notice will also contain a warning that any person responsible for the noise which is emitted from the dwelling during the period specified in the notice and which exceeds the permitted level (as measured from within the complainant's dwelling) will be guilty of an offence. The period specified in the notice must be a period:

(1) beginning no earlier than ten minutes after the time when the notice is served; and

(2) ending with the following 7 am.

12.10.9 As to service, a warning notice must be served:

(1) by delivering it to any person present at or near the offending dwelling and appearing to the local authority officer to be responsible for the noise; or

(2) if it is not reasonably practicable to identify the responsible person, by leaving it at the offending dwelling.

The warning notice must state the time at which it was served.

12.10.10 The 1996 Act and Circular do not contain a standard form of warning notice but a suggested form has been published by the Chartered Institute of Environmental Health.

Failure to comply with a warning notice

12.10.11 Where a warning notice has been served, then any person responsible for noise emitted from the offending dwelling which:

(1) is emitted from the dwelling in the period specified in the notice and

(2) exceeds the permitted level, as measured from within the complainant's dwelling, is guilty of an offence.

A person found guilty of a night noise offence under s 4 will be liable on summary conviction to a fine not exceeding level 3 on the standard scale (currently £1,000).

12.10.12 The 1996 Act contains a defence that a person charged with a night noise offence may show that there was a reasonable excuse for the act, default or sufferance in question.

Evidence

12.10.13 Where the local authority officer intends to rely on noise measurements taken in any proceedings for failing to comply with a warning notice, he may make use of the provisions of s 7 of the Act, which can reduce the formalities required at trial. Section 7 allows the production of a document signed by an officer of a local authority giving particulars of the measurement of noise by a device and of the fact that the device used was an approved device (s 7(2)). It also allows a document to be produced proving that the dwelling in question was the source of the noise (s 7(3)).

12.10.14 A document produced under s 7(2) or (3) must be served not less than seven days before the hearing or trial on the person charged with the offence. It will not be admissible as evidence of anything other than the matters shown on the record produced automatically if, not less than three days before the hearing or trial, the defendant serves a notice on the prosecutor requiring attendance at the hearing or trial of the person who signed the document (ie the authority's witnesses). The magistrates have a power to extend this three-day period.

Fixed penalty notice

12.10.15 As an alternative to prosecution under s 4 (failure to comply with a warning notice), a local authority officer has an option of serving a fixed penalty notice under s 8 if he has reason to believe that a person is committing or has just committed a s 4 offence. The fixed penalty notice is given to the responsible person, or, if this is not reasonably practical, it can be left at the address of the offending dwelling. The current fixed penalty sum is set at £100 although the Secretary of State may change this by order.

12.10.16 Where a fixed penalty notice has been served the local authority cannot issue proceedings for that offence within 14 days of the date of service of the notice. If the person responsible pays the fixed penalty before the end of that period he cannot be convicted of the offence.

12.10.17 The fixed penalty notice must state:

(1) that proceeding will not be taken for 14 days from the date of service of the notice;

(2) the fixed penalty sum is £100;

(3) details of the address at which the fixed penalty sum should be paid.

It should also give details of the circumstances alleged to constitute the offence.

12.10.18 The Secretary of State has power to specify a specific form of fixed penalty notice. Although this has not been done, a suggested form has been prepared by the Chartered Institute for Environmental Health.

12.10.19 If the fixed penalty is not paid within the 14-day period, the local authority may take proceedings against the responsible person (s 8(3)(b)).

Powers of entry and seizure

12.10.20 Where a warning notice has been served on an individual or dwelling and the noise emitted from the premises exceeds the permitted level at any time specified in the notice, local authority officers have powers to enter the dwellings and seize or remove the source of the noise (s 10 of and the Schedule to the 1996 Act).

12.10.21 Where entry is refused, an application may be made to a Justice of the Peace for a warrant enabling the local authority officer to gain access. This can include the use of force if necessary. The warrant will remain in force until such time as the equipment has been seized or until the purpose for which entry is required has been satisfied. If the premises are secure but unoccupied, the local authority is subject to a duty to leave them in a similar secure state following removal of the equipment.

12.10.22 Any person who wilfully obstructs a local authority officer attempting to enter premises or seize noise-making equipment may be liable on conviction to a fine up to level 3 on the standard scale.

Retention of noise-making equipment

12.10.23 A local authority may retain any noise-making equipment which has been seized for a period of up to 28 days from the date of seizure (para 2 of the Schedule). Where proceedings for an offence are instigated during that period, the equipment may be held until the responsible person is sentenced, acquitted, the case discontinued or otherwise dealt with.

12.10.24 Where the fixed penalty notice procedure is used, the seized equipment must be returned as soon as the fixed penalty is paid.

Forfeiture and disposal of forfeited equipment

12.10.25 Where a person has been convicted of a night noise offence, a Magistrates' Court may take a forfeiture order for any related equipment which has been used in connection with the offence (para 3 of the Schedule). This order can be made whether or not the offender is dealt with in any other way by the court.

12.10.26 When considering whether or not to make such an order the magistrates must take into consideration the value of the equipment and the likely financial and other effects on the offender if such an order is made.

12.10.27 Where the equipment is owned by another party (ie hire-purchase or lease company) the Schedule contains provisions enabling its return within six months of the date of the forfeiture order.

Checklist – late night revellers and night time neighbour noise

- Remedies
  - the Noise Act 1996 introduces a new offence based on a permitted level of noise
  - the noise may be a statutory nuisance (see chapter 3)
  - nuisance at common law may provide a remedy if noise is persistent.
- Investigating a complaint under the 1996 Act
  - check that the Act applies in the area
  - the local authority is obliged to take reasonable steps to investigate a complaint
  - the noise must occur during night hours (11 pm to 7 am)
  - a complaint can only be made by a person present in a dwelling
  - the noise must come from another dwelling.
- Issuing a warning notice
  - the notice must state that an EHO considers that a noise is being emitted from a dwelling in excess of the permitted level
  - there must be a warning that an offence may be committed
  - the notice must be served according to the rules for service and stating the time at which it was served.

- Failing to comply with a warning notice, fixed penalty notices and powers of search, seizure and disposal
  - it is an offence to fail to comply with a warning notice
  - there is a defence of reasonable excuse for the act or default or sufferance in question
  - there are abbreviated rules allowing for the admissibility of evidence in a prosecution
  - a fixed penalty notice is an alternative to prosecution
  - local authority officers have extensive powers of entry, seizure and retention. A warrant securing access can be obtained
  - magistrates have power after conviction to order the disposal and forfeiture of equipment.

12.11 Entertainment licences

12.11.1 Clubs and public houses which propose to hold public dancing, music or similar entertainments need to obtain a music and dancing licence from the relevant local authority. Such a licence will be obtained under the London Government Act 1963 as amended where the premises are situated within Greater London, or under the Local Government (Miscellaneous Provisions) Act 1982 for premises situated outside London.

12.11.2 Local authorities may grant, renew or transfer a licence subject to various terms and conditions which can include noise insulation. Licences normally last for one year or less. Where complaints have been received from local residents the local authority may decide to revoke the licence on an application for renewal or impose noise conditions.

12.11.3 A music and dancing licence does not cover the performance of stage plays where a separate theatre licence is required. Confusion has arisen over the use of karaoke machines since it is arguable that a music and dancing licence is also required to permit their use.

12.12 Waste management licences and integrated pollution control

12.12.1 The Environment Agency or relevant local authority (where appropriate) has power to impose conditions to control noise caused by licensed operations which are the subject of a waste management licence (for instance landfill tip or waste transfer station), an integrated pollution control authorisation or a local authority air pollution control authorisation. If the condition is breached enforcement and/or prosecution action may follow. The appropriate regulatory body is also likely to have powers to take action under the relevant governing legislation. Copies of the licence/authorisation will be held on a public register maintained by the appropriate regulatory body.

12.13 Noise abatement zones

12.13.1 Sections 63–67 of the Control of Pollution Act 1974 (the 1974 Act) deal with the establishment and operation of noise abatement zones. These powers have been rarely used except in the case of noise from industrial premises. The purpose of a noise abatement zone is to prevent a deterioration in environmental noise levels and to achieve a reduction in noise levels. The effect of such a zone is intended to be to control noise from classes of premises specified in the Noise Abatement Order by establishing the current noise levels and using these as reference levels to control noise emitted from those premises in future.

12.13.2 The existence of a noise abatement zone may affect proposals for development. For example, where a planning application has been submitted for consent to construct new industrial premises, consideration will be given to the noise abatement zone in that area.

12.13.3 Section 63 enables a local authority (principally a district council or London borough council) to designate all or part of its area as a noise abatement zone. The Noise Abatement Order must specify the classes of premises to which it will apply. The Order will only apply to selected classes of premises within the area of the zone. Details can be found on a public register. It is not intended to control noise emanating from all premises in that area as this would be impractical. The broad classes which can be subject to an Order may include industrial premises, commercial premises, places of entertainment or assembly, agricultural premises, transport installations and public utility installations. Domestic premises are not included as the statutory nuisance provisions are considered to be more appropriate in such a case.

12.13.4 In addition, a person may appeal to the Secretary of State within 21 days of the date of service by the local authority of the record of the noise measurements which are recorded in the public register.

Prosecution

12.13.5 It is an offence to exceed the noise level recorded in the register except with the local authority consent (s 65(1)) or to breach any condition in a consent.

Appeal

12.13.6 The applicant may lodge an appeal to the Secretary of State against the local authority's decision within three months beginning from the day the local authority notifies him of the decision. Where the local authority has failed to give notification of its decision within the two-month period, the authority shall be deemed to have refused it at the end of that period and the three-month period will then start to run (s 65).

Noise reduction notice

12.13.7   Where it appears to the local authority that the level of noise emanating from premises situated within a noise abatement zone is not acceptable, and where it is of the opinion that the reduction in noise level is practicable at a reasonable cost and would afford a public benefit, the local authority may serve a noise reduction notice on the responsible person. This will require a reduction in the level of noise in accordance with the levels specified in the Noise Abatement Order. The minimum period of compliance is six months, although the notice may provide some flexibility (for example by requiring different noise levels at different times of the day).

Failure to comply with a noise reduction order

12.13.8   Failure to comply with a noise reduction notice without reasonable excuse is a criminal offence although it is a defence in such proceedings that the best practical means had been used to prevent or to counteract the effect of the noise where the noise is caused in the course of a trade or business.

12.13.9   Where the person fails to comply with a noise reduction notice, the local authority may execute any necessary works in accordance with the Notice or a Magistrates' Court Order obtained under s 69 of the 1974 Act. The local authority may recover its costs from the responsible person for any expenditure incurred unless that person shows that the cost was unnecessary in the circumstances.

Checklist – noise abatement zones

- Noise abatement zones can be set up under the Control of Pollution Act 1974.
- The issuing of a Noise Abatement Order is intended to prevent a deterioration in local noise levels in industrial areas.
- A noise reduction notice can be utilised to require the owner of premises to reduce the level of noise to that specified in the noise abatement order.
- Various criminal penalties and rights of appeal exist.

12.14   Planning control and noise

12.14.1   The town and country planning legislation governs the development of land. The potential for a noise nuisance is a material consideration which a local planning authority must take into account when deciding whether or not to grant planning permission for the development of land. Guidance on noise can be found in DoE Planning Policy Guidance Note PPG24. Planning policies on noise are now found in development plans, for instance Unitary Development Plans, Borough Plans and Structure Plans. Where an environmental impact statement is required to be submitted in support of a planning application, the level of noise produced must also be considered. If relevant, any mitigation, reduction and preventative measures must be described in detail.

12.15 Major projects

12.15.1 Mandatory and discretionary grants are available under the Land Compensation Act 1973 and the Noise Insulation Regulations 1975 as amended for householders affected by airport, road or rail projects or other public works. In particular there may be a requirement to provide sound insulation or make a contribution towards its provision in accordance with any regulations made under s 20 of the Land Compensation Act 1973. Consideration should also be given to the Noise Insulation (Railways and Other Guided Transport Systems) Regulations 1996 in relation to buildings near railways and tramways, and to s 6(3) and Schedule 2, Part III of the Channel Tunnel Act 1987 for noise compensation for disturbance caused by the Channel Tunnel development.

Chapter 13

Air Pollution

13.1 Overview

13.1.1 A considerable amount of legislation exists to protect the quality of air. Although the common law rules in respect of private and public nuisance may be relevant to a complainant, a more likely starting-point is the statutory nuisance provisions described in chapter 3 and contained at Part III (ss 79–85) and Schedule 3 of the Environmental Protection Act 1990 (the EPA 1990) (smoke, fumes, gas, dust and steam emitted from premises which are prejudicial to health or nuisance). It will always be necessary, however, to determine exactly which legislation applies.

13.1.2 This section will consider specific statutory regimens relating to the following:

(1) Air pollution controls under Part I of the EPA 1990

(2) 'Dark smoke' from chimneys and industrial premises

(3) Emissions of smoke, grit, dust and fumes from non-domestic furnaces

(4) Smoke control areas

(5) Traffic

(6) Agriculture

(7) Air quality monitoring.

13.2 Part I, Environmental Protection Act 1990

Introduction

13.2.1 Part I of the EPA 1990 provides that certain substances and the carrying out of certain processes are to be regulated and controlled by two enforcement bodies, the Environment Agency (in relation to Integrated Pollution Control (IPC)) and local authorities (in relation to air emissions only). Substances and processes which are required to be regulated by these bodies are prescribed by statutory instrument. In order to carry out any operation in respect of such items, Part I of the EPA 1990 sets out a system of authorisations which must be obtained by the appropriate enforcement body. Where industrial, trade or commercial premises are the source of air pollution, a check should be carried out to ascertain whether there is a power of enforcement available under this Part of the EPA 1990.

Enforcement where a Part I authorisation has been issued

13.2.2 It should be noted that where the industrial process is governed by an authorisation granted under Part I, the local authority is precluded from initiating statutory nuisance proceedings under Part III of the EPA 1990 without the consent of the Secretary of State. Nevertheless in most situations the relevant enforcement body will have powers under Part I to deal with circumstances which amount to a statutory nuisance.

Enforcement under Part I

13.2.3 To check whether the process is regulated by Part I the first step is to contact the Environmental Health Officer (EHO) at the local authority. Alternatively it will be possible to go and inspect the public register maintained by the Environment Agency and/or relevant local authority to establish whether or not an authorisation has been granted. If an authorisation has been granted, it would normally contain conditions governing emissions into the atmosphere.

Options open to an enforcement body

13.2.4 The next step is to inform the appropriate enforcement bodies who will have several options:
  (1) Failure to comply with a condition may result in the service of an enforcement notice issued under s 13 of the EPA 1990 which will specify the steps that must be taken to remedy the contravention within a specified time period.
  (2) Where the enforcing body is of the opinion that the carrying on of the prescribed process involves an imminent risk of serious pollution of the environment the enforcing body may serve a prohibition notice on the person carrying on the process (s 14).
  (3) The authorisation may be revoked under s 12.
  (4) Initiate prosecution proceedings under s 23(1). (This option can be instead of or in addition to the three options referred to above.)

Prohibition notices

13.2.5 It should be noted that a prohibition notice under s 14 may be served whether or not the process is operated in breach of a condition of the authorisation. A prohibition notice is similar to a stop notice in planning and land use terms and it must direct that the authorisation shall, until the notice is withdrawn, cease to have effect. This means that the activity must stop pending the withdrawal of the notice after the enforcement body is satisfied that the steps required by the notice have been taken.

Appeals against an enforcement or prohibition notice

13.2.6 There is a right of appeal against the service of an enforcement or prohibition notice under the Environmental Protection (Applications, Appeals and Registers) Regulations 1991 (as amended). However, the bringing of the appeal does not suspend the operation of the enforcement or prohibition notice.

Failure to comply with an enforcement or prohibition notice

13.2.7 Failure to comply with, or contravention of, any requirement or prohibition imposed by an enforcement notice or prohibition notice is a criminal offence, and a person found guilty shall be liable on summary conviction to a fine not exceeding £20,000 or on conviction on indictment to a fine or term of imprisonment not exceeding two years or both (s 23(2)). Where a person is convicted of the offence which, in the opinion of the court, involves matters which the defendant can remedy, the court may, in addition to or instead of imposing any punishment, order the defendant to remedy the situation within a specific time period (s 26).

Injunctive proceedings

13.2.8 If the enforcing body is of the opinion that criminal proceedings would afford an effectual remedy, it may apply for an injunction in the High Court for an Order to stop the contravention (s 24). It may also in extreme cases decide to revoke the authorisation.

Failing to obtain an authorisation

13.2.9 It may be that the activity causing the air pollution should be, but is not, the subject of an authorisation. However, determination of this question will be the responsibility of the appropriate enforcing body. The most that a complainant can do is to make them aware of the situation and then the enforcing body will decide what course of action is appropriate. This could involve the service of an abatement notice under the statutory nuisance provisions and/or a prosecution.

Checklist – control under Part 1, Environmental Protection Act 1990

- Preliminary observations
  - where air pollution has been caused as a result of a process governed by an authorisation under Part I, statutory nuisance proceedings cannot be commenced without the consent of the Secretary of State

— check that there is in fact an authorisation in existence. Checks can be carried out with the environmental health officer or by examining the public register at the relevant regulatory body (Appendix A2.16).
- Options open to the enforcement body:
  — the issuing of an enforcement notice
  — service of a prohibition notice
  — revocation of the authorisation
  — prosecution
  — injunction proceedings.

13.3 Dark smoke – Part I, Clean Air Act 1993

13.3.1 Another piece of major legislation dealing with atmospheric pollution is the Clean Air Act 1993 (the 1993 Act) which consolidates the Clean Air Acts 1956–1968 and Part IV of the Control of Pollution Act 1974. The 1993 Act has contributed to the reduction of pollution by regulating specific emissions and introducing smoke control areas. Part I of the Act covers dark smoke emissions.

Enforcement

13.3.2 The appropriate enforcement officers for this Part are the Environmental Health Officers of the relevant local authorities. Where an offence has been committed contrary to either s 1 or s 2 of the 1993 Act (see below), a local authority may institute proceedings for an offence even if the emission arises from premises situated outside their area, so long as the smoke affects their district (s 55).

General exemptions to Parts I–III of the Act

13.3.3 Parts I–III of the Act do not apply to certain activities specified in Part VI, for example prescribed processes under Part I of the EPA 1990 (s 41), refuse from mining or quarrying of coal or slate (s 42), railway engines (s 43), vessels (s 44), Crown premises (s 46). There are also exemptions for investigations and research (s 45).

Prohibitions of dark smoke from chimneys

13.3.4 Section 1(1) prohibits the emission of dark smoke from a chimney of any building. This prohibition includes both industrial and residential houses although it does not extend to all smoke, gases or sulphurous fumes. Section 1(2) prohibits the emission of dark smoke from any other chimney which serves the furnace of any fixed boiler or industrial plant. The appropriate defendant in respect of an offence under s 1(1) is the occupier. The appropriate defendant in respect of an offence under s 1(2) is the person having possession of the boiler or plant. The burden of proof is on the defendant to show that it is not dark smoke which is being emitted.

'Dark smoke'

13.3.5 'Dark smoke' is defined as smoke which would appear dark or darker than shade figure 2 in the Ringelmann Chart (s 3(1)). The Ringelmann Chart contains five shades of grey by reference to cross hatching black lines on a white background from clear (number 0) to black (number 4). The chart is used by EHOs. It is rectangular in shape and can be held up by the operator or EHO and compared with the smoke from a distance of at least 15 metres. Nevertheless, a court may be satisfied that the smoke is not dark smoke notwithstanding there has been no actual comparison with the Ringelmann Chart (s 3). This is necessary since it would be impossible to prove the presence of dark smoke after dark. The question of 'dark smoke' was considered by the High Court in *O'Fee v Copeland Borough Council* (1995) *The Times*, 22 April.

Other definitions

13.3.6 A chimney is defined by s 64(1) to include:

> structures and openings of any kind from or through which smoke, grit, dust or fumes may be emitted, and in particular . . . flues.

If a chimney serves the whole or any part of the building, it is immaterial that it may be structurally separate from that building. A 'fireplace' includes 'any furnace, grate or stove, whether open or closed' (s 64(1)). A furnace is not defined in the legislation.

13.3.7 'Premises' includes land (s 64(1)) and 'industrial or trade purpose' includes premises used for any industrial or trade purposes, or any other premises on which matter is burnt in connection with any industrial or trade premises (s 2(6)).

Prohibition of dark smoke from industrial or trade premises

13.3.8 It is an offence under s 2 to emit dark smoke from any industrial or trade premises other than from a chimney. The occupier of the building and any person who causes or permits the emission shall be guilty of an offence. By s 2(3):

> there shall be taken to have been an emission of dark smoke from industrial or trade premises in any case where (a) material is burned on those premises; and (b) the circumstances are such that the burning would be likely to give rise to the emission of dark smoke, unless the [defendant] shows that no dark smoke was emitted

Permitted emissions of dark smoke

13.3.9 It is important to check whether any exemptions have been granted under any regulations made by the Secretary of State, for instance the Dark Smoke (Permitted Periods) Regulations 1958 which permit the emission of dark smoke in certain circumstances. The prohibitions in s 2(1) are also subject to exemptions contained in the Clean Air (Emissions of Dark Smoke) (Exemption) Regulations 1969 which allow the burning of certain exempted materials (for example demolishing buildings, road materials being burnt off prior to resurfacing and animal carcases).

Penalties

13.3.10 Where a person is found guilty of emitting dark smoke from a chimney under s 1 he will be liable on summary conviction where it concerns a chimney of a private dwelling to a fine not exceeding level 3 on the standard scale and in any other case to a fine not exceeding level 5 on the standard scale (s 1(5)). Where a person is found guilty of an offence under s 2 he will be liable under summary conviction to a fine not exceeding £20,000.

Defences to a s 1 prosecution (prohibition of dark smoke from premises)

13.3.11 It is a defence in any proceedings brought under s 1 to prove that the emission:
(1) was solely due to the lighting up of a furnace which was cold and that all practicable steps had been taken to prevent or minimise the emission of dark smoke (s 1(4)(a));
(2) was solely due to some failure of a furnace, or apparatus used in connection with a furnace and that
  (a) the failure could not reasonably have been foreseen or, if foreseen, could not reasonably have been provided against and
  (b) the alleged emission could not reasonably have been prevented by action taken after the failure occurred (s 1(4)(b));
(3) was solely due to the use of unsuitable fuel and that
  (a) suitable fuel was unobtainable and the least unsuitable fuel which was available was used and
  (b) all practicable steps had been taken to prevent or minimise the emission of dark smoke as a result of the use of that fuel (s 1(4)(c));
(4) was due to a combination of two or more of the causes specified in (1)–(3) above and that the other conditions specified were satisfied in relation to each of those causes respectively.

'Practicable' for the purposes of s 1(4)(a) is interpreted to mean:

> reasonably practicable having regard, amongst other things, to local conditions and circumstances, to the financial implications and to the current state of technical knowledge (s 64(1)).

Defences to a s 2 prosecution (prohibition of dark smoke from industrial or trade premises)

13.3.12   It is a defence to prove in proceedings for an offence under s 2 that the alleged emission was inadvertent and that all practical steps had been taken to prevent or minimise the emission of dark smoke (s 2(4)).

Checklist – dark smoke

- Part I of the Clean Air Act 1993 covers the enforcement of dark smoke emissions:
    - Environmental Health Officers have powers under this Act, even where the emission arises from premises situated outside their authority's area
    - check that the activity is not covered by an exemption under ss 41–45
    - 'dark smoke' is defined under the Act (s 3(1)).
- Emissions of dark smoke from chimneys are prohibited under s 1(1)
    - this prohibition applies to industrial and domestic premises
    - the appropriate defendant is the occupier.
- Emissions of dark smoke from chimneys serving furnaces of fixed boilers or industrial plant are prohibited under s 1(2)
    - the appropriate defendant is the person having control of the boiler or plant
    - the burden of proof is on the defendant to show that the emission is not dark smoke.
- Emissions of dark smoke from industrial or trade premises other than from a chimney are prohibited under s 2
    - the appropriate defendant is the occupier
    - certain emissions are exempted from prohibition.
- The Act sets up certain statutory defences to prosecutions under ss 1 and 2: do these apply?

13.4   Smoke, grit, dust and fumes – Part II, Clean Air Act 1993

Introduction

13.4.1   Part II of the Clean Air Act 1993 deals with emissions of smoke, grit, dust and fumes and is mostly concerned with the use of non-domestic furnaces. Domestic furnaces are treated separately, being defined as any furnace which is designed solely or mainly for domestic purposes, and used for heating a boiler with a maximum heating capacity of less than 16.12 kilowatts (s 64). Any furnaces which are in the occupation of the same person and are served by a single chimney are, for the purposes of most of the provisions in this part of the Act, considered to be one furnace (s 64(b)).

13.4.2   The objective of Part II is to ensure that new industrial furnaces are, so far as practicable, operated continuously without emitting smoke when burning fuel of a type for which the furnace was designed (see s 4(2) below).

Requirement that new furnaces shall be smokeless

13.4.3   No furnace can be installed in a building or in any fixed boiler or industrial plant unless the local authority has been notified (ss 4(1) and (4)). Failure to notify or install the furnace without local authority approval is a criminal offence and the responsible person will be guilty on summary conviction to a fine not exceeding level 3 on the standard scale.

13.4.4   By s 4(2) no furnace is to be installed in a building or fixed boiler or industrial plant unless the furnace is so far as practicable capable of being operated continuously without emitting smoke when burning fuel of a type for which the furnace was designed. Where the furnace does emit smoke in breach of s 4(2) the guilty person will be liable to a fine not exceeding level 5 on the standard scale.

Limits on the rate of emissions of grit and dust

13.4.5   The Secretary of State can prescribe regulations on the rates of emission of grit and dust from chimneys (s 3(2)). When purchasing a new furnace or boiler it is important to ensure that its operation complies with these regulations. Where the furnace is installed with the approved plans and specifications it shall be deemed to comply with the requirements of the regulations.

Exceeding the limit for emissions of dust and grime

13.4.6   Where the regulations apply, it is an offence under s 5 for the occupier to exceed the prescribed limits of dust and grit, although it is a defence to prove that the best practicable means had been used for minimising the emission.

Arrestment plant

13.4.7   The 1993 Act also contains provisions regarding arrestment plant to be installed when burning certain fuels (s 6).

Height of chimneys

13.4.8   The height of a chimney furnace may also need approval from the local authority (ss 14–15).

Checklist – smoke, grit, dust and fumes

- Part II of the Clean Air Act 1993 seeks to deal with emissions mainly from non-domestic furnaces. The aim is to ensure the installation of smokeless furnaces
  - local authorities must be informed of the installation of a new chimney (to fail to do so is a criminal offence)
  - so far as practicable, new furnaces shall be smokeless
  - operators must check that new furnaces comply with regulations as to emissions
  - it is an offence to exceed the prescribed rate of emissions
  - the height of a chimney may need approval from the local authority.

13.5 Smoke control area – Part III of the Clean Air Act 1993

13.5.1 Part III of the Clean Air Act 1993 (ss 18–29 and Schedules 1 and 2) contains provisions relating to smoke control areas which enable local authorities and the Secretary of State to declare the whole or any part of their area to be a smoke control area. The local authorities' order must be confirmed by the Secretary of State (s 19).

Prohibitions on emissions of smoke in smoke control area

13.5.2 If smoke is emitted in breach of an order from a chimney in a building, the occupier will be guilty of an offence under s 20(1). Where smoke is emitted in breach of an order from any other chimney serving the furnace of a fixed boiler or industrial plant in a smoke control area, the person having possession of the boiler or plant is guilty of an offence (s 20(2)). The penalty for both offences is a fine not exceeding level 3 on the standard scale (s 20(5)).

13.5.3 As the smoke control order may be granted subject to certain limitations and exemptions it is important to read carefully the wording first to ensure that a breach has occurred. Copies can be obtained from the local authority. Although it is not a defence to state that you are unaware of the existence of the order, very few prosecutions are made under this Act now that it has largely been superseded by European legislation and the growing importance of air quality standards.

13.6 Traffic orders

13.6.1 Traffic Regulation Orders made under the Road Traffic Regulation Act 1984 can be used to prohibit, restrict or regulate vehicles or particular types of vehicle. They can apply to part of a road, a particular road or a number of roads. (See *R v Greenwich LBC, ex p W (a minor)* [1997] Env LR D2 (CA) in which a local resident representing children in the area sought a court order to require the London Borough of Greenwich to make an order under s 14 of the Road Traffic Regulation Act 1984.)

13.6.2 By s 2 of the Road Traffic Reduction Act 1997, local authorities which are local traffic authorities (defined by s 121A of the Road Traffic Regulation Act 1984) may be directed by the Secretary of State to produce a report containing an assessment of the levels of local road traffic in their area and a forecast of future growth. The report may also specify targets for a reduction in the levels of local traffic or a reduction in the rate of growth. These targets may vary according to the area and the classes of local road traffic. If the local authority considers it is inappropriate to specify targets, the report must justify its opinion. The Secretary of State may also issue guidance in the preparation and contents of the report. Copies of every report received by the Secretary of State will be made for each House of Parliament.

13.6.3 The Road Traffice (Vehicle Emissions) (Fixed Penalty) Regulations 1997 came into force on 26 December 1997 and enable certain specified local authorities (namely: Birmingham City Council; Bristol City Council; Canterbury City Council; Glasgow City Council; Middlesbrough Borough Council; the Council of the City and County of Swansea and Westminster City Council) to issue fixed penalty notices to users of vehicles within their area who contravene or fail to comply with regs 61 or 98 of the Road Vehicles (Construction and Use) Regulations 1986 (smoke and other emissions from vehicles, turning off engines of stationary vehicles to prevent noise and exhaust emissions). A £60 fixed penalty notice can be imposed in relation to a breach of reg 61 and a £20 notice in relation to a breach of reg 98. If the penalty is not paid within the specified period, the moneys can be recovered under a County Court order, but the amount of the penalty will automatically increase to £90 and £40 respectively. The car user may request a hearing in writing within 28 days of issue of the fixed penalty notice and the requirement for payment is then suspended.

13.7 Agricultural practices

13.7.1 These are subject to the same legislation as any other business. The Ministry of Agriculture, Fisheries and Food has published a Code of Agricultural Practice for the Protection of Air which highlights sources of air pollution that can arise from agricultural practices. It is a non-statutory document.

13.7.2 Section 152 of the EPA 1990 enables the appropriate minister to make regulations to prohibit and restrict the burning of crop residues on agricultural land. This has resulted in the Crop Residues (Burning) Regulations 1993. The regulations do allow burning in certain specified circumstances, and specify how this should be done. It is an offence to breach the regulations and this may result in a fine not exceeding level 5. The Burning of Crop Residues (Repeal of Byelaws) Order 1992 has repealed all local government byelaws made under s 235 of the Local Government Act 1972.

13.8 Air quality monitoring

13.8.1 Regular monitoring of the atmosphere for pollutants is carried out by local authorities and a variety of other bodies. The air quality monitoring results are available for the public and can be obtained over the telephone from the National Air Quality Advice Line on 0800 556677.

13.8.2   Part IV of the Environment Act 1995 required the Secretary of State to publish a National Air Quality Strategy setting quality standards and objectives for the country as a whole (s 80). Local authorities will be required to implement the provisions by undertaking an air quality review (s 82), to designate air quality management areas (ss 83 and 84), to undertake an air quality assessment (s 84) and to detail how they are to achieve this in an action plan.

13.8.3   The Air Quality Regulations 1997 is the first step in this exercise and sets out air quality objectives for seven pollutants which are to be achieved by 31 December 2005. Local authorities will use this to review the air quality in their areas and assess whether the objectives are likely to be achieved by the 2005 target date. If they are not likely to be met, then they must designate an air quality management area and prepare an action plan (referred to above). DETR Circular 15/97 provides guidance for local authorities. The information obtained will be relevant to and may impact upon future land use planning and traffic management.

Chapter 14

Waste on Land and Litter

14.1 Overview

14.1.1 This chapter is concerned with a variety of statutory provisions intended to protect the environment from pollution on land. At the heart of the legislation is the wide ambit of the prohibition against unlawful or harmful deposits under s 33 of the Environmental Protection Act 1990 (EPA 1990) and its corollary, the duty of care as respects waste set out in s 34. The rights and liabilities arising out of these and other relevant statutes are arranged in the following order:

(1) An introduction to the appropriate enforcement bodies
(2) The prohibition against unauthorised or harmful deposits etc of waste (s 33 of the EPA 1990)
(3) The duty of care as respects waste (s 34 of the EPA 1990)
(4) Fly-tipping
(5) Removal of refuse
(6) Abandoned vehicles
(7) Litter
(8) Abandoned shopping and luggage trolleys.

14.2 Enforcement bodies

Environment Agency

14.2.1 The majority of legislation relating to the management of waste is enforced by the Environment Agency (EA), on which are placed the following responsibilities:

(1) the control, carriage, disposal and management of waste;
(2) the issuing of waste management licences for the operation of waste disposal sites;
(3) supervision of the operation of the licence until acceptance of surrender;
(4) the determination whether or not someone is a 'fit and proper person' to hold the licence.

The EA also maintains a public register containing details of licences it issues and other information required under s 64 of the EPA 1990 and is responsible for the registration of carriers of waste and the enforcement of that legislation under the Control of Pollution (Amendment) Act 1989.

Waste Disposal Authorities

14.2.2 In England, a Waste Disposal Authority (WDA) will normally be the relevant county council or unitary authority. Functions of a WDA under s 51 of the EPA 1990 include:
(1) Making arrangements for the disposal of controlled waste collection by waste collection authorities;
(2) The provision of sites for the deposit of household waste by members of the public;
(3) The treatment and disposal of household waste.
WDAs also have powers in respect of waste recycling (s 55). WDAs do not take part in the actual disposal of waste. This is now carried out by a private company which is supervised by the WDA. The functions of the WDA are described in more detail under ss 32 and 5 of the EPA 1990.

Waste Collection Authorities

14.2.3 In England and Wales these are district or borough councils or unitary authorities. A Waste Collection Authority (WCA) is subject to the following duties:
(1) The arrangement for the collection of household waste in their area (if requested they may also make arrangements for the collection of commercial and industrial waste on premises) (s 45);
(2) The delivery of the waste that it collects or disposal at the place directed by the WDA (s 48(1));
(3) The provision of receptacles for waste (ss 45–47);
(4) The preparation of plans for recycling of household and commercial waste (s 49).
WCAs also maintain a register containing details of waste disposal operations taking place and their areas (s 64(4)(6)).

WCAs and the collection of waste

14.2.4 Generally in England and Wales, district councils, London borough councils or unitary authorities are the Waste Collection Authorities and they are required under reg 3 and Sched 1 of the Collection and Disposal of Waste Regulations 1988 to arrange for the free collection of household waste in their area except in cases prescribed in regulations made by the Secretary of State. Furthermore they do not have to collect waste which they consider is so isolated or inaccessible that the costs of collection would be unreasonably high and they are satisfied that the waste can be adequately disposed of by the person who controls it (s 45(1)(a) of the EPA 1990). A WCA is only obliged to arrange for the collection of commercial waste if the occupier of the relevant premises has requested the WCA to collect it (s 45(1)(b) of the EPA 1990). Furthermore it has no duty to arrange for the collection of industrial waste but may also do so on request if consent is given to such arrangement (s 45(2)), and may make a reasonable charge for the collection and disposal of any waste other than household waste.

14.3 The prohibition against unauthorised or harmful deposits, treatment or disposal etc of waste – s 33 of the EPA 1990

14.3.1 The general prohibition against unauthorised or harmful deposits is set out at s 33(1) of the EPA 1990. This states that:

a person shall not –
  (a) deposit controlled waste, or knowingly cause or knowingly permit controlled waste to be deposited in or on any land unless a waste management licence authorising the deposit is in force and the deposit is in accordance with the licence;
  (b) treat, keep or dispose of controlled waste, or knowingly cause or knowingly permit controlled waste to be treated, kept or disposed of
      (i)   in or on any land; or
      (ii) by means of any mobile plant
      except under and in accordance with a waste management licence;
  (c) treat, keep or dispose of controlled waste in a manner likely to cause pollution of the environment or harm to human health.

14.3.2 It is important to note that the prohibition against the unauthorised deposit of controlled waste extends not only to the person who actually deposits the waste but also to the person who 'knowingly causes or knowingly permits' the deposit. The only lawful deposit which is allowed is one in accordance with the conditions of a waste management licence granted by the Environment Agency or former Waste Regulation Authority under s 35. As to what constitutes 'controlled waste' see s 75 of the EPA 1990 as amended by Schedules 22 and 24 of the Environment Act 1995.

Statutory exceptions

14.3.3 By s 33(2):

subsection (1) above does not apply in relation to household waste from a domestic property which is treated, kept or disposed of within the curtilage of the dwelling by or with the permission of the occupier of the dwelling.

By s 33(3) subsection (1) does not apply in cases prescribed in regulations made by the Secretary of State which exclude certain types of waste.

Defences

14.3.4 By s 33(7) statutory defences are available where a defendant can prove that

(1) he took all reasonable precautions and exercised due diligence to avoid the commission of the offence,

(2) he acted under instructions from his employer and did not know that an offence was being committed,

(3) that the acts were done in an emergency and the WRA was notified.

Penalties

14.3.5 A person who contravenes s 33(1) or any condition of a waste management licence will commit an offence under s 33(6). On summary conviction the penalty is a term of imprisonment not exceeding six months or a fine not exceeding £20,000 or both and on conviction on indictment the maximum prison term is one which does not exceed two years or an unlimited fine.

14.3.6 Where the offence concerns special waste (that is the more hazardous waste as defined in the Special Waste Regulations 1996), the penalties are increased by s 33(9) in the case of a conviction on indictment, when the term of imprisonment increases from two to five years.

Civil liability

14.3.7 In addition to a criminal liability for an unlawful deposit, s 73(6) of the EPA 1990 provides that any person who deposits waste or knowingly causes or knowingly permits it to be deposited in or on land so as to commit an offence under s 33(1) (or s 63(2)) shall incur civil liability for damage caused by the waste. Damage in this connection includes the death or injury of any person (including any disease and any impairment of physical or mental condition (s 73(8)).

14.4 The duty of care as respects waste – s 34 of the EPA 1990

14.4.1 By s 34(1) of the EPA 1990:

> it shall be the duty of any person who imports, produces, carries, keeps, treats or disposes of controlled waste or, as a broker, has control of such waste, to take all such measures applicable to him in that capacity as are reasonable in the circumstances –
>
> (a) to prevent a contravention by any person of section 33 above [see 14.3.1];
> (b) to prevent the escape of the waste from his control or that of any other person;
> (c) on the transfer of the waste, to secure –
>> (i) that the transfer is only to an authorised person or to a person for authorised transport purposes; and
>> (ii) that there is transferred such a written description of the waste as will enable other persons to avoid a contravention of that section to comply with the duty under this subsection as respects the escape of waste.

The duty prescribed in s 34(1) will not apply to an occupier of domestic premises where household waste is produced on the property. The duty requires all holders of waste (except householders) to ensure that it is accompanied by a consignment note until it reaches the place of final disposal/recovery.

The criminal sanction

14.4.2 Any person who fails to comply with the duty imposed in s 34(1) above or any regulations made by the Secretary of State under s 34(5) (for instance the Environmental Protection (Duty of Care) Regulations 1991) will be guilty of an offence under s 34(6). On summary conviction he shall be liable to a fine not exceeding the statutory maximum. On conviction on indictment the penalty is an unlimited fine. Proceedings may be instigated by the Environment Agency and local authorities, although because of anomalies in the legislation the latter may experience difficulties in obtaining the relevant information to support a prosecution.

Codes of practice

14.4.3 The Secretary of State also has power under s 34(7) and (8) to issue and revise a code of practice containing advice on how to discharge the duty of care. Whilst breach of the code of practice is not a criminal offence, it can be used in evidence in court proceedings under s 34(6). The code of practice contains advice on the duty itself and responsibilities of each of the named parties, details of the record keeping requirements and other legal controls. The latest version of the code of practice was published in March 1996 by the DoE and the Scottish and Welsh Offices and copies can be obtained from HMSO.

14.4.4 In addition, further guidance on the provisions can be found in DoE Circular 19/91 (WO/63/91 and SO/25/91).

14.5 Fly-tipping

14.5.1 The Environment Agency and local authorities (although it is always assumed that the EA has sole responsibility for this aspect) can initiate proceedings against a fly-tipper for the unauthorised disposal of a lorry load of waste under s 33(1) of the EPA 1990 (see 14.3.1 above) and for failing to comply with the duty of care under s 34 of the EPA 1990 (see 14.4.1).

Tracing an operator

14.5.2 Until recently one of the main problems of controlling fly-tipping has been the inability to trace the operator of the vehicle concerned. However, s 6 of the Control of Pollution (Amendment) Act 1989 (as amended) and regs 19–24 of the Controlled Waste (Registration of Carriers and Seizure of Vehicles) Regulations 1991 (as amended) enable the Environment Agency to obtain the name and address of the keeper and user of the vehicle and may obtain a warrant under s 6 of the Control of Pollution (Amendment) Act 1989 (as amended) from a magistrate where there is reasonable grounds for believing that an offence under s 33 of the EPA 1990 has been committed and that vehicle was used in the commission of the offence.

Seizing and removing property

14.5.3 The Environment Agency has power to seize property and remove it to somewhere where it considers it appropriate to keep it and the vehicle can be driven, towed or removed by other means that appear to be reasonable in the circumstances. All or some of the contents of the vehicle may be removed separately whether it is reasonable to do so to facilitate its removal or if there is good reason for storing them in a different place.

14.5.4 It is an offence under s 6(9) of the 1989 Act intentionally to obstruct the removal of the vehicle or its contents. The vehicle and contents must be kept in the Environment Agency's custody until they are returned to someone who establishes his entitlement to them or until it lawfully disposes of them. The Environment Agency must take certain steps as are reasonably necessary to ensure the property is not stolen or vandalised.

Disposal and return of seized property

14.5.5 The Environment Agency may sell, destroy or deposit at any place property which is seized under s 6 of the 1989 Act (as amended) if it follows the requirements of reg 23 of the 1991 Regulations. Otherwise it must be returned to the person entitled to it who will be someone who produces satisfactory evidence of his entitlement, his identity or address or whether he is recovering it as an agent for someone else. The identity of the principal must also be satisfactorily identified, as must the principal's entitlement to the property and the agent's authorisation to act on the principal's behalf. If a vehicle is concerned, then the owner or keeper must produce the vehicle registration book (reg 22(1) of the 1991 Regulations).

14.5.6 If a vehicle has been disposed of, notice of disposal should be served on the chief officer of the police force in whose area it was seized.

14.5.7 If the property is sold, the proceeds of sale can be applied to meet the Environment Agency's expenses in seizing the vehicles under the 1989 Act. Any surplus should be applied to meeting the costs of investigating claims to the proceeds of sale.

Collecting evidence

14.5.8 Despite the new statutory provisions it can still be difficult for the Environment Agency to obtain details of the culprits so it relies largely on evidence supplied by members of the public who can record vital details such as the registration number and other relevant details (time and place of unauthorised disposal) to the relevant officer. It is therefore important that as much evidence is given as possible. In particular photographs are extremely helpful.

Checklist – fly-tipping

- Proceedings in respect of the unauthorised deposit of waste are taken under s 33(1) of the EPA 1990.
- Tracing an operator
  - — use s 6 of the Control of Pollution (Amendment) Act 1989 (as amended) and regs 19–24, Controlled Waste (Registration of Carriers and Seizure of Vehicles) Regulations Act 1991 (as amended)
  - — a warrant may be obtained from the magistrates' court.
- Powers in respect of vehicles and other property
  - — the Environment Agency has powers to seize and remove property (including vehicles) and then to sell or destroy it or otherwise to deposit it at any place
  - — the proceeds may be used to discharge the Environment Agency's expenses in certain cases
  - — the Agency must ensure that it follows the correct procedures when exercising its powers.

14.6   Removal of refuse/rubbish

14.6.1   In addition to the waste legislation, district, borough and unitary authorities have power to clean up refuse and rubbish dumped in their area. This section sets out the principal powers. Specific controls in respect of abandoned motor vehicles and litter are set out in separate sections below (14.7 and 14.8).

Removal of items abandoned on open land

14.6.2   By s 6(1) of the Refuse Disposal (Amenity) Act 1978 local authorities have power to remove anything which is abandoned on open land within their area without lawful authority after they have notified the occupier of their intention to remove it and no objection is received (see s 6(2)). A local authority has powers of entry under s 8 to inspect land or clear rubbish and if relevant it may sell or dispose of the property once removed to cover its cost.

Removal of rubbish seriously detrimental to the amenity of the neighbourhood

14.6.3   In England and Wales, district and London borough county councils can remove rubbish that is seriously detrimental to the amenity of the neighbourhood from any land in the open air in their area under s 34 of the Public Health Act 1961. However, these powers cannot be used in respect of a licensed site since the existing legislation under Part II of the EPA 1990 and the licence conditions should be able to deal with any problems.

14.6.4   Before taking action the authority must give at least 28 days' notice to the owner/occupier stating their intention to remove the rubbish and explaining their rights under the legislation. An owner/occupier who received the notice has the right to serve a counter notice within 28 days stating that he will clear the rubbish (s 34(2)(a)) and this will prevent the local authority from implementing action under their notice unless the owner/occupier fails to comply within a reasonable time or fails to complete the works (s 34(3)). Alternatively the person served has a right to appeal to the Magistrates' Court on the grounds that the authority is not entitled to take action under s 34 or that the steps proposed by the notice are unreasonable (s 34(2)(b)). The effect of the notice is suspended until the appeal is finally determined or withdrawn.

Power to require proper maintenance of land

14.6.5   A similar power exists under s 215 of the Town and Country Planning Act 1990 whereby a local planning authority may serve a notice on the owner or occupier of land if it is of the opinion that the amenity in any part of the area, or an adjoining area is adversely affected by the condition of the land. The notice will require the owner/occupier of that land to carry out specific steps to remedy the condition within a specified time period which cannot be less than 28 days (s 215(4)). A notice will apply to land whether it is in the open or not.

14.6.6   There is a right of appeal under s 217 on the grounds that the condition of the land does not adversely affect the amenity, that its condition results from operations carried out under a planning permission, that the requirements of the notice are excessive or that the period for compliance is too short (s 217(1)). The appeal is made to the Magistrates' Court and the effect of a notice will be suspended until the appeal is finally determined or withdrawn. The Magistrates' Court has the power to vary or quash the notice. There is a further appeal to the Crown Court from the Magistrates' Court.

14.6.7   Failure to comply with the notice within the specified period is a criminal offence and the person found guilty will be liable on summary conviction to a fine not exceeding level 3 on the standard scale (currently £1,000) (s 216(2)). Where an interest in land is assigned or transferred before the specified time for compliance has elapsed and prosecution proceedings are commenced the defendant may, by giving the prosecution three clear days' notice, have the new owner occupier brought to court (s 216(3), (4)).

14.6.8   Where land is not occupied, the owner at the time the notice is served will be held liable (s 216(4)). Where interest in land is transferred, the original defendant will be entitled to be acquitted if he can show that he took all reasonable steps to ensure compliance with the notice (s 216(5)). Failure to comply with the notice following completion is likely to result in a further daily penalty not exceeding £40 per day for each day on which the requirements of the notice remain in breach. The local authority also has the power to enter the land to take the steps required by it and to recover its reasonable expenses from the landowner as a simple contract debt (s 219).

Removal of rubbish and material from dilapidated buildings and neglected sites

14.6.9   A district, London borough council or unitary authority can also take action under s 79(2) of the Building Act 1984 to remove rubbish or other material resulting from, or exposed by, the demolition or collapse of a building or structure lying on a site (or any adjoining land) if it considers that the site or land is in such a condition as to be seriously detrimental to the amenities of the neighbourhood. The power to require the removal of rubbish and other material does not include chattels such as machinery left following the demolition (see *McVittie v Bolton Corp* [1945] KB 281). A notice will be served on the landowner requiring him to comply with steps described in the notice to clear the land within a specified time.

14.6.10   Alternatively a local authority may enter land and remove the rubbish or other materials and recover their reasonable expenses from the landowner. Failure to comply with the notice is a criminal offence and the landowner will be liable on summary conviction to a fine not exceeding level 4 on the standard scale and a further fine up to £2 for each day the rubbish remains on the site after conviction.

Removal of items so deposited on the highway as to be a nuisance

14.6.11   The highway authority (normally the county council, or London borough council or unitary authority) may require anyone who has deposited anything that constitutes a nuisance on a highway authority to remove it following the service of a notice under s 149 of the Highways Act 1980. Failure to comply with the notice enables the authority to lodge a complaint with the Magistrates' Court for an order enabling removal and disposal.

14.6.12   If the matter constitutes a danger to the users of the highway and should be removed immediately, the authority may remove the article without obtaining an order from the Magistrates' Court (s 149(2)).

14.6.13   The local authority may recover its expenses from the person who deposited the matter or claims to be entitled to it or may apply to the Magistrates' Court for an order allowing them to dispose of it. Where its reasonable expenses exceed the sums recovered from disposal, they may seek the balance from the person who deposited the matter. Sums due under s 149 can be recovered as a civil debt or as money due under statute (s 305(5)).

14.6.14   A highway authority may serve a notice under s 151 on the owner or occupier of the land who is responsible for refuse falling onto a highway maintainable at public expense from that land requiring him to execute works that will prevent him from obstructing the street or choking any sewer or gully in it. There is a right of appeal against service of a notice to the Magistrates' Court. Alternatively if the notice is not complied with within the specified period, the person on whom the notice was served will be guilty of an offence and liable on summary conviction to a fine not exceeding level 3 on the standard scale (currently £1,000). If the offence continues a daily penalty not exceeding £1 may be imposed for each day it continues (s 151(3)).

Statutory nuisance

14.6.15 The accumulation of deposited waste that is prejudicial to health or a nuisance can also be treated as a statutory nuisance under provision of Part III of the EPA 1990 referred to at 3.2.

Checklist – removal of refuse/rubbish

- Removal of items abandoned on open land
  — see s 6 of the Refuse Disposal (Amenity) Act 1978.
- Removal of rubbish seriously detrimental to the amenity of the neighbourhood
  — see s 34 of the Public Health Act 1961.
- Proper maintenance of land
  — see s 215 of the Town and Country Planning Act 1990.
- Removal of rubbish and material from dilapidated buildings
  — see s 79(2) of the Building Act 1984.
- Removal of nuisances deposited on the highway
  — see s 149 of the Highways Act 1980.
- Statutory nuisances
  — see Part III of the EPA 1990.

14.7 Abandoned vehicles

Introduction

14.7.1 There are two statutory provisions concerned with the abandonment of vehicles: the Refuse Disposal (Amenity) Act 1978 which gives local authorities powers to deal with vehicles which have been dumped in their area and ss 99–103 of the Road Traffic Regulation Act 1984, which is more concerned with the removal of vehicles that are illegally parked and causing an obstruction or have broken down (although powers to deal with abandoned vehicles are also contained in those sections). The powers exercised under the 1984 Act can be implemented by both the police and local authorities (district, borough or unitary authority).

Unauthorised dumping

14.7.2 It is an offence under s 2 of the Refuse Disposal (Amenity) Act 1978 to abandon a motor vehicle, parts of motor vehicle or any other matter on land in the open air without authority. Anyone found guilty of this offence will be liable on summary conviction to a fine not exceeding level 4 on the standard scale or imprisonment for a term not exceeding three months or both. Section

2(2) presumes that the defendant will have brought the item on land for the purpose of abandoning it there unless he can prove the contrary.

Removal of abandoned vehicles

14.7.3 In addition to the criminal penalties referred to above, local authorities have a duty under s 3(1) of the 1978 Act to remove vehicles that appear to them to have been abandoned on any land in the open air or on any other land that forms part of the highway. The police and local authorities' duties under s 3 do not extend to abandoned vehicles on a highway that is not a carriageway if they consider that the cost of getting it to the nearest convenient garage would be too great (s 3(3)). They do not have to give any notice before removing a vehicle that is actually on the highway unless they consider that its condition is such that it ought to be destroyed and in such circumstances they must fix a notice to it stating that it will be removed and destroyed at the end of a seven-day period (s 3(5) of the Refuse Disposal (Amenity) Act 1978 and s 99(4) of the Road Traffic Regulation Act 1984).

14.7.4 Similarly local authorities and police have the power to remove vehicles under Part II of the Removal and Disposal of Vehicles Regulations 1986 which were made under both the 1978 Act and s 91 and s 101 of the 1984 Act.

14.7.5 Where vehicles are on occupied land the local authority or police are required to notify the owner of their intention to remove it and may not do so if he objects within 15 days from the date of being served with the notice (reg 9(2) of the Removal and Disposal of Vehicles Regulations 1986). The notice should be in a form set out in Schedule 2 to the 1986 Regulations and addressed to the occupier of land. Objections to the notice must be made in writing and served on the local authority by post or delivery to their officers.

14.7.6 It is usual for the vehicles to be moved by the relevant Waste Collection Authority and delivered to the appropriate Waste Disposal Authority under arrangements agreed between them. It is the duty of the Waste Disposal Authority to ensure the safe custody of the vehicles they received unless it is subsequently destroyed. Similar duties are imposed in respect of vehicles under s 100 of the Road Traffic Regulation Act 1984.

14.7.7 Abandoned vehicles that have been removed by the local authority or the police may be disposed of in accordance with the provisions of s 4 of the 1978 Act or s 101 of the 1984 Act and the matters set out in Part III of the 1986 Regulations.

14.7.8 Where a notice was fixed to a vehicle before it was removed that it would be disposed of on removal, and that vehicle does not have a current excise licence, the local authority/police may dispose of it at any time after it has been removed (s 4(1)(a) of the 1978 Act and s 101(1) and (3)(a) of the 1984 Act). If the vehicle has the benefit of a current excise licence then disposal cannot take place until after it has expired.

14.7.9 In any case the local authority/police should make another attempt to find the vehicle's owner through licence records and then give the owner 21 days to collect it. In addition a check can be made by the local police on HP Information Ltd.

14.7.10 Where the police/local authority identifies someone whom it believes to be the owner of the vehicle, it should serve him with a notice stating that it has removed the vehicle and that unless he claims it within 21 days it will dispose of it (regs 12(2) and 14 of the 1986 Regulations). The notice should be served in a manner provided by reg 13, and if the attempt to find the owner fails or he does not remove it within 21 days from the time he was served with the notice, the local authority/police may proceed with its disposal once the vehicle excise licence has expired.

14.7.11 If prior to disposal an owner satisfactorily proves that he owns it, and pays the fine prescribed by the Removal Storage and Disposal of Vehicles (Prescribed Sums and Charges etc) Regulations 1989 (as amended) the authority must allow him to remove the vehicle within seven days from the time the authority accepts his claim or later as agreed.

Prohibitions on the parking of cars for cleaning the highway

14.7.12 Section 23 of the Control of Pollution Act 1974 allows a local authority to prohibit the parking of cars if it believes it necessary to facilitate the cleaning of a highway.

Checklist – abandoned vehicles

- Unauthorised dumping
  — an offence under s 2 of the Refuse Disposal (Amenity) Act 1978.
- Removal of abandoned vehicles
  — these may be removed by local authorities pursuant to s 3 of the Refuse Disposal (Amenity) Act 1978
  — an additional power is available under Part II of the Removal and Disposal of Vehicles Regs 1986.
- Highway cleaning
  — s 23 of the Control of Pollution Act 1974 permits the prohibition of parking vehicles to facilitate highway cleaning.

14.8 Litter

Introductory

14.8.1 The most important piece of legislation currently dealing with litter is Part IV of the Environmental Protection Act 1990 (EPA 1990), although the Litter Act 1983, the Control of Pollution Act 1974 and the Town and Country Planning Act 1990 should also be consulted.

Definition of 'litter'

14.8.2 There is no statutory definition of litter in the EPA 1990 or regulations. The term has been judicially interpreted as consisting of 'anything whatsoever if it is thrown down, dropped or otherwise deposited in, into or from any place . . . and left there' (*Vaughan v Biggs* [1960] 2 All ER 473).

The Litter Act 1983

14.8.3 The Litter Act 1983 places a duty on litter authorities regularly to cleanse and empty any litter bins they have provided under the 1983 Act or under s 185 of the Highways Act 1980. 'Litter authorities' means a county council, district council, London borough council, the Common Council of the City of London, a parish council, community council, joint body, Park Board, Sub-Treasurer of the Inner Temple, or the Under Treasurer of the Middle Temple (see s 10 of the Litter Act 1983). The actual cleaning of the highways *per se* is dealt with in Part IV of the EPA 1990 (see below).

14.8.4 The Secretary of State is permitted under the 1983 Act to award grants for publicity discouraging litter, and the Tidy Britain Group has benefited from this provision. Under the 1983 Act it is also the duty of litter authorities to consult voluntary bodies from time to time about the steps which should be taken to abate litter.

Offences under Part IV, EPA 1990

Offence of leaving litter

14.8.5 A person is guilty of an offence under s 87 of the EPA 1990 who:

> throws down, drops or otherwise deposits in, into or from any place to which the section applies, and leaves, any thing whatsoever in such circumstances as to cause, or contribute to, or tend to lead to, the defacement by litter of any such place to which this section applies.

14.8.6 By s 87(3),(4), s 87(1) covers a variety of places including any 'public open place', meaning:

> a place in the open air to which the public are entitled to or permitted to have access without payment, and any covered place open to the air on at least one side and available for public use shall be treated as a public open place.

Land is therefore regarded as 'open to the air' even when it is covered, so long as it is open on at least one side (for instance bus stations). Section 87(3) also includes bus stations, Crown land, land owned by a variety of statutory undertakers that has public access and a variety of educational institutions (for instance universities and schools). By s 87(3) the offence also applies to most roads and highways, land belonging to principal litter authorities and under their direct control to which the public are entitled to have access with or without payment. The maximum penalty that may be imposed in summary proceedings is £2,500.

Fixed penalty notices for leaving litter

14.8.7 As an alternative an officer of a 'principal litter authority' may serve a fixed penalty notice on a person whom he has reason to believe committed an offence under s 87 under The Litter (Fixed Penalty Notices) Order 1991.

14.8.8 A 'principal litter authority' for these purposes includes county, district and London borough councils, the Common Council of the City of London and the Council of the Isles of Scilly. The fine operates in the same manner as a fixed penalty parking ticket: providing the fine is paid within the stated period, criminal proceedings will not be instigated.

Dog faeces

14.8.9 The Litter (Animal Droppings) Order 1991 enables the provisions under Part IV, EPA 1990 which apply to refuse, to apply to dog faeces on certain land listed under the Order but which is not heath or woodland or used for the grazing of animals. The areas of land listed include: any public walk or pleasure ground; any land on which there are no buildings or of which no more than one-twentieth part is covered with buildings and the whole or remainder of which is laid out as a garden or is used for the purposes of recreation; any part of the seashore frequently used by large numbers of people and managed by persons having direct control of it as a tourist resort or recreational facility; any esplanade or promenade above the height of the tide at mean water springs; any land not forming part of the highway open to the air, which the public use on foot only, and which provides access to retail premises; a trunk road picnic area provided by the Minister under s 112 of the Highways Act 1980; a picnic site provided by a local planning authority under s 10(2) of the Countryside Act 1968. By the Dogs (Fouling of Land) Act 1996 it is an offence not to remove dog faeces from land in the open air which has been designated for the purpose by the local authority. A fixed penalty notice can be issued by an approved local authority officer.

The duty of public bodies to keep land clear of litter

14.8.10 The EPA 1990 introduces a duty on various bodies and institutions in charge of 'relevant land', so far as practicable, to keep the land clear of litter and refuse (s 89(1)). The duty is placed on the following:

(1) every local highway authority which is responsible for the maintenance and upkeep of any relevant highway;

(2) the Secretary of State in respect of any relevant trunk road which is a special road and any relevant highway or relevant road for which he is responsible;

(3) each principal litter authority;

(4) the appropriate Crown authority;

(5) each designated statutory undertaker;

(6) the governing body of each designated educational institution;

(7) the occupier of any relevant land within the litter control area of a local authority.

14.8.11 'Relevant land' is defined as land which is open to the air and which is under the direct control of a principal litter authority and to which the public are entitled or permitted to have access with or without payment (s 86(4)).

14.8.12 It is also the duty of every local authority and the Secretary of State, to ensure that a road, highway or trunk road for which they are responsible under the Highway Acts are, so far as is practicable, kept clean (s 89(2)).

Enforcement of the duty to keep land clear of litter

14.8.13 It is not in itself a criminal offence for any of the bodies or institutions to fail to comply with the duty imposed on them. Instead, any 'aggrieved person' may complain to magistrates for a 'litter abatement order'. An aggrieved person is not specifically defined in the EPA 1990, but from s 91(1) it is clear that it will be any person who makes a complaint on the grounds that he is aggrieved by any defacement, by litter or refuse, or the lack of cleanliness of any relevant road.

14.8.14 Before instituting proceedings, the complainant must give not less than five days' written notice of his intention to make a complaint (s 91(5)). Section 91(5) does not require a complaint to be laid immediately after the five-day notice period. It would appear therefore, that a complaint could be laid at any time following the notice provided that it could be said to be sufficiently proximate in time and relates to the matters addressed in the notice. If, therefore, the notice were properly worded and the authority were to clean the site but immediately thereafter failed to maintain that standard, then a subsequent notice may not be necessary.

14.8.15 If the magistrates are satisfied that the land in question is defaced by litter or refuse, it may make a litter abatement order requiring the defendant to clear the litter or refuse away. Failure to comply with the order is an offence and liable on summary conviction to a fine not exceeding level 3 on the standard scale with a daily penalty up to £50 per day for each day the offence continues. The magistrates also have the power to award costs against the defendant, where it finds that reasonable grounds existed to justify bringing the complaint.

Standards of cleanliness

14.8.16 It is not entirely clear from Part IV what standard of cleanliness is required to comply with the duty imposed under s 89. Although the standard appears to be fairly strict and precise, the words 'as far as practicable' introduce an element of uncertainty. The Act does not define what constitutes 'practicable' and in particular whether economic circumstances could make it impracticable to achieve the standards required.

14.8.17 In an effort to clarify the extent of the duty, Part IV makes provision for the Secretary of State to issue codes of practice as practical guidance on the discharge of the duty. A code of practice was issued in January 1991 and came into effect from 1 April 1991. It is being updated at the time of writing, and when agreed will replace the existing code of practice. It is understood that the new code will be issued towards the end of 1998.

14.8.18 Failure to comply with the code of practice itself is not a criminal offence but may be issued in evidence in any proceedings for a litter abatement order (see s 89(10)).

Presenting a complaint in the Magistrates' Court
14.8.19 It should be noted that even if complaints have already been made to a local authority it may be inappropriate to proceed directly to the issuing of a notice of intention to pursue a complaint. In order to bring a successful complaint, a complainant will need to show evidence that he has acted reasonably and that proceedings were instituted only as a final resort. Evidence should include copies of letters of complaint and replies, photographs and evidence from several neighbours of affected parties.

14.8.20 Written notice should be given to the chief executive of the local authority and should draw his attention to the responsibilities under Part IV. The notice should request information on how the authority intends to comply with the duties imposed on it by the Act and details about the cleaning programme. To be successful the complainant is recommended to carry out regular monitoring of the site and the authority should be informed of this. The authority should be given a reasonable period, possibly four weeks, within which to begin to carry out its duty.

14.8.21 The complainant will need to produce the following evidence in support of his case:

(1) Evidence of the status of the 'relevant land' which is under the control of the defendant local authority.

(2) Documented evidence of the state of uncleanliness of the site. This should include evidence not only of the state of the site on the date of the hearing and the date on which the complaint was filed, but also the body of evidence built up by constant monitoring up to the date of proceedings. The complainant should monitor the litter situation daily over a period of about two to four weeks. This should be supported by photographic evidence although it may not be necessary for this to be done every day. The negatives will need to be retained for evidentiary purposes.

(3) Evidence that the complainant is 'aggrieved' by the state of the site.

If the site is cleaned up within that time there may be little to be gained in proceeding with the complaint. Records should be retained in case the situation is repeated.

14.8.22 Several weeks may pass before the matter is heard in the Magistrates' Court, so the defendant local authority has plenty of time in which to remedy the complaint. If the site is cleaned up in the period of time between the issuing of the complaint and the hearing, the complainant will need to consider whether to pursue the complaint. Proceeding with the complaint will not result in an order but the court has discretion to order the defendant local authority to pay some or all of the expenses incurred in bringing the complaint if the action is proved, although there is no guarantee that this will in fact be the case.

Other remedies
14.8.23 If the above procedure does not result in an improvement in the state of the site, the complainant may be able to apply for an order of judicial review. Alternatively complaints to the local government ombudsman, the press, local councillors and the MP may help to apply sufficient pressure to force the local authority to act.

The duty of occupiers to keep land clear of litter

14.8.24 A principal litter authority (other than a county council, regional council or Joint Board) may designate by order a litter control area. The order places a duty on the occupier of the land to keep it clear of litter. It has the same effect as the duty which applies to the authorities and other bodies subject to the duty under s 89(1) of the EPA 1990.

14.8.25 The Street Litter Control Notices Order 1991 lists many categories of land which could be subject to such an order. These include:

(1) public car parks;
(2) retail shopping developments with floor space of 5,000 sq m or more excluding the retail floor space itself;
(3) open areas to which the public have access forming part of business or office premises with a gross floor space of 5,000 sq m or more;
(4) land used for indoor or outdoor sports or recreations or as an amusement arcade or centre (for instance cinemas, theatres and swimming baths);
(5) any part of an inland beach or the seashore that is frequently used and managed as a tourist resort or recreational facility;
(6) any esplanade or promenade above mean high water springs;
(7) certain aerodromes;
(8) yachting marinas and the like above mean high water springs other than boat repair yards;
(9) motorway service stations;
(10) open land to which the public are entitled or permitted to have access;
(11) land under the direct control of a wide variety of public bodies;
(12) land where markets are held, not being part of the highway or public road;
(13) camping or caravan sites used for more than 28 days a year;
(14) a variety of picnic areas on trunk roads, and those provided by planning authorities.

14.8.26 The principal litter authority may issue an order only if it considers that the presence of the litter causes the condition of the land to be detrimental to the amenities of the locality, and is likely to continue to do so unless an order designating it as a litter control area is made (s 90(4)).

14.8.27 Before designating any land as a litter control area, a principal litter authority should notify persons who will be affected by the order. Those notified are allowed to make representations within 21 days of the service of the notice. The representations will be taken into consideration by the authority when deciding whether to proceed with the designation.

14.8.28   The form of designation order can be found in the schedule to the Litter Control Areas Order 1991.

Control of premises liable to be subject to excessive litter

14.8.29   Certain types of activity on certain premises which are liable to create excessive amounts of litter are subject to the Street Litter Control Notices Order 1991, used primarily to keep shopping areas and precincts clear of litter. Premises likely to be subject to control include:

   (1) Premises used wholly or partly for the sale of food or drink for consumption either off the premises or on a part of the premises forming open land adjacent to the street;

   (2) Service stations and other premises for which fuel for motor vehicles is sold to the public;

   (3) Premises used for indoor or outdoor sports or recreations or as an amusement arcade or centre (for instance cinemas, theatres, or swimming baths);

   (4) Banks, building society offices and other premises with automated teller machines on an outside wall.

14.8.30   A principal litter authority (other than a county council, regional council or Joint Board) may exercise these controls where any of the above premises has a frontage on a street, and where:

   (1) There is a recurrent defacement by litter of any land in the vicinity that is either part of the street or open land adjacent to it;

   (2) Open land in the vicinity of the frontage of the premises is detrimental to the amenities of the locality because of the presence of litter and is likely to remain so if no notice is served;

   (3) The activities carried out on the premises result in quantities of litter likely to cause the defacement of any part of the street or open land adjacent to it in the vicinity of the premises.

14.8.31   The notice will be served on the occupier, or where the premises are unoccupied, on their owner. It may require the clearing of litter from an area adjacent to the premises, including the provision and emptying of receptacles, within a specific period or on a prescribed regular basis,

14.8.32   A notice can only cover land 100 metres from the relevant premises, and cannot be served on land which is already within a litter control area.

14.8.33   The notice should not require the recipient to perform duties which are the responsibility of the principal litter authority itself.

14.8.34   The recipient of the notice should be given at least 28 days to make representations before it is served. The recipient may appeal against the notice by way of summary application to a magistrates' court. The court may confirm, quash or vary the terms of the notice.

14.8.35   If a person fails to comply with the notice, the principal litter authority may apply to the magistrates' court for an order for compliance. Failure to comply without reasonable excuse is an offence, subject to a fine on level 4 of the standard scale.

Public registers

14.8.36 Each principal litter authority should retain copies of all designations of land as litter control areas, and make street litter control notices on registers available to the public. The copies may only be removed from the register when the designation or notice has ceased to apply. The public should be allowed to inspect the registers at all reasonable times and free of charge, although reasonable photocopying charges can be made if copies are requested.

Checklist – litter

- Provision and maintenance of litter bins
  — see Litter Act 1983.
- Leaving litter
  — an offence contrary to s 87 of the EPA 1990
  — the offence must be committed in respect of land 'open to the air' (it must be open on at least one side)
  — a fixed penalty notice may be served where an offence under s 87 has been committed.
- Dog faeces
  — provisions under Part IV of the EPA 1990 which apply to refuse apply to dog faeces on certain land, which must not be a heath, woodland or land used to graze animals etc (see the Litter (Animal Droppings) Order 1991).
- The duty of public bodies to keep land clear of litter
  — 'relevant land' must be kept clear of litter by certain public bodies (s 89(1) of the EPA 1990)
  — a private individual may make a complaint to magistrates in order to secure a 'litter abatement order' where there has been a breach of duty
  — whether the duty has been discharged must be adjudged according to codes of practice issued by the Secretary of State
  — a complainant must keep careful evidence of the alleged breach of duty.
- The duty of occupiers to keep land clear of litter
  — a 'litter control area' designated by a principal litter authority places a duty on an occupier to keep land clear of litter. The effect of such a designation is a duty similar to that of a local authority to keep land clear of litter
  — various categories of land may be designated litter control areas by the Litter Control Areas Order 1991 (for instance public car

parks, retail shopping developments, indoor or outdoor recreation grounds, motorway service stations).
- Premises liable to be subject to excessive litter
  - some premises which are likely to attract excessive litter may be subject to the Street Litter Control Notices Order 1991 (for instance shopping precincts and banks and building societies with outdoor automatic teller machines)
  - a notice under the Order may require the provision of receptacles and/or their emptying within a specified period or on a prescribed regular basis.
- Public registers
  - copies of designations of land as litter control areas and street litter control notices are retained on registers available to the public.

14.9 Abandoned shopping and luggage trolleys

14.9.1 By s 99 of the EPA 1990 local authorities (being district and London borough councils, the Common Council of the City of London and the Council of the Isles of Scilly) are permitted to resolve that Schedule 4 of the Act applies in their area. Schedule 4 concerns abandoned shopping trolleys and luggage trolleys found by authorised officers of the local authority in the open air. However, the Schedule does not apply in the following circumstances:

(1) Where a trolley is found on land in which the owner of the trolley has a legal estate;
(2) Where an off-street parking place affords facilities to the customers of shops for leaving their shopping trolleys used by them;
(3) Where any other place designated by the local authority for the purposes of the schedule affords like facilities;
(4) As respects luggage trolleys, land which is used for the purpose of their undertaking by persons authorised by an enactment to carry on any railway, light railway, tramway or road transport undertaking or by an airport operator.

14.9.2 Schedule 4 of the EPA 1990 gives local authorities the power to seize a trolley and to remove it to such place under its control as the authority thinks fit. The apparent owner should be notified as soon as is reasonably practicable and not more than 14 days after its removal. The trolley may be sold or otherwise disposed of after six weeks if it remains unclaimed by the owner, who will have to pay a reasonable charge to cover the authority's costs.

Checklist – abandoned shopping and luggage trolleys

- Section 99 of the EPA 1990
  - s 99 enables a local authority to resolve that Sched 4 of the 1990 Act should apply in its area.

- Schedule 4 of the EPA 1990
  — Sched 4 permits authorised officers to remove abandoned shopping and luggage trolleys from open land
  — apparent owners are required to be notified
  — unclaimed trolleys may be sold and a charge levied on the owners to cover the local authority's costs
  — see s 34 of the Public Health Act 1961.

Chapter 15

Water and Sewage

15.1 Overview

15.1.1 This section is concerned with statutory provisions relating to water and sewage. It seeks in particular to identify the main criminal liabilities which someone who interferes with either undertaking will face. It also seeks to identify those duties imposed on statutory undertakers by Parliament.

15.1.2 In respect of water and the water supply this chapter will seek to consider:

    (1) The main offence of polluting controlled water contrary to s 85 of the Water Resources Act 1991

    (2) Remedial and other anti-pollution powers available to the Environment Agency in respect of controlled waters

    (3) The duties and liabilities of water undertakers in respect of the water supply

    (4) Criminal sanctions for contaminating and wasting water

    (5) The duty on water undertakers to make the mains supply available for domestic purposes

    (6) Disconnection.

15.1.3 As to sewage, this section will look in particular at the following:

    (1) The principal duties of sewerage undertakers

    (2) Sewer requisitions

    (3) Connection to a public sewer

    (4) Repairs to sewers and drains.

15.2 Water pollution – Part II of the Water Resources Act 1991

15.2.1 Part II of the Water Resources Act 1991 (the WRA 1991) contains the statutory provisions relating to water pollution. These dealing with water quality objectives, pollution offences, and various powers intended to prevent and control pollution. Much of the legislation has been introduced as a means of implementing European legislation on water pollution.

Controlled waters

15.2.2 The principal water pollution offences and the duties and powers of the Environment Agency normally occur in relation to 'controlled waters'. This term covers four categories of water:
(1) relevant territorial waters
(2) coastal waters
(3) inland waters
(4) ground waters.
The full definitions are set out at s 104(1) of the WRA 1991.

Polluting controlled waters

15.2.3 The principal offence concerning the pollution of controlled waters is set out at s 85 of the WRA 1991 which provides for a series of interrelated criminal offences of 'polluting controlled waters'. An offence is committed, contrary to s 85 by any person who 'causes or knowingly permits':
(1) any poisonous, noxious or polluting matter or any solid waste matter to enter any controlled waters (s 85(1));
(2) any matter, other than trade or sewage effluent, to enter controlled waters by being discharged from a drain or sewer in contravention of a prohibition imposed under s 86 (s 85(2));
(3) any trade effluent or sewage effluent to be discharged
    (a) into any controlled waters; or
    (b) from land in England and Wales, through a pipe, into the sea outside the seaward limits of controlled waters (s 85(3));
(4) any trade effluent or sewage effluent to be discharged, in contravention of any prohibition imposed under s 86 from a building or from any fixed plant
    (a) on to or into any land or
    (b) into any waters of the lake or pond which are not inland freshwaters (s 85(4));
(5) any matter whatever to enter any inland freshwaters so as to tend to impede the proper flow of waters in a manner leading, or likely to lead, to substantial aggravation or
    (a) pollution due to other causes or
    (b) the consequences of such pollution (s 85(5)).
Any person found guilty of an offence under s 85 is liable on summary conviction to imprisonment for a term of up to three months or a fine not exceeding £20,000 or to both; on conviction on indictment, to a term of imprisonment not exceeding two years or to an unlimited fine or to both (s 85(6)).
15.2.4 In relation to the offence set out in s 85, 'causes' has been the subject of considerable case law. The leading case is *Alphacell Ltd v Woodward* [1972] AC 824 (but see also *A-G's Ref (No 1 of 1994)* [1995] 1 WLR 599, CA).
15.2.5 Acts by vandals and third parties who interfere with plant and equipment may break the chain of causation and in such a case the accused may not

be liable (see *National Rivers Authority v Wright Engineering Co Ltd* [1994] 4 All ER 281, QBD).

15.2.6 A company may be found guilty of 'causing' the entry of prohibited matter if it results from acts of an employee carried out in the course of his employment. In *National Rivers Authority v Alfred McAlpines Homes East Limited* [1994] 4 All ER 286 the defendant company was held vicariously liable for the acts of its employees who had caused wet cement to enter controlled waters from a housing development site.

15.2.7 The phrase 'knowingly permitting' has to date been the subject of far less judicial scrutiny than 'causes'. Although the case of *Price v Cromack* [1975] 1 WLR 988, was primarily concerned with the definition of 'causing', Lord Widgery also considered 'knowingly permitting'. His views (which are supported in subsequent case law) confirm that 'knowingly permitting' involves a failure to exercise powers to prevent the pollution which must be accompanied by knowledge that the polluting incident is occurring.

15.2.8 'Knowingly permitting' could also involve giving consent to, or authorising, a certain act, or a failure to take reasonable steps to prevent or stop the act in question (see also *Schulman Incorporated Ltd v NRA* [1992] 1 Env LR D1). It follows that a landlord can be at risk if aware that a tenant is undertaking a polluting activity which it has the power to stop. The same might apply to a lender who is aware that its borrower is acting in a similar manner and has the power to stop it under the terms of the loan documentation.

15.2.9 An offence under s 85(1) requires poisonous, noxious or polluting matter or any solid waste matter to enter any controlled waters. There are no definitions in the WRA 1991 of what is 'poisonous', 'noxious' or 'polluting'. They must be given their natural meanings as far as these can be ascertained for example by reference to the Oxford Dictionary or any relevant case law. The term 'polluting' was considered in the case of *R v Dovermoss Limited* [1995] Env LR 258, in which it was held that 'polluting matter' is matter capable of causing, or likely to cause, harm to the receiving waters, without the need to show actual harm to those waters. There is no need of proof of 'harm', but proof of a 'polluting effect' on the watercourse must be proved (see also *NRA v Egger (UK) Ltd* [1992] Water Law 169).

15.2.10 Something which is 'noxious' is likely to be a substance which has been proved to 'cause harm' to its receiving waters rather than merely to have a 'polluting effect' (see *R v Cramp* [1880] 5 QBD 307).

15.2.11 'Poisonous' is the most serious degree of harm out of the three headings. It need only be capable of injuring or killing animal or plant life (see *Schulman Incorporated v NRA* [1992] 1 Env LR D2).

15.2.12 Although liability for causing pollution is strict, certain defences are provided by the WRA 1991 in ss 88 and 89.

Checklist – rights and liabilities in respect of water (1)

- Polluting controlled waters (contrary to s 85 of the WRA 1991)
  — are the waters 'controlled waters'?

— has the defendant 'caused' or 'knowingly permitted' the offence?
— does it concern 'poisonous, noxious or polluting matter' (see
   s 85(1))?
— does the matter fall within s 85(1)(2)(3)(4) or (5)?

15.3 Remedial works and other pollution powers

15.3.1 Sections 161 and 162 of the WRA 1991 enable the Environment Agency to undertake anti-pollution or remedial works.

Anti-pollution works

15.3.2 Under s 161 of the WRA 1991 the Environment Agency may undertake anti-pollution works and operations where it appears that any poisonous, noxious or polluting matter is likely to enter, or is present in any controlled waters. Where the matter is likely to enter controlled waters, the works and operations can be carried out for the purpose of preventing entry. The Environment Agency may also carry out works or operations for the purpose of restoring waters, including flora and fauna dependent on the aquatic environment. However, it can only recover its expenses reasonably incurred after the works have been carried out from any person who caused or knowingly permitted the pollution or threatened entry. As a result these powers have been little used in practice.

15.3.3 This position is likely to change when provisions set out in Schedule 22 of the Environment Act 1995 come into force. These will introduce a new s 161A enabling the Environment Agency to serve a 'works notice' on the responsible person requiring him to carry out the anti-pollution works at his expense within a specified period. It is anticipated that these regulations and statutory guidance will be brought into force at the same time as the provisions on contaminated land contained in Part II of the Environment Act 1995.

Other pollution powers

15.3.4 The Environment Agency has power to undertake various kinds of work to deal with foul water and pollution on any land which it owns or over any land over which it has acquired the necessary easements or rights (ss 159(6)(b) and 162(1) of the WRA 1991). This may include the construction and maintenance of drains, sewers, watercourses etc. There are a number of powers contained in ss 92–97 of the WRA 1991 as amended preventing and controlling pollution.

Checklist – rights and liabilities in respect of water (2)

- Remedial and other powers (ss 161 and 162 of the WRA 1991)
  - the EA may undertake anti-pollution works in advance or at the time of pollution

— the EA has powers to restore waters, flora and fauna

— a new s 161A will enable a notice to be served requiring a responsible person to carry out works. Other provisions of the WRA 1991 allow the EA to deal with foul water and pollution on land.

15.4   The supply of drinking water

Introduction

15.4.1   The supply of drinking water to the general public is the responsibility of the statutory water undertakers appointed under s 6 of the Water Industry Act 1991 (the WIA 1991), namely the various Water Companies plc. Controls over the quality of drinking water are enforced by the Drinking Water Inspectorate which is an independent arm of the DETR.

The duty to develop and maintain an efficient system of water supply

15.4.2   Each water undertaker is subject to a general duty under s 37 of the WIA 1991 to develop and maintain an efficient and economical system of water supply in its area and to ensure that supplies of water are available to persons who demand it and to maintain, improve and extend the water undertakers' mains and other pipes.

Quality and sufficiency of supplies under Part III of the WIA 1991; wholesomeness

15.4.3   Part III of the WIA 1991 is concerned with the quality and sufficiency of supplies of drinking water. In particular, s 67 enables the Secretary of State to make regulations regarding the wholesomeness of water by reference to prescribed requirements.

15.4.4   'Wholesome' has been the subject of case law (see *McColl v Strathclyde Regional Council* [1984] JPL 351). Regulations will contain general and specific requirements concerning the quality of water, the substances present in it, its characteristics and sampling techniques. The Water Supply (Water Quality) Regulations 1989 contain mandatory standards for domestic drinking water, washing and cooking water and water used for food production. The regulations take into account the standards required by EC legislation (eg Directive 80/778 EC on the quality of drinking water) and other UK requirements.

Private supplies

15.4.5   The Private Water Supplies Regulations 1991 impose quality requirements on waters from private sources or waters which are supplied by an unlicensed supplier. They impose similar requirements as the 1989 Regulations.

**Remedies where the water supply is unwholesome or insufficient –
remedial notices**

15.4.6   Where the private water supply is found to be unwholesome or insufficient, the local authority (district, London borough councils or unitary authorities) may serve a notice on the owner/occupier of premises who is using the
supply or the place where the source is located or on any party which exercises
powers of management and control in relation to the source requiring remedial
action to be carried out. They may under s 80 of the WIA 1991 serve a notice
requiring certain remedial works to be carried out. If objections are received
and are not withdrawn the local authority must refer the matter to the Secretary
of State who has wide discretion under s 81 to quash or vary the notice on the
given direction to the local authority. The matter may be considered on the
basis of written representations or an inquiry may be held. The private supply
notice in force will 'run with the land' and bind subsequent owners/occupiers.

The duty to supply a wholesome water supply at the time of supply

15.4.7   In relation to water supplied by water undertakers, they are subject to a
duty under s 68 of the WIA 1991 to ensure that the water supply used for
domestic or food production purposes is wholesome at the time of supply so far
as reasonably practicable and that there is no deterioration in quality of that
water supply from time to time. Under s 68 the Secretary of State may issue
regulations requiring the statutory undertaker to take prescribed steps for the
purpose of securing compliance with s 68.

The offence of supplying water unfit for human consumption

15.4.8   Where a water undertaker supplies water that is unfit for human consumption it will be guilty of an offence under s 70. It will be liable on summary
conviction to a fine not exceeding the statutory maximum, and on indictment
to an unlimited fine. In addition, according to s 70(2), where an individual is
guilty of an offence, and is convicted on indictment, a prison sentence may be
imposed for a term not exceeding two years (see *Drinking Water Inspectorate
and Secretary of State v Severn Trent Water* [1995] (unreported)).
15.4.9   There are a number of defences available under s 70(3) to such proceedings. For example, the water undertaker may prove that it had no reasonable grounds for suspecting that the water would be used for human
consumption, or that it took all reasonable steps and exercised all due diligence
for securing that the water was fit for human consumption on leaving its pipes,
or that it was not used for human consumption.

Offences relating to contaminating and wasting water

15.4.10   Sections 71–76 of the WIA 1991 deal with the contamination or
waste of water. Under s 71 it is an offence to cause or allow any underground

water to run to waste from any well, borehole, or other work or to abstract from any well, borehole or other water in excess of a person's reasonable requirements. Section 72 creates an offence of committing any act of neglect whereby the water and any waterworks which is used or is likely to be used for human consumption or domestic purposes for the manufacture of food or drink for human consumption is polluted or likely to be polluted. The offence will not prohibit any method of conservation of land which is in accordance with the principles of good husbandry, nor will it be construed to restrict or prohibit the reasonable use of all oil or tar by a Highway Authority.

15.4.11 Any person who does not comply with s 72 will be guilty of an offence and liable on summary conviction to both a fine not exceeding the statutory maximum and a continuing daily penalty not exceeding £50 for each day the offence continues. On conviction on indictment a defendant is liable to a term of imprisonment of two years or to an unlimited fine or to both.

15.4.12 Section 73 specifies a further offence which is committed by any owner or occupier of premises who causes or permits (intentionally or negligently) any of his water fittings to be out of repair or misused, thereby causing contamination or waste of water. Section 74 gives the Secretary of State power to make regulations concerning water fittings and s 75 confers emergency powers on water undertakers to prevent damage to persons or properties with a contamination of waste water.

'Hosepipe bans'

15.4.13 Section 76 enables water authorities to impose a 'hosepipe ban' if in its opinion there is, or is threatened, a serious water deficiency.

General duties of water undertakers – water mains for domestic purposes

15.4.14 The general duties of the water undertakers are described in Part III of the WIA 1991.

15.4.15 In particular, Chapter II describes the duties to supply water, including provisions under s 40 relating to the bulk supply of water. The water undertaker is subject to a duty to provide a water main to be used for supplying water to premises in its area for domestic purposes on receipt of a notice in accordance with the provisions in s 41.

Remedies for failing to provide a water mains

15.4.16 Where the water undertaker fails to comply with its duty and the person seeking the water main suffers loss or damage he may bring proceedings against the water undertaker under s 41(4). It is a defence to such proceedings for the undertaker to show it took all reasonable steps and exercised all due diligence to avoid the breach.

Ancillary matters connected with the provision of a water main

15.4.17 Detailed provisions in ss 42 and 43 describe the financial obligations which relate to the provision of a water main. The water undertaker has three months in which to determine whether or not it can provide the services requested in the area in accordance with s 44.

Serving a notice requiring a supply of water for domestic purposes

15.4.18 Further, the water undertaker is subject to a duty under s 45 where the owner or occupier of the premises within its area serves a notice on it requiring a supply of water for domestic purposes to a building or part of a building to connect a service pipe to those premises with one of the water undertaker's mains. Where the water undertaker is required to connect a water supply to the person's premises in pursuance of a connection notice it is also under a duty to carry out any necessary ancillary works to enable the connection although the cost of such works is recoverable from the person who requires the connection (s 46).

The duty to maintain a supply of water for domestic purposes

15.4.19 A water undertaker is under a duty to maintain a supply of water for domestic purposes under s 52. A similar duty is imposed to supply water for non-domestic purposes under s 55. Failure to comply with the duty imposed under s 52 will enable any person who sustains loss or damage to take action against the water undertaker.

Disconnection

15.4.20 A water undertaker is entitled to disconnect a service or cut off the water supply to any premises under s 60 except in cases of emergency or where the reduction is immaterial and only after the undertaker has served a notice on the consumer describing its intentions.

15.4.21 By reason of s 61, a water undertaker may disconnect the service where the occupier of the premises has failed to pay charges to the undertaker in respect of the water supply following seven days after service of a notice and providing no counter notice is served (s 61). Furthermore a customer may ask the undertaker to disconnect the water supply under s 62. General duties are imposed on undertakers in respect of disconnections described in s 63.

15.4.22 Sections 64–66 contain provisions ensuring the means of supply, consistency and water pressure and maintaining water pressure.

Checklist – the supply of drinking water

- Duties imposed on statutory undertakers and private suppliers under the WIA 1991:

— to develop and maintain an efficient and economical supply of water (s 37)

— to ensure that supplies are available to those who demand it (s 37)

— to maintain, improve and extend mains and other pipes (s 37)

— the water supply must be sufficient and wholesome (see Part III generally, the power to make regs under s 67 and the Water Supply (Water Quality) Regulations 1989

— to supply a wholesome water supply at the time of supply (s 68)

— the Private Water Supplies Regulations 1991 impose quality requirements on waters from private supplies

— a local authority has wide powers to serve a notice requiring remedial works to be carried out in respect of private supplies

— the duties in relation to water mains are set out in Part III, especially chapter II

— a person who has suffered loss because of the failure to provide a suitable mains can recover compensation (s 41(4))

— an owner or occupier of premises can require a domestic supply of water under s 45

— duties exist requiring an undertaker to maintain a supply of water for domestic and non-domestic purposes (ss 52 and 55)

— special provisions relate to disconnection (ss 60–63)

— special provisions relate to the means of supply, consistency and water pressure (ss 64–66).

• Main criminal penalties

— supplying water unfit for human consumption (s 70)

— contaminating and wasting water (ss 71–76).

15.5 Sewage and effluent disposal

Introduction

15.5.1 Part IV of the WIA 1991 contains provisions relating to the provision of sewerage services, describing the principal duties and standards of performance of sewerage undertakers, functions by local authorities, the ability to requisition a public sewer, the powers of adoption, communication drains and general connection provisions. Section 6 of the WIA 1991 describes the powers relating to the appointment of a water and sewerage undertaker in England and Wales which is likely to be a Water Company plc.

The principal duties of sewerage undertakers

15.5.2 Section 94 describes the principal duties and standards of performance of every sewerage undertaker, for example, it must provide, improve and extend the public sewerage system, clean and maintain the sewers and ensure the area is effectively drained; it must make provision for employing those services and further provide for an effective way of dealing with the contents of sewers via sewerage disposal works. Section 94(2) states that the sewerage undertaker must have regard to existing and future obligations to discharge trade effluent into its sewers and also to dispose of trade effluent.

15.5.3 The duty of a sewerage undertaker is enforceable in accordance with s 18 of the WIA 1991 by the Secretary of State or the Director General for Water Services (OFWAT). By ss 23 and 24 the Secretary of State or the Director General may apply to the High Court for a special administration order if there has been a contravention of any principal duty. The effect of such an order is to enable the court to appoint an administrator who will take over the management of the company. Section 97 enables local authorities to act as agents for the sewerage undertakers in the poor performance of their functions. However, this does not provide the sewerage undertaker with immunity from failure to comply with its duties (*King v London Borough of Harrow* [1994] EGCS 76).

The system of sewer requisitions

15.5.4 A sewerage undertaker is subject to a duty to comply with sewer requisitions served under s 98(1) WIA 1991 to provide a public sewer for the drainage of domestic premises.

15.5.5 Section 98(2) describes the categories of people who are entitled to require the provision of a public sewer for any locality. These include:

(1) the owner of any premises in the locality;
(2) the occupier of any premises in the locality;
(3) the local authority within whose area the whole or any part of the locality is situated;
(4) the Commission for the New Towns if the area is a new town;
(5) Local Government Planning and Land Act 1980 where the area is an urban development area.

15.5.6 Where the sewerage undertaker fails in its duty to provide a public sewer and the person who is entitled to it sustains loss or damage, proceedings may be brought against it. It will be a defence for the sewerage undertaker to show that it took all reasonable steps and exercised all due diligence to avoid the breach of duty (s 98(4)). Section 101 describes when a sewerage undertaker will be in breach of the duty imposed under s 98.

15.5.7 Para 103 of Schedule 22 to the Environment Act 1995 amends the provisions relating to the requisition of the sewers under the WIA 1991. In particular it introduces a further duty to a sewerage undertaker under a new s 101A to provide a public sewer to be used for the drainage of domestic sewage purposes for premises in its locality without receiving a requisition, provided that certain conditions provided in s 101A(2) are satisfied. These conditions are:

(1) the erection of the building before 20 June 1995;
(2) the fact there is no connection with a public sewer;

(3) the fact that the present drainage of the premises is giving or is likely to give rise to adverse effects to the environment or amenity, having regard to any guidance issued under s 101A by the Secretary of State.

Disputes arising between the sewerage undertaker and an owner or occupier will be referred to and determined by the Environment Agency.

Connection to public sewer

15.5.8   Section 106(1) allows the owner or occupier of any premises in the area of a sewerage undertaker to be entitled to have his drains or sewer connect with a public sewer. The owner or occupier will not be allowed to discharge any liquid from a factory or manufacturing process (s 106(2)(a)).

15.5.9   Section 106(3) requires that a person who wishes to connect to the public sewer must give notice of proposals to the sewerage undertaker. The undertaker may refuse if it feels that the mode of construction or condition of the drain or sewer would be prejudicial to the undertaker's sewerage system (s 106(4)).

15.5.10   There is a right of appeal to the Magistrates' Court against the undertaker's refusal to give consent (s 106(6)). The sewerage undertaker may wish to examine the private sewer or drain and if necessary require it to be laid open (s 106(5)). Again, there is a right of appeal to the Magistrates' Court.

15.5.11   Connection to a public sewer without consent is a criminal offence under s 109, and the fine on summary conviction shall not exceed level 4 on the standard scale.

Repairs to sewers and drains

15.5.12   Section 114(1) gives the sewerage undertaker the power to investigate a defective drain or sewer if it has grounds to believe it is in a condition which may be injurious or likely to cause injury to health or nuisance or if it is defective and admits subsoil water. The sewerage undertaker has the power to open the ground to investigate and test the sewer if reasonable. Section 114(2) states that if the sewer is found to be in a proper condition, the undertaker must reinstate the ground as soon as possible.

Similar powers are available under s 48 of the Public Health Act 1936 where there is a connection to a public sewer and in all other cases the local authority can rely on the provision to examine and test drains, private sewers etc believed to be defective.

15.5.13   A local authority has power to repair any drain, private sewer, water-closet, waste or soil pipe that has not been sufficiently maintained provided the costs do not exceed £250. Furthermore, under s 101(3), if the same is stopped up, it may serve a notice on the occupier or owner of the premises requiring the defect to be remedied within 48 hours of the service of the notice. If the notice is not complied with, the local authority may do the work and recover its reasonable expenses. By virtue of s 101 of the Building Act 1984, local authorities have the same s 114(1) and (2) powers to break open streets as sewerage undertakers. Section 278 of the Public Health Act 1936 renders the local authority liable to pay 'full compensation' where a person has sustained damage due to the exercise of their powers under that Act through no fault of his own.

15.5.14 Section 108 of the WIA 1991 confers on individuals the right to reconstruct, repair or alter the course of an underground drain. Section 61 of the Building Act 1984 states that the local authority must be given 24 hours notice except in the case of an emergency. An officer of the local authority must be permitted access during the works (s 62(2)).

15.5.15 A person who fails to comply with this section is liable on summary conviction to a fine not exceeding level 3 on the standard scale.

15.5.16 Section 48 of the Public Health Act 1936 gives a local authority power to examine and test drains and private sewers that are believed to be defective. This is only if they have reasonable grounds for believing that they may be 'prejudicial to health or a nuisance'. If the ground is found to be defective then action can be taken.

15.5.17 Under s 59(1) of the Building Act 1984, if it appears that a cesspool, private sewer or drain provided for the building is insufficient, or if the drain communicating directly or indirectly with a public sewer is so defective as to admit subsoil water or cesspool, or if any other work or appliance is prejudicial to health or a nuisance, the local authority can by notice require the owner or occupier of the building to do such work as is necessary for renewing or cleansing the sewer, drain or cesspool. Section 59(1) does not apply in relation to a building belonging to the statutory undertakers. As an alternative, the local authority can serve an abatement notice under the normal statutory nuisance procedure. If the drain, once repaired, is a nuisance or prejudicial to health, the person who undertook or executed the construction or repair commits an offence. That person is liable on summary conviction to a fine not exceeding level 1 on the standard scale unless shown that reasonable care was taken (s 63(1), Building Act 1984).

15.5.18 Under s 17(1) of the Public Health Act 1961, the local authority can give not less than seven days' notice of repair to any person owning any premises drained by means of a drain or a private sewer. The same period of notice requiring repairs to be carried out can be given to the owner of the sewer, if the sewer appears not to be in good repair and can be repaired for less than £250. Further, if it appears to the local authority that a drain, private or waste pipe on any premises is stopped up, they may require the owner or occupier of the premises by notice in writing to remedy the defect within 48 hours from the service of the notice (s 17(3)). If the notice under s 17(3) is not complied with, the local authority may themselves carry out the work necessary to remedy the defect. The provisions of s 17 are without prejudice to s 59 of the Building Act 1984 which empowers the local authority to serve notices as regards defective drains.

Disconnection

15.5.19   Section 116 enables the sewerage undertaker to discontinue and pro-hibit the use of any public sewer which is vested in the undertaker. Before the undertaker is allowed to do this it must provide a sewer which is equally effec-tive for use for that purpose and carry out work necessary to make that person's drains or sewers communicate with the sewer provided (s 116(3)).

Trade effluent

15.5.20   Section 118(1) states that the occupier of any trade premises may not discharge any trade effluent into the public sewer without the consent of the undertaker. If trade effluent is discharged without consent, the occupier of the premises shall be guilty of all offence and liable on summary conviction to a fine not exceeding the statutory maximum, and on conviction on indictment, to an unlimited fine.

Checklist – sewage and effluent disposal

- Sewer requisitions (under the WIA 1991)
  - — a sewage undertaker is obliged to comply with a sewage requisition (s 98(1))
  - — only certain categories of person are entitled to require the provision of a public sewer (see s 98(2))
  - — compensation may be recovered from an undertaker who fails to comply with a requisition
  - — NB a sewerage undertaker is required to provide a public sewer for the drainage of domestic sewage without a requisition in certain circumstances (s 101A).
- Connections to the public sewer
  - — s 106 sets out a mechanism for the connection of premises with the public sewer. Where an undertaker refuses consent there is an appeal procedure to magistrates.
- Repairs to sewers and drains
  - — a sewerage undertaker has powers to investigate the condition of drains and sewers (s 114(1))
  - — a local authority has a power to repair drains and sewers which have not been properly maintained and to require an owner to remedy any defects of the same if they have become stopped
  - — s 17 of the Public Health Act 1961 and s 59 of the Building Act 1981 contain provisions providing for notices requiring private individuals to carry out works of repair, renewal or cleansing of sewers, drains or cesspools.
- Disconnection
  - — public sewers can be disconnected (s 116(3)).

- Trade effluent
  — an occupier may not discharge trade effluent into the public sewer
  without the consent of the undertaker (s 118(1)). It is an offence to
  discharge trade effluent without consent.

Chapter 16

Remedies

16.1 Overview

16.1.1 This chapter seeks to identify a variety of specific issues relating to remedies. The focus of these issues throughout this chapter are tortious claims connected with the use of land and its appurtenant rights, although the general principles will be applicable to many causes of action.

16.1.2 Some observations will be made about the correct measure of damages in claims which are the subject of this book. This is an issue which is comparatively straightforward. More difficult questions are raised by the remedy of injunction: will one be granted, will damages be awarded in lieu, should an application be made for an interlocutory order? Some assistance can be given on the principles by which the courts exercise their discretion, but this is no substitute for experience and good judgment.

16.1.3 It is not intended in this chapter to give any assistance with procedure. The correct methods of making an application are well summarised in both the Green and the White Books. Some important observations will be made, however, on costs and pleading.

16.1.4 The issues discussed in this chapter concerning damages are:

16.2 The correct measure of damages where there has been actual damage to land and its appurtenant rights

16.3 The recovery of damages for annoyance, inconvenience and distress

16.4 Consequential loss

16.5 Damages in trespass where there has been no actual damage

16.6 Damages for interference with light

16.7 Continuing damage

16.8 Recovering compensation for damage occurring after the issue of proceedings but before judgment

16.9 Nominal damages.

16.1.5 The issues dealt with which consider injunctions include:

16.11 Final prohibitory injunctions and damages in lieu

16.12 Mandatory injunctions

16.13 Mandatory *quia timet* injunctions

16.14 Mandatory *quia timet* injunctions at an interlocutory stage

16.15 Injunctions and trespass to land.

16.2 Actual damage to land and its appurtenant rights – the correct measure of damages

Introduction

16.2.1 It can be forgotten that the usual measure of damages to compensate a plaintiff for an injury resulting from a tort concerning the use of land is diminution in value rather than cost of reinstatement. In general this does not in fact pose a problem. Where, for instance, a brick wall is damaged the loss is arguably the same. A theoretical buyer of the plaintiff's premises would say: 'I will not pay your asking price – I require a deduction reflecting the cost to me of repairing that wall'. Where the diminution in value of the premises is vastly different from the cost of reinstatement, however, then the figure reflecting the diminution in value is generally to be preferred.

Restitutio in integrum – but the award as between the parties must be reasonable

16.2.2 The underlying principle is that a plaintiff should be put in the position he was in before the tort occurred (*restitutio in integrum*). This is subject to the further principle that damages as between a plaintiff and defendant should be reasonable (*CR Taylor (Wholesale) Ltd v Hepworths Ltd* [1977] 1 WLR 659). The principles in contract as well as in tort are applicable.

Diminution in value the usual measure

16.2.3 Damages to compensate a plaintiff who has suffered some actual harm to his land or its appurtenant rights are most commonly assessed according to the diminution in value of the land in question. Examples include:

(1) *Jones v Gooday* (1841) 8 M&W 146, 151 ER 985: The defendant removed a strip of land from a field in making a ditch. He was awarded the difference in value of the land and not the amount it would have cost to restore it to its original condition.

(2) *Ough v King* [1967] 1 WLR 1547: £300 awarded, representing the difference in value of the house before and after the interference. The evidence before the court was that £60 was required to provide extra lighting.

(3) *Cecilia McGrath v The Munster and Leinster Bank Ltd* [1959] IR 313: Damages were awarded representing the reduction in the letting value of the affected office.

Reinstatement value may be appropriate where circumstances require

16.2.4 In the case of special or unique premises, the plaintiff may be entitled to recover the full reinstatement value, without an allowance for betterment.

(1) *Harbutt's Plasticine Ltd v Wayne Tank and Pump Co Ltd* [1970] 1 QB 447: The plaintiff's factory was damaged by fire. It sought to get back into production as quickly as possible. The new premises were better than the old but no better than planning officers would have insisted upon. The plaintiff was awarded the full reinstatement value.

(2) *Hollebone v Midhurst and Fernhurst Builders Ltd* [1968] 1 Lloyd's Rep 38: The plaintiff owned a house unique to its area. The defendant was ordered to pay the full cost of reinstatement (£19,000) rather than the diminished value of the premises (£15,000).

A defendant with no intention of reinstating land

16.2.5 Where it can be demonstrated that a defendant had no intention of reinstating premises, he will not recover more than the diminution in its value and in some circumstances he may be awarded less.

(1) *CR Taylor (Wholesale) Ltd v Hepworths Ltd* [1977] 1 WLR 659: The plaintiff owned an empty billiard hall in a run-down area which it maintained for its future redevelopment potential. The cost of reinstatement was £28,000 and the diminution in value £2,500. The plaintiff was awarded nothing for diminution in value because it would have cost at least that amount to clear the site to the extent that it was cleared by the fire which damaged it. The plaintiff recovered £2,600 representing the cost of remedial and safety work, £74 for damage to fixtures and fittings and £650 for removal of debris.

(2) *Hole & Son (Sayers Common) Ltd v Harrisons of Thurnscoe Ltd* [1973] 1 Lloyd's Rep 345: The plaintiff owned three cottages which it intended to demolish as soon as the statutory tenant had moved out. It was only entitled to the cost of temporary repairs and loss of rent.

When is the correct date on which to assess the reinstatement value?

16.2.6 In general, damages will be assessed as of the date on which the cause of action arose (*Miliangos v George Frank (Textiles) Ltd* [1976] AC 443). The real question is: 'when could the works first reasonably be undertaken?', given that a plaintiff is not obliged to do that which he cannot afford to do in order to mitigate his loss (*Dodd Properties Ltd v Canterbury CC* [1980] 1 WLR 433). Accordingly reinstatement costs can be recovered as of the date of judgment, even though the intervening years have seen a rise in the price of materials and other expenses. Thus in *Bunclark v Herts CC* (1977) 243 EG 455 reinstatement costs were awarded at the later date and not when the cause of action arose. The uncertainty of succeeding in a contested case as well as financial resources are relevant factors when determining whether a plaintiff has acted reasonably (see *Bunclark's* and *Dodd's* cases).

16.3 Damages for annoyance, inconvenience and distress

16.3.1 Damages under the above head are recoverable and in the case of nuisance by intangible damage may well be the only remedy sought. The amount of damages recoverable must be 'reasonable'.

(1) *Halsey v Esso Petroleum Co Ltd* [1961] 1 WLR 683: £200 awarded for a 'gross inconvenience with comfort and enjoyment of property' by noise and smell from a refinery over a five-year period. (£200 would be worth some £2,500 in 1998.)

(2) *Bone v Seale* [1975] 1 WLR 797 (CA): £1,000 awarded for 12 years' intermittent nuisance by noise and smell from pigs. (£1,000 would be worth some £6,200 in 1998.)

(3) *Kennaway v Thompson* [1981] QB 88: £1,000 awarded in respect of past noise nuisance by power boats. There had been an increase in the amount of noise created by these boats from 1972 until 1977, when races were held most weekends between early April and late October. (£1,000 would be worth about £2,500 in 1998.)

(4) *Bunclark v Herts CC* (1977) 243 EG 455: A block of flats was extensively damaged by the action of tree roots. The court allowed a claim for general damages based on (a) reduction in rent and (b) the 'unsaleability' of the flats. The award was made to recognise the ten years during which the plaintiffs had had to put up with constant damage to their flats, inconvenience and anxiety and the fact that the residents had been unable to move. (The cost of reinstatement was also ordered.)

16.4 Consequential loss

16.4.1 So far as consequential losses are concerned the relevant question is always: 'Is the damage complained of the natural and reasonable result of the defendant's act?' (See *Theyer v Purnell* [1918] 2 KB 333 at 340). In that case sheep with scab strayed on to the plaintiff's farm. The sheep had to remain there for several months subject to a Notice of Detention order. The plaintiff claimed a variety of expenses and was held to be entitled to the cost of keep of the sheep and 'damage directly caused to the plaintiff's sheep under this detention notice'. In *Horton v Colwyn Bay & Colwyn UDC* [1908] 1 KB 327 at 341 Buckley LJ held:

> If an actionable wrong has been done to the claimant he is entitled to recover all the damage resulting from that wrong, and nonetheless because he would have had no right of action for some part of the damage if the wrong had not also created a damage which was actionable.

In each case, however, where consequential losses are sought to be recovered, the question whether the losses are too remote is a question which must be considered carefully in each case.

16.4.2 Loss of profits and expenses are recoverable as consequential costs. In an action for private nuisance, compensation for personal injury or damage to chattels may also be recovered as a consequential losses.

16.5 Damages in trespass where there has been no actual damage

16.5.1 Special rules apply to acts of trespass to land since the trespass may be committed without the plaintiff suffering any actual harm to his property. A wrongdoer who keeps an owner from his land must pay a fair rental for it based on the value to the wrongdoer, even though he causes no damage (*Whitwham v Westminster Brymbo Coal and Coke Co* [1896] 2 Ch 538. The plaintiff does not need to call any evidence that he would have been able to let the land (*Swordheath Properties Ltd v Tabet* [1979] 1 WLR 285). At the same time the defendant is not required to disgorge any profits he may have received from the use to which he in turn put the land (*Strand Electric and Engineering Co Ltd v Brisford Entertainments Ltd* [1952] 2 QB 246). (See also 5.5.2 and 5.5.3.)

16.5.2 By reason of the fact that trespass is a cause of action which is complete without any proof of actual damages the court has wide power to order consequential damages, including economic loss (*Midland Bank v Bardgrove Property Services Ltd* (1992) 60 BLR 1 and *Maher v Nazir* Construction Industry Law Letter – May 1977 1257).

16.5.3 In *Griffiths v Kingsley-Stubbs* (CA) [1987] CLY 1227 £400 was awarded for trespass by footings of a bathroom extension (one and a half inches on to the plaintiff's land).

16.6 Damages for interference with light

16.6.1 Two methods of assessing compensation for loss of light are in general use by practitioners. An action for loss of light generally requires the engagement of a surveyor familiar with such work and his fees are likely to be very high.

16.6.2 The conventional method of calculation is usefully set out in *The Valuation of Rights to Light* (J Anstey) published by the College of Estate Management. This requires a calculation of the measurement of loss of light by reference to the movement of the Sky Factor contour (see 8.4.6). The amount of loss is then compared with a rental value of the property per square metre according to a valuation graph in common use between the leading experts (information will also be needed from a valuer to assist with the local rental value). A multiplier is then applied to this to determine the years' purchase in perpetuity.

16.6.3 An alternative method is to calculate the development gain to the tortfeasor. An experienced expert will claim a percentage of the development value according to the degree of loss of light.

16.6.4 It should be noted that although these are conventional calculations which will be particularly helpful in seeking to settle an action before it goes to trial, the judge will be asked to award a figure for general damages (to include loss of amenity) based on the actual evidence of the lay witnesses (see *Carr-Saunders v Dick McNeil Associates Ltd* [1986] 2 All ER 888 (in which £8,000 was awarded in lieu of an injunction (worth about £13,000 in 1998)) and *Deakins v Hookings* [1994] 1 EGLR 190 (HHJ Cooke)). Expert evidence can be of assistance but is not determinative.

16.7 Continuing damage

16.7.1 Prospective damages can never be recovered in an action (the exception being where damages are awarded in lieu of an injunction – see 16.11 below). Some causes of action, notably trespass and nuisance by intangible damage, may give rise to a fresh cause of action every day. Thus in *Darley Main Colliery Co v Mitchell* (1886) 11 App Cas 127, the plaintiff had succeeded in recovering damages in an initial action as a result of mine workings by his lessee. When further subsistence manifested itself more than six years later, the plaintiff was entitled to recover further damages, the cause of action not being complete until damage had occurred.

16.8 Recovering compensation for damage occurring after the issue of proceedings but before judgment

16.8.1 Where a plaintiff sues for damages to compensate him for a past injury, and after the date of issue but before the date of judgment he suffers further damage, he is entitled to judgment with an inquiry as to the appropriate level of compensation for all the damage sustained up to the date of judgment, so long as the damage arises from the same offending act. Thus in *McCombe v Read* [1955] 2 QB 429 the plaintiff sued for subsidence caused by the abstraction of water by trees. He sought an injunction and damages to compensate him for underpinning works already carried out. After the issue of proceedings further works became necessary. The judge gave the plaintiff the option of recovering the special damages claimed in the proceedings or an inquiry into damages to include the subsequent injuries.

16.9 'Nominal damages'

Introduction

16.9.1 A particular concern for a plaintiff is the question whether he will recover more than nominal damages. There appears to be some confusion especially in the county court between 'nominal' and 'small' damages and whether a successful litigant in either case will get his costs at all.

Meaning of 'nominal damages'

16.9.2 An award of 'nominal damages' represents a token amount. It is 'a sum of money that may be spoken of, but that has no existence in point of quantity' (*Beaumont v Greathead* (1846) 2 CB 494 at 499). It is a sum which can be said to be of no value to the plaintiff.

Nominal damages distinguished from small damages

16.9.3 Nominal damages 'does not mean small damages' (*The Mediana* [1900] AC 113). In *Pamplin v Express Newspapers Ltd (No 2)* [1988] 1 All ER 282 at 289 'a small award of damages' was described as a sum 'such as £50 or even £10' and was to be distinguished from 'an award of a derisory or contemptuous sum'.

Nominal damages and costs – plaintiff at risk

16.9.4 Costs should follow the event when damages are small (see *Pamplin's* case above – a sum as low as £10 'in the ordinary way would carry the costs'). Where the damages are nominal on the other hand, not only is the plaintiff unlikely to recover his own costs, but in a rare case he may be ordered to pay those of the other side. See Devlin J in *Anglo-Cyprian Trade Agencies Ltd v Paphos Wine Industries Ltd* [1951] 1 All ER 874:

> No doubt, the ordinary rule is that, where a plaintiff has been successful, he ought not to be deprived of his costs, or, at any rate, made to pay the costs of the other side, unless he has been guilty of some sort of misconduct. In applying that rule, however, it is necessary to decide whether the plaintiff really has been successful, and I do not think that a plaintiff who recovers nominal damages ought necessarily to be regarded in the ordinary sense of the word as a 'successful' plaintiff.

In the County Court the amount of damages recovered may be reflected by the scale of costs used to assess the costs to be paid to the winner.

Nominal damages irrelevant where plaintiff seeks to establish a legal right

16.9.5 Where part of the plaintiff's object in taking proceedings is to establish a legal right, he should recover his costs even though the damages he recovers are nominal (*Armstrong v Sheppard & Short Ltd* [1959] 2 QB 384). In that event he can properly be considered a successful plaintiff since he has recovered something of benefit to him (Lord Halsbury in *The Mediana* at 116 and *Anglo-Cyprian Trade Agencies v Paphos Wine Industries* above). An example of such a case is a case in trespass where the plaintiff seeks to establish his right to the land in question. It is better practice, however, to include a claim for a declaration in the pleadings at the same time as the claim for damages.

16.10 Injunctions – introductory

16.10.1 Where an infringement of a proprietary right is proved a plaintiff is *prima facie* entitled to an injunction. However, this is 'not an unqualified right' so that where the infringement is trivial or has caused the plaintiff no inconvenience or where the plaintiff has misled either the court or the defendants, then as a matter of its discretion, the court may decline to grant relief (*Armstrong v Sheppard & Short Ltd* [1959] 2 QB 384).

16.11   Final prohibitory injunctions and damages in lieu

Introduction

16.11.1   One of the central questions for anyone contemplating an action based on the use and enjoyment of land is whether the judge will award an injunction or damages in lieu. Whether or not an injunction is granted can have important consequences in costs, especially in the county court where a low award may attract an award of costs on a lower scale.

16.11.2   This section considers only prohibitory injunctions and damages in lieu, a prohibitory injunction being one which has the effect, if granted, of prohibiting conduct which may occur in the future. The principles relating to mandatory injunctions are considered in outline at 16.12 below.

A presumption in favour of the grant of an injunction

16.11.3   Where the facts establish that a plaintiff is entitled to an injunction there is a presumption that the court will exercise its discretion to grant injunctive relief. The underlying policy is to prevent a defendant from being able to purchase a legal wrong by an award of money. See AL Smith LJ in *Shelfer v City of London Electric Lighting Co* [1895] 1 Ch 287 at 322:

> Many judges have stated, and I emphatically agree with them, that a person by committing a wrongful act ... is not thereby entitled to ask the court to sanction his doing so by purchasing his neighbour's rights, by assessing damages in that behalf, leaving his neighbours with the nuisance, or his lights dimmed as the case may be.

So too in *Cowper v Laidler* [1903] 2 Ch 337 at 341 it was said that:

> to refuse to aid the legal right by injunction and to give damages instead is in fact to compel the plaintiff to part with his easement for money.

It should be clearly understood that the starting point for the court is the grant of an injunction.

Special circumstances – damages in lieu

16.11.4   For a defendant to persuade a court that damages should be awarded in lieu of an injunction he must bring his case within the criteria laid down by AL Smith LJ in *Shelfer's* case at 322:

> In my opinion, it may be stated as a good working rule that – (1) if the injury to the plaintiff's legal rights is small, (2) and is one which is capable of being estimated in money, (3) and is one which can be adequately compensated by a small money payment, (4) and the case is one in which it would be oppressive to the defendant to grant an injunction:- then damages in substitution for an injunction may be given.

Moreover, in order to bring a case within these criteria 'special circumstances' or 'very special circumstances' must apply (*Shelfer v City of London Electric Lighting Co* [1895] 1 Ch 287, *Jaggard v Sawyer* [1995] 1 WLR 269 at 287B and *Wiltshire Bacon Co Ltd v Associated Cinema Properties Ltd* [1937] 4 All ER 80). The possible benefit or amenity value to a wider group is irrelevant (*Kennaway v Thompson* [1981] QB 88).

Is the injury to the plaintiff's rights 'small'?

16.11.5 No mechanistic approach can be adopted to the application of AL Smith LJ's criteria and everything will depend on the facts. Whether an injury to a plaintiff's rights can be described as 'small', for instance, is a matter of degree. AL Smith LJ gave the following example in *Shelfer's* case at 323:

> An injury to the plaintiff's legal right to light to a window in a cottage represented by £15 might well be held to be not small but considerable; whereas a similar injury to a warehouse or other large building represented by ten times that amount might be held to be inconsiderable.

At the same time it must be recognised that 'an injunction [is] a formidable legal weapon which ought to be held for less trivial occasions' (Cozens-Hardy J in *Llandudno UDC v Woods* [1899] 2 Ch 705 at 710).

Overhanging cranes

16.11.6 In cases involving the overhanging booms of cranes it is settled that an operator must ensure that he has the permission of the owners of the surrounding land (*Woollerton and Wilson v Costain Ltd* [1970] 1 WLR 411). The damage caused by a trespass to a person's airspace by an overhanging crane can therefore not be described as small, since the owners of the surrounding properties have been deprived of the opportunity to bargain as they wish for the grant of rights over their property (*Anchor Brewhouse Developments Ltd v Berkley House (Docklands Developments) Ltd* (1987) 38 Build LR 82).

Is the injury capable of being estimated in money?

16.11.7 The more difficult it is to estimate the value of an infringement of a right, the less likely the court will be to grant damages in lieu of an injunction. However, the courts have attempted to devise methods of assessing the monetary value of an injury.

16.11.8 One method adopted by the courts is to assess the market value of the amount which it would have cost the defendant in order to have obtained the consent of the plaintiff to the injury (*Bracewell v Appleby* [1975] Ch 408 and *Jaggard v Sawyer* [1995] 1 WLR 269). This approach was also adopted by Millet J in *Carr-Saunders v Dick McNeil Associates Ltd* [1986] 1 WLR 922 (a right to light case), pointing out that the justification for an award on this basis is the extra value that the plaintiff's agreement would have had to a defendant if the defendant had bothered to ask before carrying out his works: 'he would have [had] a bargaining position because, unless he were bought out, the defendants would [have been] inhibited in their development'. See also *Gafford v Graham* (1998) *The Times*, 1 May.

16.11.9 It must be remembered that if the court intends to make a monetary award of damages in lieu of an injunction then the amount of the award must reflect the fact that the court is sanctioning an indeterminate number of injuries to the plaintiff's right in the future. In *Leeds Industrial Co-operative Society Ltd v Slack* [1924] AC 851 the House of Lords sanctioned the award of damages under Lord Cairns' Act in respect of an injury which was threatened but had not yet occurred. See at 857:

> Does [the Court have power] to award damages in lieu of an injunction when injury is threatened but has not yet been done?
>
> In my opinion this question must be answered in the affirmative. The power given is to award damages to the party injured, either in addition or in substitution for an injunction. If the damages are given in addition to the injunction they are to compensate for the injury which has been done and the injunction will prevent its continuance or repetition. But if damages are given in substitution for an injunction they must necessarily cover not only the injury already sustained but also the injury that would be inflicted in the future by the commission of the act threatened. If no injury has yet been sustained the damages will be solely in respect of the damage to be sustained in the future by injuries which the injunction, if granted, would have prevented.

See also the judgment of Millett LJ in *Jaggard's* case.

Is it oppressive to grant an injunction?

16.11.10 A defendant who wishes to persuade the court that it would be oppressive to grant an injunction has an uphill struggle. This is because of the importance which the courts attach to the recognition of an individual's private law rights (see *Elliott's* case at 16.12.4 below). In *Kelsen v Imperial Tobacco Co Ltd* [1957] QB 334 the court was not impressed by the considerable cost to the defendant of erecting the overhanging advertising sign, the judge noting (at 347) that:

> Cases in which an injunction has not been granted on the ground of hardship have, I believe, been mostly cases in which there has been some accidental invasion of the plaintiff's rights.

Additional considerations – the conduct of the defendant

16.11.11 Even where the four *Shelfer* criteria are satisfied it does not follow that the plaintiff will be denied an injunction. The conduct of the plaintiff is a highly relevant factor:

> There may also be cases in which, though the four above-mentioned requirements exist, the defendant by his conduct, as for instance, hurrying up his buildings so as if possible to avoid an injunction, or otherwise acting in deliberate disregard to the

plaintiff's rights, has disentitled himself from asking that damages may be assessed in substitution for an injunction.

(AL Smith LJ in *Shelfer's* case at 323). In *Kelsen's* case (16.11.10) MacNair J found it relevant that the defendant had adopted an attitude that it had a right to display the offending advertisement.

Should a plaintiff apply for an interim injunction?

16.11.12 An objection is often made to an application for a permanent injunction that the plaintiff did not apply for an interlocutory order. This is not a conclusive factor (see *Anchor Brewhouse Developments v Berkley House Ltd* 38 BLR 82 and the *dicta* in *Wrotham Park Estate Co Ltd v Parkside Homes Ltd* [1974] 1 WLR 798). On the other hand, where there has not been a prompt application for an interlocutory injunction it is an easy peg from which to hang the discretionary refusal of a final order (see for instance *Bracewell v Appleby* [1975] Ch 408). At the very least the litigant who does not apply for an interlocutory order takes on the risk that the court will be presented with a *fait accompli*, the reality of which the court cannot ignore (see *Jaggard v Sawyer* [1995] 1 WLR 269). A party who stands by for years without any complaint may well find himself being held to have acquiesced in the wrong done to him, his acquiescence being a bar to relief in respect of those matters (*Gafford v Graham* (1998) *The Times*, 1 May).

Pleading

16.11.13 A plaintiff who seeks an injunction makes a false move if his pleading asserts a right to 'an injunction, alternatively damages'. The correct course is to make the claim for an injunction without claiming damages. As Millett LJ put it in *Jaggard's* case (at 285D):

> It would be absurd as well as misleading to insist on the plaintiff including a claim for damages in his writ when he is insisting on his right to an injunction and opposing the defendant's claim that he should be content to receive damages instead.

The discretion is that of the judge and the matter should be put off for an inquiry into the damages if the judge decides that compensation is appropriate.
16.11.14 At the same time it is of course important that if there is a claim for damages for a loss which has already been sustained, then that claim is separately pleaded. Such a claim is for damages for past loss and is entirely different for damages in substitution for an injunction.

16.12 Mandatory injunctions

16.12.1 A mandatory injunction is:

> an order compelling a Defendant to restore things to the condition in which they were at the time when the Plaintiff's complaint was made

(*Isenberg v East India House Estate Co Ltd* 3 De GJ & Sm 263, 46 ER 637, 641). It has been said that the court will only exercise the power to make such an order with 'the greatest possible caution'.

16.12.2 *Isenberg's* case was a right to light case in which various well recognised principles applied today were first clearly set out, notably the fact that the grant of a mandatory order:

> is confined to cases where the injury done to the Plaintiff cannot be estimated and sufficiently compensated by a pecuniary sum.

In *Kelsen v Imperial Tobacco Co* [1957] QB 334 an advertising sign was attached to a wall above the plaintiff tobacconist's shop. It trespassed over the plaintiff's airspace by a very small space. MacNair J held that the injury was small but that it was impossible to estimate the damage in terms of money, because if they were to be calculated at all they would probably be nominal. He granted a mandatory order for the removal of the sign.

16.12.3 In general the court prefers to make an order of compensation and will be alive to the danger that it must not:

> deliver over the Defendants to the Plaintiff bound hand and foot, in order to be made subject to any extortionate demand that he may by possibility make

(Lord Westbury in *Isenberg's* case at 641). Where an injunction is refused the usual form of order will be, if possible, an inquiry into the damages sustained by the plaintiff.

16.12.4 The interests of the wider public are irrelevant. In *Elliott v Islington LBC* [1991] 1 EGLR 167 an ancient horse chestnut was causing a nuisance by extending over the plaintiff's wall. The Court of Appeal decided that the wider amenity value to the public of retaining the tree was not to be preferred to the specific private rights of the plaintiff. Lord Donaldson stated (at 169D):

> The Defendants if they want to have tree here, can go out and buy themselves a mature tree. They can dig a hole in which to put it rather further away from the plaintiff's wall. It is his wall, it is his garden and there is no reason why he should not have full enjoyment of it.

16.13 Mandatory *quia timet* injunctions

16.13.1 A mandatory *quia timet* injunction is an injunction requiring a defendant to take positive steps to avert the threat or likelihood of damage. The leading authority is *Redland Bricks Ltd v Morris* [1970] AC 652 in which the following principles were set out at 665F–666:

(1) There must be a very strong probability on the facts that grave damage will accrue in the future;

(2) The jurisdiction is one to be exercised sparingly;

(3) The plaintiff must demonstrate that damages will not be a sufficient remedy if such damage does happen;

(4) The question of cost is highly relevant (unlike a prohibitory injunction), so that the court will take into account the fact that, in spite of gloomy expert opinion, damage may never occur or that it may occur on a much smaller scale than expected. The defendant will still be able to recover damages at a later stage and it will still be open to him to apply for an injunction if it becomes appropriate;

(5) Where the defendant has sought to steal a march on the plaintiff or otherwise acted wantonly and unreasonably he is more likely to be ordered to do positive works to restore the status quo, even where the expense is out of all proportion to the advantage accruing to the plaintiff;

(6) The defendant must know exactly what he has to do so that he can instruct contractors accordingly.

In the *Redland Bricks* case £35,000 work would have been required to repair damage to land estimated at £1,500–£1,600 per acre. The injunction was discharged.

16.14 Mandatory *quia timet* injunctions at an interlocutory stage

16.14.1 A mandatory *quia timet* injunction will be granted at the interlocutory stage where the court is satisfied to a high degree of assurance that the trial judge would consider that the injunction had been rightly granted (*Locobail International Finance Ltd v Agroexport* [1986] 1 WLR 657). Where, exceptionally, the court cannot be so satisfied, but it is clear that by withholding the injunction there would be a high risk of injustice, the order should in any event be granted (*Rover International Ltd v Canon Film Sales Ltd* [1987] 1 WLR 1597).

16.14.2 In *Daniel v Ferguson* [1891] 2 Ch 27 the defendant discovered that the plaintiff had entered a motion for an injunction to prevent the defendant from erecting a building which the plaintiff claimed interfered with his right to light. The defendant then employed a gang of men to work day and night over the weekend to hurry up the building, which attained a height of 40 feet. The defendant then applied *ex parte* and obtained an order compelling the defendant to tear down the wall. The order was granted 'without regard to what the result of the trial may be'.

16.14.3 In practice a court may grant a mandatory *quia timet* injunction at an interlocutory stage, paying particular regard to the following:

(1) high-handed conduct by the defendant;

(2) the sufficiency of the evidence – would the evidence in fact be any better at trial?;

(3) the question whether the defendant could be adequately compensated at the final hearing.

16.15 Injunctions and trespass to land

Dispossession – final injunctions

16.15.1 Where a plaintiff has been dispossessed by a trespasser, for instance by the erection of a building on his property, the plaintiff is entitled to a final order as of right. *Shelfer v City of London Electric Lighting Co* [1895] 1 Ch 287 with its four exceptions has no application (see 16.11.4 above). Thus in *Harrow LBC v Donohue* [1993] NPC 49 (CA) D had built a garage (for which he had planning consent), half of which was on P's land. The County Court judge ordered damages in lieu. It was said by Waite LJ, overturning the judge's decision that:

> where a defendant has acted in breach of the property rights of the plaintiff by dispossessing him altogether by erection of a building, the court has no alternative but either to grant the plaintiff possession of the building or ordering the demolition of the trespassing part. The court has a discretion as to which of those remedies but no further.

In the County Court, a mandatory order has been made where a 'granny flat' trespassed seven-eighths of an inch over the plaintiff's airspace on the basis that it was a 'festering sore' (*Cudmore-Ray v Pajouheshnia* [1993] CLY 4040).

Interim injunctions

16.15.2 In *Patel v Smith Ltd* [1987] 1 WLR 853 it was held that where title is not in issue, a landowner is *prima facie* entitled to an injunction to restrain a trespass even if the trespass does not harm him. Only if the defendant could show an arguable case that he had a right to do what the plaintiff sought to prevent, should the court go on to consider the balance of convenience, the preservation of the status quo and the adequacy of damages as a remedy.

Environmental Law – Regulatory Bodies and Enforcement

Introduction

A1.1 Environmental law in England and Wales has developed in an ad hoc manner, largely in response to changing conditions and this situation is reflected in the large number of government departments, agencies and bodies who have responsibility for the environmental matters set out in the relevant chapters of this book.

A1.2 Despite the amalgamation of Her Majesty's Inspectorate of Pollution, the National Rivers Authority and Waste Regulation Authorities into the Environment Agency in April 1996, a considerable number of agencies and bodies still remain with responsibility for environmental issues.

Regulatory bodies

The Environment Agency

A1.3 The Environment Agency for England and Wales (EA) was created on 8 August 1995 by the passing of the Environment Act 1995 (EA 1995). It took up its statutory duties on 1 April 1996 and is a non-departmental public body.

A1.4 The EA is organised in three tiers: head office, regions and sub-regions or area head offices. Operational activities are carried out at regional and area level. There are eight regions, each comprising three or four designated areas. Each region has a Regional General Manager. The regional contacts are listed at the end of this appendix.

A1.5 The EA brings together the functions previously carried out by the National Rivers Authority, Her Majesty's Inspectorate of Pollution, local waste regulation authorities and some units of the Department of the Environment dealing with aspects of waste regulation and contaminated land.

A1.6 In addition to the responsibilities carried out by its predecessor bodies, the EA has new responsibilities for other areas such as contaminated land, producer responsibility, national waste strategy and the production of annual environmental reports.

A1.7 The EA 1995 has a new principal aim. This is described in s 4(1) as:

... in discharging its functions so to protect or enhance the environment, taken as a whole, as to make the contribution towards attaining the objective of achieving sustainable development.

A1.8   Section 9 states that the EA in deciding whether to exercise a power must take into account the likely costs and benefits of the exercise or its non-exercise or its exercise in the manner in question.

A1.9   The EA has a written policy statement on enforcement and prosecution (see A1.17 below).

Sewerage/water undertakers

A1.10   The privatised sewerage/water undertakers are responsible for
  (1) the grant of trade effluent discharge consents, enabling dischargers to discharge into public sewers and
  (2) the supply of water.

Their functions and duties are described in the Water Industry Act 1991 (as amended). In turn discharges from sewage treatment works operated by sewerage undertakers into controlled waters are regulated by the EA. Local authorities can be appointed to act as agents for the sewerage/water undertakers.

Local authorities and other bodies

A1.11   Local authorities have a considerable number of environmental responsibilities at all levels, ie county, district, London borough or unitary authorities. They are mainly concerned with emissions into air, general sanitary and public health matters. In addition there are a number of countryside bodies, for example, English Nature, which are responsible for matters relating to nature conservation. In Wales and Scotland the Countryside Commission and the Countryside Councils have responsibility for nature conservation issues.

Enforcement of environmental law

A1.12   Environmental law can be enforced in a variety of ways, for example, through administrative action by issuing or refusing environmental consents and permits, serving notices (eg enforcement, prohibition, variation, suspension and revocation notices), sending warning letters, making site visits, taking samples, requiring clean up works and the appeals procedure.

A1.13   Criminal proceedings can be instigated in the Magistrates' or Crown Court where fines and/or jail sentences may be imposed.

The personal liability of directors and other officers

A1.14   In addition most environmental, health and safety and town planning statutes contain a standard clause stating that a director, manager, secretary or other similar officer may be held personally liable for an offence committed by the company if it has been carried out with their consent, connivance or neglect (see: s 157 of the Environmental Protection Act 1990; s 37 of the Health and Safety at Work Act 1974; s 217 of the Water Resources Act 1991; s 210 of the Water Industry Act 1991; s 331 of the Town and Country Planning Act 1990; s 52 of the Clean Air Act 1993; s 36 of the Radioactive Substances Act 1993; s 7 of the Control of Pollution (Amendment) Act 1989).

Civil liabilities

A1.15 Many of the statutes referred to above also contain clauses imposing civil liability (see: s 73 of the Environmental Protection Act 1990; s 209 of the Water Industry Act 1991; s 208 of the Water Resources Act 1991; s 12 of the Nuclear Installations Act 1965).

Private prosecutions

A1.16 Individuals can instigate private prosecutions in relation to most environmental offences. Prior to the Environmental Information Regulations 1992 a private prosecutor incurred considerable difficulty in obtaining sufficient evidence to mount an effective case. This was because his right of access to environmental information was very limited and in some cases non-existent. A discussion of the 1992 Regulations is set out at Appendix A2.

EA enforcement and prosecution policies

A1.17 On 2 April 1998 the Environment Agency published a consultation paper containing its draft Enforcement and Prosecution Policy. Unlike earlier drafts the Policy does not expressly indicate the audience to which it is directed. Publications of the Interim Draft Enforcement Statement made it clear that the guidance was aimed at warranted agency officers although this does not appear to be stated in this case. Nevertheless the intention is to provide the principles which the EA will adopt when considering enforcement and prosecution action since they are given a wide discretion. In particular it requires warranted officers of the Agency to explain the following to any person on whom enforcement action is contemplated:
    (1) suggested remedial action;
    (2) its intention to take immediate enforcement action;
    (3) right to make representations; and
    (4) right of appeal, if applicable.
A1.18 The Draft Policy places great emphasis on the role of giving informal advice, negotiation and regulation. It recommends that prosecutions should only be used as a last resort after the issue of warnings, cautions, notices, including the suspension of operations and variation of licence conditions. Nevertheless in serious cases, prosecution for breaches of legislation may be the only recourse.

A1.19 It is unclear what status the Draft Policy has and whether failure to follow its advice would have any impact on Court proceedings. It certainly cannot be used as a ground of defence but could be used as a useful negotiating tool when discussing what enforcement actions should be taken and in worst cases referred to in a plea of mitigation. It does not ensure absolute consistency in approach throughout the regional offices of the EA.

The impact of the European Union

A1.20 The European Union, formerly the European Community, is a major driving force in the development of much of the environmental law and policy within Europe and thereby within individual member states.

A1.21 Following the UK's membership of the European Community in 1973, EC Regulations automatically become law in the UK, whereas EC Directives generally do not apply until implementing legislation is passed although there are exceptions.

A1.22 A Directive which has direct effect will apply to a member state as soon as it takes effect. Where this applies it could enable individuals to take proceedings against government bodies and public authorities for any damage that has resulted following the government's failure to implement EU legislation within the prescribed time limit or to correctly implement the provisions of the Directive.

A1.23 Proceedings for failing to implement a directive may be taken against a member state or an emanation of the state and not against a private body or person (see *Foster v British Gas* [1991] 2 CMLR 217). However, on 25 August 1994 the High Court held in *Griffin & Others v South West Water* (unreported) that South West Water Co Plc was an 'emanation of the state' because it provided a public service controlled by a state appointed regulator (OFWAT).

A1.24 A national law, which is contrary to the provisions of a directive, can be declared null and void and a national court can prohibit a government from implementing legislation which is in breach of EU Law (*R v Secretary of State for Transport, Ex Parte, Factortame Limited & Others* [1990] 3 CMLR 375). National laws must be interpreted as far as possible in the light and wording of a directive even if it originated before the adoption of the directive. It is also possible, in certain circumstances, for private citizens to take action against a member state if they have suffered loss as a result of a member state's failure to implement the Directive.

The effect of incorporation of the European Convention on Human Rights

A1.25 The announcement in the Queen's speech in May 1997 that incorporation of the Council of Europe's European Convention on Human Rights is to form part of the government's forthcoming legislative programme is likely to have a direct impact on environmental issues.

A1.26 The Convention is currently not binding on domestic courts (although it is binding on the government in international law) but this is all set to change. Article 1 of Protocol 1 embodies the right to peaceful enjoyment of one's possessions, Article 2 confers a right to life: Article 3 a right not to be subject to degrading treatment and Article 8 guarantees the right to respect for private life, home and correspondence. Although the Convention does not confer a right to a clean environment, the articles referred to above have all been relied on to support various cases on environmental grounds.

Environment Agency regions addresses and contact numbers

North East Region	Southern Region
Rivers House 21 Park Square South Leeds LS1 2QG Tel: (0113) 244 0191	Guildbourne House Chatsworth Road Worthing BN11 1LD Tel: (01903) 832000
Anglian Region	**South-West Region**
Kingfisher House Goldhay Way Orton Goldhay Peterborough PE2 5ZR Tel: (01733) 371811	Manley House Kestrel Way Exeter EX2 7LQ Tel: (01392) 444000
Thames Region	**Midlands Region**
Kings Meadow House Kings Meadow Road Reading RG1 8DQ Tel: (01734) 535000	Sapphire East 550 Shreetsbrook Road Solihull B91 1QT Tel: (0121) 7112424
Welsh Region	**Head Office**
Rivers House/Plas-yr-Afon St Mellons Business Park St Mellons Cardiff CF3 0LT Tel: (012222) 770088	Rio House Waterside Drive Aztec West Almondsbury Bristol BS12 4UD Tel: (01454) 624400

North West Region

Richard Fairclough House
Knutsford Road
Warrington
WA4 1HG
Tel: (01925) 653999

Environmental Law and Access to Information

The Environmental Information Regulations 1992

A2.1 The Environmental Information Regulations 1992 implement EC Directive 90/313. The Directive makes it possible to access environmental information held by public authorities whilst imposing conditions on the availability of such information.

A2.2 The 1992 Regulations replace any restrictions on the access to environmental data which were imposed by statutory provisions which existed prior to the Regulations coming into force. If, however, a pre-existing statutory requirement allows for greater disclosure than under the Regulations, the more generous requirement will prevail (reg 2(1)(c)).

The duty to make information available

A2.3 The central requirement under the 1992 Regulations is that 'a relevant person' who holds any information relating to the environment which is covered by the 1992 Regulations must make that information available to anyone who requests it (reg 3(1)).

The meaning of 'relevant person'

A2.4 The 1992 Regulations divide the term 'relevant person' into two categories. The first category includes all Ministers of the Crown, government departments, local authorities and other persons carrying out public administration at national, regional or local level whose responsibilities relate to the environment.

A2.5 The second category includes any body with public responsibilities for the environment outside the previous category, but which is nevertheless under the 'control' of any body or individual in the first category. The guidance states that 'control' means a relationship constituted by statute, contracts or other means, which either separately or jointly confer the responsibility of directly or indirectly exercising a decisive influence on a body. This would be the case for most public sector bodies, some private bodies with statutory duty and also some government-owned companies.

A2.6 There is still very much a live debate whether bodies such as the water and sewerage undertakers should be regarded as 'bodies with public responsibilities for the environment and under the control of public authorities' and are therefore subject to the same duty of disclosure (see *Griffin & Others v South West Water* (unreported)).

Information relating to the environment

A2.7 For the present purposes information relates to the environment if it falls within one of the three following categories (reg 2(2)(a),(b)):

(1) *Category One*: relates to the state of any water or air, flora or fauna, soil or natural site or other land.

(2) *Category Two*: relates to any activities or measures (including activities giving rise to noise or any other nuisance) which adversely affect anything in the first category or may do so.

(3) *Category Three*: relates to any activities or administrative or other measures (including environmental management programmes) designed to protect any of the environmental media mentioned in the first category.

The meaning of 'information' and 'records'

A2.8 'Information' includes anything contained in any records. 'Records' are defined to include registers, reports and returns as well as computer records and other records kept otherwise than in a document (reg 2(1),(4)). If information is not obtained as a result of a body's environmental responsibilities it is assumed that it is governed by the present 1992 Regulations. The 1992 Regulations also cover information collected before the 1992 Regulations came into force on 31 December 1992. What is not included is the following:

> ... non-existing information that could be created by manipulating existing information ... does not include information destroyed in accordance with established office procedures.

A2.9 The issue what information is covered by the 1992 Regulations was considered in *R v British Coal Corp ex p Ibstock Building Products Ltd* [1995] Env LR 277. It was held the 1992 Regulations covered not only details of possible dumping of munitions in a mine but also the name of the person who had informed British Coal about the dumping.

Procedural limitations

A2.10 The 1992 Regulations require the relevant body or agency to respond to a request for information as soon as possible. The response must not come more than two months after the request was made. If a refusal is made it must be in writing accompanied by reasons (reg 3(2)). The two-month limit can be too long in many cases especially where the information is required urgently.

Charges

A2.11   The relevant body or agency can charge the applicant for the supply of information to cover its reasonable costs. No charge, however, may be made to inspect a public register, but the supply of copies of information can be charged for.

Refusal of access

A2.12   The body or agency can refuse the application if the request is too general or unreasonable (reg 3(3)).

Grounds for refusal of information

A2.13   Generally the body subject to the duty of disclosure must make the information they hold available to every person who requests it (reg 3(1)). The information must be provided to any natural or legal person at his request 'without having to prove an interest'.

A2.14   Nevertheless these are exceptions to the right to information and reg 4 creates two categories of grounds for refusal. First, information that is *capable* of being treated as confidential (in the relevant body's opinion) but only if it relates to matters listed in category 1 in reg 4. Second, information which *must* be kept confidential is described in category 2.

A2.15   There is no right of appeal against a refusal to supply the information and any challenge would have to be made by way of an application for judicial review. However, the costs can be considerable so this remedy is only likely to be sought in the most extreme cases. Alternatively the matter could be referred to a senior level within the relevant organisation who may respond more positively. Where a local authority is involved, a complaint may be made to the local government ombudsman. The information held on the public register can be very technical and a lay person may find it difficult to understand, as there is no objection to provide a non technical summary.

Public registers

A2.16   Most of the environmental statutes contain provisions requiring the relevant body to establish and maintain a public register containing environmental information. A list of the primary environmental registers and where they can be found is set out below. In view of the large and varied number of public registers it is unusual to find in this age of the computer that this information is not held by a central body.

Public registers

Register and information held on it	Statutory bases and other major legislation	Held by

1. **Chemical Release Inventory**
– collates information on chemical releases and radioactive discharges, not site specific
– annual releases of specific substances
– analysis on
  – substance basis
  – geographical basis
  – industrial sector basis
– information comparing actual releases with authorised limits
– quantities and sources of unauthorised discharges
	Pt 1 of the Environmental Protection Act 1990	EA

2. **Waste Management** – registrations claiming exemptions – applications for waste management licences – licences granted – consultees responses on licence applications – variation application and notices – consultees responses on variation applications – notices of revocation or suspension of licences – applications for surrender – surrender application inspections and Certificates of Completion – applications for transfer – appeal documents – convictions of licence holders – offences under EPA Pt II – notices under EPA	ss 64–67, of the Environmental Protection Act 1990; reg 10 of the Waste Management Licensing Regulations 1994	EA

Register and information held on it	Statutory bases and other major legislation	Held by
3. **Waste Carriers** – registered carriers inc business details – registration numbers – dates on which registration takes effect – details of convictions for offences – details of disposal or waste management licences held	Controlled Waste (Registration of Carriers and Seizure of Vehicles) Regs 1991	EA
4. **Integrated Pollution Control (IPC) and Local Authority Air Pollution Control (LAAPC)** – applications for authorisation following request under EPA, Sched 1, para 1(3) – consultees responses – authorisations – variation notices, enforcement notices or prohibition notices – particulars of notices withdrawing a prohibition notice – applications for variations of authorisations – revocations of authorisations – appeal information – details of convictions of offences under the EPA, Part I. – particulars of monitoring by the enforcing authority or by holders – environmental assessment reports published by the enforcing authority – details of directions given to the enforcing authority by the Secretary of State under EPA, Pt 1	s 20 of the Environmental Protection Act 1990 and reg 15 of the Environmental Protection (Applications, Appeals and Registers) Regs 1991	EA & local authorities with Part A prescribed processes, copies of IPC entries for that area held by the local authority for Part B processes the information is held by the relevant local authority

Register and information held on it	Statutory bases and other major legislation	Held by
5. **Water: discharge consents** – water quality objective notices – application for discharge consents, variation consents and formal requests under WRA Sched 10, para 1 – particulars of consents granted – sampling information – taken by EA or former NRA and other persons includes particulars of any analysis – certificates of exemption from register entry – enforcement notices served under s 90B of the WRA – revocations of discharge consents (Sched 10 para 7, WRA) – appeals under s 91 WRA – directions given by Secretary of State Re: Water Pollution – convictions for offences of those holding discharge consents – consent conditions – works notices, appeals and convictions for work notices offences	ss 190 and 209 of the Water Resources Act 1991; Control of Pollution (Applications, Appeals, and Registers) Regulations 1996 (SI No 2971)	EA
6. **Water: trade effluent consents** – trade effluent consents granted under WIA – directions made by sewerage undertake (WIA, Pt IV, Ch III) – trade effluent agreements – notices served by the Secretary of State under s 132 of the WIA	s 196 of the Water Industry Act 1991	Sewerage Undertakers

Register and information held on it	Statutory bases and other major legislation	Held by
7. **Water flow information** – information on flow, level and volume of water in inland waters and ground-water acquirers	s 197 of the Water Resources Act 1991	EA
8. **Water: Abstraction and Impounding Licenses**	s 189 of the Water Resources Act 1991	EA
9. **Water: Drinking Water Quality**	reg 29 of the Water Supply (Water Quality) Regulations 1989	Water Undertaker
10. **Water: Water/Sewerage Undertakers**	s 195 of the Water Industry Act 1991	Director General of Water Services
11. **Radioactive substances** – applications for registration and authorisation under the Act – all documents issued by the EA – records for convictions under Radioactive Substances (Records of Convictions) Regulations 1992 – annual reports of EA monitoring information – monitoring data of operators under s 12(4) of the Radioactive Substances Act	Radioactive Substances Act 1993	EA and local authorities
12. **Health and Safety at Work** – notices served under Health and Safety at Work Act 1974 and Fire Precautions Act 1971	Environmental and Safety Information Act 1988	Health and Safety Executive and Local Authorities

Register and information held on it	Statutory bases and other major legislation	Held by
13. **Town and Country Planning** – applications for planning permission – decisions on planning permission including appeals – details of permission granted on an enforcement appeal	Town and Country Planning (General Development Procedure) Order 1995	Local Planning Authorities and Local Land Charges Register
– mineral planning permission applications – details of established use certificates and certificates of lawful use or development – register of stop and enforcement notices – hazardous substances consent register – details of advertisement consents	Planning (Hazardous Substances) Regs 1992 Town and Country Planning (Control of Advertisements) Regs 1992	Local Planning Authority Local Planning Authority
14. **Local Land Charges** – part 3 Planning Charges – part 4 Miscellaneous Charges – part 10 Listed Building Charges	Land Charges Act 1972 and Local Land Charges Rules 1977	Local Land Charges Register
15. **Genetically Modified Organisms** – importation, marketing etc – directions by Secretary of State – prohibition notices – consent applications and consents and conditions – convictions under s 118 of the Environmental Protection Act 1990	Pt VI of the Environmental Protection Act 1990 and Genetically Modified Organisms (Deliberate Release) Regulations 1992	EA
16. **Noise abatement zones** – details noise level measurements – details measuring equipment – addresses of premises from which noise was emanating	s 63 of the Control of Pollution Act 1974 and reg 64 of the Control of Noise (Measurement and Registers) Regulations 1976	Local Authorities – noise level register

Register and information held on it	Statutory bases and other major legislation	Held by
17. Local Government – includes committee reports – background materials	Local Government (Access to Information) Act 1985 and Environmental Information Regulations 1992	Local Authorities
18. Atmospheric Pollution – Information obtained by authorities under their powers s 79(2) of Control of Pollution Act 1974 (the Act) – appeals under s 81 of the Act – information re: notice provisions s 80 of the Act – directions made by Secretary of State under s 81(2) of the Act	Clean Air Act 1993, Pt V	Local Authorities
19. Litter Control – orders made by litter authority under s 90(3) of the EPA – Litter Control Areas – offences and duties relating to litter – street litter control notices under s 93 of the EPA	Environmental Protection Act 1990 and Litter Control Areas Order 1991	Principal Litter Authorities ie all local authorities but with county councils having limited powers as well (s 95 of the Environmental Protection Act 1990)

A Note on Disputes Involving Trees

A3.1 Most disputes involving trees covered by this book will fall into one of two categories: subsidence claims (arising out of the extraction of water from the soil adjacent to a building) and boundary disputes (generally encroachment of either roots or the overhead canopy). Tree which fall on to the public highway causing a dangerous obstruction represent a third category of claim.

A3.2 This appendix is intended to alert litigants to some other statutory provisions, many of which are relevant whatever the cause of action.

A3.3 As to the three categories of claim, in summary:

(1) Claims for subsidence are properly framed in the law of nuisance, the principles of which are set out in chapter 1. Some caution needs to be taken about the question whether it was reasonably foreseeable by the tree-owner, if a private individual, that the roots of the tree would cause the damage about which the plaintiff claims. Normally some correspondence or verbal exchanges take place between the parties before the relevant cause of action arises.

(2) Boundary dispute actions will generally be claims in trespass although they can be brought in private nuisance. The principles of trespass are set out at chapter 5, whilst help can also be obtained at 1.5 (nuisance by encroachment) and at chapter 6 (boundary disputes, especially 6.7).

(3) Hazards on the highway. These are actions in public nuisance and the principles are set out at chapter 2 (6.7.8–6.7.11 are also relevant).

Subsidence and other claims against local authorities – trees growing in the highway – s 96, of the Highways Act 1980

A3.4 If pursuing the owner of a tree growing in the highway it will be necessary to identify the correct defendant. To do this it will be necessary to refer to s 96(1) of the Highways Act 1980 since this is the section which gives an authority (the highway authority) the power to plant trees and to 'do anything expedient' to maintain trees (see also 6.7).

A3.5 Trees are conventionally divided into three categories:

(1) trees planted prior to dedication or adoption of the highway by the authority 'pre-adoption trees',

    (2) those planted after dedication or adoption of the highway but not planted under statutory powers ('post-adoption trees') and

    (3) those planted under express statutory powers ('planted trees').

A3.6 The relevant question is: does property in the tree vest in the highway authority? Planted trees clearly vest in the highway authority as a result of s 96. *Hurst v Hampshire CC* ((1997) LGR 27, (1997) *The Times*, 26 June) holds that:

    (1) post-adoption trees vest in the authority,

    (2) (*obiter*) pre-adoption trees also vest in the authority.

A3.7 Some note should also be taken of s 96(6) (no tree shall be planted or allowed to remain if it hinders the use of the highway or causes a nuisance or injury to an adjoining owner of property) and s 96(7) (a person damaged by anything done by an authority in pursuance of its s 96 powers is entitled to compensation). The question whether s 96 imposes a statutory duty on an authority has not yet been decided and there is some doubt as to the scope of s 96(7) (see *Hurst's* case).

Statutory control on the felling and lopping etc of trees

A3.8 Anyone intending to fell, lop, top or otherwise deal with a tree should beware of a variety of statutory schemes covering trees:

    (1) *Tree Preservation Orders (ss 197–214 of the Town and Country Planning Act 1990*: A local authority has power in the interest of amenity to make a tree preservation order (TPO) in respect of trees. When the order is made it becomes a criminal offence to carry out any of these activities if permission is not obtained in advance. There is a statutory defence if the action is taken to avoid a nuisance or the causing of damage to property or person. To avoid the risk of appearing in the dock it would be a sensible course to write to the authority telling them what is proposed to be done and inviting the authority to apply on notice of an injunction.

    (2) *Conservation Areas*: In areas of special architectural or historic interest an area may be designated a conservation area. In such an area where a tree is not the subject of a TPO, six weeks' prior notice is required to be given to the local authority of works intended to be carried out.

    (3) *Restrictions on Felling under the Forestry Act 1967*: A felling licence is required by the Forestry Commissioners to fell any growing trees whose diameter exceeds 15 centimetres, unless it is a fruit tree or a tree growing in an orchard, garden, churchyard or public open space (s 9(1)(2) of the Forestry Act 1967). Certain other exceptions apply, and by s 9(4) a licence is not required where felling is required to prevent or abate a nuisance. It is a criminal offence to fell without a licence, the penalty for which is a fine not exceeding level 4 on the standard scale or twice the value of the tree felled.

Access to Neighbouring Land Act 1992

A3.9 Where it is necessary to carry out certain works to trees owned by a landowner and the works cannot be carried out (or would be substantially more difficult to carry out) without being able to enter on to neighbouring land, the County Court has jurisdiction to authorise access on to that neighbouring land for the purpose of effecting those works (Access to Neighbouring Land Act 1992, s 1). By s 1(4)(c) such works include:

> the treatment, cutting back, felling, removal or replacement of any hedge, tree, shrub or other growing thing which is [comprised in, or situate on, the neighbouring land] and which is, or is in danger of becoming, damaged, diseased, dangerous, insecurely rooted or dead.

By s 1(7) of the 1992 Act the County Court also has power to approve an inspection of the neighbouring land for the purposes of ascertaining whether such works may be reasonably necessary.

Standard Scale of Fines in the Magistrates' Courts

A4.1

LEVEL	MAXIMUM FINE (£)
1	200
2	500
3	1,000
4	2,500
5	5,000

Appendix A5

Precedents and Specimen Forms

A selection of representative pleadings is set out in this appendix. They are best used as a guide to identifying the key requirements of an appropriate cause of action or statutory defence and should be used in conjunction with the main text.

Pleading is an art requiring skill and experience. Amendments are unpopular with judges. It is generally far better to commence a case on the correct footing, even if it means front-loading the expenses.

Special damages must be pleaded in full and interest calculations should be set out in detail.

Draft pleadings and specimen forms

A (1) **Private nuisance** – Defendant owner of adjoining land and in occupation – claim for compensation for damage already sustained and an injunction for the removal of the nuisance

(2) **Private nuisance** – Defendant leasehold owner of adjoining land and in occupation – claim for compensation for damage already sustained, economic loss and an injunction

(3) **Private nuisance** – First Defendant absent owner of adjoining land – Second Defendant in occupation – claim against both defendants for compensation for damage already sustained, economic loss and an injunction

(4) **Private nuisance** – failure to abate a dangerous hazard

B (5) **Private nuisance (intangible damage)** – First Plaintiff absent owner of premises, Second Plaintiff tenant of premises – claims for compensation for loss to value of reversion, inconvenience and an injunction

C (6) **Public nuisance (highway)** – economic loss caused by public nuisance – obstruction of the highway

D (7) **Fire** – *Rylands v Fletcher* and negligence

E (8) **Trespass to land** – boundary dispute – claim for an injunction

F (9) **Right to light** – windows poorly lit prior to interference

G (10) **Withdrawal of support** – easement of support by building

H (11) **Animal damage** – animal dangerous by nature and animal with abnormally dangerous characteristics
(12) **Animal damage** – statutory defences: fault of plaintiff and *volenti non fit injuria*

I (13) **Subsidence damage caused by tree roots** – defendant highway authority

J **Specimen Forms**
(14) **RSC Ord 113** – draft summons
(15) **RSC Ord 113** – draft affidavit in support
(16) **RSC Ord 113** – draft order
(17) **RSC Ord 113** – draft writ of possession
(18) **CCR Ord 24** – application for recovery of possession (specimen form)
(19) **CCR Ord 24** – notice to respondent (specimen form)
(20) **Party Wall etc Act 1996** – s 1 – Line of Junction Notice (specimen form)
(21) **Party Wall etc Act 1996** – s 3 – Party Structure Notice (specimen form)
(22) **Party Wall etc Act 1996** – s 6 – Three Metre/Six Metre notice (specimen form)

A. Claim alleging damage to property by private nuisance

A5.1 Defendant owner of adjoining land and in occupation – claim for compensation for damage already sustained and an injunction for the removal of the nuisance

[FULL TITLE]

Statement of Claim

1. The Plaintiff is the freehold owner of premises known as Gilbey Hall, London E38.
2. The Defendant is the freehold owner of premises known as 10 Mariah Street, London E38.
3. The Plaintiff's and the Defendant's premises are separated by a brick wall running north to south on the Plaintiff's land.
4. On about 15ᵗʰ March 1998 in the course of landscaping works carried out by the Defendant's contractors, a mound of topsoil was left piled against the wall on the Defendant's land.
5. Moisture has percolated through the mound and has cause damage to the wall, wearing away both the surface of the brickwork and the lime mortar separating the bricks.
6. Further, if the Defendant is not ordered to remove the mound of topsoil the wall will collapse.
7. In the premises the Plaintiff is entitled to and claims:

(a) damages to compensate the Plaintiff for the damage already sustained to the wall, to be assessed as the amount required to rectify the said damage;

(b) an injunction ordering the Defendant to remove the mound of topsoil.

8. The Plaintiff is further entitled to interest [set out in full]

AND the Plaintiff claims:

(1) damages
(2) an injunction ordering the Defendant to remove the mound of topsoil.
(3) interest pursuant to . . .

A5.2 Defendant leasehold owner of adjoining land and in occupation – claim for compensation for damage already sustained, economic loss and an injunction

[FULL TITLE]

Statement of Claim

1. The Plaintiff is the freehold owner of premises known as Gilbey Hall, London E38 and carries on the trade of market gardening.
2. The Defendant carries on the retail trade of buying and selling motor vehicles and is the occupier of premises known as 10 Mariah Street, London E38 under the terms of a lease dated 15th March 1994.
3. The Plaintiff's and the Defendant's premises are separated by a brick wall running north to south on the Plaintiff's land.
4. On about 15th March 1998 in the course of landscaping works carried out by contractors acting on behalf of the Defendant, a mound of topsoil was left piled against the wall on the Defendant's land.
5. (a) Moisture has percolated through the mound and has caused damage to the wall, wearing away both the surface of the brickwork and the lime mortar separating the bricks.
   (b) Oil and other chemicals used by the Defendant in the course of its trade have percolated through the wall and on to the Plaintiff's land, destroying all the Plaintiff's brassica crops planted in 1997.
6. Further, if the Defendant is not ordered to remove the mound of topsoil the wall will collapse.
7. In the premises the Plaintiff is entitled to and claims:
   (a) damages to compensate the Plaintiff for the damage already sustained to the wall, to be assessed as the amount required to rectify the said damage;
   (b) damages to compensate the Plaintiff for the loss of his brassica crop

Particulars

[set out claim in full, including amount required to remove and destroy crop and loss of profits]

(c) an injunction ordering the Defendant to remove the mound of topsoil.

8. The Plaintiff is further entitled to interest [set out in full]

AND the Plaintiff claims:

(1) damages
(2) an injunction ordering the Defendant to remove the mound of topsoil
(3) interest pursuant to . . .

A5.3 First Defendant absent owner of adjoining land – Second Defendant in occupation – claim against both defendants for compensation for damage already sustained, economic loss and an injunction

[FULL TITLE]

Statement of Claim

1. The Plaintiff is the freehold owner of premises known as Gilbey Hall, London E38 and carries on the trade of market gardening.
2. The First Defendant is the freehold owner of premises known as 10 Mariah Street, London E38 demised to the Second Defendants under the terms of a ten year lease dated 15th June 1996 ('the Mariah Street Premises') and commencing on 10th June 1996.
3. At all material times the Mariah Street Premises have ben used by both the First and Second Defendants for the storage and retail sale of motor vehicles.
4. The Plaintiff's premises and the Mariah Street Premises are separated by a brick wall running north to south on the Plaintiff's land.
5. On about 15th March 1995 in the course of landscaping works carried out by contractors acting on behalf of the First Defendant, a mound of topsoil was left piled against the wall on the First Defendant's land.
6. (a) Moisture has percolated through the mound and has caused damage to the wall, wearing away both the surface of the brickwork and the lime mortar separating the bricks.
   (b) Oil and other chemicals used by the First and Second Defendant in the course of their trade have percolated through the wall and on to the Plaintiff's land, destroying all the Plaintiff's brassica crops planted in 1997.
7. Further, if the First and/or Second Defendant is not ordered to remove the mound of topsoil the wall will collapse.
8. In the premises the Plaintiff is entitled to and claims:
   (a) damages to compensate the Plaintiff for the damage already sustained to the wall, to be assessed as the amount required to rectify the said damage;
   (b) damages to compensate the Plaintiff for the loss of his brassica crop.

Particulars

[set out claim in full, including amount required to remove and
destroy crop and loss of profits]

   (c)   an injunction ordering the First and/or Second Defendant to remove
the mound of topsoil.

9.   In the premises the Plaintiff is entitled to an injunction ordering the
First and/or Second Defendant to move the topsoil and to make good
any damage to the wall and to the Plaintiff's land.

10.   The Plaintiff is further entitled to interest [set out in full]

AND the Plaintiff claims:

(1)   damages
(2)   an injunction ordering the First and/or Second Defendant to remove the
topsoil
(3)   interest pursuant to . . .

A5.4   Failure to abate a dangerous hazard

[FULL TITLE]

Statement of Claim

1.   The Plaintiff:
   (a)   is the owner of land known as 'Spring Common', Shropshire,
   (b)   carries on the trade of grower and wholesale supplier of Christmas
trees grown on the said land.

2.   The Defendant:
   (a)   is the owner of land known as 'The Business', West Stoke, Rutland,
   (b)   carries on business as the owner of a health farm built on his land.

3.   On 15th March 1998 a beech tree on the Defendant's land within 100
metres of the Plaintiff's land spontaneously combusted.

4.   The Defendant knew of the fire occasioned by the tree, the Plaintiff
having advised his agent and professional woodsman John Amelanch-
ier at about 12.00 p.m. of the existence of the fire.

5.   In the premises the Defendant owed a duty to the Plaintiff to take reasonable steps to remove or abate the nuisance occurring on his land.

6.   At about 2.00 p.m. the Defendant chopped down the tree and cut it into
pieces. The remains were left smouldering.

7.   At some time between 3.00 and 4.00 p.m. the fire was rekindled by the
wind and travelled on to the Plaintiff's land, destroying his entire crop
of Christmas Trees.

8.   By reason of the foregoing the Plaintiff has suffered loss and damage.

Particulars

[set out full claim for loss of profits and any other consequential losses]

9. The Plaintiff's loss was caused by the breach of the Defendant's duty set out at paragraph 5 above.

Particulars

The Defendant should have ensured that the fire was extinguished. He employs sufficient staff at his health farm to have been able to take steps to convey water from the lake on his property to the burning tree.

10. By reason of the foregoing the Plaintiff is entitled to and claims (a) damages as set out in paragraph 8 above and (b) interest [set out in full].

AND the Plaintiff claims:

(1) damages
(2) interest . . .

B. Claim alleging interference with enjoyment of property (nuisance by intangible damage)

A5.5 First Plaintiff absent owner of premises, Second Plaintiff tenant of premises; – claims for compensation for loss to value of reversion, inconvenience and an injunction

[FULL TITLE]

Statement of Claim

1. The First Plaintiff is the freehold owner and entitled to the reversion of a dwelling-house known as 'Blossom', Sugar Road, London E38 ('the Premises') which are let to the Second Plaintiff and his family under the terms of a lease dated 15th April 1996.
2. The Defendant is the owner and occupier of a dwelling-house known as 'Pristine', Sugar Road, London E38, adjacent to 'Blossom' and separated by a party wall forming part of both dwelling-houses.
3. Since 15th April 1996, when the Second Plaintiff and his family first moved in to the Premises, the Defendant has interfered with the Second Plaintiff's ordinary use and enjoyment of the Premises as a family home in that the Defendant:

Particulars

(a) has played her tenor saxophone from 2 to 3 o'clock in the morning every morning,
(b) has been seen waiting every evening at 6 o'clock at the end of Sugar Road soliciting passers-by and then taking them to 'Pristine' for the purposes of prostitution,
(c) on or about 10th January 1998 moved two Gloucester Old Spot pigs into an outbuilding on her land at 'Pristine', the permanent smell from which is offensive and intolerable.

4. Despite repeated requests from the First and Second Plaintiffs the Defendant has refused to discontinue the activities referred to in paragraph 3 above.
5. In the premises:
   (a) the First Plaintiff is entitled to and claims (i) damages representing the loss in value to his reversion caused by the Defendant's activities and (ii) an injunction whereby [set out terms in full]
   (b) the Second Plaintiff is entitled to and claims (i) damages for his anxiety and inconvenience to date and (ii) an injunction in the same terms as those set out in paragraph 5(b) above.
6. The Plaintiff is further entitled to interest [set out in full]

AND the Plaintiffs claim:

(1) damages
(2) an order [set out terms in full]
(3) interest pursuant to . . .

C. Claim alleging public nuisance

A5.6 Economic loss caused by public nuisance – obstruction of the highway

[FULL TITLE]

Statement of Claim

1. At all material times:
   (a) the Plaintiff was the leasehold owner of premises known as 'Sans Serif', Gazpacho Road, Islington, London EC4,
   (b) the Plaintiff's premises were located in a cul-de-sac, which could only be approached from Stalin Road, Hackney, London EC4,
   (c) the Plaintiff traded as a motorcycle messenger service and delivery agency. Motorbikes were kept at the Plaintiff's premises and the Plaintiff's employees came to its premises to await orders during the day.
2. On or about 10th February 1998 the Defendant, who trades as a circus entertainer, brought his circus vehicles to a halt in Stalin Road so that it was impossible for the Plaintiff's employees to manoeuvre their motorbikes out of the Plaintiff's premises between the hours of 6 o'clock in the morning and 3 o'clock in the afternoon.
3. By reason of the obstruction of Stalin Road by the Defendant the Plaintiff suffered damage beyond the inconvenience suffered by other users of the highway.

Particulars

[set out calculation of loss of profits]

4. In the premises the Plaintiff is entitled to and claims damages for its loss set out in paragraph 3 above and interest [in full].

AND the Plaintiff claims:

(1) damages
(2) interest . . .

D. Claim alleging damage by fire

A5.7 *Rylands v Fletcher* and negligence

[FULL TITLE]

Statement of Claim

1. The Plaintiff is the owner and occupier of premises known as 'The Yard', London E38.
2. The Defendant is the owner and occupier of adjoining premises known as 'The Hall', London E38.
3. (a) At all material times the Defendant used his premises for the storage of used car and machinery parts which he sold to dealers of used motor vehicles,
   (b) The car and machinery parts were wrapped in waxed paper and kept in wooden boxes in an area of about two acres in total.
4. In the premises the Defendant's use of land was neither a natural nor an ordinary use of the land.
5. The Defendant owed a duty to the Plaintiff (a) to ensure that no fire was ignited amongst the packing cases containing used car and machinery parts and (b) to ensure that the packing cases were kept safe from fire.
6. At about 2.00 p.m. on 10th April 1998 a contractor engaged by the Defendant to clear his premises of rodents started a fire under a packing case. The packing case caught fire and the flames rapidly spread from the Defendant's premises to the Plaintiff's premises, razing them to the ground.
7. Further, the lighting of the fire by the Defendant's contractor was a breach of the duties set out at paragraph 5 above.
8. By reason of the foregoing the Defendant is liable to the Plaintiff in damages.

Particulars

(a) 'Pristine' was a 16th century dwelling of great historic interest which had been in the Plaintiff's family since it was built. It had unrivalled views across the river Thames and was unique. In the premises the Plaintiffs are entitled to claim the cost of rebuilding their property in the sum of . . .

(b) The Plaintiff is entitled to the cost of housing his family in the Luxus hotel from the date of the fire to the date of completion of the works to 'Pristine' in the sum of . . .

(c) The Plaintiff further claims general damages for anxiety and distress.

9.   The Plaintiff is further entitled to and claims interest [set out in full]

AND the Plaintiff claims:

(1) damages
(2) interest . . .

NOTE: this pleading demonstrates (1) the liability of a party in an action for damage caused by fire for the acts of his independent contractors (see 4.3.5) and (2) the requirement that where an application is made for an injunction on the basis *inter alia* that the Plaintiff cannot be compensated in money, damages in lieu of an injunction should not be claimed in the pleading.

E. Claim alleging trespass (boundary dispute)

A5.8   Trespass to land – claim for an injunction

[FULL TITLE]

Statement of Claim

1.   The Plaintiffs are the owners and occupiers of premises known as 1, Haven's Rest, London E38 ('the Plaintiffs' Property').
2.   The Defendants are the owners and occupiers of premises known as 3, Haven's Rest, London E38 ('the Defendant's Property').
3.   In December 1997 a metal fence post was erected by the Defendants at about the northernmost point of the boundary between the Plaintiffs' Property and the Defendants' Property. The post leans over the Defendants' Property so that the top of the post is some 1 m over the Defendants' land. This constitutes a trespass.
4.   At about the southernmost point of the boundary between the Plaintiffs' Property and the Defendants' Property the roots and branches of the vegetation planted on the Defendants' side of the boundary have grown so that they are pushing the ornamental concrete brick-style blocks belonging to the Plaintiffs over the boundary between the two premises. This constitutes a trespass.
5.   (a) At the rear and to the south of the Defendants' property there is a strip of land belonging to the Plaintiffs. The Defendants have appropriated part of this land as their own by placing a wire fence along it and by planting shrubs along a line plotted between points X and Y on the plan at Appendix 1 attached hereto. The wire fence and the shrubs were put in place in about March 1998.

   (b) The land annexed by the Plaintiffs in this way is located between points X, Y and Z on the said plan. The distance between X and Y is about 12 mm. The distance between Y and Z is about 40 mm. X is marked at the site by a wooden post. The appropriation of the land in this way constitutes a trespass.

6. The Plaintiffs are entitled to and claim an order that the Defendants:
   (a) remove the fence post referred to in paragraph 3 above,
   (b) remove the concrete brick-style blocks referred to in paragraph 4 above or trim the roots and branches of the aforesaid vegetation, alternatively remove the said vegetation,
   (c) remove the fence and shrubs referred to in paragraph 5 above.

7. The Plaintiffs are further entitled and claim a declaration that they are the owners of the land located between points X, Y and Z on the plan annexed hereto as Appendix 1.

8. Further, the Plaintiffs claim damages together with interest thereon [set out in full]

AND the Plaintiffs claim:

(1) damages and interest pursuant to . . .
(2) an order that the Defendants:
   (a) remove the fence post referred to in paragraph 3 above,
   (b) remove the concrete brick-style blocks referred to in paragraph 4 above or trim the roots and branches of the aforesaid vegetation, alternatively remove the said vegetation,
   (c) remove the fence and shrubs referred to in paragraph 5 above.
(3) a declaration that they are the owners of the land located between points X, Y and Z on the plan annexed hereto as Appendix 1.

F. Interference with right to light

A5.9   Windows poorly lit prior to interference

[FULL TITLE]

Statement of Claim

1. The Plaintiffs are the freehold owners of a dwelling house known as 'Boron', Rutland.

2. The Defendants are the freehold owners of a dwelling house known as 'Xenon', Rutland.

3. (a) The Plaintiffs' house has windows facing a garage built on the Defendants' property. The windows provide light to the Plaintiffs' hallway and have been in place for a period of at least 20 years prior to 1st March 1998.
   (b) The Plaintiffs are entitled by prescription under s 3 of the Prescription Act 1832 to the use and enjoyment of light to and from the hallway windows of the Plaintiffs' house.

4. On 1st March 1998 the Defendants commenced building works to their garage, which they have extended by some 600 mm in height.
5. The extension of the garage referred to in paragraph 4 above was completed on about 12th March 1998 and has substantially interfered with the amount of light enjoyed by the Plaintiffs in their hallway. The hallway is a significant and important part of the Plaintiff's house and did not enjoy good lighting even before the Defendants commenced their building works.
6. By reason of the foregoing the Plaintiffs are entitled to and claim:
   (a) damages for their past loss together with interest thereon [set out in full]
   (b) an injunction compelling the Defendants to remove the extension to their garage.

AND the Plaintiffs claim:

(1) damages and interest thereon pursuant to . . .
(2) an order compelling the Defendants to remove the extension to their garage.

G. Claim alleging withdrawal of support

A5.10 Easement of support by building

[FULL TITLE]

Statement of Claim

1. The Plaintiff is the owner and occupier of a dwelling-house known as 21, Rose Lane, London E38 ('the Plaintiff's property').
2. The Defendant is the owner and occupier of a dwelling-house known as 22, Rose Lane, London E38 ('the Defendant's property), which is adjacent to the Plaintiff's property.
3. (a) The Plaintiff's and Defendant's properties, which were both constructed in 1955, were separated by a party wall.
   (b) The party wall had enjoyed support from the front and rear walls of the Defendant's property.
   (c) In the premises and by reason of s 2 of the Prescription Act 1832, the Plaintiff had acquired an easement of support provided by the front and rear walls of the Defendant's property;
   (d) The Plaintiff will further rely on the doctrine of lost modern grant.
4. On 26th March 1998 the Defendant withdrew the support provided to the party wall by demolishing his property. The party wall fell down and caused damage to the Plaintiff's property.

Particulars

[set out nature of damage in full]

5. By reason of the foregoing the Plaintiff is entitled to and claims damage.

Particulars

[set out claim in full, providing details of cost and repair/diminution
in value as appropriate and consequential expenses,
for instance hire of other premises]

6. The Plaintiff is further entitled to and claims interest on such sums as may be awarded to him [set out in full].

AND the Plaintiff claims:

(1) damages
(2) interest pursuant to . . .

H. Claim alleging damage by animal

A5.11 Animal dangerous by nature and animal with abnormally dangerous characteristics

[FULL TITLE]

Statement of Claim

1. At all material times:
    (a) the Plaintiff was the owner and occupier of 'Cunninghams', London E38
    (b) the Defendant was the owner and occupier of 'The Ark', London E38, a property adjacent to 'Cunninghams'
    (c) 'Hunter' was a labrador dog looked after by Justin Green, a boy under the age of 16 years,
    (d) Justin Green is a member of the Defendant's household.
2. On 26th March 1998 the Plaintiff was walking towards the driveway leading to Cunninghams when she was bitten on the left leg by Hunter, who was being directed by Justin Green to the rear of the Defendant's motor vehicle.
3. The Plaintiff then ran on to the driveway of Cunninghams where she was bitten on the right ankle by an adder which had escaped from the Defendant's garage where it was kept by Justin Green.
4. The Defendant is the keeper of Hunter and of the adder by reason of s 6 of the Animals Act 1971.
5. The Plaintiff sustained injuries. The skin of her left leg was punctured in several places, requiring sutures. The right ankle was punctured and became extremely swollen. Particulars are set out in the report of Dr Smith dated 1st May 1998 annexed hereto.
6. By reason of the fact that the adder is an animal which belongs to a dangerous species within the meaning of s 2(1) of the Animals Act

1971, the Defendant is liable to the Plaintiff for the damage to her right foot.

7. Further and by reason of s 2(2) of the Animals Act 1971 the Defendant is liable to the Plaintiff for the damage to her left leg because:

(a) the bite to the leg was of a kind which Hunter, unless restrained, was likely to cause, and

(b) the likelihood of the bite was due to a characteristic not normally found in dogs, namely that Hunter reacts ferociously to passers-by when he is being directed into the Defendant's motor car because he considers that the passers-by are encroaching on to his territory, and

(c) the Defendant knew that Hunter reacts to passers-by in this manner since there have been previous incidents when Hunter has lunged at the Plaintiff whilst being directed by Justin Green and the Defendant into the Defendant's motor vehicle.

8. In the premises the Plaintiff claims damages from the Defendant together with interest [set out in full]

AND the Plaintiff claims:

(1) damages
(2) interest

A5.12 Statutory defences: fault of plaintiff and *volenti non fit injuria*

1. Paragraphs 1, 2 and 3 of the Particulars of Claim are admitted.
2. As to paragraphs 4 and 5:

(a) it is denied that the Defendant is liable to the Plaintiff;

(b) the injuries sustained by the Plaintiff were wholly due to the fault of the Plaintiff within the meaning of s 5(1) of the Animals Act 1998 since the Plaintiff approached, knowing that she was likely to be attacked by Hunter and that the adder had escaped from the garage in which it was kept. Further or in the alternative the Plaintiff voluntarily accepted the risk of the injuries she suffered within the meaning of s 5(2) of the 1971 Act.

I. Claim for subsidence damage caused by tree roots

A5.13 Claim for subsidence damage caused by tree roots – defendant highway authority

[FULL TITLE]

Statement of Claim

1. (a) At all material times the Plaintiff has been the owner and occupier of premises known as 21 Slough Street, London E38 ('the Premises').

(b) The premises are adjacent to the highway known as Slough Street ('the Highway').

2. The Defendant is the highway authority with a duty to maintain the Highway.

3. In about 1993 the Defendant planted a tree of the Rosaceae family just outside the Plaintiff's premises approximately in line with the boundary between the Plaintiff's premises and 22 Slough Street.

4. (a) Property in the aforesaid tree vests in the Defendant.
   (b) The Defendant is under a duty by reason of s 96(1) of the Highways Act 1980 ('the 1980 Act') to maintain the tree.

5. By s 96(6) of the 1980 Act the Defendant is prohibited by statute from allowing the tree to remain where it was planted if it causes a nuisance or is injurious to an owner or occupier of premises adjacent to the Highway.

6. (a) The tree has caused damage by subsidence to the front of the Plaintiff's premises due to moisture extraction of the clay soil by its roots. This type of damage was foreseeable by the Defendant from the time when it was planted.
   (b) The nature and extent of the damage can be seen in the four photographs annexed hereto. A sketch map also annexed hereto is intended to assist in identifying the retaining wall.

7. The Defendant is liable to the Plaintiff:
   (a) for the nuisance the Plaintiff has suffered both at common law and under s 96(6) of the 1980 Act, particulars of which are set out in paragraph 5 above,
   (b) for the breach of duty owed by the Defendant to the Plaintiff under s 96(1) of the 1980 Act. The Defendant failed to maintain the tree by failing (i) to prune or lop, or adequately to prune or lop the branches of the tree, (ii) to prune or adequately to prune the roots.

8. If not removed the tree will cause further substantial damage to the Plaintiff's property.

9. The Plaintiff's claim is for:
   (a) damages together with interest [set out in full]. The Plaintiff is entitled to the reimbursement of the expense to which he will be put in order to reinstate the front area of the premises, the stairs and the retaining wall. The cost will be determined as of the date of the assessment of damages by the court
   (b) an injunction compelling the Defendant to remove or adequately to maintain the tree

AND the Plaintiff claims:

(1) damages together with interest thereon pursuant to . . .
(2) interest . . .

J. Specimen forms

A5.14 O.113r2   Draft Originating Summons – based on Prescribed
                          Form 11A

199 – [A] No [ ]

IN THE HIGH COURT OF JUSTICE
[QUEEN'S BENCH]/[CHANCERY] DIVISION

IN THE MATTER of LAND SITUATE AT [address of land]
and
IN THE MATTER of ORDER 113

B E T W E E N

ABC PLC

Plaintiff

–and–
[insert names of any known occupiers] (1)
[PERSONS UNKNOWN] (2)

Defendants

TO [Named defendants] [and] [Persons Unknown] occupying the land situate
at [address sufficient to identify the land]

LET all parties concerned attend before Master   in Chambers in
Room   , Royal Courts of Justice, Strand, London WC2A 2LL on   day,
the   day of January 199[ ] at   o'clock in the   noon on the hearing
of an application by the Plaintiff for an order that it recovers possession of the
land situate at [address sufficient to identify the land] [shown edged in red on
the H M Land Registry office copy of the filed plan dated [   ] in respect
of title number [   ] attached hereto], on the grounds that it is entitled to
possession and that the persons in occupation are in occupation without licence
or consent.

(No application is made by this Summons in respect of residential premises).

DATED the   day of   199

THIS SUMMONS was taken out by [Firm name, address, reference and telephone
number] Solicitors for the Plaintiff whose address is [insert address of Plaintiff]

NOTE Any person occupying the premises who is not named as a Defendant by this
Summons may apply to the Court personally or by Counsel or Solicitor to be joined as a
Defendant. If a person occupying the premises does not attend personally or by Counsel

or Solicitor at the time and place above-mentioned, such Order will be made as the Court may think just and expedient.

A5.15 Draft affidavit in support

Sworn   199–
Deponent: [Name] [Number]
Filed: Plaintiff

199– – A No

IN THE HIGH COURT OF JUSTICE
[QUEEN'S BENCH]/[CHANCERY] DIVISION

IN THE MATTER of LAND SITUATE AT [description of land as in Originating Summons]
and
IN THE MATTER of ORDER 113

B E T W E E N

ABC PLC

Plaintiff

–and–
[Named Defendants] (1)
PERSONS UNKNOWN (2)

Defendants

I, [Name, address and description of deponent] **MAKE OATH** and say as follows:

1. I am [description of Plaintiff's representative] and am authorised to make this affidavit on the Plaintiff's behalf. I make this affidavit from matters within my own knowledge save as otherwise expressly appears. Where any of the matters to which I depose are not within my own knowledge they are to the best of my information and belief true.

2. The Plaintiff is the freehold owner [insert details of the Plaintiff's interest in the land] of land situate at [as in Originating Summons] ('the Land') which is the subject of these proceedings. [I] have the responsibility of [managing] the Land for the Plaintiff.

3. The Land is shown edged [colour of edging] on the H M Land Registry office copy filed plan dated [   ] and forms part of the title number [   ]. There is now produced and shown to me marked 'ACD 1' a true cop of this filed plan. The Land comprises [   ]. There are no residential dwellings upon the Land.

4. On [   ] it was brought to my attention by [   ] that the defendants had taken up occupation of the Land. Neither the Plaintiff nor its authorised agents have given anybody licence or consent to occupy the Land. [Insert any other details of the circumstances in which the land has been occupied without licence or consent].

5. I visited the Land myself on [   ] and noted that present on the Land were [details]. I do not know the names of any of the persons who are in wrongful occupation of the Land [who are not named in the Originating Summons].

6. I respectfully submit to the Court that in the circumstances an Order for Possession should be made in favour of the Plaintiff against the Defendants in respect of the Land and that such Order should be made forthwith on the grounds that the Plaintiff is alone entitled to possession and that the Defendants have occupied the Land and continue to occupy it without any licence or consent of the Plaintiff or anyone authorised to grant such a licence or consent on its behalf.

SWORN at   )
)
in the   )
)
this   day of   199   )

Before me,

A Solicitor Empowered to Administer Oaths
This affidavit is filed on behalf of the Plaintiff

A5.16 O.113r6   Draft Order for Possession – based on Prescribed
                            Form 42A

                                                          199 –[ ] No [ ]

IN THE HIGH COURT OF JUSTICE
[QUEEN'S BENCH]/[CHANCERY] DIVISION
MASTER [name] MASTER IN CHAMBERS

IN THE MATTER of LAND SITUATE AT [description as in Originating Summons]
and
IN THE MATTER of ORDER 113

BETWEEN
                            ABC PLC
                                                            Plaintiff
                            –and–
                    [NAMED DEFENDANTS] (1)
                    [PERSONS UNKNOWN] (2)
                                                            Defendants

UPON HEARING the solicitors for the Plaintiff

AND READING the affidavit of [deponent of supporting affidavit] filed this
day of   199

IT IS ORDERED that the Plaintiff, ABC PLC, do recover possession of the
land described in the Originating Summons as the land situate at [description
as in the Originating Summons] and the Defendants do give possession of the
said land forthwith.

DATED the   day of   199

A5.17   O.113r7   Draft Writ of Possession – based on Prescribed
                          Form 66A

                                                199 –[A] No [ ]

IN THE HIGH COURT OF JUSTICE
[QUEEN'S BENCH]/[CHANCERY] DIVISION

IN THE MATTER of LAND SITUATE AT [description as in Originating
Summons]

and

IN THE MATTER of ORDER 113

B E T W E E N

ABC PLC

                                                          Plaintiff

–and–
[Named Defendants] (1)
PERSONS UNKNOWN (2)

                                                          Defendants

ELIZABETH THE SECOND, by the Grace of God, of the United Kingdom
of Great Britain and Northern Ireland, and of Our other Realms and Territories,
Queen, Head of the Commonwealth, Defender of the Faith.

TO the Sheriff of [County] Greeting:

WHEREAS in the above-named action it was on the [   ] day of [   ]
199 ordered that the Plaintiff, ABC PLC, do recover possession of the land
situate at [description as in Originating Summons]

WE COMMAND you that you enter the said land and cause ABC PLC to
have possession of it.

AND WE ALSO COMMAND you that you endorse on this Writ immediately after execution thereof a statement of the manner in which you have executed it and send a copy of the statement to ABC PLC

WITNESS, The Right Honourable Lord Irvine of Lairg Lord High Chancellor of Great Britain, the [   ] day of [   ] 199

This Writ was issued by [Solicitors name, address and reference] Solicitors for the Plaintiff, ABC PLC whose address is [address]

The Defendants are presently residing on the land situate at [address] and the Plaintiff has no other address[es] for them.

A5.18   Originating application for possession under Order 24 (Form N312, Order 24, rule 1)

In the   County Court
                                                                     Case No.

In the matter of

                                                                     Solicitor's ref
Between   Applicant
                                                                     Solicitor's ref
and   Respondent[1]

I
of[2]

hereby applies to the Court for an order for recovery of possession of[3]

on the ground that [he] [she] is entitled to possession and that the person[s] in occupation of the premises [is] [are] in occupation without licence or consent.

[The person[s] in occupation who [is] [are] intended to be served individually with this application [is] [are]:-[4]

[There are other persons in occupation whose names are not known to the Applicant]][5]

[It is not intended to serve any person individually with notice of this application.][6]

The Applicant's address for service is:-[7]

Dated
Signed
[Solicitor for the] Applicant
of

Address all communication to the Chief Clerk **and quote the above case number**

The Court Office at

is open from 10 a.m. to 4 p.m. Mondays to Fridays

Notes
1. If any whose name is known to the Applicant.
2. State address and occupation of Applicant.
3. Here describe the property.
4. Here state the name of every person in occupation whose name the Applicant knows. (Delete if it is not intended to serve any person individually with notice of this application.)
5. Delete if not applicable.
6. Delete if the Applicant intends to serve the occupants individually.
7. Here state the Applicant's address for service.

A5.19 N.8(1) Notice to Respondent when a Matter will be heard under Order 24

Order 3, Rule 4(4)(b), Order 24, rule 4

[Royal Arms]   Seal
[*General Title – Form N.8*]

To [named respondent and] every [other] person in occupation of

A sealed copy of an originating application to the Court is attached.
This matter will be heard by this Court at
          on   at   o'clock when you should attend.

Failure to attend may result in an order being made in your absence.

TAKE NOTICE. Any person occupying the premises mentioned in the application, who is not named as a respondent, may apply to the Court to be joined as a Respondent.

DATED

A5.20 Line of Junction Notice, Party Wall etc. Act, 1996 Section 1
To: (Adjoining Owner)
of

*I/We   (Building Owner)
of

as owner(s) of the land known as

which adjoins your land known as

HEREBY SERVE YOU WITH NOTICE THAT
*Under Section 1 (2), subject to your written consent
it is intended to build on the line of junction of the said lands a *party
wall/party fence wall.
*Under Section 1 (5)
it is intended to build on the line of junction of the said lands a wall wholly
on *my/our own land.
*Under Section 1 (6)
it is intended to place projecting footings and foundations on your land
at *my/our expense.
*Under Section 7 (4) *is/is not proposed to employ special foundations, which
would require your written consent.

The proposed works *as shown on the accompanying drawings/are:

It is intended to commence works *after one month/on the
or earlier by agreement.
In the event of matters arising for settlement *I/we would appoint as *my/our
surveyor Mr
of (address)

Signed
*Authorised to sign
on behalf of   (date)

*Delete as appropriate

A5.21   Party Structure Notice, Party Wall etc. Act, 1996 Section 3

To: (Adjoining Owner)
of

*I/We   (Building Owner)
of

as owner(s) of

which adjoins your premises known as

HEREBY SERVE YOU WITH NOTICE THAT, IN ACCORDANCE WITH
*MY/OUR RIGHTS:
Under Section 2 Sub-section (2), paragraphs . . .
and with reference to the **party structure/party fence wall** separating the
above premises, it is intended to carry out the works detailed below after the
expiration of **two months** from service of this notice

The proposed works are:

It is intended to commence works *as soon as notice has run/on the
or earlier by agreement.
Under Section 5, if you do not consent to the works within 14 days you are
deemed to have dissented and a difference is deemed to have arisen. In such
case Section 10 of the Act requires that both parties should concur in the
appointment of a surveyor or should each appoint one surveyor and in those
circumstances
*I/we would appoint Mr
of (address)

Signed   (date)
*Authorised to sign
on behalf of   (Building Owner)

*Delete as appropriate

A5.22   Three Metre/Six Metre Notice, Party Wall etc. Act, 1996 Section 6

To: (Adjoining Owner)
of

*I/We   (Building Owner)
of

as owner(s) of

which adjoins your premises known as

HEREBY SERVE YOU WITH NOTICE THAT
*Under Section 6(1)
it is intended to build within 3 metres of your building and to a lower level than the bottom of your foundations, by carrying out the works detailed below, after the expiration of one month from the service of this notice
or
*Under Section 6(2)
it is intended to build within 6 metres of your building and to a depth as defined in the Act, by carrying out the works detailed below, after the expiration of one month from the service of this notice.

IT *IS/IS NOT PROPOSED TO UNDERPIN OR OTHERWISE STRENGTHEN IN ORDER TO SAFEGUARD THE FOUNDATIONS OF YOUR BUILDING.

The accompanying plans and sections show the site and the excavation depth proposed.
The intended works are:

It is intended to commence works *as soon as notice has run/on the
or earlier by agreement.

Under Section 6(7), if you do not consent to the works within 14 days you are deemed to have dissented and a difference is deemed to have arisen. In such case Section 10 of the Act requires that both parties should concur in the appointment of a surveyor or should each appoint one surveyor and in those circumstances

*I/we would appoint Mr
of (address)

Signed   (date)
*Authorised to sign
on behalf of   (Building Owner)

*Delete as appropriate

Index

All references are to paragraph number. Those prefixed A refer to the Appendices.

Abatement notices—
appeals, 3.12.2, 3.13, 12.2.11
costs, 3.13.4, 3.13.7
defences, 3.14.4–9, 12.2.14–16
emissions, 13.2.9
further breach, 3.14.12
grounds of appeal, 3.13.3
industrial premises, 3.14.3
information requirements, 3.12.3–4
issue, 3.12.1–4
lack of funds, 3.14.6
local authority powers and duties, 3.12–14,
   12.2.10
loudspeakers, 12.6.6
no lawful requirement, 3.14.7
noise, 3.13.3, 3.14.9, 12.6.6
offences, 3.14, 12.2.12, 12.2.13
penalties, 3.14.2–3
persons responsible, 3.12.5–6
powers of magistrates, 3.13.4
removal or interference, 12.2.12
service, 3.12.5–8, 12.2.7–9
suspension, 3.13.5–6
use of force, 12.2.10
vehicles, machinery or equipment, 3.13.3,
   12.2.6–16
Abatement orders—
costs, 3.18.7
defences, 3.18.9
litter, 14.8.13, 14.8.15
local authority powers and duties,
   3.18.10–11
locus standi, 3.18.2–4
offences, 3.18.8
penalties, 3.18.5, 3.18.8, 14.8.15
persons aggrieved, 3.18.3–4, 3.18.6
persons responsible, 3.18.6
powers of magistrates, 3.18.3, 3.18.5,
   3.18.7, 3.18.8, 3.18.10–11
prejudice to health, 3.18.3
private proceedings, 3.18
procedure, 3.18.5–7
Accumulations—
contaminated land, 3.6.1
dangerous escapes, 4.2.7–9
liabilities, 4.2.9

Act of God—
dangerous escapes, 4.2.14
fire, 4.3.6
floods, 4.2.14
hazards, 1.11.3
Adverse possession—
burden of proof, 5.7.5
Crown property, 5.7.3
equitable interests, 5.7.12
evidence, 5.7.6
foreshore, 5.7.3
future plans of owner, 5.7.7
land registration, 5.7.11
leases, 5.7.9–10
limitations, 5.7.3
overriding interests, 5.7.11
police powers, 5.5.14
rights of possessor, 5.7.11
series of trespassers, 5.7.4
tenants, 5.7.8
title, 5.7.1–2, 5.7.11
trespass, 5.7, 16.15.1
Agency, private nuisance, 1.9.16, 1.9.17
Agriculture—
air pollution, 13.7
burning crop residues, 13.7.2
livestock *see* Animals
Air pollution—
agriculture, 13.7
air quality monitoring, 13.8
dark smoke *see* Smoke
domestic property, 3.4.1
dust, 3.5, 13.4.1, 13.4.5–6
emissions—
   abatement notices, 13.2.9
   appeals, 13.2.6
   authorisations, 13.2.1–5, 13.2.8, 13.2.9
   chimneys *see* Chimneys
   enforcement, 13.2
   enforcement notices, 13.2.4, 13.2.6–7
   furnaces *see* Furnaces
   injunctions, 13.2.8
   integrated pollution control, 13.2.1
   local authority powers and duties, 3.3.4,
      3.5.2, 13.2.1, 13.2.3
   motor vehicles, 13.6

Air pollution—*contd*
  emissions—*contd*
    offences, 13.2.7
    prescribed limits, 13.4.5–6
    prohibition notices, 13.2.4–7
    smoke control areas, 13.5
    statutory nuisances, 3.3.4, 3.4.1, 3.5.2,
      13.2.2
  fumes, 3.4.1
  gases, 3.4.1
  grit, 13.4.1, 13.4.5–6
  industrial premises, 3.5, 13.2, 13.3, 13.4
  odours *see* Smell
  overview, 13.1
  smoke *see* Smoke
Aircraft—
  certificates, 12.9.3
  international law, 12.9.4
  noise, 12.9
  noise abatement, 12.9.2
  trespass, 5.2.5, 12.9.1
Airspace—
  advertising signs, 16.12.2
  aircraft, 5.2.5, 12.9.1
  flats, 5.3.2
  light *see* Right to light
  overhanging cranes, 16.11.6
Ancient monuments, trespass, 5.6.4, 5.6.13–17
Ancillary relief, occupation orders, 10.5.18
Animals—
  abnormal characteristics—
    circumstances, 9.3.15
    experts, 9.3.16
    failure to restrain, 9.3.12
    identity, 9.3.17
    knowledge, 9.3.1, 9.3.9–10, 9.3.18–20
    likelihood of damage, 9.3.11–15
    scienter rule, 9.3.1
    statutory requirements, 9.3.9–10
  camels, 9.3.6
  causes of action, 9.2, A5.11
  common land, 9.5.4
  contributory negligence, 9.3.22
  dangerous—
    by nature, 9.3.1, 9.3.5–8
    characteristics, 9.3.1, 9.3.9–20
    escapes, 9.2.3
  defences, 9.3.21–5
  defendants, 9.3.2–4
  dogs—
    appeals, 9.6.6
    bred for fighting, 9.7
    burden of proof, 9.7.4, 9.9.1
    complaints, 9.6.1–4
    dangerous, 9.2.1, 9.6–7
    destruction, 9.6.1, 9.6.5, 9.7.5–7
    faeces, 14.8.9
    guard dogs, 9.3.23, 9.3.25, 9.6.13, 11.3.7

Animals—*contd*
  dogs—*contd*
    identity, 9.3.17, 9.6.3
    information requirements, 9.6.2–3
    injury to livestock, 9.8
    local authority powers and duties,
      9.10.1–4
    locus standi, 9.6.4
    London, 9.6.11–12
    muzzles, 9.6.7, 9.6.11–12, 9.7.2
    normal characteristics, 9.3.15
    notice of shooting, 9.9.2
    offences, 9.6.5, 9.6.8–13, 9.7, 9.10.4
    out of control, 9.6.8
    owners, 9.6.3
    penalties, 9.6.1, 9.6.5, 9.6.7, 9.6.8,
      9.6.11, 9.6.12, 9.7.2, 9.7.6–7, 9.8.3–4
    personal injuries, 9.6.8
    pit bull terriers, 9.7
    police powers, 9.10.1–4
    prohibited places, 9.6.10
    registration, 9.7.3
    remedies, 9.6.1, 9.6.5–7
    road traffic, 9.2.1, 9.5.1
    seizure, 9.10.2
    shooting, 9.9.1, 9.9.2
    statute law, 9.6–10
    strays, 9.10
    strict liability, 9.6.9
    unmuzzled, 9.6.11–12, 9.7.2
    volenti non fit injuria, 9.3.23–4, 11.3.7,
      A5.12
  duty of care, 9.2.1, 9.4.11, 9.5.1
  elephants, 9.3.6, 9.3.7
  employees, 9.3.24
  evidence, 9.3.8, 9.3.16–20
  fences, 6.3.9, 9.4.6, 9.5.2–4
  foreseeable damage, 9.2.1, 9.2.2
  highways, 9.4.4, 9.5
  horses—
    foreseeable damage, 9.2.2
    normal characteristics, 9.3.14
    road traffic accidents, 9.2.1
  keepers, 9.3.2–3, 9.3.18–20
  liabilities—
    common law, 9.2
    statute law, 9.3, 9.8
    strict, 9.3.5
  livestock—
    definition, 9.4.3
    injured by dogs, 9.8
    protection from worrying, 9.9
    trespass, 9.4, 9.8.4
    worrying defined, 9.8.3
  lost, 9.3.3
  negligence, 9.1.1, 9.2.1–2
  normal characteristics, 9.3.14–15
  overview, 9.1

Animals—*contd*
  pigs, smell, 1.6.22, 1.6.25, 16.3.1
  private nuisance, 1.6.22, 1.6.25, 9.2.3
  sheep, 16.4.1
  statutory nuisances, 3.7.1
  trespass—
    causes of action, 9.2.3
    compensation, 9.4.4, 9.4.5, 9.4.7
    damage to goods, 9.4.5
    defendants, 9.4.2
    detention, 9.4.7–9
    duty of care, 9.4.11
    expenses, 9.4.9, 9.4.10
    fences, 9.4.6
    from highway, 9.4.4
    livestock worried, 9.8.4
    notices, 9.4.7
    plaintiffs, 9.4.4–6
    right of sale, 9.4.8
    statute law, 9.4
  trespasser injured, 9.3.25
  voluntary risk, 9.3.23–4, 11.3.7
Appeals—
  abatement notices, 3.12.2, 3.13, 12.2.11
  dangerous dogs, 9.6.6
  enforcement notices, 13.2.6
  Land Registry, 6.12.26
  noise abatement zones, 12.13.6
  party wall disputes, 7.5.1, 7.5.12
  prohibition notices, 13.2.6
  refuse removal, 14.6.4, 14.6.6
  s 60 notices, 12.3.6–9
  s 61 consents, 12.3.16
  sewage connection, 15.5.10
Arrest—
  contempt of court, 10.5.28
  non-molestation orders, 10.5.23–7
  occupation orders, 10.5.23–7
  police powers, 10.5.25
  restraining orders, 10.4.9
  warrants, 10.4.9, 10.5.26–7
Assault—
  clinical injury, 10.2.8, 10.3.1
  offences, 10.2.3, 10.2.6–12
  penalties, 10.2.6
  psychiatric injury, 10.2.3, 10.2.7–8,
    10.2.11, 10.2.12
  telephone calls, 10.2.3, 10.2.11, 10.2.12
  trespass to the person, 10.3.2

Best practical means—
  burden of proof, 3.14.4
  defences, 3.14.4, 12.2.14–15
  definition, 3.14.4
Boats, premises, 3.2.3
Boundaries—
  cadastral system, 6.2.4
  civil, 6.5.5

Boundaries—*contd*
  communication with neighbours, 6.2.7
  conveyances, 6.6.4, 6.6.5, 6.12.1, 6.12.3,
    6.12.7
  disputes, A5.8
  ditches *see* Ditches
  Electronic Distance Measurement, 6.2.3,
    6.12.34
  evidence, 6.12
  fences *see* Fences
  foreshore, 6.10
  General Boundaries Rule, 6.2.3
  hedges *see* Hedges
  highways, 6.8
  lakes, 6.11.5
  measurement, 6.2.2–3, 6.12.34
  new boundaries, 6.2
  overview, 6.1
  party walls *see* Party walls
  photographs *see* Photographs
  presumption of ownership, 6.3.2, 6.3.4,
    6.3.7, 6.6.2–6, 6.8.1–4, 6.11.1
  railways, 6.9
  rivers, 6.6.4, 6.11.1–4, 6.11.6
  surveyors, 6.12.33–4
  T-marks, 6.3.8, 6.6.3, 6.12.9
  tidal rivers, 6.11.6
  tidal waters, 6.10.1
  trees *see* Trees
  walls, 6.4.1
Building Research Establishment, 8.4.23
Buildings—
  absent owners, 1.9.10, 2.3.18
  acts of trespassers, 1.10.11
  Building Regulations, 12.4
  construction *see* Construction works
  danger to highway, 2.3.15–18
  industrial *see* Industrial premises
  interests in land, 1.3.4
  light *see* Right to light
  noise control, 12.4
  party walls *see* Party walls
  physical damage, 1.2.7, 1.6.16, 8.3.7–8
  repairs, 1.9.11–12, 8.3.7
  right of support, 8.3.5–8
  trespass, 16.5.3, 16.15.1
  see also Premises
Burden of proof—
  adverse possession, 5.7.5
  best practical means, 3.14.4
  building and demolition operations, 1.6.29
  dangerous dogs, 9.7.4
  dark smoke, 13.3.4
Burglar alarms—
  codes of practice, 12.7.1, 12.7.2
  local authority powers and duties, 12.7.2,
    12.7.3
  London, 12.7.2

Burglar alarms—*contd*
noise, 12.7
police powers, 12.7.2, 12.7.3
powers of entry, 12.7.2

Cadastral system, boundaries, 6.2.4
Caravan sites—
dangerous objects, 4.2.6
human rights, 5.4.10
licences, 5.4.10
local authority powers and duties, 5.4.9,
5.4.11
planning permission, 5.4.10
unauthorised campers, 5.6.18–21
Causes of action—
animals, 9.2, A5.11
damage *see* Damage
injunctions, 10.3.6–7
private nuisance, 1.1.1, 1.2, 1.3–8
right to light, 8.4.1, 8.4.3
trees, A3.1–7
Charging orders, local authority powers and
duties, 3.15.2
Chartered Institute of Environmental Health,
12.10.10, 12.10.18
Chattels *see* Goods
Chimneys—
dark smoke, 13.3.4
definition, 13.3.6
emission rates, 13.4.5–6
furnaces, 13.4.5, 13.4.8, 13.5.2
height, 13.4.8
Codes of practice—
agricultural air pollution, 13.7.1
burglar alarms, 12.7.1, 12.7.2
controlled waste, 14.4.3
litter, 14.8.17–18
loudspeakers, 12.6.6
s 60 notices, 12.3.5
Compensation—
party walls, 7.3.6, 8.3.17
straying livestock, 9.4.4, 9.4.5, 9.4.7
Complaints—
construction works, 12.3.3
dangerous dogs, 9.6.1–4
entertainment licences, 12.11.2
information requirements, 3.11.5, 12.3.3
investigation, 3.11.2, 3.11.6, 3.11.8,
3.14.10, 12.10.4–7
litter, 14.8.13, 14.8.14, 14.8.19–22
local authority powers and duties, 3.11.4–8,
3.14.10, 3.18.1, 12.3.3
loudspeakers, 12.6.6
night time noise, 12.10.4–7
procedure, 3.11.4
Consequential loss—
loss of profit, 16.4.2
private nuisance, 1.3.4, 1.7.6, 16.4.2

Consequential loss—*contd*
sheep, 16.4.1
trespass, 16.5.2
Construction works—
burden of proof, 1.6.29
complaints, 12.3.3
conflict of interest, 1.6.27–8
liabilities, 1.9.17, 2.3.16–17, 12.3.12
local authority powers and duties, 12.3
noise, 12.3
party walls, 8.3.11–17
private nuisance, 1.6.27–9, 1.9.17
right to light, 8.4.17
s 60 notices—
appeals, 12.3.6–9
codes of practice, 12.3.5
grounds of appeal, 12.3.7–8
injunctions, 12.3.10, 12.3.13
magistrates courts, 12.3.6
offences, 12.3.11
penalties, 12.3.11
personal liabilities, 12.3.12
service, 12.3.4–5
suspension, 12.3.9
s 61 consents—
appeals, 12.3.16
applications, 12.3.14
offences, 12.3.15
penalties, 12.3.15
types controlled, 12.3.2
see also Buildings
Contaminated land—
accumulation or deposit, 3.6.1
statutory nuisances, 3.2.2
Contempt of court—
non-molestation orders, 10.5.28
occupation orders, 10.5.28
restraining orders, 10.4.10
Contractors—
building and demolition operations,
1.6.27–9, 1.9.17, 2.3.16–7
highways, 2.3.12
liabilities—
fire, 4.1.3, 4.3.5
private nuisance, 1.9.4, 1.9.17, 1.11.4,
2.3.17
public nuisance, 2.3.17
see also Construction works
Contributory negligence—
animals, 9.3.22
highways, 2.3.20
private nuisance, 1.11.10
trespass, 5.5.5
see also Negligence
Conveyances—
boundaries, 6.6.4, 6.6.5, 6.12.1, 6.12.3,
6.12.7
easements, 8.2.5

Costs—
abatement notices, 3.13.4, 3.13.7
abatement orders, 3.18.7
environmental information, A2.11
injunctions, 16.11.1
nominal damages, 16.9.4, 16.9.5
party wall disputes, 7.5.10–13
recovery by local authority, 3.15.2–3
Covenants—
fences, 6.3.9
party walls, 7.2.7
Cranes, airspace, 16.11.6
Criminal law—
offences see Offences
penalties see Penalties
police see Police powers
Crown property—
adverse possession, 5.7.3
foreshore, 6.10.2, 6.11.3
litter, 14.8.6
noise, 3.8.2, 3.9.2
sea bed, 6.10.3
smoke, 3.3.2, 13.3.3
tidal rivers, 6.11.3
Curtilage, definition, 6.12.5

Damage—
after proceedings issued, 16.8
annoyance, inconvenience and distress, 16.3
balancing exercise, 1.3.3
buildings, 1.2.7, 1.4, 1.6.16
consequential loss, 1.3.4, 1.7.6, 16.4, 16.5.2
continuing, 16.7
culpability, 1.3.2–3
damages in lieu of injunction, 16.11.4,
16.11.7–9, 16.12.3
dangerous escapes, 4.1.1–2, 4.2.11–12
diminution in value—
date of assessment, 16.2.6
examples, 16.2.3
no intention to reinstate, 16.2.5
reinstatement value, 16.2.1, 16.2.4,
16.2.6
restitutio in integrum, 16.2.2
distress damage feasant, 11.3.5
encroachment, 1.5
evidence, 1.4
fire see Fire
foreseeable see Foreseeable damage
goods, 1.1.3, 1.3.4, 1.7.1, 4.2.12
intangible see Intangible interference
measure of damages, 16.2
nominal see Nominal damages
not private nuisance, 1.1.3, 1.3.4, 1.7
overview, 1.3
party walls, repairs and works, 7.3.8–10
personal see Personal injuries
physical, 1.4

Damage—contd
pleadings, 16.11.12
proof, 1.1.3, 1.3.1
public nuisance, 2.2.3, 2.3.8
real property, 1.1.3, 1.1.5, 1.3–8
reversionary interests, 1.2.4, 1.2.7, 1.6.7,
A5.5
right of support, 8.3.2, 8.3.4
right to light, 16.6
special, 2.2.3, 2.3.8
trespass, 5.5.2–4, 16.5
unlawful waste deposit, 14.3.7
weather, 7.3.7, 7.6.2
Dangerous escapes—
accumulations, 4.2.7–9
act of God, 4.2.14
animals, 9.2.3
damage, 4.1.1–2, 4.2.11–12
dangerous substances, 4.2.6
defences, 4.2.14–16
electricity supply, 4.2.8
escape, 4.2.10
explosions, 4.2.6, 4.2.10, 4.2.15
fire see Fire
foreseeable consequences, 4.1.2, 4.2.13,
9.2.3
goods damaged, 4.2.12
malicious acts, 4.2.15
natural or ordinary user, 4.2.3, 4.2.4, 4.2.5
negligence, 4.2.16
non-natural user, 4.1.1, 4.2.3
overview, 4.1
personal injuries, 4.2.11
private nuisance, 1.7.8
Rylands v Fletcher, 4.1–2
strict liability, 4.1.2, 4.2
trespass, 4.2.15–16
Dangerous hazards see Hazards
Dark smoke see Smoke
Deeds—
conveyances, 6.6.4, 6.6.5, 6.12.1, 6.12.3,
6.12.7
evidence, 6.12.3–10
original documents, 6.12.10
parcel clause, 6.12.4–6
plans, 6.12.4, 6.12.7
pre-registration, 6.12.16–17
T-marks, 6.3.8, 6.6.3, 6.12.9
Defences—
abatement notices, 3.14.4–9, 12.2.14–16
abatement orders, 3.18.9
act of God, 1.11.3
best practical means, 3.14.4, 12.2.14–15
coming to a nuisance, 1.11.5–6
contractors, 1.11.4
contributory negligence, 1.11.10, 2.3.20,
9.3.22
dangerous escapes, 4.2.14–16

Defences—*contd*
    dark smoke, 13.3.11–12
    failure to maintain highway, 2.3.20
    fire damage, 4.3.6–7
    night time noise, 12.10.12
    noise, 3.14.9
    private nuisance, 1.11
    statutory immunity, 1.11.7–9
    statutory nuisances, 12.3.10
    trespass, 1.11.2, 9.3.25
    unfit drinking water, 15.4.9
    vehicles, machinery or equipment, 3.14.8
    volenti non fit injuria, 9.3.23–4, 11.3.6–7,
        A5.12
    waste management, 14.3.4
Defendants—
    animals, 9.3.2–4
    dark smoke, 13.3.4
    hazards, 1.10.5–10, 1.11.2, 1.11.3
    injunctions, 16.11.11, 16.14.2, 16.14.3
    possession proceedings, 5.5.20, 5.5.22,
        5.5.28
    private nuisance, 1.9
    straying livestock, 9.4.2
    trespass, 5.4
Demolition, private nuisance, 1.6.27–9
Demonstrations—
    hunt saboteurs, 5.6.10
    noise, 3.9.2, 12.2.4
Director General for Water Services, 15.5.3
Directors—
    personal liabilities, 12.3.12, A1.14
    s 60 notices, 12.3.12
Disclosure—
    environment *see* Environmental information
    trade secrets, 3.14.11
Displaced residential occupiers—
    definition, 5.5.10
    trespass, 5.5.9, 5.5.10, 5.5.14
Dispossession *see* Adverse possession
Ditches—
    access to neighbouring land, 6.6.6
    conveyances, 6.6.4, 6.6.5
    filled in, 6.12.28
    hedge and ditch presumption, 6.6.2–6, 6.8.4
    maintenance, 6.6.6
    not original boundary, 6.6.4
    Ordnance Survey, 6.6.4–5, 6.12.14
    rebuttal of presumption, 6.6.4, 6.8.4
    streams, 6.6.4
    T-marks, 6.6.3
    see also Boundaries
Dogs *see* Animals
Domestic property—
    air pollution, 3.4.1
    boundaries *see* Boundaries
    curtilage, 6.12.5
    dark smoke, 13.3.4

Domestic property—*contd*
    dwelling house, 6.12.5
    furnaces, 13.4.1
    leases, 5.4.4
    noise—
        insulation, 12.9.2, 12.15.1
        night time, 12.10
        seizure of equipment, 3.8.4, 3.11.3,
            12.10.20–2
    occupation, 5.5.9–14
    possession, 5.4.4
    power to enter, 3.8.4, 12.7.2, 12.10.20–2
    repossession *see* Possession
        proceedings
    semi-detached houses, 7.2.5
    sewers, 15.5.7
    water supply, 15.4.19
Dust—
    air pollution, 3.5, 13.4.1, 13.4.5–6
    statutory nuisances, 3.5
Duty of care—
    animals, 9.2.1, 9.4.11, 9.5.1
    negligence *see* Negligence
    occupiers, 5.8.1–4
    tenants, 5.8.2
    waste management, 14.4
Dwellings—
    definition, 6.12.5, 12.10.4
    see also Domestic property

Easements—
    acquisition—
        conveyances, 8.2.5
        express grant, 8.2.4
        grant of land, 8.2.5
        implied grant, 8.2.5
        manner, 8.2.3
        protection against, 8.4.25–6
        reservation, 8.2.4
    assignment, 8.2.2
    characteristics, 8.2.2
    dominant and servient tenement—
        freeholds, 8.2.9
        leases, 8.2.14
        presumption, 8.2.6
        requirements, 8.2.2
        right of support, 8.3.6–7
        right to light, 8.4.11, 8.4.12, 8.4.26
        uninterrupted use, 8.2.12
    establishing existence, 8.2
    highways, 2.3.2–3
    light *see* Right to light
    prescription *see* Prescription
    presumption, 8.2.6–7, 8.2.11
    support *see* Right of support
    walls, 8.3.10
Effluent—
    industrial, 3.5, 15.5.20, A1.10

Effluent—*contd*
  see also Sewage
Ejectment, trespass, 5.2.3
Electricity supply, dangerous escapes, 4.2.8
Electronic Distance Measurement, boundaries, 6.2.3, 6.12.34
Emissions *see* Air pollution
Employees—
  keepers of animals, 9.3.24
  victims of harassment, 10.1.5
  water pollution, 15.2.6
Employers—
  economic torts, 10.3.3
  liabilities, 1.9.17, 2.3.12, 2.3.17
Encroachment—
  private nuisance, 1.5
  trees—
    highways, 6.7.10
    roots, 6.7.6
Enforcement—
  duty to keep land clear of litter, 14.8.13–15
  emissions, 13.2
  environmental law, A1.12–19
  notices, 13.2.4, 13.2.6–7
  offences *see* Offences
  penalties *see* Penalties
  police *see* Police
  statutory nuisances *see* Local authority powers and duties
  waste management, 14.2
  see also Environment Agency
Entertainment—
  complaints, 12.11.2
  karaoke, 12.11.3
  licenced events, 5.6.6, 5.6.9, 12.11
  local authority powers and duties, 5.6.6, 5.6.9, 12.11.2
  London, 12.11.1
  music and dancing, 12.11.1, 12.11.3
  music defined, 5.6.6
  police powers, 5.6.9
  raves *see* Raves
  theatre, 12.11.3
Environment—
  air pollution *see* Air pollution
  character of locality, 1.6.17–20, 1.6.24, 8.4.3
  conservation, A1.11
  contamination *see* Contaminated land
  dangerous hazards *see* Hazards
  escapes *see* Dangerous escapes
  European law, A1.20–4
  human rights, A1.25–6
  integrated pollution control, 3.3.4, 12.12.1, 13.2.1
  liabilities, A1.14, A1.15
  noise *see* Noise
  nuisance *see* Statutory nuisances

Environment—*contd*
  odours *see* Smells
  private prosecutions, A1.16
  sewage *see* Sewage
  smoke *see* Smoke
  waste *see* Waste management
  water *see* Water
Environment Agency—
  aims, A1.7
  controlled waters, 15.2.2, 15.3, A1.10
  creation, A1.2, A1.3
  disposal and return of property, 14.5.5–7
  enforcement and prosecution policies, A1.17–19
  exercise of powers, A1.7
  functions, A1.5, A1.6
  integrated pollution control, 3.3.4, 12.12.1, 13.2.1, 13.2.3
  loudspeakers, 12.6.2
  obstruction, 14.5.4
  organisation, A1.4
  rivers, 6.11.4
  seizure, 14.5.3–7
  waste management, 14.2.1, 14.3.2, 14.4.2, 14.5.3–8
Environmental health officers, 3.11.3, 3.11.4, 3.11.6–7, 3.18.1, 5.6.9, 13.2.3, 13.3.2
Environmental information—
  categories, A2.7
  confidentiality, A2.14
  costs, A2.11
  European law, A2.1
  information defined, A2.8
  judicial review, A2.15
  mines, A2.9
  pre-existing disclosure, A2.2
  records defined, A2.8
  refusal of access, A2.12–15
  registers, A2.15, A2.16
  relevant persons, A2.3–6
  time, A2.10
Equipment—
  forfeiture, 12.10.25–7
  meaning, 12.2.3
  noise, 3.9, 3.13.3, 3.14.8, 12.2.2–3, 12.6, 12.10.20–7
  retention, 12.10.23–4
  seizure, 3.8.4, 3.9.2, 3.11.3, 5.6.8, 12.10.20–2
  VME *see* Vehicles, machinery or equipment
Erosion—
  foreshore, 6.10.2
  right of support, 8.3.4
  rivers, 6.11.3
Escapes *see* Dangerous escapes
European law—
  drinking water, 15.4.4
  environment, A1.20–4

European law—*contd*
  environmental information, A2.1
  impact on UK, A1.20–4
  motor vehicles, 12.8.1
Eviction, reasonable force, 5.5.6, 5.5.7
Evidence—
  adverse possession, 5.7.6
  best evidence rule, 6.12.2
  boundaries, 6.12
  clinical injury, 10.2.8, 10.3.1
  conveyances, 6.6.4, 6.6.5, 6.12.1, 6.12.3,
    6.12.7
  damage, 1.4
  dangerous animals, 9.3.8, 9.3.16–20
  deeds, 6.12.3–10
  existing features, 6.12.27–8
  experts *see* Expert witnesses
  fly-tipping, 14.5.8
  hearsay, 6.12.2
  litter complaints, 14.8.21
  night time noise, 12.10.13–14
  noise, 3.8.3, 12.1.2
  photographs *see* Photographs
  proof of title, 5.5.22, 5.5.26
  tribunal rules, 6.12.2
Excavations, party walls, 7.1.5, 7.1.7
Exclusion zones—
  injunctions, 10.3.10–11
  occupation orders, 10.5.18
Expert witnesses—
  civil procedure, 6.12.29–32
  dangerous animals, 9.3.8, 9.3.16
  photographs, 6.12.23
  practice statement, 6.12.30
  psychiatric injury, 10.2.8
  surveyors, 6.12.30, 6.12.33–4
Explosions, dangerous escapes, 4.2.6, 4.2.10,
  4.2.15

Family law—
  Law Commission recommendations, 10.5.5
  molestation, meaning, 10.5.6
  non-molestation orders—
    applicants, 10.5.10
    arrest, 10.5.23
    children, 10.5.9, 10.5.10
    contempt of court, 10.5.28
    effect, 10.5.12
    ex parte applications, 10.5.21, 10.5.24
    grounds, 10.5.11
    jurisdiction, 10.5.7
    persons protected, 10.5.8–9
    remand, 10.5.27
    undertakings, 10.5.22
  objectionable conduct, 10.5.1, 10.5.2
  occupation orders—
    ancillary relief, 10.5.18
    arrest, 10.5.23

Family law—*contd*
  occupation orders—*contd*
    cohabitation, 10.5.16–17
    contempt of court, 10.5.28
    ex parte applications, 10.5.21, 10.5.24
    exclusion zones, 10.5.18
    grounds, 10.5.14
    jurisdiction, 10.5.13
    no existing right of occupation, 10.5.15
    remand, 10.5.27
    time limits, 10.5.18
    undertakings, 10.5.22
Fault *see* Contributory negligence
Fees—
  possession proceedings, 5.5.21
  wheel clamping release, 11.3.10
Fences—
  animals, 6.3.9, 9.4.6, 9.5.2–4
  covenants, 6.3.9
  duty, 6.3.9
  erection, 6.3.2–5
  highway authorities, 6.8.5–6
  highways, 6.3.9, 6.3.10, 6.8.5–6
  larch lap, 6.3.4
  liabilities, 6.3.10
  mines, 6.3.9
  party fences, 6.3.6
  posts—
    concrete, 6.3.5
    holes, 6.3.2
    position, 6.3.3
  presumption of ownership, 6.3.2, 6.3.4,
    6.3.7, 6.8.4
  quarries, 6.3.9
  railways, 6.3.9, 6.9.5, 6.9.9
  repairs, 6.3.8
  replacement, 6.3.5
  T-marks, 6.3.8
  types, 6.3.1
  see also Boundaries
Fire—
  accidents, 4.3.8
  act of God, 4.3.6
  burning crop residues, 13.7.2
  contractors, 4.1.3, 4.3.5
  defences, 4.3.6–7
  furnaces *see* Furnaces
  knowledge, 4.3.4
  London, 4.3.8–10
  negligence, 4.1.3, 4.3.2, 4.3.4, 4.3.9
  party walls, 7.1.2
  Rylands v Fletcher, 4.3.2, 4.3.3, 4.3.10,
    A5.7
  strict liability, 4.1.3, 4.3.1
  trespass, 4.3.7
Fixed penalties—
  dog faeces, 14.8.9
  litter, 14.8.7–8

Fixed penalties—*contd*
  motor vehicles, 13.6.3
  night time noise, 12.10.17–18
  see also Penalties
Floods, act of God, 4.2.14
Floor partitions, party walls, 7.2.13–15
Fly-tipping *see* Waste management
Footpaths—
  aerial photographs, 6.12.25
  trespass, 5.2.4
Foreseeable damage—
  animals, 9.2.1, 9.2.2
  dangerous escapes, 4.1.2, 4.2.13
  encroachment by tree roots, 6.7.6
  horses, 9.2.2
  liabilities, 1.8.2
  private nuisance, 1.1.4, 1.3.2, 1.8
  public nuisance, 2.3.9
  standard, 1.8.3
Foreshore—
  adverse possession, 5.7.3
  boundaries, 6.10
  Crown property, 6.10.2, 6.11.3
  dog faeces, 14.8.9
  erosion, 6.10.2
  litter, 14.8.25
  moving freehold, 6.10.2
  Ordnance Survey, 6.10.1
  prescription, 6.10.2
  sewage discharge, 1.2.5
  tidal waters, 6.10.1
Foundations, party walls, 7.3.5, 7.3.6, 7.4.4
Fumes, definition, 3.4.1
Furnaces—
  arrestment plant, 13.4.7
  chimneys, 13.4.5, 13.4.8, 13.5.2
  domestic, 13.4.1
  emissions, 13.4.1–6
  grit and dust, 13.4.1, 13.4.5–6
  local authority powers and duties, 13.4.3
  new installations, 13.4.2–5
  offences, 13.4.3, 13.5.2
  requirements, 13.4.3–5

Gases, definition, 3.4.1
General Boundaries Rule, 6.2.3
Goods—
  damage—
    dangerous escapes, 4.2.12
    private nuisance, 1.1.3, 1.3.4, 1.7.1
    straying livestock, 9.4.5
  distress damage feasant, 11.3.5
  interference, 10.3.2, 11.3.6, 11.3.10
  possession proceedings, 5.5.39
  trespass, 5.1.4, 10.3.2
Grit, air pollution, 13.4.1, 13.4.5–6
Gypsies—
  definition, 5.4.7

Gypsies—*contd*
  squatters, 5.4.8
  trespass, 5.4.7–11
  unauthorised campers, 5.6.18–21

Harassment—
  assault *see* Assault
  civil remedies, 10.3–4
  course of conduct, 10.4.2, 10.4.3
  definition, 10.4.2
  fear of violence, 10.2.9–11, 10.2.23
  indecent or obscene letters, 10.2.21
  injunctions, 10.1.6, 10.3.1, 10.4
  intentionally causing emotional distress,
    10.3.2
  intimidation, 10.3.3
  matrimonial *see* Family law
  nuisance calls *see* Telephone calls
  offences, 10.1.7–8, 10.2, 10.3.1, 10.4.1,
    10.4.5
  overview, 10.1
  penalties, 10.4.5
  private nuisance, 10.3.4
  psychological damage *see* Psychiatric
    injury
  public order offences, 10.2.22–5
  restraint *see* Restraining orders
  second offences, 10.2.2
  stalkers *see* Stalkers
  threatening to kill, 10.2.18
  torts, 10.3.4, 10.4.8
  trespass, 10.3.2
  unlawful interference, 10.3.3
  victims—
    employees, 10.1.5
    employers, 10.3.3
    ex partners *see* Family law
    merits of criminal proceedings, 10.1.7,
      10.2.2, 10.3.1
Hazards—
  act of God, 1.11.3
  adoption, 1.10.9, 1.11.2
  defendants duty, 1.10.6–8, 1.11.2
  escapes *see* Dangerous escapes
  highway obstruction, 2.3.13
  knowledge, 1.10.10, 1.11.2
  latent defects, 1.10.12
  natural, 1.10.5–7, 1.11.3, 2.3.13
  private nuisance, 1.7.8, 1.9.17, 1.10, 1.11.2,
    1.11.3, 8.3.7, A5.4
Health, prejudice *see* Prejudice to health
Hedges—
  beech, 6.5.2
  civil boundaries, 6.5.5
  cupressocyparis leylandii, 6.5.1
  hedge and ditch presumption, 6.6.2–6, 6.8.4
  modern, control, 6.5.1–2
  new planting, 6.5.3

Hedges—*contd*
  Ordnance Survey, 6.5.5–6, 6.6.4–5,
    6.12.12–14
  replaced with fence, 6.8.5–6
  returned clippings, 6.5.8, 6.7.4
  rootline, 6.5.5–6, 6.6.4, 6.12.12, 6.12.14
  rural, 6.5.4, 6.5.7
  T-marks, 6.6.3
  width, 6.5.5–7
  see also Boundaries, Trees
Highways—
  access and egress, 2.3.10
  boundaries, 6.8
  building and demolition operations,
    2.3.16–17
  cleaning, 14.7.12
  contractors, 2.3.12
  contributory negligence, 2.3.20
  dangerous buildings, 2.3.15–18
  easements, 2.3.2–3
  failure to maintain, 2.3.19–20
  fences, 6.3.9, 6.3.10, 6.8.5–6
  footpaths *see* Footpaths
  highway authorities, 6.7.8–11, 6.8.5–6
  litter, 14.8.12
  nature of nuisance, 2.3.1
  noise, 3.9, 12.2, 12.3.1
  obstruction, 2.3.6, 2.3.11–13, A5.6
  personal injuries, 2.3.8
  public nuisance, 2.3
  reasonable user, 2.3.4–7
  refuse removal, 14.6.11–14
  road traffic accidents, 9.2.1, 9.5.1
  roadworks, 12.3.1
  straying livestock, 9.4.4, 9.5
  streets *see* Streets
  subsoil—
    successors in title, 6.8.3
    usque ad medium filum viae, 6.8.2
  trees *see* Trees
HM Land Registry *see* Land Registry
Horses *see* Animals
Human rights—
  caravan sites, 5.4.10
  environment, A1.25–6
Hunt saboteurs, trespass, 5.6.10

Industrial disputes, noise, 12.2.4
Industrial premises—
  abatement notices, 3.14.3
  air pollution, 3.5, 13.2, 13.3, 13.4
  definition, 3.14.3
  delicate trades, 1.6.16
  noise abatement *see* Noise abatement zones
  trade effluent, 3.5, 15.5.20, A1.10
Information requirements—
  abatement notices, 3.12.3–4
  complaints, 3.11.5, 12.3.3

Information requirements—*contd*
  dangerous dogs, 9.6.2–3
  environment *see* Environmental information
  party walls, 7.4.2–4, 8.3.15
Injunctions—
  1997 Act, 10.4
  causes of action, 10.3.6–7
  contempt of court, 10.4.10, 10.5.28
  costs, 16.11.1
  damages in lieu, 16.11.4, 16.11.7–9,
    16.12.3
  defendants conduct, 16.11.11, 16.14.2,
    16.14.3
  emissions, 13.2.8
  exclusion zones, 10.3.10–11
  final, 16.15.1
  harassment, 10.1.6, 10.3.1, 10.4
  interlocutory, 10.3.5–9, 10.4, 16.11.12,
    16.15.2
  jurisdiction, 10.3.5–7
  local authority powers and duties, 3.16.1
  mandatory—
    compensation preferred, 16.12.3
    defendants conduct, 16.14.2, 16.14.3
    definition, 16.12.1
    interlocutory stage, 16.14
    quia timet, 16.3, 16.4
    small injury, 16.12.2
    threat of damage, 16.13.1
    wider public interest, 16.12.4
  matrimonial *see* Family law
  oppression, 16.11.10
  pleadings, 16.11.13
  presumption in favour, 16.11.3
  relief refused, 16.10.1
  restraint *see* Restraining orders
  s 60 notices, 12.3.10, 12.3.13
  small injury, 16.11.5–6, 16.12.2
  special circumstances, 16.11.4
  stalkers, 10.3.8, 10.3.10–11
  telephone calls, 10.3.8, 10.3.10
  threat of injury, 16.11.19, 16.13.1
  trespass, 16.15
  undertakings, 10.3.9
  value of infringement, 16.11.7–9
  wrongful interference with goods, 10.3.2
Intangible interference—
  building and demolition operations,
    1.6.27–9, 1.9.17
  character of locality, 1.6.17–20, 1.6.24
  comfortable enjoyment, 1.6.5, 1.6.9, 1.6.10
  cumulative effect, 1.6.19–20
  delicate trades, 1.6.16
  examples, 1.6.6
  flexible test, 1.6.8
  hypersensitive plaintiffs, 1.6.16
  inconvenience minimised, 1.6.23
  intermittent, 1.6.26

Intangible interference—*contd*
  landlords, 1.6.7
  malice, 1.6.11–14
  material damage distinguished, 1.6.2
  noise, 1.6.11–14, 1.6.20, 1.6.21, 1.11.5
  planning permission, 1.6.24–5
  real property, 1.1.3, 1.6
  reasonable activities, 1.6.3, 1.6.4, 1.6.15
  reasonable user, 1.6.21–3
  smell, 1.6.22, 1.6.25
  standard of tolerance, 1.6.9, 1.6.10, 1.6.15,
    1.6.28
  temporary, 1.6.26
  trivial, 1.6.10
Integrated pollution control—
  emissions, 13.2.1, 13.2.3
  noise, 12.12.1
  smoke, 3.3.4
  see also Air pollution
Interests in land—
  buildings, 1.3.4
  plaintiffs, 1.1.2, 1.1.5, 1.2.1–7
  public nuisance, 2.2.4
  reversionary, 1.2.4, 1.2.7, 1.6.7, 1.9.13,
    A5.5
  rights and privileges, 1.2.6, 8.3.2–4
  scope of protection, 5.2.4
Interference—
  goods, 10.3.2, 11.3.6, 11.3.10
  intangible *see* Intangible interference
  unlawful, 10.3.3
Interim orders—
  interlocutory injunctions, 10.3.5–9, 10.4,
    16.11.12, 16.15.2
  possession proceedings, 5.5.34–40
Intimidation, harassment, 10.3.3

Judicial review—
  environmental information, A2.15
  local authority powers and duties, 3.17.1,
    14.8.23

Keepers—
  animals, 9.3.2–3, 9.3.18–20
  definition, 9.3.2
  knowledge, 9.3.18–20
  see also Animals
Knowledge—
  absent owners, 1.9.10
  acts of trespassers, 1.10.11, 1.11.2, 4.2.16
  actual, 1.9.6, 1.9.7
  constructive, 1.9.6, 1.9.8
  controlled waste, 14.3.1, 14.3.2
  danger to trespassers, 5.8.3
  dangerous animals, 9.3.1, 9.3.9–10,
    9.3.18–20
  fire, 4.3.4
  hazards, 1.10.10, 1.11.2

Knowledge—*contd*
  landlords, 1.9.16
  latent defects, 1.9.9, 1.9.6
  private nuisance *see* Private nuisance
  tree damage, 6.7.5
  water pollution, 15.2.3, 15.2.7–8
  wheel clamping, 11.3.2, 11.3.8

Lakes, boundaries, 6.11.5
Land—
  contaminated *see* Contaminated land
  definition, 5.6.10, 6.12.5
  nuisance *see* Private nuisance
  occupation *see* Occupation
  premises *see* Buildings, Premises
  property *see* Real property
  proprietary interest *see* Interests in land
  registration, 5.7.11
  relevant, 14.8.10–11, 14.8.21
  support *see* Right of support
  trespass *see* Trespass
  waste *see* Waste management
Land Registry—
  appeals, 6.12.26
  Filed Plan, 6.12.12, 6.12.15
  first registration, 6.12.16
  leaflets, 6.12.11
  Ordnance Survey, 6.12.12–15
  original deeds, 6.12.16–17
  rivers, 6.11.2
Landlords—
  authorisation of nuisance, 1.9.14
  building repairs, 1.9.11–12
  implied authority, 1.9.15
  intangible interference, 1.6.7
  knowledge, 1.9.16
  leases *see* Leases
  liabilities, 1.9.1, 1.9.11–16
  private nuisance, 1.2.7, 1.6.7, 1.9.1,
    1.9.11–13
  reversionary interests *see* Reversion
  trespass, 5.3.2
  see also Tenants
Latent defects—
  hazards, 1.10.12
  knowledge, 1.9.9, 1.9.16
  trees, 1.10.12
Leases—
  adverse possession, 5.7.9–10
  domestic property, 5.4.4
  servient tenements, 8.2.14
  termination, 5.4.2
  trespass, 5.3.2, 5.4.1–2, 5.4.4, 5.7.9–10
Liabilities—
  absent owners, 1.9.10, 2.3.18
  accumulations, 4.2.9
  acts—
    contractors *see* Contractors

Liabilities—*contd*
  acts—*contd*
    tenants, 1.9.14–17
    trespassers, 1.10.3, 1.10.4, 1.10.11,
      1.11.2, 4.2.16, 4.3.7
  animals *see* Animals
  construction works, 1.9.17, 2.3.16–17,
    12.3.12
  criminal *see* Offences
  current occupiers, 1.9.6–8
  dangerous buildings, 2.3.15–18
  directors, 12.3.12, A1.14
  employers, 1.9.17, 2.3.12, 2.3.17
  environment, A1.14, A1.15
  fences, 6.3.10
  highway authorities, 6.7.10–11
  landlords, 1.9.1, 1.9.11–17
  natural hazards, 1.10.5–7
  negligence *see* Negligence
  original tortfeasors, 1.9.2–5
  party walls, 7.3.3–4
  private nuisance, 1.9, 1.10
  reasonably foreseeable damage, 1.8.2
  reversion, 1.9.13
  s 60 notices, 12.3.12
  strict *see* Strict liability
  waste management, 14.3.7
Licences—
  caravan sites, 5.4.10
  entertainment, 5.6.6, 5.6.9, 12.11
  private nuisance, 1.2.3, 1.2.4
  trees, 6.7.9, A3.8
  trespass, 5.2.4, 5.3.1, 5.4.1–3, 5.5.3
  waste management, 14.2.1, 14.3.2, 14.3.5
Limitations, adverse possession, 5.7.3
Litter—
  abatement orders, 14.8.13, 14.8.15
  control areas—
    notices, 14.8.29–35
    registers, 14.8.36
  definition, 14.8.2
  dog faeces, 14.8.9
  duty of occupiers—
    categories of land, 14.8.25
    control areas, 14.8.24–8
    notices, 14.8.27
    representations, 14.8.27
  duty of public bodies—
    codes of practice, 14.8.17–18
    complaints, 14.8.13, 14.8.14, 14.8.19–22
    enforcement, 14.8.13–15
    evidence, 14.8.21
    highways, 14.8.12
    notices, 14.8.14, 14.8.19–20
    relevant land, 14.8.10–11, 14.8.21
    standards of cleanliness, 14.8.16–18
  fixed penalties, 14.8.7–8, 14.8.9
  foreshore, 14.8.25

Litter—*contd*
  litter authorities, 14.8.3, 14.8.4, 14.8.6,
    14.8.7, 14.8.8, 14.8.24, 14.8.26–7, 14.8.30,
    14.8.33, 14.8.36
  offences, 14.8.5–9, 14.8.35
  overview, 14.8.1–4
  penalties, 14.8.6, 14.8.7, 14.8.8
  premises subject to excessive litter—
    notices, 14.8.29–35
    offences, 14.8.35
    representations, 14.8.35
  public open place, 14.8.6
  shopping centres, 14.8.29
  see also Waste management
Livestock *see* Animals
Local authority powers and duties—
  abatement notices, 3.12–14, 12.2.10
  abatement orders, 3.18.10–11
  air quality, 13.8.2, 13.8.3
  burglar alarms, 12.7.2, 12.7.3
  caravan sites, 5.4.9, 5.4.11
  charging orders, 3.15.2
  complaints, 3.11.4–8, 3.14.10, 3.18.1,
    12.3.3
  construction works, 12.3
  dark smoke, 13.3.2
  directions, 5.6.18–21
  drinking water, 15.4.6
  duties under 1990 Act, 3.11.2–3
  emissions, 3.3.4, 3.5.2, 13.2.1
  entertainment licences, 5.6.6, 5.6.9, 12.11.2
  entry—
    night time noise, 12.10.22
    refuse removal, 14.6.2
  environmental health officers, 3.11.3,
    3.11.4, 3.11.6–7, 3.18.1, 5.6.9, 13.2.3,
    13.3.2
  environmental law, A1.11
  furnaces, 13.4.3
  injunctions, 3.16.1
  instalment payments, 3.15.3
  judicial review, 3.17.1, 14.8.23
  litter *see* Litter
  loudspeakers, 12.6.3–4, 12.6.6
  motor vehicles, 3.9.4, 5.6.18–21, 12.2.10,
    14.7
  night time noise, 12.10
  noise, 3.9.4, 12.3, 12.10.2
  noise abatement *see* Noise abatement zones
  ombudsman, 3.17.2
  planning *see* Planning
  prejudice to health, 3.10.1
  private remedies, 3.17–18
  recovery of costs, 3.15.2–3
  refuse removal, 14.6
  responsibility for enforcement, 3.11.1
  seizure—
    equipment, 3.8.4, 3.9.2, 3.11.3

Local authority powers and duties—*contd*
  seizure—*contd*
    shopping trolleys, 14.9.2
    stray dogs, 9.10.2
  self-help, 3.15
  sewers, 15.5.12, 15.5.13, 15.5.15–18
  shopping trolleys, 14.9
  smoke control areas, 13.5.1
  stray dogs, 9.10.1–4
  straying livestock, 9.4.10
  summary proceedings, 3.5.2
  trade secrets, 3.14.11
  traffic orders, 13.6
  trees, 6.7.7, 6.7.8–11
  trespassory assemblies, 5.6.14
  unauthorised campers, 5.6.18–21
  vehicles, machinery or equipment, 3.9.2,
    3.9.4, 12.2.3, 12.2.7–10
  waste *see* Waste management
  wheel clamping, 12.2.10
  wilful obstruction, 3.14.10
Locus standi—
  abatement orders, 3.18.2–4
  dangerous dogs, 9.6.4
  trespass, 5.3.1–2
London—
  burglar alarms, 12.7.2
  dangerous dogs, 9.6.11–12
  entertainment licences, 12.11.1
  fire, 4.3.8–10
  floor partitions, 7.2.15
  party walls, 7.1.2, 7.1.3, 7.1.5, 7.1.6, 7.2.15
  trespassory assemblies, 5.6.15
Loudspeakers—
  abatement notices, 12.6.6
  codes of practice, 12.6.6
  complaints, 12.6.6
  consents, 12.6.3–4, 12.6.6
  exemptions, 12.6.2, 12.6.5
  ice cream and burger vans, 12.6.5, 12.6.6
  local authority powers and duties, 12.6.3–4,
    12.6.6
  noise, 12.6

Machinery—
  noise, 12.5
  VME *see* Vehicles, machinery or equip-
    ment
Magistrates courts—
  abatement notices, 3.13.4
  abatement orders, 3.18.3, 3.18.5, 3.18.7,
    3.18.8, 3.18.10–11
  dangerous dogs, 9.6.1–4
  fines, A4
  litter, 14.8.13–14, 14.8.19–22
  refuse on highway, 14.6.11–14
  restraining orders, 10.4.6
  s 60 notices, 12.3.6

Magistrates courts—*contd*
  sewage connection, 15.5.10
Malice—
  dangerous escapes, 4.2.15
  intangible interference, 1.6.11–14
Mandatory injunctions *see* Injunctions
Matrimonial law *see* Family law
Measurement—
  boundaries, 6.2.2–3, 6.12.34
  dark smoke, 13.3.5
  night time noise, 12.10.6
  right to light, 8.4.4–10, 16.6.2
Metropolis *see* London
Mines—
  continuing damage, 16.7.1
  dark smoke, 13.3.3
  environmental information, A2.9
  fences, 6.3.9
Mobile homes, premises, 3.2.2
Molestation, meaning, 10.5.6
Motor vehicles—
  abandoned—
    disposal, 14.7.7–8, 14.7.10–11
    excise licences, 14.7.8, 14.7.10
    local authority powers and duties, 14.7
    notices, 14.7.3, 14.7.5, 14.7.8, 14.7.10
    penalties, 14.7.2
    police powers, 14.7.3–5, 14.7.7–10
    removal, 14.7.3–11
    unauthorised dumping, 14.7.2
  emissions, 13.6
  European law, 12.8.1
  fixed penalties, 13.6.3
  fly-tipping, 14.5.2–7
  highway cleaning, 14.7.12
  immobilisation *see* Wheel clamping
  local authority powers and duties, 3.9.4,
    5.6.18–21, 12.2.10, 14.7
  noise, 3.9.2–4, 3.13.3, 3.14.8, 12.2.2–3,
    12.8
  penalties, 13.6.3, 14.7.2
  seizure, 5.6.2, 5.6.8, 14.5.2–7
  traffic orders, 13.6
  trespass, 5.6.2
  unauthorised campers, 5.6.18–21
  VME *see* Vehicles, machinery or equipment
Music—
  definition, 5.6.6
  entertainment licences, 12.11.1, 12.11.3
  raves *see* Raves

National Air Quality—
  Advice Line, 13.8.1
  strategy, 13.8.2
Negligence—
  animals, 9.1.1, 9.2.1–2
  contributory *see* Contributory negligence
  dangerous escapes, 4.2.16

Negligence—*contd*
  duty of care, 1.1.4, 1.10, 9.2.1
  fire, 4.1.3, 4.3.2, 4.3.4, 4.3.9
  private nuisance, 1.1.4, 1.8.1, 1.10, 1.11.10
Neighbouring land—
  communications, 6.2.7
  ditches, 6.6.6
  night time noise, 12.10
  trees, A3.9
  walls, 6.4.2, 8.3.9
Night time noise—
  complaints, 12.10.4–7
  DoE circulars, 12.10.6
  entry—
    obstruction, 12.10.22
    powers, 12.10.20–2
    warrants, 12.10.21
  equipment—
    forfeiture, 12.10.25–7
    retention, 10.10.23–4
    seizure, 12.10.20–2
  evidence, 12.10.13–14
  fixed penalties—
    content, 12.10.17–18
    non-payment, 12.10.19
    payment, 12.10.16
    seizure of equipment, 12.10.24
    service, 12.10.15
  investigations, 12.10.4–7
  local authority powers and duties, 12.10
  measurement, 12.10.6
  neighbours, 12.10
  overview, 12.10.1–3
  permitted levels, 12.10.1, 12.10.6–7
  warning notices—
    content, 12.10.8, 12.10.10
    defences, 12.10.12
    offences, 12.10.11
    penalties, 12.10.11
    service, 12.10.9
Noise—
  abatement notices, 3.13.3, 3.14.9
  abatement zones—
    appeals, 12.13.6
    local authority powers and duties, 12.13
    necessary works, 12.13.9
    noise reduction notices, 3.14.9, 12.13.7–9
    offences, 12.13.5, 12.13.8–9
    Orders, 12.13.1, 12.13.3, 12.13.6
    planning applications, 12.13.2
    purpose, 12.13.1
    registers, 12.13.3, 12.13.4, 12.13.5
  aircraft, 12.9
  building control, 12.4
  burglar alarms, 12.7
  construction works, 12.3
  Crown property, 3.8.2, 3.9.2
  defences, 3.14.9

Noise—*contd*
  definition, 3.8.1
  domestic property *see* Domestic property
  equipment, 3.9, 3.13.3, 3.14.8, 12.2.2–3,
    12.6, 12.10.20–7
  evidence, 3.8.3, 12.1.2
  highways, 3.9, 12.2, 12.3.1
  industrial disputes, 12.2.4
  intangible interference, 1.6.11–14, 1.6.20,
    1.6.21, 1.11.5
  integrated pollution control, 12.12.1
  local authority powers and duties, 3.9.4,
    12.3, 12.10.2
  machinery, 12.5
  major projects, 12.15
  motor vehicles, 3.9.2–4, 3.13.3, 3.14.8,
    12.2.2–3, 12.8
  night time *see* Night time noise
  overview, 12.1
  planning applications, 12.13.2, 12.14.1
  political demonstrations, 3.9.2, 12.2.4
  power boats, 16.3.1
  prejudice to health, 3.2.7, 3.8.1
  raves *see* Raves
  reduction notices, 3.14.9
  roadworks, 12.3.1
  seizure of equipment, 3.8.4, 3.9.2
  single events, 3.8.1
  statutory nuisances, 3.2.1, 3.7.1, 3.8–9,
    3.13.3, 3.14.9, 12.2
  streets, 12.2
  VME *see* Vehicles, machinery or equipment
  waste management, 12.12
Nominal damages—
  costs, 16.9.4, 16.9.5
  definition, 16.9.2
  legal right established, 16.9.5
  small damages distinguished, 16.9.3
Non-molestation orders *see* Family law
Notices—
  abandoned vehicles, 14.7.3, 14.7.5, 14.7.8,
    14.7.10
  abatement *see* Abatement notices
  dangerous structures, 7.4.7
  detained livestock, 9.4.7
  dogs—
    seizure, 9.10.2
    shooting, 9.9.2
  enforcement, 13.2.4, 13.2.6–7
  litter—
    complaints, 14.8.14, 14.8.19–20
    control areas, 14.8.27
  noise reduction, 3.14.9, 12.13.7–9
  notional obstruction, 8.4.26
  party walls *see* Party walls
  prohibition, 13.2.4–7
  refuse removal, 14.6.2, 14.6.4, 14.6.5–8,
    14.6.9, 14.6.10

Notices—*contd*
  remedial works, 15.4.6
  s 60 *see* Construction works
  sewer repairs, 15.5.13, 15.5.17, 15.5.18
  street litter control, 14.8.29–35
  warnings *see* Night time noise
  water—
    connection, 15.4.18
    pollution, 15.3.3
    remedial works, 15.4.6
Nuisances—
  air pollution *see* Air pollution
  harassment *see* Harassment
  hazards *see* Hazards
  intangible *see* Intangible interference
  litter *see* Litter
  private *see* Private nuisance
  public *see* Public nuisance
  stalkers *see* Stalkers
  statutory *see* Statutory nuisances
  telephone calls *see* Telephone calls

Obstruction—
  definition, 2.3.11–12
  discontinue or abate, 2.3.14
  highways, 2.3.6, 2.3.11–13, A5.6
  natural hazards, 2.3.13
  wilful, 3.14.10, 12.10.22, 14.5.4
Occupation—
  adopting a hazard, 1.10.9, 1.11.2
  adverse *see* Adverse possession
  displaced residential occupiers, 5.5.9,
    5.5.10, 5.5.14
  domestic property, 5.5.9–14
  drinking water, 15.4.12
  duties to trespassers, 5.8.1–4
  knowledge—
    danger, 5.8.3
    nuisance, 1.11.2
  liabilities, 1.9.6–8
  litter *see* Litter
  parcels clause, 6.12.6
  permissive, 1.1.2, 1.2.2
  protected intending occupiers, 5.5.9,
    5.5.11–12, 5.5.14
  tenants *see* Tenants
Occupation orders *see* Family law
Offences—
  abatement notices, 3.14, 12.2.12, 12.2.13
  abatement orders, 3.18.8
  aggravated trespass, 5.1.3, 5.6.10–12
  assault, 10.2.3, 10.2.6–12
  criminal damage, 11.3.2–3
  dark smoke, 13.3.8
  dogs—
    dangerous, 9.6.5, 9.6.8–13, 9.7
    faeces, 14.8.9
    strays, 9.10.4

Offences—*contd*
  enforcement notices, 13.2.7
  false statements, 5.5.12, 5.5.40
  furnaces, 13.4.3, 13.5.2
  harassment, 10.1.7–8, 10.2, 10.3.1, 10.4.1,
    10.4.5
  hoax warnings, 10.2.16
  indecent or obscene letters, 10.2.21
  litter, 14.8.5–9, 14.8.35
  noise—
    abatement zones, 12.13.5
    machinery, 12.5
    night time *see* Night time noise
    reduction notices, 12.13.8–9
    s 60 notices, 12.3.11
    s 61 consents, 12.3.15
  police directions, 5.6.3, 5.6.8, 5.6.17
  possession proceedings, 5.5.35, 5.5.37,
    5.5.40
  prohibition notices, 13.2.7
  protected intending occupiers, 5.5.12
  public order, 10.2.22–5
  restraining orders, 10.4.7, 10.4.11
  sewage—
    connection, 15.5.11
    repairs, 15.5.14–15, 15.5.17
    trade effluent, 15.5.20
  smoke control areas, 13.5.2
  squatters, 5.5.35, 5.5.37
  stalkers *see* Stalkers
  telephone calls, 10.2.3, 10.2.12, 10.2.13
  threatening to kill, 10.2.18
  tree felling, A3.8
  trespass, 5.1.3, 5.5.14, 5.6.10–17
  trespassory assembly, 5.1.3, 5.6.13–17
  vagrancy, 10.2.10, 10.2.19
  violence, entering premises, 5.5.8–9
  water—
    drinking, 15.4.8–12
    pollution, 15.2.3–12
    unfit, 15.4.8
  wilful obstruction, 3.14.10, 12.10.22,
    14.5.4
Ombudsman, local authority powers and
  duties, 3.17.2
Ordnance Survey—
  ditches, 6.6.4–5, 6.12.14
  field numbers and acreages, 6.6.4
  foreshore, 6.10.1
  hedges, 6.5.5–6, 6.6.4–5, 6.12.12–14
  Land Registry, 6.12.12–15
  tie-marks, 6.6.4
Owners—
  absent, 1.9.10, 2.3.18, A5.3
  definition, 3.12.5, 7.4.6
  landlords *see* Landlords
  occupiers *see* Occupation
  party walls, 7.3, 7.4.6

Party fence wall—
  definition, 7.2.10
  height, 7.3.7
  notices, 7.4.5
  projections supporting wall, 7.2.11
  repairs and works, 7.3.7
Party walls—
  1996 Act, 7.1.5, 7.2–6, 8.3.9–17
  access to neighbouring land, 8.3.9
  boundary within, 7.2.3
  compensation, 7.3.6, 8.3.17
  conservatories, 7.3.7
  covenants, 7.2.7
  definition, 7.2
  dispute resolution—
    appeals, 7.5.1, 7.5.12
    awards, 7.5.10–12
    costs and expenses, 7.5.10–13
    surveyors, 7.5.1–11
  enclosure, 7.2.7–9
  excavations, 7.1.5, 7.1.7
  excavations and construction, 8.3.11–17
  fire, 7.1.2
  foundations, 7.3.5, 7.3.6, 7.4.4
  London, 7.1.2, 7.1.3, 7.1.5, 7.1.6, 7.2.15
  new building—
    expenses, 7.3.3, 7.3.4
    foundations, 7.3.5, 7.3.6
    intention, 7.3.2
    liabilities, 7.3.3–4
    line of junction, 7.3.1–6, A5.20
    no consent, 7.3.5
    notices, 7.3.2, 7.4, A5.20
    rights and duties, 7.3.1–6
  notices—
    counternotices, 7.4.8
    dangerous structures, 7.4.7
    deemed disputes, 7.4.9, 8.3.16
    excavations and construction, 8.3.12–16
    information requirements, 7.4.2–4, 8.3.15
    security for expenses, 7.6.1
    service, 7.4.6
    special foundations, 7.4.4
    three metre, 8.3.13, A5.22
    time, 7.4.5
  overview, 7.1
  owners, 7.3, 7.4.6
  party fence walls, 7.2.10–12, 7.3.7
  party structures—
    damage to adjoining property, 7.3.8–10
    definition, 7.2.13
    floor partitions, 7.2.13–15
    height, 7.3.7, 7.3.9
    London, 7.2.15
    notices, 7.4, A5.21
    rebuilding, 7.3.7
    repairs and works, 7.3.7–10, 8.3.9
    rights of building owner, 7.3.7

Party walls—contd
  party structures—contd
    weather protection, 7.3.7, 7.6.2
  projections supporting wall, 7.2.2, 7.2.4,
    7.2.11
  right of support, 7.1.4, 7.1.5, 7.2.8, 8.3.9–17
  rights and duties, 7.3
  security for expenses, 7.6.1–2
  semi-detached houses, 7.2.5
  separating buildings, 7.2.6
  six metre, 8.3.13, 8.3.14
  surveyors, 7.1.6, 7.2.15, 7.5
  trespass, 7.2.8
  type (a), 7.2.2, 7.2.3–5
  type (b), 7.2.6–9
Penalties—
  abandoned vehicles, 14.7.2
  abatement notices, 3.14.2–3
  abatement orders, 3.18.5, 3.18.8, 14.8.15
  aggravated trespass, 5.6.12
  assault, 10.2.6
  controlled waste, 14.4.2
  dangerous dogs, 9.6.1, 9.6.5, 9.6.7, 9.6.8,
    9.6.11, 9.6.12, 9.7.2, 9.7.6–7, 9.8.3–4
  dark smoke, 13.3.10
  false statements, 5.5.12, 5.5.40
  fines, A4
  fixed see Fixed penalties
  furnaces, 13.4.4
  harassment, 10.4.5
  hoax warnings, 10.2.16
  litter, 14.8.6, 14.8.7, 14.8.8
  motor vehicles, 13.6.3, 14.7.2
  noise—
    machinery, 12.5
    night time, 12.10.11, 12.10.15–19
    s 60 notices, 12.3.11
    s 61 consents, 12.3.15
  police directions, 5.6.3, 5.6.8, 5.6.17
  possession proceedings, 5.5.35, 5.5.40
  public order offences, 10.2.23, 10.2.24,
    10.2.25
  refuse removal, 14.6.7, 14.6.8, 14.6.10,
    14.6.14
  restraining orders, 10.4.7, 10.4.11
  sewer repairs, 15.5.15, 15.5.17
  sleeping rough, 10.2.19
  smoke control areas, 13.5.2
  squatters, 5.5.35
  telephone calls, 10.2.13
  trespassory assembly, 5.6.16
  unauthorised campers, 5.6.19, 5.6.20
  vagrancy, 10.2.19
  waste management, 14.3.5–6, 14.4.2,
    14.6.7, 14.6.8, 14.6.10, 14.6.14
  water—
    pollution, 15.2.3
    supply, 15.4.8, 15.4.11

Personal injuries—
  dangerous dogs, 9.6.8
  dangerous escapes, 4.2.11
  highways, 2.3.8
  private nuisance, 1.1.3, 1.3.4, 1.7.2
  psychological *see* Psychiatric injury
Persons responsible—
  abatement notices, 3.12.5–6
  abatement orders, 3.18.6
  meaning, 3.12.6
  vehicles, machinery or equipment, 3.9.3,
    12.2.7–9
Photographs—
  aerial, 6.12.22–6
  civil procedure, 6.12.20–1
  expert witnesses, 6.12.23
  flash, 6.12.21
  gates, 6.12.25
  oblique, 6.12.24
  old, 6.12.19
  photographic log, 6.2.5–6
  provenance, 6.12.18
  recent, 6.12.20–1
  rights of way, 6.12.25
  stereo-plotting, 6.12.23, 6.12.26
  vertical, 6.12.23, 6.12.26
Pigs *see* Animals
Plaintiffs—
  causes of action *see* Causes of action
  coming to a nuisance, 1.11.5–6
  hypersensitive, 1.6.15
  interests in land, 1.1.2, 1.1.5, 1.2.1–7
  locus standi see Locus standi
  straying livestock, 9.4.4–6
  trespass, 5.3.1–3
Planning—
  amenity policies, 8.4.20, 8.4.22
  applications, noise, 12.13.2, 12.14.1
  conservation areas, A3.8
  permission—
    caravan sites, 5.4.10
    intangible interference, 1.6.24–5
    walls, 8.4.25
  PPG24, 12.14.1
  refuse removal, 14.6.5–8
  right to light, 8.4.20–4
Plans—
  deeds, 6.12.4, 6.12.7
  surveyors, 6.12.10
  T-marks *see* T-marks
Pleadings—
  damage, 16.11.12
  injunctions, 16.11.13
  see also Precedents
Police powers—
  abandoned vehicles, 14.7.3–5, 14.7.7–10
  adverse occupation, 5.5.14
  aggravated trespass, 5.6.10–12

Police powers—*contd*
  arrest, 10.5.25
  burglar alarms, 12.7.2, 12.7.3
  civil trespass, 5.6.5
  directions, 5.6.2, 5.6.3, 5.6.8, 5.6.17
  dogs—
    dangerous, 9.6.4
    strays, 9.10.1–4
    worrying livestock, 9.8.2
  licensed entertainment, 5.6.9
  non-molestation orders, 10.2.25
  occupation orders, 10.2.25
  raves, 5.6.6–9
  removal of trespassers, 5.5.14–15, 5.6.2–5
  seizure, 5.6.2, 5.6.8, 9.10.2, 14.5.6
  straying animals, 9.4.7, 9.10.1–4
  trespass, 5.5.14–15, 5.6.1–17
  trespassory assemblies, 5.6.14–17
  wheel clamping, 11.2
Pollution—
  air *see* Air pollution
  control *see* Integrated pollution control
  noise *see* Noise
  water *see* Water
Port Health Authorities, functions, 3.2.3
Possession—
  de facto, 1.2.5
  domestic property, 5.4.4
  exclusive rights, 1.2.4, 1.2.5
  leases, 5.3.2
  peaceable re-entry, 5.4.3, 5.4.6
  real property, 1.1.2, 1.2.1–7
  repossession, 5.5.16–40
  trespass, 5.3.1, 5.5.16
Possession proceedings—
  affidavits—
    filing, 5.5.21, 5.5.31, 5.5.36, A5.15
    service, 5.5.22, 5.5.23, 5.5.24, 5.5.26,
      5.5.32
  CCR Ord 24 Part I, 5.5.30–3, A5.18,
    A5.19
  CCR Ord 24 Part II, 5.5.34–40
  defendants, 5.5.20, 5.5.22, 5.5.28
  false statements, 5.5.40
  fees, 5.5.21
  immediate right to possession, 5.5.38
  interim orders, 5.5.34–40
  occupier's goods, 5.5.39
  offences, 5.5.35, 5.5.37, 5.5.40
  originating application, 5.5.31, 5.5.37
  originating summons, 5.5.19, 5.5.21, 5.5.22,
    5.5.26, A5.14
  persons unknown, 5.5.20
  proof of title, 5.5.22, 5.5.26
  RSC Ord 113, 5.5.18–28, A5.14–17
  service of process, 5.5.23–6, 5.5.32
  summary orders, 5.5.30–3, A5.16
  tenants, 5.5.17, 5.5.18, 5.5.30

Possession proceedings—*contd*
  time, 5.5.25, 5.5.28, 5.5.32, 5.5.33, 5.5.37,
    5.5.38
  undertakings, 5.5.37, 5.5.39
  warrant of possession, 5.5.33
  writ of possession, 5.5.28, A5.17
Precedents—
  CCR Ord 24—
    application for possession, A5.18
    notice to respondent, A5.19
  damage by animal—
    claim, A5.11
    defence, A5.12
  fire, *Rylands v Fletcher*, A5.7
  party walls—
    line of junction notice, A5.20
    party structure notice, A5.21
    three/six metre notice, A5.22
  private nuisance—
    absent owner of adjoining land, A5.3
    dangerous hazards, A5.4
    intangible interference, A5.5
    leasehold owner of adjoining land, A5.2
    occupier of adjoining land, A5.1
  public nuisance, obstruction of highway,
    A5.6
  right to light, A5.9
  RSC Ord 113—
    draft affidavit, A5.15
    draft order, A5.16
    draft summons, A5.14
    draft writ of possession, A5.17
  trees, subsidence, A5.13
  trespass, boundaries, A5.8
  withdrawal of support, A5.10
Prejudice to health—
  abatement orders, 3.18.3
  definition, 3.2.5
  local authority powers and duties, 3.10.1
  noise, 3.2.7, 3.8.1
  personal discomfort, 3.2.4, 3.2.7, 3.8.1
  statutory nuisances, 3.2.4–7, 3.8.1, 3.10.1
  vehicles, machinery or equipment, 12.2.2
Premises—
  boats, 3.2.3
  danger to trespassers, 5.8.1–4
  definition, 13.3.7
  domestic *see* Domestic property
  industrial *see* Industrial premises
  mobile homes, 3.2.2
  sailing vessels, 3.2.3
  scope, 3.2.3
  smoke, 3.3
  unfit property, 3.2.8
  see also Buildings
Prescription—
  absolute and indefeasible right, 8.2.13,
    8.2.15, 8.4.17

Prescription—*contd*
  adverse possession distinguished, 5.7.2
  claims, 8.2.9
  common law, 8.2.6–9
  foreshore, 6.10.2
  lost modern grant, 8.2.8
  motor vehicles, 5.2.7
  presumption, 8.2.6–7, 8.2.11
  rebuttal, 8.2.7
  statute law, 8.2.10–17
  time, 8.2.7, 8.2.8, 8.2.9, 8.2.11–14,
    8.2.15–16
  time immemorial, 8.2.7, 8.2.8, 8.2.11
  uninterrupted enjoyment, 8.2.12, 8.2.15–16
  see also Easements
Presumption—
  easements, 8.2.6–7, 8.2.11
  fences, 6.3.2, 6.3.4, 6.3.7, 6.8.4
  hedge and ditch, 6.6.2–6, 6.8.4
  injunctions, 16.11.3
  prescription, 8.2.6–7, 8.2.11
  rebuttal, 6.6.4, 6.8.4
  tidal rivers, 6.11.6
  usque ad medium filum viae, 6.8.2, 6.11.1
Private nuisance—
  act of God, 1.11.3
  agency, 1.9.16, 1.9.17
  animals, 1.6.22, 1.6.25, 9.2.3
  building and demolition operations,
    1.6.27–9, 1.9.17
  contractors, 1.6.27–9, 1.9.4, 1.9.17, 1.11.4
  contributory negligence, 1.11.10
  damage *see* Damage
  dangerous escapes, 1.7.8
  defences, 1.11
  defendants, 1.9
  duty not to continue, 1.9.8, 1.10.3
  emanating from land, 1.9.5
  encroachment, 1.5
  goods damaged, 1.1.3, 1.3.4, 1.7.1
  harassment, 10.3.4
  hazards, 1.7.8, 1.9.17, 1.10, 1.11.2, 1.11.3,
    8.3.7, A5.4
  intangible *see* Intangible interference
  isolated incidents, 1.7.7
  knowledge—
    absent owners, 1.9.10
    acts of trespassers, 1.10.11, 1.11.2
    actual, 1.9.6, 1.9.7
    constructive, 1.9.6, 1.9.8
    hazards, 1.10.10, 1.11.2
    landlords, 1.9.16
    latent defects, 1.9.9, 1.9.6
    not imputed, 1.9.9
    trees, 6.7.5
  landlords, 1.2.7, 1.6.7, 1.9.1, 1.9.11–17
  latent defects, 1.9.9, 1.9.16, 1.10.12
  liabilities, 1.9, 1.10

Private nuisance—*contd*
 licensees, 1.2.3, 1.2.4
 negligence, 1.1.4, 1.8.1, 1.10, 1.11.10
 overview, 1.1
 personal injuries, 1.1.3, 1.3.4, 1.7.2
 plaintiffs—
  causes of action, 1.1.1, 1.2, 1.3–8
  coming to a nuisance, 1.11.5–6
  interests in land, 1.1.2, 1.1.5, 1.2.1–7
 precedents *see* Precedents
 reasonably foreseeable damage, 1.1.4, 1.3.2,
  1.8
 right of support, 8.3.7–8
 right to a view, 1.7.3
 statutory immunity, 1.11.7–9
 strict liability, 1.1.3
 television reception, 1.7.4–5
 tenants, 1.2.2, 1.9.11, 1.9.14–17
 trees, 1.5, 1.9.9, 1.10.12, 6.7.5
 trespass, 1.10.3, 1.10.4, 1.10.11, 1.11.2
Property—
 buildings *see* Buildings
 chattels *see* Goods
 land *see* Real property
Protected intending occupiers—
 definition, 5.5.11
 offences, 5.5.12
 trespass, 5.5.9, 5.5.11–12, 5.5.14
Psychiatric injury—
 assault, 10.2.3, 10.2.7–8, 10.2.11, 10.2.12
 expert witnesses, 10.2.8
 telephone calls, 10.2.3, 10.2.11, 10.2.12
Public nuisance—
 actionable civil wrong, 2.2.1
 class of people affected, 2.1.1, 2.2.1–2
 common law actions, 2.2
 definition, 2.1.1, 2.2.1
 examples, 2.2.2
 highways *see* Highways
 hoax warnings, 10.2.16
 interests in land, 2.2.4
 overview, 2.1.1–2
 reasonably foreseeable damage, 2.3.9
 special damage, 2.2.3, 2.3.8
 telephone calls, 2.2.2, 10.2.14–16
 trees, 2.3.13, 6.7.8–11
Public open place, definition, 14.8.6

Quarries—
 dark smoke, 13.3.3
 fences, 6.3.9
 natural support to land, 8.3.3

Railways—
 accommodation works, 6.9.6–9
 boundaries, 6.9
 Channel Tunnel, 12.15.1
 compulsory purchase, 6.9.2

Railways—*contd*
 fences, 6.3.9, 6.9.5, 6.9.9
 history, 6.9.3
 locomotives—
  smoke, 3.3.3, 13.3.3
  steam, 3.5.1
 major projects, 12.15.1
 plans, 6.9.4
 Railtrack Plc, 6.9.3, 6.9.9
 rights of passage, 6.9.8
 subsoil, 6.9.2
Raves—
 directions, 5.6.8
 licenced events, 5.6.6, 5.6.9
 meaning, 5.6.6
 police powers, 5.6.6–9
 unlicensed events, 5.6.7
Real property—
 airspace, 5.2.5, 5.3.2, 12.9.1, 16.11.6,
  16.12.3
 damage, 1.1.3, 1.1.5
 duty of care, 1.1.4
 intangible interference *see* Intangible interference
 light *see* Right to light
 natural or ordinary user, 4.2.3, 4.2.4, 4.2.5
 natural state, 3.2.3
 non-natural user, 4.1.1, 4.2.3
 nuisance emanating, 1.9.5
 permissive occupation, 1.1.2, 1.2.2
 possession *see* Possession
 property rights, 1.1.1, 5.2.5
 proprietary interests *see* Interests in land
 repossession *see* Possession proceedings
 residential *see* Domestic property
 support *see* Right of support
 trespass *see* Trespass
Reasonable user—
 highways, 2.3.4–7
 intangible interference, 1.6.21–3
Reasonably foreseeable damage *see*
 Foreseeable damage
Refuse—
 litter *see* Litter
 waste *see* Waste management
Registers—
 environmental information, A2.15, A2.16
 integrated pollution control, 3.3.4, 12.12.1,
  13.2.3
 litter control areas, 14.8.36
 noise abatement zones, 12.13.3, 12.13.4,
  12.13.5
 waste management licences, 14.2.1
Relevant land, definition, 14.8.11
Relevant person, definition, A2.4–6
Remedies—
 abatement *see* Abatement orders
 damage *see* Damage

Remedies—*contd*
  dogs, 9.6.1, 9.6.5–7
  failure to provide sewers, 15.5.6
  harassment, 10.3–4
  injunctions *see* Injunctions
  local authority powers and duties, 3.17–18
  matrimonial law *see* Family law
  overview, 16.1
  restraint *see* Restraining orders
  trespass, 5.5
  water supply, 15.4.16, 15.4.19
Repairs—
  access to neighbouring land, 6.4.2, 6.6.6,
    8.3.9
  buildings, 1.9.11–12, 8.3.7
  fences, 6.3.8
  landlords, 1.9.11–12
  party fence wall, 7.3.7
  party structures, 7.3.7–10
  party walls, 7.3.8–10, 8.3.39
  right of support, 8.3.7
Residential property *see* Domestic property
Restraining orders—
  arrest, 10.4.9
  contempt of court, 10.4.10
  double jeopardy, 10.4.12
  magistrates courts, 10.4.6
  offences, 10.4.7, 10.4.11
  penalties, 10.4.7, 10.4.12
  remedies, 10.4.6–12
Reversion—
  damage, 1.2.4, 1.2.7, 1.6.7, A5.5
  interests in land, 1.2.4, 1.2.7, 1.6.7, 1.9.13,
    A5.5
  liabilities, 1.9.13
Right of support—
  categories, 8.3.1
  damage, 8.3.2, 8.3.4
  easements, 7.2.8, 8.2.5, 8.2.10–14, 8.3.6–7,
    8.3.10, A5.10
  erosion, 8.3.4
  interferences, 8.3.3
  natural support to land, 8.3.1, 8.3.2–4
  negative obligation, 8.3.2
  overview, 8.1.1, 8.1.2
  party walls, 7.1.4, 7.1.5, 7.2.8, 8.3.9–17
  prescription *see* Prescription
  private nuisance, 8.3.7–8
  statute law, 8.2.10–14
  support to buildings, 8.3.5–8
  withdrawal, 8.3
Right to light—
  50/50 working rule, 8.4.7, 8.4.8
  abandonment, 8.4.16–19
  alteration to premises, 8.4.16–19
  causes of action, 8.4.1, 8.4.3
  character of locality, 8.4.3
  comfortable use, 8.4.2

Right to light—*contd*
  damage, 16.6
  development gain, 16.6.3
  easements, 1.7.3, 8.2.4, 8.2.5, 8.2.15–17,
    8.4.2–19, 8.4.25–6
  express grant, 8.2.4
  interference, 8.4, A5.9
  light—
    ancient, 8.4.16, 8.4.18
    from different sources, 8.4.11
    measurement, 8.4.4–10, 16.6.2
    poor, 8.4.13–15
    remaining, 8.4.3, 8.4.14
    unusually good, 8.4.12
  Local Land Charge, 8.4.26
  mandatory injunctions, 16.12.2
  notional obstruction, 8.4.26
  overview, 8.1.1, 8.1.2
  planning guidelines, 8.4.23–4
  prescription *see* Prescription
  protection against, 8.4.25–6
  reconstruction of premises, 8.4.17
  reference point, 8.4.6
  right to a view, 1.7.3
  scope, 8.4.2–3
  sky factor percentage, 8.4.6, 16.6.2
  statute law, 8.2.15–17
  surveyors, 8.4.6, 8.4.7, 8.4.10, 16.6.1–2
  town planning, 8.4.20–4
  working plane, 8.4.6, 8.4.7
Rights of way, photographs, 6.12.25
Rivers—
  accretion or erosion, 6.11.3
  boundaries, 6.6.4, 6.11.1–4, 6.11.6
  Environment Agency, 6.11.4
  fishing rights, 6.11.4, 6.11.6
  Land Registry, 6.11.2
  riparian rights, 1.2.6, 6.11.4, 6.11.6
  streams, 6.6.4, 6.11.1–4
  tidal, 6.11.6
  usque ad medium filum viae, 6.11.1
Roads *see* Highways
Rylands v Fletcher rule—
  escapes *see* Dangerous escapes
  fire *see* Fire

Sailing vessels, premises, 3.2.3
Scotland, wheel clamping, 11.3.8
Sea bed, Crown property, 6.10.3
Seashore *see* Foreshore
Seizure—
  disposal and return of property, 14.5.5–7
  Environment Agency, 14.5.3–7
  equipment, 3.8.4, 3.9.2, 3.11.3, 5.6.8,
    12.10.20–2
  fly-tipping, 14.5.3–7
  local authority powers and duties, 3.8.4,
    3.9.2, 3.11.3, 9.10.2, 12.10.20–2, 14.9.2

Seizure—*contd*
  motor vehicles, 5.6.2, 5.6.8, 14.5.2–7
  police powers, 5.6.2, 5.6.8, 9.10.2, 14.5.6
  retention of equipment, 12.10.23–4
  shopping trolleys, 14.9.2
  stray dogs, 9.10.2
  vehicles, machinery or equipment, 3.9.2
Self-help—
  local authority powers and duties, 3.15
  trespass, 5.5.6–15
  wheel clamping, 11.3.4
Service—
  abatement notices, 3.12.5–8, 12.2.7–9
  affidavits, 5.5.22, 5.5.23, 5.5.24, 5.5.26,
    5.5.32
  fixed penalty notices, 12.10.15
  party walls notices, 7.4.6
  possession proceedings, 5.5.23–6, 5.5.32
  s 60 notices, 12.3.4–5
  warning notices, 12.10.9
Sewage—
  Director General for Water Services, 15.5.3
  disposal, 15.5
  drains, 15.5.12–18
  foreshore, 1.2.5
  principal duties, 15.5.2–3
  sewers—
    appeals, 15.5.10
    connection, 15.5.8–11
    disconnection, 15.5.19
    domestic purposes, 15.5.7
    entitlement, 15.5.5
    failure to provide, 15.5.6
    investigations, 15.5.12
    local authority powers and duties,
      15.5.12, 15.5.13, 15.5.15–18
    maintenance, 15.5.2
    notices, 15.5.13, 15.5.17, 15.5.18
    offences, 15.5.11, 15.5.14–5, 15.5.17
    penalties, 15.5.15, 15.5.17
    remedies, 15.5.6
    repairs, 15.5.12–18
    requisitions, 15.5.4–7
    trade effluent, 15.5.20, A1.10
  special administration orders, 15.5.3
  see also Waste management
Shops—
  litter, 14.8.29
  shopping trolleys, 14.9
  squatters, 5.4.6
Smell—
  intangible interference, 1.6.22, 1.6.25
  pigs, 1.6.22, 1.6.25, 16.3.1
  statutory nuisances, 3.2.1, 3.5, 3.7.1
Smoke—
  chimneys *see* Chimneys
  control areas—
    exemptions, 13.5.3

Smoke—*contd*
  control areas—*contd*
    local authority powers and duties, 13.5.1
    offences, 13.5.2
    penalties, 13.5.2
  Crown property, 3.3.2, 13.3.3
  dark smoke—
    air pollution, 13.3
    burden of proof, 13.3.4
    chimneys, 13.3.4, 13.3.6
    defences, 13.3.11–12
    defendants, 13.3.4
    definition, 13.3.5
    domestic property, 13.3.4
    enforcement, 13.2.3
    exemptions, 13.3.3, 13.3.9
    local authority powers and duties, 13.3.2
    measurement, 13.3.5
    offences, 13.3.8
    penalties, 13.3.10
    premises defined, 13.3.7
  definition, 3.3.1, 13.3.5
  furnaces *see* Furnaces
  integrated pollution control, 3.3.4
  premises, 3.3
  railway locomotives, 3.3.3, 13.3.3
  s 79 exclusions, 3.3.2–3
  statutory nuisances, 3.3
Special damage—
  definition, 2.2.3
  public nuisance, 2.2.3, 2.3.8
Special foundations, definition, 7.4.4
Squatters—
  definition, 5.4.5
  eviction, 5.5.7
  gypsies, 5.4.8
  offences, 5.5.35, 5.5.37
  repossession *see* Possession proceedings
  shops, 5.4.6
  see also Trespass
Stalkers—
  ex partners *see* Family law
  injunctions, 10.3.8, 10.3.10–11
  intentionally causing emotional distress,
    10.3.2
  offenders, 10.1.2
  trespass, 10.3.2
  see also Harassment
Statutory nuisances—
  abatement *see* Abatement notices
  accumulations or deposits, 3.6.1
  ambit of 1990 Act, 3.2.1
  animals, 3.7.1
  contaminated land, 3.2.2
  declared by enactment, 3.10.1
  defences, 12.3.10
  dust, 3.5
  emissions, 3.3.4, 3.4.1, 3.5.2, 13.2.2

Statutory nuisances—*contd*
  enforcement *see* Local authority powers and
    duties
  environment, 3.2
  fumes, 3.4.1
  gases, 3.4.1
  highways *see* Highways
  industrial emissions, 3.5
  material discomfort, 1.6.30
  noise, 3.2.1, 3.8–9, 3.13.3, 3.14.9, 12.2
  overview, 3.1
  prejudice to health or nuisance, 3.2.4–7,
    3.8.1, 3.10.1
  s 79 exclusions, 3.3.2–3, 3.9.2
  smell, 3.2.1, 3.5, 3.7.1
  smoke, 3.3
  steam, 3.5
  unfit property, 3.2.8
  VME *see* Vehicles, machinery or equip-
    ment
  waste, 14.6.5
  water, 3.10.1
Steam—
  industrial emissions, 3.5
  railway locomotives, 3.5.1
Strangers *see* Trespass
Streets—
  definition, 3.9.1, 12.2.5
  litter, 14.8.29–35
  noise, 12.2
  see also Highways
Strict liability—
  animals, 9.3.5
  dangerous dogs, 9.6.9
  fire, 4.1.3, 4.3.1
  private nuisance, 1.1.3
  Rylands v Fletcher, 4.1.2, 4.2, 4.3.3
  water pollution, 15.2.12
Surveyors—
  aerial photographs, 6.12.23
  boundaries, 6.12.33–4
  expert witnesses, 6.12.30, 6.12.33–4
  party walls, 7.1.6, 7.2.15, 7.5
  plans, 6.12.10
  practice statement, 6.12.30
  right to light, 8.4.6, 8.4.7, 8.4.10, 16.6.1–2

T-marks—
  boundaries, 6.3.8, 6.6.3, 6.12.9
  ditches, 6.6.3
  fences, 6.3.8
  hedges, 6.6.3
Telephone calls—
  assault, 10.2.3, 10.2.12
  electronic machines, 10.1.3
  fear of violence, 10.2.11
  hoax warnings, 10.2.16, 10.2.20
  injunctions, 10.3.8, 10.3.10

Telephone calls—*contd*
  intentionally causing emotional distress,
    10.3.2
  menacing, 10.2.13
  Nuisance Call Bureau, 10.1.3
  obscene, 10.2.13
  offences, 10.2.3, 10.2.12, 10.2.13
  offenders, 10.1.4
  penalties, 10.2.13
  psychiatric injury, 10.2.3, 10.2.11, 10.2.12
  public nuisance, 2.2.2, 10.2.14–16
  silence, 10.2.12
Television reception, private nuisance, 1.7.4–5
Tenants—
  adverse possession, 5.7.8
  duty of care, 5.8.2
  possession proceedings, 5.5.17, 5.5.18,
    5.5.30
  private nuisance, 1.2.2, 1.9.11, 1.9.14–7
  trespass, 5.3.2, 5.4.1–4, 5.5.3–4
  see also Landlords
Time—
  environmental information, A2.10
  occupation orders, 10.5.18
  party wall notices, 7.4.5
  possession proceedings, 5.5.25, 5.5.28,
    5.5.32, 5.5.33, 5.5.37, 5.5.38
  prescription, 8.2.7, 8.2.8, 8.2.9, 8.2.11–14,
    8.2.15–16
Title—
  adverse possession, 5.7.1–2, 5.7.11
  deeds *see* Deeds
  possession proceedings, 5.5.22, 5.5.26
Torts—
  consequential loss, 1.7.6, 16.4
  escapes *see* Dangerous escapes
  harassment, 10.3.4, 10.4.8
  intentionally causing emotional distress,
    10.3.2
  intimidation, 10.3.3
  liability *see* Liabilities
  private nuisance *see* Private nuisance
  trespass *see* Trespass
  unlawful interference, 10.3.3
  wrongful interference with goods, 5.1.4,
    10.3.2, 11.3.6, 11.3.10
Town planning *see* Planning
Trade effluent, 3.5, 15.5.20, A1.10
Trade secrets, local authority powers and
    duties, 3.14.11
Traffic orders, local authority powers and
    duties, 13.6
Travellers *see* Gypsies
Trees—
  access to neighbouring land, A3.9
  beech, 6.5.2
  boundaries, 6.7
  causes of action, A3.1–7

Trees—contd
  conservation areas, A3.8
  cupressocyparis leylandii, 6.5.1
  encroachment—
    highways, 6.7.10
    roots, 6.7.6, A5.13
  hedges *see* Hedges
  highways—
    adjoining property, A3.7
    authorities, 6.7.8–11, A3.4, A5.13
    planted, A3.5
    post-adoption, A3.5
    pre-adoption, A3.5
    statutory nuisance, 2.3.13
  latent defects, 1.10.12
  licences—
    felling, A3.8
    planting, 6.7.9
  local authority powers and duties, 6.7.7,
    6.7.8–11
  overhanging branches, 6.7.4–5
  ownership, 6.7.1
  planting, 6.7.2, 6.7.9, 6.7.11
  Preservation Orders, 6.7.7, A3.8
  private nuisance, 1.5, 1.9.9, 1.10.12, 6.7.5
  public nuisance, 2.3.13, 6.7.8–11
  returned clippings, 6.7.4
  selection, 6.7.2–3
  trespass, 5.1.2
  wider public interest, 16.12.4
Trespass—
  adverse possession, 5.7, 16.15.1
  aggravated, 5.1.3, 5.6.10–12
  airspace, 5.2.5, 5.3.2, 12.9.1
  ancient monuments, 5.6.4, 5.6.13–17
  animals *see* Animals
  boundary disputes, A5.8
  buildings, 16.5.3, 16.15.1
  consequential loss, 16.5.2
  contributory negligence, 5.5.5
  damage, 5.5.2–4, 16.5
  dangerous escapes, 4.2.15–16
  defences, 1.11.2, 9.3.25
  defendants, 5.4
  displaced residential occupiers, 5.5.9,
    5.5.10, 5.5.14
  duration, 5.2.6–7
  ejectment, 5.2.3
  fire, 4.3.7
  footpaths, 5.2.4
  goods, 5.1.4, 10.3.2
  gypsies, 5.4.7–11
  harassment, 10.3.2
  hunt saboteurs, 5.6.10
  injunctions, 16.15
  intermittence, 5.2.7
  landlords, 5.3.2
  leases, 5.3.2, 5.4.1–2, 5.4.4, 5.7.9–10

Trespass—contd
  licences, 5.2.4, 5.3.1, 5.4.1–3, 5.5.3
  locus standi, 5.3.1–2
  mere presence sufficient, 5.2.1
  motor vehicles, 5.6.2
  no actual damage, 16.5
  occupiers duties, 5.8.1–4
  offences, 5.1.3, 5.5.14, 5.6.10–17
  open land, 5.6.4
  overview, 5.1
  party walls, 7.2.8
  permission exceeded, 5.2.4
  plaintiffs, 5.3.1–3
  police powers, 5.5.14–15, 5.6.1–17
  possession, 5.3.1
  presence of articles, 5.2.2
  private nuisance, 1.10.3, 1.10.4, 1.10.11,
    1.11.2
  protected intending occupiers, 5.5.9,
    5.5.11–12, 5.5.14
  protection of land, 5.2.5
  reasonable force, 5.5.6, 5.5.7
  remedies, 5.5
  repossession *see* Possession proceedings
  scheduled monuments, 5.6.4
  scope, 5.2.1–3
  self-help, 5.5.6–15
  squatters *see* Squatters
  stalkers, 10.3.2
  tenants, 5.3.2, 5.4.1–4, 5.5.3–4
  trees, 5.1.2
  trespassory assembly, 5.1.3, 5.6.13–17
Trespass to the person—
  assault, 10.3.2
  meaning, 5.1.5

Undertakings—
  injunctions, 10.3.9
  non-molestation orders, 10.5.22
  occupation orders, 10.5.22
  possession proceedings, 5.5.37, 5.5.39
Unlawful interference, harassment, 10.3.3
Usque ad medium filum viae—
  highways, 6.8.2
  rivers, 6.11.1

Vagrancy—
  fear of violence, 10.2.10
  penalties, 10.2.19
Vehicles, machinery or equipment—
  abatement notices, 3.13.3, 12.2.6–16
  defences, 3.14.8
  DoE circulars, 3.9.1, 12.2.6, 12.2.7
  exemptions, 3.9.2, 12.2.4
  local authority powers and duties, 3.9.2,
    3.9.4, 12.2.3, 12.2.7–10
  noisy activities, 3.9.2
  persons responsible, 3.9.3, 12.2.7–9

Vehicles, machinery or equipment—*contd*
    prejudice to health, 12.2.2
    roadworks, 12.3.1
    seizure, 3.9.2
    special abatement procedure, 12.2.6–16
    unattended, 12.2.6, 12.2.8–9
Violence—
    assault *see* Assault
    entering premises, 5.5.8–9
    fear, 10.2.9–11, 10.2.23
    psychological *see* Psychiatric injury
    public order offences, 10.2.23

Walls—
    access to neighbouring land, 6.4.2, 8.3.9
    boundaries, 6.4.1
    easements, 8.3.10
    lateral support, 8.3.10
    party *see* Party walls
    planning permission, 8.4.25
    preservation or renewal, 6.4.2
Warrants—
    arrest, 10.4.9, 10.5.26–7
    entry to property, 12.7.2, 12.10.21
    fly-tipping, 14.5.2
    possession, 5.5.33
Waste management—
    abandoned vehicles *see* Motor vehicles
    civil liability, 14.3.7
    controlled waste—
        codes of practice, 14.4.3
        consignment notes, 14.4.1
        disposal, 14.2.2
        DoE circulars, 14.4.4
        duty of care, 14.4
        penalties, 14.4.2
        unlawful deposit, 14.3.1–2
    defences, 14.3.4
    enforcement, 14.2
    Environment Agency, 14.2.1, 14.3.2,
        14.4.2, 14.5.3–8
    fly-tipping—
        evidence, 14.5.8
        motor vehicles, 14.5.2–7
        seizure, 14.5.3–7
        tracing operators, 14.5.2
        unauthorised disposal, 14.5
        warrants, 14.5.2
    household waste—
        collection, 14.2.3, 14.2.4
        disposal, 14.2.2, 14.3.3
    industrial waste, collection, 14.2.3, 14.2.4
    licences, 14.2.1, 14.3.2, 14.3.5
    litter *see* Litter
    noise, 12.12
    overview, 14.1
    penalties, 14.3.5–6, 14.4.2, 14.6.7, 14.6.8,
        14.6.10, 14.6.14

Waste management—*contd*
    refuse removal—
        abandoned items, 14.6.2
        appeals, 14.6.4, 14.6.6
        detrimental to amenity, 14.6.3–8
        dilapidated buildings, 14.6.9
        highways, 14.6.11–14
        local authority powers and duties, 14.6
        neglected sites, 14.6.9
        notices, 14.6.2, 14.6.4, 14.6.5–8, 14.6.9,
            14.6.10
        open land, 14.6.2
        penalties, 14.6.7, 14.6.8, 14.6.10, 14.6.14
        planning, 14.6.5–8
        unoccupied land, 14.6.8
    sewage *see* Sewage
    shopping trolleys, 14.9
    special waste, 14.3.6
    statutory nuisances, 14.6.5
    unlawful deposits, 14.1.1, 14.3
    Waste Collection Authorities, 14.2.3–4,
        14.7.6
    Waste Disposal Authorities, 14.2.2, 14.7.6
Water—
    controlled waters—
        definition, 15.2.2
        Environment Agency, 15.2.2, 15.3,
            A1.10
        offences, 15.2.3–12
        sewage, A1.10
    drinking water—
        connection notices, 15.4.18
        contamination and waste, 15.4.10–12
        disconnection, 15.4.20–1
        domestic supply, 15.4.19
        Drinking Water Inspectorate, 15.4.1
        European law, 15.4.4
        hosepipe bans, 15.4.13
        local authority powers and duties, 15.4.6
        occupiers, 15.4.12
        offences, 15.4.8–12
        penalties, 15.4.8, 15.4.11
        pressure, 15.4.22
        private supplies, 15.4.5
        quality and sufficiency, 15.4.3–7
        remedial works notices, 15.4.6
        remedies, 15.4.16, 15.4.19
        supply, 15.4
        unfit, 15.4.8–9
        unwholesome or insufficient, 15.4.6
        water mains, 15.4.15–17
        wholesome, 15.4.3, 15.4.4, 15.4.7
    floods, 4.2.14
    lakes, 6.11.5
    overview, 15.1
    pollution—
        employees, 15.2.6
        foul water, 15.3.4

Water—*contd*
  pollution—*contd*
    knowingly permitting, 15.2.3, 15.2.7–8
    noxious matter, 15.2.3, 15.2.9, 15.2.10
    offences, 15.2.3–12
    penalties, 15.2.3
    poisonous matter, 15.2.3, 15.2.9,
      15.2.11
    polluting matter, 15.2.3, 15.2.9
    statute law, 15.2
    strict liability, 15.2.12
    vandalism, 15.2.5
  remedial work—
    anti-pollution works, 15.3.2–3
    statutory powers, 15.3
    works notices, 15.3.3
  rivers *see* Rivers
  sewage *see* Sewage
  statutory nuisances, 3.10.1

Water—*contd*
  streams, 6.6.4, 6.11.1–4
Wheel clamping—
  criminal damage, 11.3.2–3
  disabled persons, 11.2.2
  distress damage feasant, 11.3.4–5
  knowledge, 11.3.2, 11.3.8
  local authority powers and duties, 12.2.10
  overview, 11.1.1
  parking meters, 11.2.2
  police powers, 11.2
  private land, 11.3
  recaption, 11.3.4
  release fees, 11.3.9
  Scotland, 11.3.8
  self-help, 11.3.4
  volenti non fit injuria, 11.3.6–7
Writ of possession, possession proceedings,
  5.5.28, A5.17